Wealth of Wisdom

Wealth of Wisdom

THE TOP 50 QUESTIONS WEALTHY FAMILIES ASK

Tom McCullough
Keith Whitaker

WILEY

This edition first published 2018

Registered office
John Wiley & Sons Ltd, The Atrium, Southern Gate, Chichester, West Sussex, PO19 8SQ, United Kingdom

For details of our global editorial offices, for customer services and for information about how to apply for permission to reuse the copyright material in this book please see our website at www.wiley.com.

Library of Congress Cataloging-in-Publication Data is available:

ISBN 978-1-119-33153-7 (hardback)
ISBN 978-1-119-33154-4 (ePDF)
ISBN 978-1-119-33152-0 (ePub)

V7D9DBEFE-5C68-4FFA-868D-E78E60838AE1_092519

Cover Design: Wiley
Cover Image: © Nikitina Olga/Shutterstock

Set in 11/13pt NewBaskervilleStd by SPi Global, Chennai, India
Printed in the USA

Tom dedicates this book to Karen, Kate, Ben, and Miranda.

Keith dedicates this book to the many trusted advisors who, over the past two decades, have invited him to share with them the journey of helping enterprising families.

Contents

Foreword

Dirk Jungé, Chairman, Pitcairn Company

For parents, there is no greater imperative or joy than creating a better life for your children. For families that have generated considerable wealth through family business or investing, this objective comes with unique opportunities and challenges. Wealth creators have the chance to sustain not just family wealth, but also to pass on the values and education future generations need to find success and satisfaction in their pursuits. Yet wealth is an amplifier of all things. If not properly cultivated, the very resources intended to perpetuate a family's legacy can be its undoing.

As Tom McCullough and Keith Whitaker and their contributing authors so articulately detail in this book, succession planning encompasses far more than simply transitioning assets. It requires constant tending, including clear communication, good governance, effective education, and shared values. It's not about providing the next generation with financial independence, it's about providing them with the tools to be truly independent.

I was fortunate enough to grow up in a family that nurtured true independence from an early age. My father learned about hard work as a child by planting, weeding, watering, and harvesting crops in his family garden during the Great Depression. When I was 12, he started instilling that same work ethic in me. My father provided an advance on my allowance for the capital investment in a small garden at our family's summer home in the Catskill Mountains. I set about digging up the hard brown clay and the seemingly endless rocks under the soil. After weeks of preparing for planting, my humble plot had a name – Rock Acres.

I can still remember the crop rotation I selected for that first summer – corn, eggplant, squash, cucumber, lettuce, and tomatoes. Before long, my garden started yielding strong produce, which I sold to friends and family near my home. Early in the summer, I'd get frustrated when I pictured my friends buying popsicles and candy from the market on their way to the pool, while I pulled weeds. But come August, as I began to see a considerable return on the time I'd put into Rock Acres, I started to appreciate my summer's worth of hard work.

I learned more that summer than I thought possible, and many of the lessons wouldn't be fully apparent to me until decades later when I had children of my own and my perspectives on family changed. My father put me on the path toward a life fueled by the values that drove his success and have sustained our family for generations. Those hard-earned values, including work ethic, patience, and business fundamentals have been invaluable in my work helping our family protect and grow its wealth. For more than 40 years, the Pitcairn Company has given me a front row seat to how wealth impacts families, both my own family and others we serve as a multi-family office.

There's no substitute for a summer of hard work, but this book, *Wealth of Wisdom*, and its countless lessons and insights comes close. Tom and Keith draw from their distinguished careers to identify the key questions that families are asking. What makes this work truly stand apart is the impressive group of voices Tom and Keith have brought together to share their knowledge. They have curated established best practices and bold new thinking from the leading thinkers and advisors in the family wealth field. The observations and practical advice on family transitions and succession planning are a concise and powerful resource for families.

Tom and Keith are the perfect guides to synthesize all this knowledge into a single work. Their perspectives and approaches elevate this work into something greater – a master class in sustaining family wealth, backed by decades of experience and generations of insights.

While reading this book, I found myself highlighting entire passages and flagging pages to revisit with colleagues and family members. It held countless takeaways I am eager to share and put into practice. Many of these insights coalesced around three themes all families can derive value from in an ever-changing world.

One of those themes is the changing demographics and their impact on family dynamics. Individuals, particularly affluent individuals, are living longer, thus reshaping expectations around lifestyles and legacy. With this longevity, first-generation wealth creators and subsequent generations face new opportunities and obstacles. This reality adds increased pressure for families to foster meaningful conversations about difficult issues all families must grapple with. This book addresses this emerging issue of longevity from a variety of meaningful perspectives and offers a roadmap for those conversations.

Another highly relevant, emerging theme is the shifting role of investments within the family structure. As the primary financial tool for many families, it's difficult to overstate the importance of a well-constructed portfolio. But as Tom, Keith, and other experts convincingly illustrate, recent and emerging approaches, such as goals-based investing, are creating a meaningful intersection between family priorities and financial strategy. Investing can be a powerful tool in educating future generations and defining family values, in addition to sustaining financial wealth into the future.

As families celebrate and adapt to longer life expectancy and craft a values-driven investment strategy, the importance of trusted advisors is another clear theme in this work. Families need experts to provide information and guidance, but they also need partners to tell the difficult truths and ask the right questions.

With this book, Tom and Keith provide those trusted services in abundance. Crucially, they take the next steps beyond just offering thoughtful insights on the issues facing affluent families. They have gathered a select group of experts in family wealth who offer practical advice and exercises families can use to define and perpetuate a legacy. Every chapter is structured around thoughtful questions for further reflection on the topic, creating a natural process for family leaders to foster conversations around these issues.

Questions fuel families. They're how younger generations learn family traditions; they're how priorities are set and how decisions are made; they're how conflict is identified and ultimately resolved. By providing actionable activities and essential questions, *Wealth of Wisdom* takes universal challenges and gives families a personal way to work through them. The result is an interactive framework for advancing family relationships and legacy.

From the first pages of their introduction, Tom and Keith's lifelong passion for helping families maintain the success they've worked so hard to achieve and pass those values on to future generations is readily apparent. They have dedicated their careers to supporting families in achieving these goals, and that commitment and experience comes through in every passage of this book. With *Wealth of Wisdom*, Tom, Keith, and their cadre of experts offer families the tools and resources they need to move into the future with clarity, confidence, and control.

Families reading this book have access to the best thinking and strategies on creating a better life for their heirs, and increasing the chances of a legacy and positive impact that last far into the future.

Acknowledgments

From Tom and Keith

In the creation of any book of this breadth, it is impossible to identify and thank every person who has had an influence on its conception and content.

There are literally countless people who – directly and indirectly – have provided inspiration, encouragement, insight, and ideas that have found their way into this book in some way. We would like to thank all of them for their contributions to this labor of love, which we hope will be of benefit to families of wealth around the world.

Specifically, we would like to thank the contributing authors. They are really the stars of this show. They are the best in the world in their fields and have a wealth of experience to share. We are fortunate to have them in this volume. Among them there are family members and family advisors, authors and speakers, inheritors and entrepreneurs, professors and practitioners, investors and initiators, and mentors and sages. We thank them for freely sharing their wisdom, understanding and practical answers to the questions that so many families wrestle with.

We gratefully acknowledge and express our appreciation to: Patricia Angus, Patricia Annino, Josh Baron, Doug Baumoel, Christopher Brightman, Jean Brunel, Ashvin Chhabra, Randolph Cohen, Charles Collier, Robert Dannhauser, John Davis, Fernando del Pino, Heidi Druckemiller, Mary Duke, Jennifer East, Coventry Edwards-Pitt, Charles Ellis, Peter Evans, Jamie Forbes, Dean Fowler, James Garland, Kelin Gersick, Hartley Goldstone, Katherine Grady, James Grubman, Alasdair Halliday, Barbara Hauser, Lee Hausner, Scott Hayman, Andrew Hier, Stephen Horan, James Hughes, Dennis Jaffe, Nina Kumar, Rob Lachenauer, Ivan Lansberg, Suniya Luthar, Philip Marcovici, Howard Marks, Barnaby Marsh, Susan Massenzio, Robert Maynard, Greg McCann, Anne McClintock, Scotty McLennan, Lisa Parker, Ellen Miley Perry, Ellen Remmer, Kirby Rosplock, Paul Schervish, Alex Scott, Jill Shipley, Meir Statman, Christian Stewart, Blair Trippe, Thayer Willis, and Kathy Wiseman. We are also grateful to Christine Lagarde for giving us permission to use a condensed version of one of her most memorable speeches.

From Tom

I would like to thank the partners and staff at Northwood Family Office who work tirelessly to understand and resolve the important issues and questions of our client families. I would also like to thank the families who have entrusted their lives and wealth to Northwood's care. Particular appreciation to Scott Dickenson and Mia Cassidy for their assistance on getting this book across the finish line.

I would also like to thank my many colleagues in the private wealth industry, too numerous to mention, who have contributed to and honed my thinking about these important issues of family, wealth and the thoughtful management of both. It has allowed me to develop an approach to family wealth management that puts the family and their goals back at the center of the wealth management process, where they have always belonged.

I would also like to express my appreciation to my colleagues at the Rotman School of Management for the vision and foresight they have shown in introducing a professional, integrated private wealth management program in the MBA program at the University of Toronto, and to the students who have contributed to the program.

I would also like to express special thanks to my co-editor, Keith Whitaker, who, as an experienced author and family advisor, brought wisdom, perspective, humanity, integrity, and enjoyment to a challenging but stimulating task.

And finally, much love and appreciation to Karen, Kate, Ben, and Miranda for their support and encouragement – and for giving me the freedom to pursue my passions, including writing this book.

From Keith

I want to begin by thanking my co-editor, Tom, who invited me on this journey and who has made it so enjoyable – one could not ask for a better partner in such an undertaking.

I also want to thank my colleagues at Wise Counsel Research for their continual emphasis not just on seeking the right answers but also on first discovering the right questions.

I give special thanks to my family and my beloved partner for their encouragement and for their willingness to share the journey of money, family, and life with me.

Finally, a deep bow of appreciation to the families who have inspired these words and who will read these pages. May we pray always to receive not what we want but, rather, to want what is best for us.

Introduction

How Did This Book Begin?

Managing significant family wealth is a complex affair, offering both opportunities and challenges. And those challenges have been on the rise with an unprecedented transfer of wealth across generations, shifting definitions of family, globalization, evolving family dynamics, increasing longevity as well as historically low interest rates, increasing tax demands, and massive wealth creation.

Many family leaders are not well prepared for management of wealth or family issues. It is often not their full-time vocation and they may not have had much training in the relevant disciplines. And even if they do have some of the required technical skills (investments, tax, legal, or business), they usually don't feel equipped to handle the vast number of non-technical "soft" issues that seem to arise (values, family relationships, succession, and decision-making). The challenges are similar for advisors.

In our travels around the world, speaking with thousands of families of wealth and advisors to families, we have heard many questions about the issues that confront them every day. Often these questions are tinged with a sense of hopelessness and frustration, and these feelings reflect the number of times that the questioners have tried to find good solutions and have come up empty. Here are just a few of the common questions that originally sparked our interest in creating this book:

- How much money should we leave our children, and when?
- How do we raise responsible, independent, and productive children (versus entitled trust fund babies)?
- How can we manage conflict in our family?
- How can we ensure the success of our successors?
- What's the best way to think through the prenuptial process?
- What return should we actually expect from our investments?
- What does passing values to the next generation really look like?

Hearing such questions repeatedly led us to think about how we could bring answers to these families in a way that would be helpful, practical, and easily accessible to them. There is a lot of information already written on some of these topics (and very little on others), but it can be hard to find, is typically too general, and it is definitely not all in one place. We decided to pull it all together into one volume so a family leader, family member, or family advisor could sit down and review all the key questions at one time.

Who Are the Contributors?

But who would answer these 50 questions? We might have written all of the responses ourselves, but we wanted to offer a diversity of perspectives, tone, and experience. In our travels, we have also had the privilege of meeting and getting to know an amazing group of people who regularly work with wealthy families on these key issues. These thought leaders, practitioners, advisors, writers, and teachers are among the most thoughtful people in the world on the topics that are most important to families of wealth. They understand the issues and challenges, but also the nuances of how difficult it can be to uncover workable solutions.

So we set about finding one or two uniquely talented and experienced people to answer each of the 50 questions. The people we found are business advisors, professors, consultants, speakers, and/or family members themselves. They are all leaders in their respective fields, they have significant practical experience, and they have earned the respect of their peers and the appreciation of many families who have benefited from their wisdom over the years.

Over the space of about a year we researched, winnowed and ultimately selected the key questions common to most families of wealth. We then painstakingly matched questions with contributors and worked with the authors to hone their answers so they best addressed the practical needs of families on the particular topics they took on.

We also asked each author to include some questions for further reflection at the end of their essay so that readers could continue thinking about the particular question and make as many applications as possible to their own family. These essays and questions for reflection also are designed to make possible family-wide discussions. In addition, we asked the authors to include a list of books and articles on the topic so readers could go deeper on any particular issue if they so desired.

The result? A wonderful collection of responses to 50 of the most often-asked questions about wealth and family, written by some of the most thoughtful, practical, and insightful family wealth experts in the world.

What Are the Questions?

As we analyzed the 50 questions, we found that they fell nicely into nine categories.

1. *Thinking through what matters most.* The questions in this section address the basic existential issues of life and wealth, and we encourage readers to read the essays and make the application to their own families.

The questions deal with the definition of wealth, what it actually means to live well, what difference our family history makes, and how we pass on values and a legacy. We wanted to start with the things that define us as families and communities, believing that this understanding will act as a foundation and reference point for all questions to follow.

2. *Planning thoughtfully.* This section is about the issues that almost every family will face as they plan for and pass through the various stages of life – planning for good years and bad, seeing children married, transitioning farms and cottages, retirement, living into older ages (with all the good and bad that it entails), and finally death. Having wealth can add comfort, but also complication, to these life milestones, and many families wonder how best to plan for and deal with them as they come into view.
3. *Investing wisely.* In this section, we help wealthy families think through the most important questions about their investments and the risks they need to take. We start by looking at how to identify and calculate goals, what are reasonable market return expectations, and how that can all come together into a practical asset mix and investment portfolio. For some reason, many investment practitioners like complexity, but most clients don't, so we provide some perspectives on simpler approaches to investing. We also address questions that family investors have about risk in the context of investing. And we look at the issue of whether investors should invest through active investment managers or pursue index investing, with an article on each side of the issue.
4. *Raising the rising generation.* One of the biggest areas of concern for families is in the area of children, wealth, and succession. There is much concern about raising responsible, independent, productive offspring versus entitled trust fund babies. Families worry about raising children in a culture that is so focused on success, about how much money to leave their kids and when they should do it, and what the actual impact of large gifts could be. We address all these issues, as well as questions about how to have good family conversations about financial inheritance, financial literacy, and helping children find the balance between independence and staying connected to the family.
5. *Making shared decisions.* Wealthy families, more than others, have shared decisions to make, due to common pools of wealth, shared business ownership, and communal assets. These can be significant challenges, both with and without the presence of the founder. In this section, we answer families' questions about how to make decisions as a group, how to improve family communication, and what practical steps they can take to build healthy families. We also look at the issues of governance, family meetings, and conflict management, and answer the question

of whether families should keep their assets together or go their separate ways.

6. *Combining family and business.* Many wealthy families have operating businesses, or have made most of their wealth from a business that has since been sold. It permeates family history, relationships, and decision-making. Many families still retain a family "enterprise" of some sort, whether that is a company, a pool of investments, a trust, or a foundation. Understanding and integrating the roles of family, ownership, and management is an ongoing challenge, epitomized by the classic Three Circle Model.[1] In this section, we look at questions of how to engage children in the family enterprise, how to develop leaders and make successors successful, and the importance of business family unity. We also identify the signs that owners might be losing control of their business, and ask whether a family can stay together after the business is sold. Even if you don't have an operating business, these questions and answers contain rich veins of valuable insight.
7. *Giving well.* Philanthropy is a central part of the lives of most families of wealth. Charitable giving is a natural option for families with excess capital beyond their needs, but more than that it is an expression of their values, vision, and commitment to their communities. In this section we address some philosophical questions about how to decide on your charitable choices, and some practical questions about how charitable goals can be best achieved – giving, investing, or a combination. We also address the important questions about how to encourage generosity among succeeding generations, and how to engage children and grandchildren in philanthropy.
8. *Seeking sound advice.* Managing families and wealth is complicated and it is hard to be good at every aspect of it yourself. As such, most wealthy families will seek some advice, but good advisors can be hard to find. In this section, we look at questions about advisors, including what types of advisors you should consider, and how you can find qualified, trustworthy ones and avoid the bad ones. We also look at some specific questions about whether a family should choose a single-family office or a multi-family office, and how they might choose an excellent trustee.
9. *Facing the future.* Finally, we look at questions about how families of wealth will face the future. We know from experience that the future is uncertain and things that seem certain now may be completely (and surprisingly) different in just 5, 10, or 20 years' time. This could apply to the world, the market in which the family business operates, capital markets, global equality/inequality, or the family itself. It might also apply to the

---

[1]Renato Tagiuri and John Davis, "Bivalent Attributes of the Family Firm," *Family Business Review* 9, no. 2 (Summer 1996): 199–208.

way in which you think about your own goals and desires. The practical (and eclectic) answers to these questions are not definitive (by design). Rather they are intended to provoke reflection and discussion within your own family, and to help you find the balance between family stability and resilience over the generations.

How Might You Use This Book?

The primary use of this book is to spark reflection, deepen your thinking, and educate your choices, whatever your role in your family is – patriarch, matriarch, son, daughter, brother, sister, cousin, shareholder, trustee, beneficiary, or advisor.

Don't feel the need to read through this book the way you would a novel. Each section, each essay, is meant to stand on its own. Take a moment to think about what your main concerns or questions are. Then look through the table of contents and identify the chapters that speak most to those thoughts. At the same time, don't hesitate to dip into essays that may seem further afield. If you feel knowledgeable already about investments or planning, try some of the chapters on raising the rising generation or making shared decisions. Our hope is that these chapters will hold unexpected discoveries for even the most experienced readers.

Beyond personal reflection, we have designed these chapters to spark family conversations. These can happen most readily in two ways. First, we encourage you to share chapters that you find meaningful with one or another family member (e.g. a spouse or a sibling or a cousin). Then set up a time to discuss what you learned, what new questions or thoughts your learning prompted, and how you want to apply your learning to your family.

Second, these essays – and particularly the questions for further reflection with which each one ends – are short enough to form the basis of a family discussion (for example, at a family meeting). So often, families hesitate to hold family meetings out of a fear that they lack a common vocabulary – that the meeting will be over some members' heads and beneath others'.

If you are facing particular choices or challenges as a family – for example, around the management of a family business, or planning for a family vacation home, or evaluating investment managers – use one or more of these essays to provide a shared point of departure. Ask family members to read it before the meeting, provide a synopsis at the meeting, and then discuss each member's reaction. Even if you don't resolve the particular matter at hand, this process will educate family members in an important topic and, most importantly, about each other.

For the advisors among our readers, we encourage you to borrow liberally from the suggestions that our contributors make and apply the lessons they have learned to your own client families' situations. Further, we encourage you to use specific chapters to prompt conversations with your clients about these topics. Even if you disagree with an author's recommendation, or the conclusion does not fit your client's specific needs, talking over the chapter can deepen your understanding of your client and their appreciation for your care.

Finally, for both families and advisors, we have included at the end of each chapter a biography of the author or authors. Feel free to reach out to them for a conversation or consultation, if you find their thoughts speak to your situation. Likewise, as cultivators of this orchard, we are ready to share the fruits of this labor – the best practices, the lessons learned – with individual families or audiences of multiple families.

Summary

This book is intended to be a practical, on-the-ground, how-to guide that will answer the key questions that every family of wealth wrestles with on a regular basis and provide common lessons and practical steps that families can take away and employ today. It brings together the most creative ideas and insightful thinking from the best minds in the world on topics of wealth and family. It also provides additional resources that families can access if they want more information and depth on a particular topic.

We hope your enjoy this book as much as we enjoyed creating it.

P.S. Attentive readers will note that this collection of answers to the top 50 questions wealthy families ask has 52 chapters. The reason is that we have included two chapters on the question of how to define investment risk (chapters 17 and 18) as well as two chapters on the question of whether to employ active or passive investment strategies (chapters 19 and 20). There is so much debate around these questions that we thought including at least two different views of each would benefit our readers, even at the cost of offering 52 answers to 50 questions.

SECTION 1

THINKING THROUGH WHAT MATTERS MOST

While he was Dean of Religious Studies at Stanford University, one of our contributors (Scotty McLennan) would invite guests to lecture to the university community on the topic, "What matters most to you and why?" His invitees, who were all well-spoken and accomplished leaders in their fields, regularly reported that this lecture was one of the most difficult – and most rewarding – that they had ever been asked to give.

It is in a similar spirit that we begin this collection: with a focus not on the experts or the answers but on you, the reader, and your questions. Business, wealth, family, and life itself all have a way of drawing our attention away from what matters most to what matters now, from the important to the urgent. The essays in this first section are meant to help correct that natural tendency.

Patricia Angus begins that process with the question, "Are you wealthy?" This question may seem at first blush easy to answer, just a quantitative matter. But of course it all depends on what you mean by "wealth." She invites readers to think through that question in ways far beyond money, including the impact that each of us has on the world around us.

Scotty McLennan then offers a different way to think through these large matters: engagement with serious literature. He shares several examples that touch upon the relationships between parents and children, meaningful work, and death. He closes with several lessons that he has drawn from decades of such reading as concerns that enormous question, "What are the most important factors in living well?"

The next two essays then focus more closely on thinking through what matters most within the context of significant wealth. Thayer Willis takes on the large topic of legacy: What is it? She offers a path to answering that question for yourself that begins with identifying and clarifying your values and moves to specific ways to speak about your values with your heirs. Building upon this approach, Ellen Miley Perry then offers five lessons for passing on values to children and grandchildren, lessons that concern modeling desired behaviors, telling stories, and attending to the growth of human capital.

In the fifth essay in this section, Paul Schervish introduces readers to the Ignatian practice of "spiritual discernment," which provides a framework for thinking through – and "feeling through" – the questions facing someone who has resources that exceed his or her personal needs, such as questions about how much to give to charity and how much to leave to children or other heirs.

Finally, for most people, the answer to the question "What matters most?" depends not only on where we are going but also where we have come from. This is particularly true when the context is family. Heidi Druckemiller explores how important stories are – even or especially stories of adversity and loss – when it comes to building a legacy and connecting families across generations. Indeed, such stories might be one of the largest "asset classes" of our true wealth.

CHAPTER 1

Are You Wealthy?

Patricia Angus

If there's one truth that I've learned in nearly three decades of working with many of the world's "wealthiest" families, it's that the questions you ask are far more important than the answers you might find. Indeed, it has become clear that wisdom is about asking the right questions, knowing what can be answered, and becoming comfortable with all that cannot. This should come as no surprise, but often in "wealth management," this truism is overlooked or given short shrift. Further, it is more important than ever to face this reality as we progress through a period of rapidly increasing disparity of income and wealth.

I've found it useful to help clients understand that they are not alone when they ask questions that do not have simple answers. In fact, many of these same questions have been asked by philosophers, religious thinkers, and spiritual seekers since time immemorial. Nor is it unusual to feel discomfort when facing the fact that there are no simple, and certainly not quantifiable, answers. Coming to terms with this reality is in fact the first step forward in developing a "wealthy" life. Here are some thoughts on this exploration based on my research, readings, and work with clients.

What Is Wealth?

In each new engagement, I ask a series of questions to get to know all members of a family. One of the first questions I ask is, "How do you define wealth?" The responses have been quite enlightening. Only rarely is the answer "money." I hear words such as "love," "health," "family," and "well-being." I hear silence and hesitation and more questions. Even the few family members who answer that they equate wealth with money or material resources quickly elaborate on the definition as they realize that the term encompasses more than that. These reflections can very quickly open up deeper conversations about meaning and purpose.

While the term *wealth* is often used interchangeably with money, its etymology shows that its origin is in well being, not in material resources.[1] Further, the concept itself has been a subject of inquiry in all the world's religions, spiritual traditions, literature, and philosophy. I've found that asking family members what has informed their view of wealth is critical. For some, the Torah or the Bible provide insights. For others, wealth is deeply connected to a spiritual tradition that might have its origins in Taoism, Confucianism, Hinduism, or Buddhism. Most can refer to early childhood messages from their family. It matters far less which tradition is the source, and far more how the individual defines the concept. Whereas professionals and firms in private wealth management today might emphasize that wealth is complex, and use helpful metaphors such as multiple capitals (e.g., human, intellectual, financial, social, etc.), I find that each person must undergo an individual exploration and come up with terms that resonate personally. So, start with "what does wealth mean to you?" and then proceed from there.

Are You Wealthy?

A couple of years ago, I attended a conference focused on the challenges and opportunities of families with "great wealth." For several days, consultants, lawyers, accountants, and financial service executives discussed how families with extraordinary financial, business, and philanthropic resources could ensure that this "wealth" would last many generations into the future. As discussions veered toward questions of "how much is enough?" and "how can we make sure that our wealth doesn't adversely impact heirs?" I felt a sense of discomfort that had been growing in me for some time. These questions are not profound. They are also based on implicit assumptions that deserve further exploration. There are moral, ethical, and societal questions underlying the pursuit of ensuring the consolidation of wealth within such a small percentage of the population. I left feeling disturbed and alone.

I took the backseat of a taxi with these questions and concerns swirling in my mind and heart. My silence was broken when the taxi driver pointed to one of the tallest buildings we were about to pass. He then shared a story with me. Some time ago, his son had asked, "Papa, is there a man who owns that building?" The father replied, "Well, yes, I think so." The son continued, "Papa, do you think that man is happy?" The soft-spoken taxi driver replied, "I am in doubt," then asked, "Son, do you think I am happy?" His son quickly answered, "Yes, I think you are very happy." The father replied, "You are right. I am very happy."

The taxi driver then proceeded to tell me why and how he was happy and, as he said, "wealthy." He'd left his home country, where his family had been financially successful, to start over in this new land. He made his living as a

[1] See *Oxford English Dictionary*.

taxi driver, sending his two children through college and on to receive Master's degrees. He stated, "I am a very wealthy man. I have a pillow to sleep on, a beautiful wife of 32 years, and children I love and speak with all the time. I am a rich man."

I couldn't have asked for a better antidote to the conversations I'd just left. We proceeded to have a deep exchange about the nature of family and wealth, challenges and opportunities. We were able to openly question and explore what it means to be truly "rich." This was not a simple story of how "poor people are wealthier than the rich." Rather, it reminded me of how often the most important questions are not asked by wealth management professionals, especially those who work with the few families who now control so much of the world's resources. Are you wealthy? It's a question that's rarely asked, and my fellow traveler opened the door to that discussion in a way that I rarely hear.

After our conversation, I thought of all that I'd read on the subject, including F. Scott Fitzgerald: "He remembered poor Julian and his romantic awe of [rich people] and how he had started a story once that began, 'The very rich are different from you and me.' And how someone had said to Julian, 'Yes, they have more money.'"[2] I thought of the line in the Bible: "It is easier for a camel to go through the eye of a needle, than for a rich man to enter into the kingdom of God."[3] I remembered how difficult it can be to be "affluent" – the financial complexity, the identity and trust issues, the family dynamics, the burdens, and responsibilities. I thought about the assumption that private ownership can allocate resources better than government and the inherent threat to the social compact[4] that such private control entails. I wondered whether one can be wealthy in a world of such great disparity of ownership and control of the world's resources. I thought, "I am in doubt."

What's the Purpose of Wealth?

There are many ways that the question of "purpose" arises in the context of wealth – material otherwise. Often, family members ask "Now what?" after selling a business or coming to the realization that they've accumulated more financial resources than they'll need for the rest of their lives, and even for the lifetimes of their children and grandchildren. Making money is no longer a driving motivation. Others might reach this moment when they inherit a trust or other funds from a parent, spouse, or ancestor. They look at a bank account statement, a luxurious house, people attending to their needs, and ask, "What's it all for?"

---

[2]Ernest Hemingway, "The Snows of Kilimanjaro," in *The Fifth Column and the First Forty-nine Stories* (New York: Scribner's, 1938).

[3]*King James Bible.* Matthew 19: 24.

[4]Jean-Jacques Rousseau, *The Social Contract; or, Principles of Political Right* (1762).

Once again, these are not new questions and they are not asked solely by those with substantial resources. This is the human condition. Living a life of purpose, connection, and meaning is at the core of these questions. It has always been there. So, what does the world's wisdom and literature say about this?

In Judaism, Christianity, and Islam there is the Golden Rule: "Do unto others as you'd have others do unto you." This is a bedrock principle and guide to living a good life. It has nothing to do with gold and accumulation of material resources. Yet, in my experience, those in private wealth management more often refer to it via the tongue-in-cheek version: "He who has the gold rules." Again, the profound nature of one's place in the world, connection with others, and responsibility toward fellow humans is pushed aside, albeit with humor. The story of Buddhism's origins sheds light as well. Buddha was a wealthy young man who decided to see what life was like outside the confines of the family compound. In his journey beyond, he discovered suffering and proceeded to spend the rest of his life contemplating how best to handle this aspect of the human condition. He concluded that it was best to acknowledge that suffering exists, avoid attachment, and strive to relieve all others from suffering.

There are multiple passages in the Bible addressing wealth and money. There's an admonition against worshiping material wealth. And, there's the simple statement that "The love of money is the root of all evil."[5] In this tradition, money itself is not evil, but rather, how one feels and acts with it is what matters. In these religious texts we find the questions that can help one explore purpose and thereby meaning. What is the purpose of wealth in your life?

Philosophy has something to say about this, especially as it relates to perhaps the most important question about the human condition: How do we face our mortality? Back in 545 BCE, Theognis warned, "No man takes with him to Hades all his exceeding wealth."[6]

So, what is one to do with material wealth? On this topic, I find that my graduate students (many of whom are values-driven millennials) are especially attracted to the line, "Money is like muck, no good except to be spread."[7] The reality is that most traditions tie good fortune to responsibility. Money is to be used for others even in – and especially during – its accumulation beyond one's needs. And, again, the answers are not simple. Balancing philanthropic impulses with the requirements of the social compact is complex work.

Wealth and family are at the core of some of the most profound and perplexing aspects of the human condition. I encourage all my clients, and all readers of this book, to ask themselves the unanswerable questions – and to be open to the exploration. I've found that the *wealthiest* people I know are those who stay

---

[5] *King James Bible.* 1 Timothy 6: 10.

[6] Theognis. *Elegies,* 1. 725.

[7] Francis Bacon, *Essays. Of Seditions and Troubles* (1625).

in community, connected, and are concerned about the balance of the world's wealth. They never cease to ask questions, including,

- What is wealth?
- Am I wealthy?
- What is the purpose of wealth?
- Is my life, community, and world in balance?
- Is the world wealthy?
- Can I be wealthy if those around me are not?

Additional Resources

Philip Novak, *The World's Wisdom: Sacred Texts of the World's Religions* (New York: HarperOne, 1995).

Luc Ferry, *A Brief History of Thought: a Philosophical Guide to Living* (New York: Harper Perennial, 2011).

Mary Catherine Bateson, *Composing a Life* (New York: Grove Press, 2001).

Biography

Patricia Angus is the CEO and founder of Angus Advisory Group LLC, a family enterprise consulting firm. She is an adjunct professor and founding director of the Family Business Program at Columbia University Graduate School of Business. For nearly three decades, she has advised global families with substantial assets on issues including estate planning, succession, governance, wealth management, strategic planning, intergenerational transition, and community engagement. She is the author of numerous articles, case studies, and *The Trustee Primer.* She has been consistently recognized as a global thought leader and is known for her critical analysis, strategic planning, and compassionate guidance.

CHAPTER 2

What Are the Most Important Factors in Living Well?

Scotty McLennan

Good literature is a wonderful resource for exploring the most important factors in living well. For almost two decades at Stanford University I have had the opportunity to teach a class modestly called "The Meaning of Life" to undergraduate and graduate students, as well as to older adult learners in continuing studies. We have explored novels, plays, and short stories with the aim of seeing how their fictional characters, as portrayed by great authors, strive to attain fulfilled lives – with varying levels of success. By looking at several of the 50 works considered over the years, I believe we can identify some of the key factors in building meaningful lives for ourselves.

Shakespeare's *King Lear* is deeply instructive on familial love, in particular between parent and child. The King of Britain in this play has three daughters: Goneril, Regan, and Cordelia. King Lear asks them who loves him most, as he is deciding how to divide his kingdom among them in his old age. That is a bad start for a parent right there. Unconditional parental love does not have a *most*, nor expect a *most.* Goneril responds, "I love you more than word can wield the matter … As much as child e'er loved, or father found; A love that makes breath poor, and speech unable."[1] Regan in turn claims, "[M]y sister … comes too short, that I profess myself an enemy to all other joys … And find that I am alone felicitate in your dear Highness' love." Cordelia is the only one to speak honestly and truthfully: "[M]y lord, you have begot me, bred me, loved me. I return those duties back as are right fit, Obey you, love you, and most honor you. [But] Why have my sisters husbands if they say They love you all? Haply, when I shall wed, That lord whose hand must take my plight shall carry Half my love with him, half my care and duty." King Lear's response is immediately to disinherit Cordelia: "Let it be so, thy truth then be thy dower! … Here I disclaim

[1]Quotations from William Shakespeare, *King Lear* (New York: Washington Square Press, 1957).

all my paternal care … And as a stranger to my heart and me Hold thee from this for ever."

Of course, it is Cordelia who turns out to be the loyal, loving daughter. By contrast, Goneril and Regan take everything from their father, even stripping him of all symbols of authority. Later in the play, King Lear ends up staggering about outside in a raging storm, ultimately going mad. He is then tenderly ministered to by his daughter Cordelia, and they reconcile before their tragic deaths. Cordelia never wavers throughout the whole play in her unconditional love for her father. It is the kind of love one would like to hope that a parent would have for a child too.

In Arthur Miller's play *Death of a Salesman*, Willie Loman seems to have a lot of love for his son, Biff, at least through his high school years (he favors him over his younger son, Happy). He sees Biff as having great potential – athletically as a football star, academically as headed to the University of Virginia, physically as an "Adonis," and as someone who will "make an appearance in the business world"[2] and get ahead. He feels adored by Biff – that is, until his son catches him having an affair out of town in his work as a traveling salesman. Then Biff loses his personal drive to emulate his father.

As Biff heads out West from his family home in New York City – to work outdoors as a ranch hand well into his thirties – a serious parent–child conflict develops. Biff realizes he is not cut out for a white-collar career in the city but is trying to be who he really is, rather than force himself into a mold that doesn't fit. The parent–child conflict is a classic of the child trying to discover his or her true identity, vocation, and calling, in the face of strong parental expectations. It is familiar to many parents who want the best for their children but are also desperately concerned that their children are striking off in directions that won't realize their potential, much less put enough bread on the table in the long run for their families.

As readers of the play, or as theatregoers, we come to learn Willie's deep flaws. First of all, he is not really suited to being in business himself. His own personal passion, like his son's, is working with his hands: in his garden and as a handyman. Perhaps he should have been a contractor. When he is fired at the age of 63, he is too proud to take a job offered by his best friend. He is not able to look very deeply within himself in order to plumb his own soul. Biff says his father blew him so full of hot air as a child that he could never find his way as an adult. At his graveside at the end of the play, Willie is remembered by Biff as having the wrong dreams and never knowing who he really was. Despite it all, though, Biff retains his love for his father, and Willie is able to feel it at the end of his life and return it in a partial way.

Leo Tolstoy in his novel *The Death of Ivan Ilyich* shows us, by contrast, a successful professional – a lawyer who has done well in school and goes on to become a magistrate and then a judge in prerevolutionary Russia. He is not

[2]Quotation from Arthur Miller, *Death of a Salesman* (New York: Penguin Books, 1988).

only proficient at his work, but also highly ethical, taking care never to abuse his power. He marries an attractive woman, from a good family, whom he loves. They have two children who seem to be growing up well. Ivan achieves high social ranking and a coveted position in St. Petersburg. But in his early 40s he contracts a terminal illness and is dead within two years.

Unfortunately, his death is long and painful, and he has considerable opportunity to look back and ask if his life was ever "real." That is, he realizes that he has pursued a socially and professionally correct life and done "everything one is supposed to," but he has been living superficially and missing the essence of a true life. He is not quite sure what that essence is until his young son comes into the bedroom where he is dying, grasps his hand, and kisses it as Ivan is flailing his arms and screaming in pain. The narrator of the novel tells us that at that moment "it was revealed to him that his life had not been what it should have been but that he could still rectify the situation."[3] The real thing for him now seems to be active, unconditional love for others, which he has always been too busy and too preoccupied to give to his family. He explicitly grieves for his son and wife in his final moments on his deathbed, understanding their loss of a father and husband, and tries to ask their forgiveness.

Reading fiction like this, and discussing it with others, is one of the best ways to identify the most important factors in living well. For example, here are some of the answers proposed by students in one of my classes when I asked what they had learned about living a "real" life from reading *The Death of Ivan Ilyich*: (1) Strive to become extraordinary in your life, not just ordinary. Live with passion. (2) Don't get so absorbed in climbing ladders to success that you start missing rungs. Enjoy and appreciate each aspect of your life day to day. (3) Pursue your role in life without getting attached to externals. (4) Develop personal values to live by authentically, rather than trying to fulfill conventional societal expectations. (5) Only the examined life is worthwhile. Set up a regimen for self-examination and truly get to know yourself. (6) See pain and suffering as a positive force for growth and insight.

I would give these students an "A" for effort, but I think there are more factors in living well, potentially of even greater importance, because Ivan had lived his whole life without ever truly learning how to get outside of himself in love for someone else. Finally, in the end, his schoolboy son taught him how to do so. Only then was he able to transcend himself in concern for others. Other students in my classes expanded on this in the class by adding to the list: (7) Become selfless, thinking of others' needs first and building for posterity. (8) Develop depth relationships with others as your first priority. (9) Hold other people when and as they need to be held, just as Ivan's son holds his hand. (10) Develop a spiritual life, looking for light beyond yourself.

Read well. Live well.

---

[3]Quotations from Leo Tolstoy, *The Death of Ivan Ilyich* (New York: Bantam Books, 1981).

Questions for Further Reflection

1. What are the respective roles of nature and nurture in striving to live well?
2. What is the difference, as David Brooks has asked, between the resume virtues and the eulogy virtues?
3. Why are we here?
4. Does it matter how we face death?
5. What if there is no overarching meaning of life?

Additional Resources

Joseph L. Badaracco, Jr., *Questions of Character: Illuminating the Heart of Leadership Through Literature* (Boston: Harvard Business Review Press, 2006).

Robert Coles, *The Call of Stories: Teaching and the Moral Imagination* (Boston: Houghton Mifflin, 2006).

Hubert Dreyfus and Sean Dorrance Kelly, *All Things Shining: Reading the Western Classics to Find Meaning in a Secular Age* (New York: Free Press, 2011).

Biography

Scotty McLennan is Lecturer in Political Economy at the Stanford Graduate School of Business (GSB), where he teaches in the areas of business ethics and business and spirituality. From 2000 to 2014 he was the Stanford University Dean for Religious Life, as well as Lecturer at the GSB starting in 2003. He was the University Chaplain at Tufts University from 1984 to 2000, as well as Lecturer at the Harvard Business School during 10 of those years.

Scotty received a BA from Yale University in 1970 as a Scholar of the House working in the area of computers and the mind. He received MDiv. and JD degrees from Harvard Divinity and Law Schools in 1975. In 1975, he was ordained to the ministry (Unitarian Universalist) and admitted to the Massachusetts bar as an attorney.

From 1975 to 1984, Scotty practiced church-sponsored poverty law in the Dorchester area of Boston. He represented low-income people in the general practice of law, including consumer, landlord-tenant, government benefits, immigration, family, and criminal law.

At Stanford, Scotty has taught undergraduate courses through the Ethics in Society Program ("Ethics and the Professions" and "The Meaning of Life"), Urban Studies ("Spirituality and Nonviolent Social Transformation"), the Masters of Liberal Arts Program ("The Meaning of Life"), Continuing Studies ("Exploring Liberal Christianity"), and the Graduate School of Business ("The Business World: Moral and Spiritual Inquiry Through Literature" and "Finding Spiritual Meaning at Work: Business Exemplars" and "Global Business: Unspoken Rules of the Game").

Scotty is co-author with Laura Nash of *Church on Sunday, Work on Monday: The Challenge of Fusing Christian Values with Business Life* (Jossey-Bass, 2001) and the author of *Finding Your Religion: When the Faith You Grew Up With Has Lost Its Meaning* (San Francisco: Harper, 1999) and *Jesus Was a Liberal: Reclaiming Christianity for All* (Palgrave Macmillan, 2009).

CHAPTER 3

What Are the Key Considerations in Crafting Your Legacy?

Thayer Willis

What is the legacy you have already created? How will you be remembered? Do you like it?

Why would you even care about your legacy? You'll be gone, right? Yes, when your legacy comes into sharp focus, you will be gone, probably recently gone. So, what is it you care about as you consider your legacy?

For almost everyone, the answer is *values.* Most of us care passionately about passing on our values. If we can pass on substantial financial capital, this reflects our values. And if we can pass on values that we consciously and intentionally associate with our financial capital, so much the better. In fact, many people care about these values above the financial legacy. Whether it is hard work, entrepreneurial spirit, a love of learning, family unity, service to God, service to others, a love of numbers or words, or whatever it might be that you value, this is where you can sharpen your focus now.

How can you enhance your legacy to exemplify your values and priorities better? Many years ago, when I taught stress management, I learned the most basic definition from Emmett Miller, MD: (1) Identify your values; (2) prioritize them; (3) Base your actions on your priorities.

This three-step method is the perfect approach to identify what is important to you and to begin your legacy management. There are many exercises available on the Internet to help you identify and clarify your values. Most of these exercises will get you started. On pages 33–34 of my book, *Beyond Gold: True Wealth for Inheritors,* there is an excellent Values Identification and Clarification Exercise that you can use for this purpose (see Exercise 3.1).

Exercise 3.1 Values Identification and Clarification

This is a very useful exercise to bring your values into sharp focus. Read through the instructions below and then use the following list of values to identify your answers.

1. **Circle** the strongest values in your life. Do not be overly analytical. Just mark the values that resonate with you intuitively. As much as possible, employ your heart more than your mind as you choose the values that are most meaningful to you. You may add to the list if there are important words you do not find there.
2. Next, **star your top 10 values**, the ones that are so important that you would be dissatisfied if you did not have them. If you wish to analyze further, prioritize your top 10.
3. Finally, **underline** the values you have not yet fully developed but *aspire* to have. These words describe the person you want to become. Some of these may be values you have already identified as the ones you have in your life. They may already be circled and starred. You may add an underline as well. It is possible to have a value *and* to aspire to it. An example of this is integrity. You may have it already in much that you do, yet you may still aspire to it in a few more areas of your life.

Abundance	Control	God	Knowledge
Acceptance	Courage	Grace	Laughter
Accomplishment	Creativity	Gratitude	Leadership
Adventure	Dedication	Health	Learning
Affection	Dependability	Healthy lifestyle	Love
Athleticism	Enjoyment	Helping others	Loyalty
Authenticity	Equality	Honesty	Mercy
Beauty	Ethics	Honor	Moderation
Being outdoors	Excellence	Hope	Morals
Belonging	Expertise	Humility	Objectivity
Candor	Faith	Humor	Open-mindedness
Challenging work	Family	Impeccability	Originality
Charity	Financial wealth	Inclusivity	Passion
Communication	Forgiveness	Independence	Patience
Community	Fortitude	Integrity	Peacefulness
Compassion	Freedom	Intelligence	Perfection
Competence	Friendliness	Joy	Personal growth
Competition	Generosity	Justice	Philanthropy
Contributing	Gentleness	Kindness	Power
Rationality	Self-discipline	Status	Unselfishness
Relaxation	Self-reliance	Success	Vulnerability
Religion	Sense of purpose	Support	Wisdom

Resilience	Sensitivity	Surrender	Working alone
Respect	Sensuality	Taking charge	Working with others
Responsibility	Significance	Tenacity	Youthfulness
Risk	Spirituality	Tradition	_____
Safety	Spontaneity	Trust	_____
Security	Stability	Truthfulness	_____

Take some time to look over the groups you came up with. You may be surprised at your observations.

You can take off some of the pressure to commit to the lists you are creating by realizing that this is merely a snapshot of you today. If you were to do this exercise again tomorrow or in a year, the values you identify may be somewhat different. However, you would find the majority of the same values show up for you time after time. A few will change as you evolve and grow, but many of your values will not change, especially your top three. Certain others will always show up in your top 10.

After you have identified and clarified your values, you can write your personal mission statement. When you define your own personal mission statement, you will see your top values come to life. Your mission statement is a chance for you to identify what it is that's important that you're doing with your precious time.

These two steps, values identification and clarification, and writing your personal mission statement, will show you how much work you have to do on crafting your legacy.

Your legacy is the character, qualities, and deeds that come to mind when people remember you. Your legacy is not your estate plan. Your estate plan is a legal and financial arrangement that governs how your assets pass to others when you die. You can manage your legacy by making your estate plan support it and reflect it.

To illustrate how easily this can go wrong, let's say you have worked hard in your life to be fair to your children, taking care to give both of them support for their hopes and dreams. And let's say your daughter has squandered opportunities, has been deceitful, and has failed to exemplify the values you modeled for her. Your son has behaved well, has gratefully pursued opportunities, has been open and honest with you, and has developed a lifestyle you respect. You decide to leave everything to your daughter "because she needs help" and nothing to your son because he is self-sufficient. Ultimately, this estate plan does not reflect your values or the legacy of fairness you intend. Most of us would not want to reward the bad and punish the good.

Another example of your estate plan failing to reflect your values is to teach your children that you expect them to complete education and training, and find their way in the world making a purposeful life and a living wage for themselves. Then you give them substantial financial wealth in their early twenties. Most young adults cannot weather this kind of gift well. It shows up as cross-purpose and at best, it is confusing. At worst it leads to self-destruction. This is in direct conflict with the legacy you intend.

Once in a great while I have seen successful young inheritors who receive financial wealth when they are in their twenties. The most successful among them are the ones who had the wisdom to create a foundation and devote themselves to work for which they are passionate. This is extremely rare and cannot be "effectively" mandated. Your estate plan will not create your legacy. It is up to you to take charge of your legacy, and then work to create an estate plan that supports what you intend.

If you find, as many do, that you still have work to do on shaping your legacy, consider the following:

Have an individual, in-person meeting with each of your heirs.

A. **Ask each heir, to describe to you *your legacy*.** What do you think of what you are told? If you like it, great. If you don't, fix it (see the following steps).
B. **Ask each heir, "What are your hopes and dreams?"** Does your legacy to this person support their hopes and dreams? It is a great topic for discussion. Think about, "how can I enhance his or her hopes and dreams with my estate planning?" Asking them each to discuss this with you will give you the chance to examine the way your legacy and your estate plan gifts to them will be likely to affect them.
C. **Ask yourself, "Am I damaging the initiative of my heir in any way?"** If you worry that the answer to this question is "yes," alter your estate plan.

Add to *your legacy*, the attitudes and behaviors you want to establish in yourself. Adding attitudes and behaviors will be easier than eliminating, so start with adding. If you have found that there are qualities that you aspire to that don't show up in the reality of the legacy you have created, add them. For instance, if you value your relationships with family members and this is a high priority for you, make sure your actions reveal this.

Eliminate from *your legacy* attitudes and behaviors you want to eliminate in yourself. Once you have added those you aspire to, eliminating will be easier.

Ask yourself, "Am I leaving heirs attached to each other legally and/or financially, who wouldn't want this restrictive arrangement?" If they don't want it, don't do it. It is common for wealth creators and their offspring to leave rising generations financially and legally attached to each other. The legal and financial attachment could be, for example, a family business, a family real estate investment, or a family foundation.

Usually, this is a bad idea. It sounds good and could be the wealth creator's dream, but there are just too many variables in the future. The one and only exception is the instance in which offspring are already working well together, can see benefits in pooling their resources, and have a substantial history of working out their differences well.

Be creative with the negativity of those in your legacy sphere. You cannot force anyone to get along well or have positive relationships if they want to be separate or engage in destructive behaviors. Undocumented loans and gifts can muddy the waters and result in a lopsided legacy and estate plan. Heirs are likely to experience resentment and enmity. This is easily managed by keeping careful documentation of any assets that change hands.

If in doubt, err on the side of separation of heirs, clear and transparent records, and restricted resources for those practicing negative behaviors. There is no constructive way to force anyone to do work they don't want to do. Let your heirs find their strengths and enjoy using them. If you find that you have damaging negativity in your legacy sphere – for example, family members who refuse to speak to each other, who are addicted to drugs or alcohol, or who are crippled by entitlement, who won't work or persistently drain family resources, take the high road and commit yourself to strengthening the family. Remember the parable of the lost sheep. Make sure your lost sheep knows you are there for him or her, looking for how you can help. Do not give up.

If you prefer that your unmarried and childless heirs leave their inherited assets to rising generations, nieces, nephews, and cousins, tell them. Hire a patient consultant to facilitate relationships if necessary. No one has a crystal ball. If you have a preference about where your assets go beyond those in your estate plan, say so. In fact, if you don't have a preference, it would be considerate to say this too. Be kind if relationships are lacking. Offer to help or to hire someone to help.

Consult with an experienced, creative tax and estate lawyer to coordinate your legacy and your estate plan. This is a defining step, which will deliver substance into your legacy.

To recap:

1. Clarify and identify your values.
2. Write your personal mission statement.
3. Have an individual, in-person meeting with each of your heirs.
4. Add to *your legacy* those attitudes and behaviors you want to establish in yourself.
5. Eliminate from *your legacy* those attitudes and behaviors you want to eliminate in yourself.

6. Ask yourself, "Am I leaving heirs attached to each other legally and/or financially, who wouldn't want this restrictive arrangement?" If they don't want it, don't do it.
7. Be creative with the negativity of those in your legacy sphere.
8. If you prefer that your childless and unmarried heirs leave their inherited assets to rising generations, nieces, nephews, cousins, tell them.
9. Consult with an experienced, creative tax and estate lawyer to coordinate your legacy and your estate plan.

Many people have shed tears over their legacies. It can be that the legacy each of us wants to impart has been poorly perceived or has been rejected. This makes the effort of tuning up your legacy even more important. If you can sow with passion that brings you to tears, you can reap with joy. The overall goal is to be kind.

As James Hughes has said many times, we want to enhance the lives of our heirs and not hurt them in any way. The qualifier is that in order to enhance the lives of our heirs, it usually takes considerable time and attention. Plus, it can be very difficult to get it right, difficult but ultimately rewarding to know that you put everything you had into getting it right.

It is entirely within your power to take responsibility for your legacy management. There is no reason to wait another day. Consider the preceding steps and you will know where to begin. Make sure your legacy is clearly based on your values, and you will know you have it right.

Questions for Further Reflection

1. What work do I have to do on my legacy?
2. What will I tune up first?
3. Given the endless possibilities, what new quality would I add to my legacy?

Additional Resources

Thayer Willis, *Navigating the Dark Side of Wealth: A Life Guide for Inheritors* (Portland, OR: New Concord Press, 2003).

Thayer Willis, *Beyond Gold: True Wealth for Inheritors* (Portland, OR: New Concord Press, 2012).

Jim Stovell, *The Ultimate Gift* (Colorado Springs, CO: David C Cook, 2007).

Biography

Thayer Willis is an internationally acclaimed author, educator, speaker, and leading authority in the area of wealth counseling. She has been a licensed, practicing psychotherapist since 1990, and her primary focus is on facilitating the work of inheritors and their families as they cope with the psychological challenges of wealth. A child of wealth herself, born into the founding family of the multi-national Georgia-Pacific Corporation, she brings to her field a unique insider's perspective on contending with family dynamics as they relate to the mental and emotional challenges of wealth.

Accredited with an MA from the University of Oregon and an MSW from Portland State University, Thayer is a licensed clinical social worker (LCSW) specializing in wealth-related issues. Thayer offers 28 years of experience in a field she helped pioneer and dominates as one of its most prominent, foremost authorities. Working privately with a global client base, she has helped thousands of inheritors and their families in eight countries and four continents resolve wealth-related family conflicts.

Thayer is the author of *Navigating the Dark Side of Wealth: A Life Guide for Inheritors,* an invaluable introduction for families on the difficult journey to freedom beyond wealth, and *Beyond Gold: True Wealth for Inheritors,* which focuses on how individuals can be responsible with the financial wealth in their lives, keep it in perspective, and be free to take on the tough, rewarding task of enhancing relationships.

CHAPTER 4

What Does Passing on Values to the Next Generation Really Look Like?

Ellen Miley Perry

If you are reading this chapter in hopes of obtaining strategies and ideas on how to have your children and grandchildren embrace many of the same life priorities and values that you have, you are not alone. I have worked with very successful and affluent families for more than 25 years and the issue of passing on values is among the most frequent topics on which I am consulted. The process of deeply understanding your own values, being intentional about how to instill some of those in your children, embracing their unique values, and taking the many steps necessary to create a legacy is indeed a life's work.

During these many years, and through the candidness of my clients, I have learned five important lessons about values transmission:

- Values are caught, not taught.
- Values are different than beliefs, preferences, choices, and principles.
- Leading a life that is consistent with one's values is the greatest predictor of happiness.
- Storytelling is a powerful means of sharing values.
- If the family is to flourish for multiple generations, the attention to human capital should be as serious as that to financial capital.

Values Are Caught, Not Taught

We all heard as children that "actions speak louder than words." That turns out to be true. Our values are on display every day, in so many ways, for our friends, family, and community to observe. We demonstrate our values most clearly in the ways we choose to spend our time, our money, and our energy. Families often decide to develop a family mission statement or family values statement. They hope that these documents will teach the future generations what is important to them, what the family legacy is, and what values they hold dear. Such formal statements may help the family crystallize its thinking. But what many thoughtful, committed families have discovered is that what is most meaningful is how you actually live your life, not what can be communicated in a written document.

Children are keen observers. They watch their parents, they listen to their interactions, and they have an almost unerring ability to discern dissonance between what their parents say and what they do.

As adults, we unmistakably demonstrate – in large ways and in small, seemingly inconsequential ways – through our actions who we are, what we truly believe, and what is really important to us.

Our core values are revealed for example, not just through the philanthropic passions we pursue but in how we treat others, the time and devotion we give to our family, the generosity of spirit we show to friends, family, service providers, and others and the priorities we make clear to others. Dr. R. Kelly Crace, of Duke University, author of the Life Values Inventory (www.lifevaluesinventory.org) and a highly respected researcher on values and life satisfaction, says that "If I followed you around for three weeks I could tell you exactly what your top five values are." He believes that it is not what we say we care about, but rather what we *do* that most clearly and accurately informs others about our values.

Parents who are clear about the values that matter most to them are also more able to be intentional about passing on those values. Their words and actions are consistent. This enables them to communicate the connection between their specific values and the actions they believe will effectively promote those values.

For example, parents who wish to pass on the value of responsibility create opportunities for their children to be dependable and accountable. Families who wish to pass on the value of productivity create real work experiences (e.g. expecting children to work for non-family employers).

Wealth can bring with it a sort of gravitational pull – an energy around the money and privilege that is powerful and frequently distracting. Too often, children in affluent families have few household chores, no summer jobs, and few consequences to their actions. Jobs that do exist may be obtained through parental connections and children may lose the value of external, objective feedback. Summers may be used for travel, vacations, and camp, which can be wonderful experiences, but children then miss the opportunity for employment. It is no surprise then that parents experience an uncomfortable disconnect between their own values of productivity, responsibility, and hard work and the values that their children display.

Parents who wish to pass on the value of commitment must commit to keeping their children engaged in activities long enough for them to experience a sense of satisfaction. Dr. Edward Hallowell, author and noted expert on attention deficit disorder and parenting, points to this experience in his book *The Childhood Roots of Adult Happiness.* Dr. Hallowell observes that children must have the opportunity to explore various activities, choose those that are interesting to them, practice them to proficiency or mastery, and then be recognized, even in small ways, for that skill. Affluence may make children more comfortable quitting a sport or music lessons than middle-class children would, for whom the financial costs of these activities are more meaningful.

If parents hope to raise children who are productive, motivated, grounded, and compassionate, as I believe most do, then actions that foster those values must occur consistently throughout the child-raising years.

Values Are Different from Beliefs, Preferences, and Choices

Values are the compass that each of us uses to direct our behavior, often unconsciously. They are the core defining elements of our being, without which we are not ourselves. They are the organizing principles of our lives.

You will likely pass on money rather than values unless you have a plan and attend to this task with the same thoughtfulness as you do financial wealth management. The way that one generation passes on its values to the next usually reflects the same philosophy and attitudes as the transfer of wealth. For example, someone who passes on the value of compassion and service will likely also pass on assets to charity. Someone who passes on the value of hard work to their children likely will not create an estate plan that allows the heirs to live a life of idleness. Those who believe in generosity will be generous to their family and the world, whereas those who possess a less generous spirit might be more controlling and less able to help their children learn the joys and value of sharing their wealth responsibly.

People often use the term *values* to describe what really are beliefs, choices, or preferences. For example, spirituality is a value; the preference or choice may be Christianity or Judaism. A value is community service and civic engagement; a preference or belief may be conservatism or liberalism. Generosity is a value; a preference is environmental conservation or the arts. Families often experience great concern that their deepest values are not being embraced by the next generation, when indeed the *value* is embraced, but the *expression* of that value is different. This is not to say that troubling values are not a real cause for concern – they are. But varying expressions of the same values are healthy for the individual's own development.

Successive generations often struggle to find a sense of their own identity in wealthy families – a sense that they themselves are unique and wonderful in the shadow of a highly successful parent or grandparent. The more that these children and grandchildren can be honored and valued within their families for their own characteristics, beliefs and choices, the happier and healthier not just the individual is, but the whole family system. Those families who have a rigid definition of "who we are" often, sadly, find the younger generations creating distance and making choices that do not promote family unity in an effort to have some individuality. For some wealthy families, the notion of a common and narrow definition of family identity is deeply important, and, sadly for some, it is tied to the transmission of money. On the other hand, families who respect real differences and foster a sense of inclusion in the family find that their families are not only richer in character but also tighter and more committed through the generations. If family unity is a strong value for you, inclusion and acceptance are important allies.

Leading a Life That Is Consistent with Your Values Is the Greatest Predictor of Happiness

Most thoughtful research shows that one of the most important predictors of happiness is the congruence of one's life with one's values. Dr. Crace has shown in study after study that when people live a life aligned with their four or five core values they are happy, healthy, and resilient. When you act on your values, you feel satisfied. When you do not, these same values become a source of frustration and stress. They create a bond when they are shared, and they can be a point of contention when family members, friends, or colleagues have different core values.

Clarifying your personal values is the starting point for understanding what you want your legacy to be. Understanding your children's values can increase the chances that you will pass your legacy on in a way that is meaningful to you and to them.

Values are frames and filters for behavior and communication, and staying values-focused supports healthy parenting. So, why then is passing on values such a complicated process? The most frequent problems that parents face are the following.

Loss of Focus on Their Own Values

A life of privilege and wealth can be highly distracting for some people. These individuals may lose sight of what truly matters to them in the face of almost limitless choices. In the end, when options are so abundant, values are one of the only effective ways of narrowing the choices and leading a life that reflects your values. Families of real abundance have the opportunity to live a life that is fully reflective of their values, unlike those with financial constraints that dictate how they spend their time and available resources.

Conflicts of Values That They Need to Resolve

Parents can help their children understand their struggles to balance multiple and sometimes competing values. For example, a values conflict might exist between a goal of financial success and family unity. To have financial success, a parent must often spend significant time away from the family. This values conflict may be misunderstood by others. Often, spouses and children see the value one places on financial success or productivity as being the guiding principle of an entrepreneur's life, but to family members it feels like it impedes family togetherness and well being. Values conflicts such as these have the potential to send mixed messages to children about what's really important. This is a frequent issue in families of wealth.

Understanding That Teenagers Have a Developmental Need to Challenge Their Parents' Values

This is a healthy and normal part of child development, and parents are rewarded for patience and perspective during the trying teenage years. Differences in values are not a problem. The key is how these differences are played out. When parents have what appears to be a conflict in values with a child, they should ask: Is the conflict a sign of lack of respect for the parents' values, or is it problematic behavior? In general, children are not equipped to know how to express values or how to act on them. Parents who have thought about their own values can help their children develop the skills to communicate effectively about their own values.

Helpful questions to ask yourself, as a parent, include the following:

- What values did I have when I was younger?
- How have these values changed over time?
- What are the values that my children hold?
- How are they the same or different?

You might also want to examine these:

- What is the current state of my relationships with my children?
- What do I want these relationships to be?

Communicating values to children entails:

- Knowing your values
- Managing your fears
- Being neutral and able to accept your children's different values.

Storytelling Is a Powerful Means of Communicating Your Values

Legacy is more than financial inheritance. Its definition includes anything handed down from the past as from an ancestor or predecessor. Your legacy – and your values – are more powerfully conveyed by telling personal stories than through legal documents.

Telling stories is an opportunity to see your own life more clearly in terms of what's most important to you, what your values are, and to live your life more fully according to and in alignment with these values.

When we tell our stories, we are offering three invaluable gifts to the next generation:

1. We are giving them a better understanding of who we are and the forces that shape the values we're trying to transmit.

   The person hearing the stories receives a more complete picture of the parent as person; the teller can be seen not only as a parent, but also as a child, entrepreneur, adventurer, a learner, someone who has struggled and is making his or her way. The stories offer a broader perspective to the next generation, grounding the teller/parent and his/her values in a context.
2. We are giving them an opportunity to explore who they are and how they want to form their own journey.

   When we hear a story, we project ourselves into it; we imagine ourselves there, we identify with the hero, and we make connections to our own lives and experiences. In this act of listening, members of the next generation can imagine their own stories projected on the template of the parent's story. It offers them an opportunity to discover how they are similar or different or both, and ways they wish to emulate or ways that they wish to diverge from their parent's journey.
3. We are giving them the tools to continue passing on the family's legacy.

   By modeling the act of telling a story, we are teaching the next generation the importance of stories and legacy. They will learn to value the family legacy and be able to continue telling the stories themselves. In this way the family legacy is preserved and passed on through the generations.

If the Family Is to Flourish for Multiple Generations, the Attention to Human Capital Should Be as Serious as That to Financial Capital

Successful families often spend much of their time worrying, planning around, and attending to their financial assets. They hire and retain a team of experts to help them successfully manage their financial wealth. They spend many days each year attending to the successful management of their money. Additionally, they give much time and thought to how they will pass on that wealth.

Fewer families attend with the same intensity, energy, and commitment to the human assets of their families: the family members. And if a family is to flourish for many generations and the wealth is to be useful means for the family members in attaining happiness and accomplishment, it is exactly that kind of attention that is needed.

I have come to believe that the most important job of the second generation and beyond is to develop *human capital* with the same energy and intention that the first generation created the *financial capital*. To do this intelligently and successfully, these generations must work hard to maintain healthy family relationships, use their financial resources to enhance the life experiences and opportunities of each member of the family, welcome and integrate spouses into the family, identify and encourage the gifts that they each bring, and, lastly, develop practices and policies that create healthy connections and decision-making.

Each and every healthy multi-generational family accomplishes this task in some way. In every case, a family member, or group of family members, deeply devoted themselves to creating a healthy, committed, and vibrant family. Those family leaders acquired training and skills to assist this effort in one way or another and encouraged the robust connectivity of the family in real and meaningful ways.

The transmission of values to the next generations is indeed important life's work. Many parents, regardless of financial circumstances, worry about how to do this well. Although wealth brings with it a plethora of opportunities, it also brings with it complicating elements in the passing on of good values. Wealth allows for wonderful educational opportunities, travel, broadening experiences, and access to enriching people and choices. It also creates the possibility of entitlement, overindulgence, lack of motivation, and focus on materialism. Some successful parents overload their children with activities and too much pressure to succeed.

The nurturing of good values, regardless of whether or not they happen to be those of the parents, is vital work that is essential to the flourishing of a family for multiple generations. When wealth presents challenges, it is all the more important to be thoughtful and intentional about this process. The rewards that your family will reap are real and immeasurable. Good values are the most important asset you will ever leave your children and the best estate planning tool you will ever discover.

Questions for Further Reflection

1. What, in your view, are the most important values that you were brought up holding?
2. What would you say are the values that your children have learned from your deeds and words, including stories?
3. What steps could you take to engage your children in a conversation about your respective values, shared and different?

Additional Resources

Ellen Miley Perry, *A Wealth of Possibilities: Navigating Family, Money, and Legacy* (Washington, DC: Egremont Press, 2012).

Biography

Ellen Miley Perry is the founder and principal of Wealthbridge Partners, LLC. She has 30 years of experience serving as a strategic advisor for families of substantial wealth. During this time, she gained perspective on the many ways wealth affects families, and she developed expertise on practices that substantively enhance the life of a family and its individual members. From advice and counsel to the business founder to work on governance, succession planning, joint decision-making, conflict resolution, and next-generation flourishing, she brings wisdom, practicality, creativity, and a sense of possibility to the families with whom she works.

Before founding Wealthbridge Partners, Ellen was the co-founder and CEO of Asset Management Advisors (now GenSpring Family Offices), a multiclient family office, and Teton Trust Company, its affiliated private trust.

Ellen, author of *A Wealth of Possibilities – Navigating Family, Money, and Legacy*, is a frequent speaker, author, and advisor on strategies that create and sustain great families throughout multiple generations. Her work and opinions have been quoted in numerous publications including the *Wall Street Journal*, the *New York Times*, and *Fortune Magazine*, as well as in several books by other authors.

CHAPTER 5

How to Think Through Using Resources That Exceed My Personal Needs?

Paul Schervish

The point of the essays in this book is to help you think through a variety of topics for yourself related to wealth. But what does it mean to "think through" these things? How have the wisest and most thoughtful people – past and present – thought through important matters in their lives? They have used a process known as *discernment.* My goal here is to share with you a sketch of this process so that you can apply it yourself.

Why Discernment?

Currently, there are two trends affecting wealth holders that suggest an increase in the need for discernment. The first is the significant growth in the number of wealth holders and the magnitude of their wealth. The second is the desire of wealth holders to allocate their wealth in a way that is as effective and personally fulfilling as the process of accumulating it. Knowledge of the process of discerned decision-making is the key ingredient missing from many current efforts to enrich the quantity and quality of decisions about your allocation of wealth.

Wealth Holders Today

Increasing numbers of wealth holders are achieving and exceeding their financial goals of providing for the material needs for themselves and their families, and doing so at younger and younger ages. This phenomenon raises a significant question for wealth holders: how to allocate the growing financial resources that exceed their material needs. The major attribute of such "redundant" wealth is that it offers a greater range of choice, and the potential to be unlimited, creative, and purposeful.

No doubt, it matters much to you that the quality of your wealth-allocation decisions be conscientious. Discernment is a method by which you can figure out the wisest uses of your time, talent, and treasure, and implement your decisions in a competent manner. You are at the center of the questions you ask and the answers you seek.

Three alternatives suggest themselves as valuable destinies for your wealth. The first is to increase consumption. But when your family's material needs have been satisfied, further increasing your standard of living may not be a significant goal. The second is to increase financial or business investment, which is certainly one potential outcome.

The third is distribution to heirs and philanthropy. This option provides the opportunity to create outcomes that are of a different and perhaps more fulfilling order than those in the world of commerce.

Your Need for Discernment

Figuring out the most fruitful allocation of financial resources can feel like a daunting responsibility. A leading question for those with an exceptional level of assets is this: *How will you use your wealth as a means to deeper purposes, once raising your standard of living is no longer of high importance?*

Answering this question well requires a method of discernment. Discernment is not just thinking seriously about an idea. It is a process that leads to a *decision* to do or not do something. It combines both thinking and feeling and allows you to choose the most inspiring option among the wide range facing you today.

Ignatius of Loyola, the founder of the Society of Jesus, formulated discernment in a teachable and accessible way. His rules for discernment are laid out in his retreat manual, *Spiritual Exercises.* For Ignatius, discernment involves clarifying your preferences, making decisions about them, and implementing them. It is a matter of dispositions, decisions, and deeds.

Discernment differs from other ways of figuring things out. It encourages you to take the time and effort to figure out what most connects you (and your truest self) to your relationships – from family, to work, to people around the globe. Discernment leads you to dig beneath the surface of your everyday thinking to find those choices that bring you joy and that you can do.

Abundance of Choice

There are many people – including perhaps your children, business partners, clergy, charities, financial advisors, and attorneys – who may have a plan for you and your resources. They are not necessarily misleading you or being self-centered, and you can certainly heed their input. But discernment places the reflection (and decisions) about what to do firmly in your court. This, according to Ignatius, is not an insurmountable burden.

Discovering through discernment can be liberating and fulfilling. In fact, you can put aside what others – party politics, advisors, fundraisers, or guilt – tell you to do. Discernment helps you sift through your resources and purposes to see what they are, and then to do what you find most inspiring. It transforms the burden of uncertainty, dissatisfaction, confusion, and hopes into heartfelt decisions. This sifting process can sometimes be thorny because you can confuse outside obligation for inspiration. As Ignatius recounts from his own experience, imposed duty brings sinking feelings, resentments, and regrets.

Recall those times when you were mulling a decision about allocating assets to or from your lifestyle, children, business, or philanthropy. The hard part is not figuring out options; it's deciding among them. In addition to your own pursuit of opportunities, there are many groups seeking to put options in front of you, and your wealth adds to your abundance of choice. And here is where the elements of discernment come in to help with your deliberations.

Personal Example

Many of us pray, meditate, or ruminate in order to make decisions. The best spiritual instruction I ever received in regard to deciding what theology school to attend came from a wise Jesuit. He told me that discernment was not actually waiting for a voice from God to tell me which school (among three good choices) to attend. He recommended, instead, that I seek a peaceful connection to God. Then – in the middle of that experience of connection – then, I should choose the school *I felt I most wanted to attend.* Follow the inspiration.

Discernment Breaks into the Silence of Wise Choices

Discernment is a way for you to break into the hidden silences in your heart about what to do, and to boldly address what the Second Vatican Council calls the "joys, hopes, hurts, and anxieties" of life.

How to break into the silence? Discernment involves attending to both thoughts and feelings. It requires clear thinking, of course, but also entails monitoring your feelings about how your previous decisions worked out and what you want for the future. One technique Ignatius recommends is to list and evaluate the pros and cons of a particular decision. He suggests that you picture actually making that decision, with all the pros and cons. You then wait to see whether the inspiration (or "consolation," as he calls it) from that choice endures or evaporates over time. Sometimes a discerned decision comes about by actually experimenting with – and not just envisioning – a choice so you can see how it will work and what you feel about it. Sometimes the most authentic decision is that you are not yet ready to make a decision.

How do you decide among the many choices you have? How, for example, do you choose between giving to improve education for inner city kids, funding research to benefit cancer patients, or allocating more to your investments or children? I suggest that you think about (meditate on/dwell on) familiar experiences that, since your childhood, have defined what is important to you and others, and in that process you see what rises to your attention.

There are several such life experiences you might reflect on during a discernment exercise – empathy, gratitude, altering circumstances, and happiness. Empathy arises from identification with those whom you feel are like members of your family – and spreads over time to those who are not related to you by blood. For instance, you might think about providing for the education of your nieces and nephews, contributing to families who have suffered from a natural disaster, and helping your religious congregation.

A second experience from childhood that may surface during your discernment exercise is gratitude or "a desire to give back," as people often put it. You become conscious of the unearned advantages, good breaks, luck, and grace that have come your way, prompting you to bequeath such benefits to others. This may lead you to provide scholarships for the kids in the now inner-city school that provided you a step up in life, or to contribute to the hospital that treated your child for autism or cancer.

A third experience is your history of "wanting to make a difference," by changing your personal life and things around you. As you grew up, you strove to expand your freedom at home and in school. As an adult, you chose careers, created businesses, and built a family. As you know, this ability to shape the world (and not just take what life hands you) is especially available to those with exceptional financial capacity. This might stimulate you to change the workings of an educational system, provide your alma mater with a research center, start another business, or provide extraordinary opportunities to your children.

A fourth lifetime experience connected to discernment is the quest for fulfillment or happiness. Unlike the previous three experiences, the quest for happiness doesn't usually suggest new people or causes to focus on. Rather, it enables you to trust and confirm your decisions. Growth in happiness occurs when you close the gap between where you are and where you want to be, while helping others to do the same. In fact, a key measure of a discerned decision is whether you feel that it provides greater joy and fulfillment to you and others at the same time.

Liberty and Inspiration

Discernment allows decisions to be self-discovered in an environment of liberty and inspiration, and allows those decisions to be more wholeheartedly embraced, pursued, and sustained. *Liberty* is the freedom from unfounded assumptions, fears, and anxieties. It also includes what Ignatius calls "indifference." This indifference in no way means being blasé. Indifference is a technical term. It means that before you make a decision, you develop a sense of humility that puts aside the internalized pressures that can constrict your openness to all the possible solutions.

Inspiration is the array of desires and aspirations that lead you to make choices and commitments. Ignatius says that the will of God is found in what inspires you, not guilt or other externally imposed obligations. Every financial decision requires an objective assessment about whether you have enough money to do what you want. But a discerned allocation also yields a subjective appraisal about how inspiring the things are that you want to accomplish. You will know that you have made a discerned decision about wealth allocation when the distributions you make result from your personal inspiration and not just from your objective amount of wealth.

Examples of Family Discernment

Let's look at some examples of discernment. The names and other narrative details have been altered for confidentiality reasons. Louis and Marie Alexander discerned it was time to reduce their ownership of several Texas construction companies headquartered in Houston. Over a business career of 50 years, Louis founded separate home, office, and road construction companies. For a while, Louis had been feeling that he would be happier if he could reduce his work hours, liquidate his operating companies, and concentrate on transferring wealth to children and philanthropy.

Last year, Louis retired from actively running his businesses and sold the last of his holdings. The question then facing him was how to use his liquidated wealth of about $150 million for family and philanthropy. Up to this point, Louis and Marie's discernment process was informal and implicit, but it did follow the principles of liberty and inspiration. They had already carried out some modest transfers to children for lifestyle and the education of grandchildren. In addition, they had been involved for decades in several philanthropic causes, in line with the general norms for entrepreneurs of their wealth and stature in Houston.

Louis and Marie initiated a formal process of decision-making to put their wealth in motion. Their wealth had become a "burden" in the way that Ignatius speaks of it – an unease you too may have experienced. They had a sense of restlessness about what to do with their wealth and questions about how much additional money to give to philanthropic organizations and their adult children. They were also wondering when to tell them about it and when to distribute it.

In search of practical solutions to their concerns, we undertook "biographical conversations" with Louis and Marie, then with their children, and finally with the entire family. These conversations are open-ended interviews prompting individuals to think back to the key people and experiences that have made them who they are today, and to think forward to what they want to be and do in the future. The facilitated conversations permitted the Alexander family members to discover and enunciate for themselves what was most important.

We first turned to how much money the children would receive. Currently, the Alexanders give each child and grandchild the full amount of tax-excluded gifts each year, and they pay college tuition and expenses for each grandchild. But they have limited the amount of future trusts and inheritances to a total of $5 million. Louis and Marie felt that this amount was enough to provide their children and grandchildren with many good opportunities.

Louis and Marie also started to think about their capacity and desires for philanthropy. The question for them was whether they wanted to ratchet up gifts to their current recipients or to focus their charitable giving on a few organizations. They had for many years each contributed large gifts for research at the two hospitals that had treated both Marie's mother and Louis for cancer. They were proud of these gifts. Their energy and animation about cancer research increased to such an extent that it invited the question of whether they wanted to do something extraordinary for this particular cause. The Alexanders spent only a brief time ruminating before deciding to contribute $125 million, to be split between their two preferred hospitals for cancer centers bearing their name. Louis and Marie said that this process had helped them pinpoint something that makes them happier than anything else they've ever done with their money.

But there were complications. The children, knowing their parents' net worth and the amount of the donations, felt somewhat slighted, and raised this with their parents. The children were not being greedy. Still, many people mistake money for love. The children perceived that their parents had not appreciated the good uses to which they would put additional capital. A modest, but not threatening, disagreement ensued. The children felt scorned, whereas Louis and Marie lamented that their children had shown an unbecoming sense of entitlement. The children felt that their parents seemed to show more pride, enjoyment, and confidence in their philanthropy than in them. None of this broke the relationship with their parents. They celebrate holidays together and remain grateful for the benefits they have received. Still, they hope that more money will be set aside for them down the road.

The lesson here is that discernment that leads one family to conscientious decisions does not always or inevitably work for everyone.

Another family had a more positive outcome. The father is a religious and reflective person who quietly aligns himself in all things to what he calls the "Divine Presence." He dedicated his wealth to prison ministry, inner-city schools, universities, and providing healthcare (equal to his own) to all his employees. He had regular conversations with his married children and watched how they built their families. He concluded that his children "are better parents than I was and they are already more philanthropic than I was at their age." He was pleased to pay for educational expenses for his grandchildren. And each year he provided the maximum tax-excluded gifts for all his children, spouses, and grandchildren.

For him, freedom of choice is the practical advantage of wealth and the most profound gift of God. He trusted his kids to "make wise choices" and decided to leave them as much wealth as possible. His asked his children whether they would like him to add more money to his foundation and hand it over to them to run. They answered in the affirmative, even though that meant they would receive proportionately less in bequests.

Choose Advisors Who Coach Your Discernment

Many charitable organizations, fundraisers, community foundations, financial institutions, and independent financial advisors have also realized the need for a process of conscientious discernment. These intermediaries are recognizing an opportunity to provide new sources of value to clients and donors. Some explicitly differentiate themselves by offering specific services to help you allocate your wealth in a more self-reflective and self-chosen manner. When engaging such helpful services, remember that you and your discernment must remain at the center of every decision-making process about how you want to devote your wealth to family and philanthropy.

Discernment as Mindful Introspection

In the end, you will do most of your discernment in the quiet of your heart, in discussions with your family, and in your own investigation of what you want to allocate and to whom. Remember, discernment is a procedure of self-discovery that clarifies your financial goals – for self, family, and philanthropy, quantifies those goals, and devises plans to reach these goals and implement them. Over time and through experimentation and experience, you will build your aptitude for discernment and become your own best teacher. Your regular use of the elements of discernment will create an effective pattern for making decisions. Developing the habit of discernment will generate a set of dispositions, decisions, and deeds that are more spiritually fulfilling, emotionally engaging, and practically effective.

Today, many people are exceeding their own financial goals for consumption, and doing so at younger and younger ages. But that raises compelling questions about both the number of choices families have but also the quality of those choices. It's a matter of creating a worthwhile legacy. In the root sense of the Latin *legatus* (or "ambassador"), in leaving a legacy, you are not so much leaving purposes and wealth behind; you are sending them forward.

Ultimately, discernment is a spiritual exercise. It is a method of guiding heartfelt and useful decisions by asking yourself the deepest questions with liberty and inspiration. For those seeking better decisions, more fulfilment, and a renewed sense of peace, I heartily recommend this journey.

Questions for Further Reflection

In adopting discernment as a method to make decisions about your wealth, you should find your own answers to these foundational questions:

What are you inspired to do with your financial and personal capacities

- That meets the true needs of others and yourself?
- That brings you joy and happiness?
- That you can do well through gifts to family and philanthropy?
- And that enables you to identify with the fate of others, express gratitude for blessings, and achieve deeper effectiveness and significance for yourself and others?

Additional Resources

Paul G. Schervish and Keith Whitaker, *Wealth and the Will of God: Discerning the Use of Riches in the Service of Ultimate Purpose* (Bloomington, IN: Indiana University Press, 2010). See especially "Introduction: Moral Biography" and Chapter 3, "Ignatius: All Things Ordered to Service of God."

Paul G. Schervish, "Religious Discernment of Philanthropic Decisions in the Age of Affluence," in *Religious Giving: For Love of God,* ed. David H. Smith (Bloomington, IN: Indiana University Press, 2010), pp. 125–146.

Biography

Paul Schervish is professor emeritus of sociology and retired founder and director of the Center on Wealth and Philanthropy at Boston College. He has served as distinguished visiting professor at the Indiana University Center on Philanthropy and as Fulbright Professor of Philanthropy at University College, Cork, Ireland. He has been selected five times to the *NonProfit Times* "Power and Influence Top 50." He received the 2013 Distinguished Career Award from the section on Altruism, Morality, and Social Solidarity of the American Sociological Association. Paul is the author of *Gospels of Wealth: How the Rich Portray Their Lives* and co-author with Keith Whitaker of *Wealth and the Will of God.* With John Havens, he is the author of the 1998 report *Millionaires and the Millennium,* which predicted the now-well-known $41 trillion wealth transfer. Projections from their revised wealth transfer model were published in the 2014 report, *Great Expectations: A New Model and Metric for the Continuing Wealth Transfer.*

Paul serves as a consultant for individuals and families, and as a speaker at forums of wealth holders, financial professionals, and fundraisers. He received a bachelor's degree in classical and comparative literature from the University of Detroit, a Master's degree in sociology from Northwestern University, a Master of Divinity from the Jesuit School of Theology at Berkeley, and a PhD in sociology from the University of Wisconsin, Madison.

CHAPTER 6

Does Family History Matter?

Heidi Druckemiller

I recently watched a documentary film entitled *I Have a Message for You*, which features an oral history given by a Holocaust survivor named Klara who is currently 92 years old and lives in Tel Aviv.

I learned that Klara and her husband survived World War II by jumping out of a train that was transporting Jews from Belgium to a death camp in Poland – a train that was also carrying Klara's dying father. Wracked with guilt about leaving her father behind, Klara nevertheless took the dangerous leap that allowed her life to continue, leading up to the moment where we see her sitting on a couch in Israel in 2017 and recounting her incredible story.

Even more incredible, in 1962, while Klara was walking along Dizengoff Street in Tel Aviv, she was suddenly approached by a woman who recognized her from that terrible train. This woman had been there when Klara's father woke up from a deep sleep and realized that his daughter was gone. Before passing away, he implored anyone who might ever see Klara again to tell her that he was the happiest father in the world, knowing that she had escaped.

By the end of the film, I was amazed by Klara's tale of human suffering, loss, bravery, and survival against all odds. What particularly amazed me was the story of Klara's seemingly random encounter on Dizengoff Street decades after the end of the war. Many of us have experienced similarly magical moments of synchronicity – incidences that seem almost other-worldly or unbelievable, and yet can also feel inevitable or even fated. Such moments, impossible to predict or rationally explain, often become, somewhat counterintuitively, the most important and defining aspects of our lives.

It is the discovery of stories like Klara's encounter on Dizengoff Street that I see as the true purpose of family history. Although the process of unearthing and preserving primary source documents and other pieces of the historical record is vitally important, if we leave our efforts at just that, it's akin to creating a mere black-and-white sketch of what has the possibility of being a more colorful, nuanced, and complex work of art.

All of us have personal stories, reminiscences, and anecdotes that will never appear on the documents that officially record the events of our lives. That is not to diminish the importance of such documents or the information that they contain. As a professional historian, I relish the challenge of interpreting all the disparate data that I collect, as much as I enjoy fitting individuals' lives into larger historical contexts, and crafting compelling narratives. But why would any of us refuse, if given the opportunity, to add original, first-hand accounts to those narratives? Why would we not leave something more personal for our descendants to cherish? To give them a way, in our own words, of understanding who we were so that they might better understand themselves?

I think often of my grandmother, Lillian, who I loved dearly and about whom I also harbor a few regrets; in particular, I regret not recording some of her memories while I still had the chance. I know quite a bit about her life as well as her family's larger story: how her parents and siblings emigrated from present-day Slovakia to the United States in the early 1900s, how one of her sisters was left behind, the joys and hardships they faced as immigrants in their adopted city of Cleveland, Ohio, and so much more. The records that have survived from Slovakia, the ship manifests that document my ancestors' overseas journeys, and the naturalization records that certified them as American citizens are among my most prized possessions. But as I study my own family history, I find myself more often than not drawn to the stories that linger *behind* those documents – the individual voices that seem to whisper underneath the names and words written or typed on simple pieces of paper.

While studying my grandparents' 1937 marriage record, for instance, I think about how they met one night at a youth group event at their church and, according to Lillian, she took one look at my grandfather and knew that she was going to marry him. When she promptly stated this conviction to her mother upon returning home that evening, my great-grandmother waved it off as the naïve statement of a fanciful young woman.

The short story is, of course, that Lillian was right. "And did you know," she asked me once, *"that our two families were from neighboring villages back in Slovakia? And isn't that something?"* I nodded yes, and as I recall that conversation now I find some sort of existential comfort in the notion that Lillian would have had the same feeling of love at first sight had she encountered my grandfather for the first time on a dirt road between Lubenik and Mokra Luka instead of at a church dance in downtown Cleveland; that they were meant to meet and marry whether the winds of history had blown their families to American shores or not; that my mother was meant to be born; that I am meant to be here.

These days, it's become quite commonplace in the professional history and family dynamics space to tout ideas about why family history work matters for smart and practical reasons related to issues of governance, impact investing, and philanthropy. It is widely believed that the creation of a shared legacy is an effective way for extended families to define common purpose across generations, an idea with which I wholeheartedly agree.

But something essential is being lost amongst all the statistics and messaging surrounding the importance of legacy and its relationship to creating and sustaining wealth, and that is the assertion that family history work is equally, if not more, important for other philosophical and emotional reasons. It's important for us to record our family stories simply because *we are.* Because our ancestors lived. Because it's enlightening and meaningful to discover how we are connected to those who came before us, not simply to learn from their successes and failures, but to more fully understand that our lives are extensions of what they experienced, the decisions they made, and the chance encounters they might have had on Dizengoff Street, or while walking along a dirt road, or dancing in a church basement.

It's important for all of us to remember that we need to get personal with this subject. To sit back and wonder whether life really is just random (as you might have always thought) or whether the documents you find and the stories you hear actually imply something different – that you truly are a part of a larger story than you ever imagined. And although you might not ever completely comprehend it, taking the time to honor those who preceded you and adding your own voice to the mix for those who will follow could very well be the most important work you ever do.

It is work that can begin with the simple step of capturing and preserving the stories and experiences of aging family members, while there is still time. During periods of generational change, recording the stories of elders helps to make their achievements, struggles, and sacrifices tangible to members of the rising generation. These personal recollections also bring to light the uncertainty and drama of the past, as well as signal to young people that they, too, will become part of an ongoing story.

It is these ongoing stories and our places in them that ultimately matter. Again and again, research on happy, functional, and cohesive families has proven that the one thing they share in common is the creation of a strong family narrative. During the process of creating these narratives, authenticity is key. It is imperative to be truthful, and ask that of others, in order to capture stories that "oscillate" – meaning that they honestly convey the ups and downs of real life. Looking back, it can be deceptively easy to view past events – especially achievements – as inevitable, overlooking the moments of risk, perseverance, and luck that made them possible.

Whether you are preparing for a generational transition, celebrating a milestone, striving to improve communications, or simply curious, your family history matters. The story of your past can help you to discover your family's unique values, shape its moral purpose, and direct its strategic decision-making. It will also, inevitably, give your life meaning in ways that you can't yet imagine.

Questions for Further Reflection

1. Is there something in your family history – a particular event or the life of a certain ancestor – about which you have always wanted to know more? Start there. You are likely curious for a reason.
2. Do you have aging relatives whose stories are important to record? Don't wait until it's too late. Most of us have made this mistake and learned to regret it.
3. Do you know of something difficult – an illness, a setback, etc. – that someone in your family history faced and how her or she overcame it? Lessons and insights surrounding that event could be extremely useful to something you are grappling with right now.
4. How are particular events or people in your family history relevant to something that you and/or members of your extended family are experiencing at the given moment?
5. What makes understanding your legacy important to you at this particular time in your life?
6. Can you name all eight of your great-grandparents? Most people can't, which is interesting considering that those individuals are only three generations removed from us. Many family fortunes are also lost within three short generations. Consider whether those two things might be interrelated.
7. When you begin to uncover your family history, keep particular questions in mind – not only how did things happen and why were specific decisions made, but also: what does it all mean?

Additional Resources

Donald Ritchie, *Doing Oral History*, 2nd ed. (New York: Oxford University Press, 2003).

Victor Frankl, *Man's Search for Meaning* (Boston: Beacon Press, 2006).

Bruce Feiler, *The Secrets of Happy Families* (New York: William Morrow, 2013).

Biography

Heidi Druckemiller is a family history expert and senior consultant with The Winthrop Group, a leading history consultancy. Since 1982, Winthrop has provided history and archival services for organizations, families, and individuals, based on the idea that high-quality historical services can offer the same, if not more, value as other professional services such as investment strategies or legal advice. Prior to joining Winthrop, Heidi held the title of Senior Historian & Senior Vice President at Wells Fargo & Co., where she spent many years creating comprehensive family history projects on behalf of select clients and prospects.

Heidi also specializes in architectural and urban history and earned her BA at Brown University. She graduated with a Master's degree from Columbia University's Graduate School of Architecture, Planning, and Preservation.

SECTION 2

PLANNING THOUGHTFULLY

In principle, nobody is ever really against planning, but few of us do it. And fewer of us do it well. In a famous study, Roy Williams and Vic Preisser suggest that almost 70% of family wealth transference and business succession plans fail.[1] Reasons include lack of planning, poor follow-through, and insufficient communication. It's a common problem, but it is preventable.

Planning can mean many things to many people, but there are likely three core benefits to consider.

1. *Thoughtful decisions.* Planning can help you think through and express what you really want and how you might get there. A few well-crafted questions from an experienced guide (like some of the ones in this book) can help you make better, more thoughtful decisions, and understand the consequences of your choices. Founders, in particular, tend to be more doers than planners (given their past entrepreneurial successes) and may have to work a little harder at stepping back to think about what is most important, but may see it as worthwhile with all that is now at stake.
2. *A roadmap.* Planning can also help you create a set of key priorities and a to-do list of the critical things that need to happen to ensure success (whatever the definition is). There is a very high correlation between writing down what you want to do and doing it (or delegating it!). Vague wishes, hopes, and intentions won't do the trick.
3. *Conversations with others.* A good plan also includes conservations with and involvement of other people in your world – spouse, children, partners, co-workers, and advisors. They can't read your mind. A good plan helps bring clarity, communication, and hopefully even buy-in to the family plan.

[1]Williams and Preisser, *Preparing Heirs* (San Francisco: Robert D. Reed Publishers, 2011).

Scott Hayman writes the opening article, asking "Is it worth having a financial plan?" In it he lays out the reasons to have a plan, including a higher probability of meeting goals, improved confidence in decision-making, and lower stress, not to mention better outcomes. He also provides suggestions on how to make the plan realistic and valuable.

Meir Statman takes on the question "What is the right balance between saving and spending in retirement?" In his research interviews with couples in retirement age, he finds that many have more than enough money to pay for whatever they need, without risk of running out of money before running out of life. Yet they resist, insisting that they cannot afford these services. Why do people behave this way? Can they change? Should they change?

When your children tell you they're getting married, it is usually good news. But for families of wealth, there are often other issues and complications that come up as well, including concerns about protecting family assets in a world of marriage breakdown. Charles Collier answers the question "How do you start a family conversation about prenuptial arrangements?" and shares his many years of wisdom and experience. In fact, he turns the question on its head and suggests a conversation about how you can help the couple in their lives together.

Another blessing of wealth that can easily turn into a burden is a family vacation home. While such an estate can create positive memories for generations, it can also entangle family members in financial and emotional complications. Jamie Forbes marshals his experience as a consultant and a member of a family that has preserved a shared property for well over a century to offer concrete recommendations for the communication and shared decision-making required to successfully manage a family vacation property.

An increasingly common phenomenon in today's era is extended human longevity. Living longer seems like a good thing but it can have negative and even surprising implications. Patricia Annino answers the question "How can you prepare for longevity and mental incapacity among family members?" She tackles the tricky issues of assessing mental competence, but also the other side of that coin when parents are still so sharp in their later years that they don't step aside from family and business leadership and frustrate the next generation.

And finally, Kathy Wiseman looks at the issue of "How do you prepare for a good goodbye?" In many families and cultures, people don't like to talk about death. It's not comfortable. In addition, many hard-driving entrepreneurs want to believe they're never going to die. But in families of wealth, it is critical to plan for your goodbye and prepare for it – financially, emotionally, and relationally.

Planning is a worthwhile exercise for all families, particular those with significant wealth and complexity. In any planning, remember to use good inputs and conservative assumptions, frequent communication with key stakeholders, and lots of flexibility to accommodate the inevitable surprises!

CHAPTER 7

Is It Worth Having a Financial Plan?

Scott Hayman

Every family of wealth needs a financial plan. It allows them to build a roadmap that will help ensure they achieve their goals, and a framework to make sensible decisions over the course of their lifetime. An investment in a solid, thoughtful plan will pay dividends long into the future.

The key part of this sentence is "over the course of their lifetime." A good plan should last a long time but must be monitored and updated to reflect new facts and assumptions that arise.

Even if you have significant net worth and aren't sure the idea of a financial/cash flow plan is worth the effort, keep reading. The planning principles in this article are critical, both to ensure you have enough money to do all the things you want to do during your life and after you are gone, and to properly plan for the succession of your wealth, whether it be to future generations or to philanthropic causes. A good plan will help you identify the inevitable gaps in your strategy, and allow you to fix them before it is too late.

Planning is also important for your adult children as they make investment, saving, and spending decisions in their own lives. It allows you to help them develop the good skills and habits they need to make wise choices. Most parents want to ensure their children will have happy fulfilling lives, and a good plan is a critical building block.

Inputs to the Plan

Goals and Objectives

Whenever you start something, you typically do it with the idea of achieving a goal or objective. A financial plan is no different. The starting point in building a plan is understanding what you are trying to achieve. What is the wealth for? Who is the wealth for? When will they receive it? How much will they receive?

What Is the Wealth For? Everyone has different goals. One of the basic objectives for most families is to ensure they can live the life they want to live. Once you have decided what that life looks like, you have to decide what portion of your wealth it will take to fund those goals. Goals generally include your lifestyle expenses, capital purchases, philanthropic causes, and helping out family members.

In a recent conversation with a client who had more than enough money to live the lifestyle he wanted, he told me that he still wanted to build more wealth. When I asked him why, his answer was that he was a builder by nature. If he did not continue to build, he would feel like he was going backwards. He has spent his whole life building his company, and his wealth. I don't think his answer was about a goal. I believe it was his motivation.

When I pressed him about why he wanted to keep building beyond his own needs and those of his family, it ultimately came out that he was building his wealth so he could give more to philanthropic causes that he wanted to support. This was important in understanding how to go about building his plan. It also identified a need to spend more time deciding how he would give his wealth away. This conversation allowed him to see that giving, too, would be an important part of his "building."

Who Is the Wealth For? I believe there are only two things you do with money. You spend it, and you give it away. Whatever you do not spend or give away during your lifetime, you give away at death, either to children, future generations, friends or charity – or to the government.

When Will They Receive It? As for the money you will be giving away, you have to decide when to give it to them. A proper balance between helping others and ensuring your own security is essential. You do not want to give away too much money too soon, and leave yourself short. I often do an exercise with clients to clarify how much they require as a safety net. This exercise identifies the amount of money that they are free to give away to children or to the charities they want to support.

How Much Will (and Should) They Get? This is one of the most common questions faced by families with wealth. I think you should give your children enough to help, but not enough that will stifle their own initiative and self-development. Do not "rob" your beneficiaries of their own achievements by giving them too much. We all know stories of the "trust fund babies" who have grown up (seemingly) without a worry in the world. They often do not have a purpose and have not developed the self-esteem that comes from making their own way in life. And they have not built the "muscles" that come from hardship, failure, and sacrifice. This incapacity can come back to haunt them.

Data and Assumptions

Every financial plan has many data inputs and assumptions. The better the inputs (i.e. accurate, realistic, current), the better the analysis, and the better the framework that can be built. I think of this as "fact-based decision making." As such, it is important to use the most accurate and up-to-date financial information that the family has.

The first step is building the family balance sheet. On the left-hand side of the ledger, you can start by listing all family assets including cash, securities, real estate, operating companies and the estimated present value of future employment income, business cash flow and inheritances to be received.

On the right-hand side of the balance sheet, you list the family liabilities. For most families of wealth, this is not debt. Liabilities are, rather, self-imposed, and are more commonly known as family goals. These liabilities must be funded, either by income or by assets. They typically include (the present value of) expected lifetime spending, potential one-off cash flow requirements, planned gifts to future generations, and charitable donations. The difference between assets and liabilities is family net worth (or discretionary capital).

For a client with $50 million in assets, I calculated that their living expenses of $500,000 a year would require about $20 million of their total capital, their annual gifts to their children of $50,000 per year would require $2 million, and their philanthropic donations each year of $100,000 would require $4 million (based on different rate of return assumptions). Those goals totalled $26 million, and left another $24 million for legacy goals and discretionary capital.

The next step is the family income statement and, in my experience, this is where people have the most difficulty. An income statement, in and of itself, is quite simple. It shows gross income, less taxes, less expenses, with the balance, one hopes, being a surplus! Most people know what their income is, and taxes can be calculated relatively easily. The more elusive number seems to be expenses.

When I ask people what they spend, they often don't know or they underestimate the number. If you are not sure what you spend as a family, there is a quick way to estimate it: (A) Estimate how much income you have each year, (B) do a rough calculation estimate of the taxes you pay, and then (C) approximate how much you save each year. Then do the simple math: A minus B minus C equals the amount you spend each year. You put all of this data into a long-term cash flow model and you start to get your outputs.

As mentioned, any financial plan requires a number of assumptions, such as inflation, interest rates, life expectancy, years of work (income generation), number of descendants, and when the business might be sold, to mention just a few. And these assumptions have to be predicted over many years. They are never going to be perfect, but reasonable estimates (or even ranges) are more helpful than no plan at all.

A good financial plan identifies the all-important goalposts and a variety of possible outcomes. In other words, depending on the width of your goalposts, you should be able to kick the ball anywhere between them and be sure of successfully meeting all your family's financial goals. The best advice is to use conservative assumptions since upside surprises are better than downside surprises!

Cash Flow Alternatives and Analysis When you review the various potential outcomes in your plan based on the different assumptions you select and choices you make, you will probably be happy with some of them and not with others. It may mean changing some of the inputs to improve your cash flow results. You can change four main levers in a cash flow forecast:

1. *Income.* Income includes positive cash flow from employment, your business or your portfolio. For instance, if you can increase the returns on the portfolio or earn more employment or business income, you would expect higher cash flow.
2. *Expenses.* This is arguably the most important input to a cash flow forecast, due to the fact that expenses are paid with after tax dollars and recur every year. For example, if (for ease of calculation) your tax rate is 50%, you need two dollars of income to pay for one dollar of expense.
3. *Time.* This factor relates to how long a person will work and have income, as well as how long you will live. Working longer is good (from a cash flow perspective) and living longer is bad! In this age of increased life-spans, it is important to ensure that the plan is conservative in terms of estimating how many years you will live. In North America, there is currently almost a 50% chance that at least one member of a 65-year-old couple will live to age 90.
4. *Other Assets.* These are a family's assets that don't produce income right now, but could be sold later to add to the portfolio and produce income – e.g. a second property.

You can then tinker with the cash flow forecast to get to a place where you feel relatively comfortable. The most obvious cash flow inputs you can tweak are expenses and real investment returns. Some people with high income and high cash flow producing businesses might decide to work a few years longer or keep the business a bit longer before selling.

Assuming (and hoping for) higher rates of return on investments can be elusive (and generally not controllable) and may require taking on more risk. Therefore, it is often worth being conservative on your asset class return assumptions and use a lower-than-expected return versus a higher one.

On the other hand, people usually have the most control over the money they spend. Most families do not want to spend less, but they can sometimes adjust to make a plan work. Obviously, many other variables can be adjusted to see what works and which assumptions are reasonable and which are not.

Once you have a range of various potential outcomes, the most important part of the plan is an analysis of the pros and cons of each cash flow option and which scenario best achieves the family's goals and objectives with the highest probability. This is where the real value of the plan comes in. The analysis should help your family understand why a particular alternative is best and what the related risks are.

A cash flow analysis often highlights unexpected outcomes. Oftentimes, it shows families that their wealth is likely to grow to a very large amount over time, which may lead them to make different decisions about their money. For example, they might give away more money to charitable causes during their lifetime as it becomes clear that they are certain to have excess wealth.

On the other hand, I once had to tell a 55-year-old client who had just sold a business for $30 million (and had no significant income except from investments) that if he kept spending at his current rate, he would be out of money by age 75. He thought he had lots of money, but the plan showed him that he didn't, based on his spending patterns. He decided to scale back his lifestyle expenses.

When it turns out you cannot do everything you want, the key questions to ask are:

- What are your priorities?
- What changes will you make?
- Which of the four cash flow levers can you pull?

Other Disciplines

The cash flow analysis really looks at the "raw numbers" side of the plan – the achievability of the goals, if you will. Once you have decided on the best cash flow scenario to use, the next step is to include the tax, investment, and estate planning components. Here are some examples:

Tax planning. A family often has choices as to *who* holds assets, and *how* assets are held. A serious review of the family structure can reduce their tax burden while still achieving other objectives. For taxable investors, the appropriate structure can add return to the portfolio without adding risk, simply by reducing the overall taxes payable. Most investment managers spend a lot of time looking for added return for their investors. There are often easier solutions to increasing return by using tax planning.

Investment planning. Once you know the rate of return that makes your plan work (using conservative assumptions!), deciding on asset classes and building the investment portfolio is much easier. It also means that the portfolio links back to the family's goals since they are already incorporated into the financial plan's cash flow forecast.

Estate planning. As mentioned above, there are only two things you do with money – spend it or give it away. The estate plan section of the financial plan should answer the following "give-away" questions:

1. Who will receive the money – family, charity, etc.?
2. How much will they get?
3. When will you tell them about it?
4. When will they receive it – while you are alive, or after you have died?
5. How will they receive it – directly or through a trust?
6. How will you prepare them to receive the money – education, skills, experience, etc.?

Life insurance. Insurance should be addressed in the plan, but not everyone needs it. There is an easy way to estimate how much life insurance you need. Simply total up the cost of all of your goals and objectives (i.e. the liabilities on your family balance sheet), and compare them to your assets, after all taxes (including all estimated estate, gift, and capital gains taxes). If assets exceed goals, you do not require life insurance. If they don't, you can consider using life insurance to make up the difference.

The other reason some families use life insurance is liquidity. If you have a lot of illiquid assets, you may require life insurance to provide liquidity so your family doesn't end up having to sell assets in a hurry (at fire-sale prices) to pay taxes at your death.

Administration – A critical part of any financial plan is documentation. It is particularly important to document the details of all assets and liabilities so the plan can be easily followed after you die or are not able to make decisions. Having wills and powers of attorney and an audit trail of all of your holdings, while not directly a part of a financial plan, are important to make sure the plan can be implemented and your goals and wishes can be achieved.

Implementation

Once you have decided on a plan, you must implement it! Otherwise, you have wasted your time. From the cash flow forecasts and all the analysis that has been undertaken you can develop a prioritized to-do list. For example, if you have not updated your will since before your children were in diapers, you may want to move that to the top of the list.

Review, Adapt, Adjust

If you renovate your house room by room, by the time you get the last one done, it is probably time to go back to the first room and redo it. A financial plan is similar. It should be a dynamic document that is reviewed, adapted, and adjusted as facts and circumstances change. Many factors can change as a family goes through life. When something changes, you need to assess the impact of that new development (and the others that will inevitably arise) on your plan to see if you need to make adjustments.

Major changes in life such as births, deaths, marriages, divorces, and changes in financial assets all represent changes that should cause you to review your plan.

When the Plan Is Done

A good financial plan is a living document that is flexible and adaptable. Using the fact-based approach outlined earlier will give you comfort that you have done all your homework and you are making the best decisions you can at the time with the information you have. Don't fool yourself with erroneous information. Be realistic and conservative. Remember that upside surprises are better than downside surprises.

I believe that the biggest benefits of a plan are the direction and perspective it provides for families, which leads to better decision making. This in turn means better outcomes, fewer mistakes and increased flexibility. And this ultimately provides the confidence that everything is looked after.

Every successful business has a business plan, and every family needs a financial plan. Preparing and living by a well-constructed financial plan will dramatically increase your family's chance for success. The investment of a little bit of time and energy in the development of a plan will be one of the best decisions your family can ever make.

Questions for Further Reflection

1. Do I have all the relevant facts to draft a proper plan? What am I missing?
2. What are reasonable assumptions?
3. What has changed (or may change) in my family's life that could affect our plan? Why?
4. Is what I am about to do better than something else I have done or could do?
5. What is the worst thing that could happen, and if it does happen, how will it affect us?

Additional Resources

Mark Daniell and Tom McCullough, *Family Wealth Management: 7 Imperatives for Investing in the New World Order* (Singapore: Wiley, 2013).

Ross Levin, *The Wealth Management Index: The Financial Advisor's System for Assessing & Managing Your Client's Plans & Goals* (New York: McGraw-Hill, 1996).

Biography

Scott Hayman is president, co-founder, and head of client service at Northwood Family Office, Canada's leading multi-family office. He is a Chartered Professional Accountant (CPA, CA), a Certified Financial Planner (CFP), a Trust and Estates Practitioner (TEP), and has spent over 30 years in the financial services industry.

Prior to co-founding Northwood, Scott worked at a fee-based financial planning firm and in senior roles at two major national investment firms. In 2003, Scott co-founded Northwood Family Office with partner Tom McCullough. Scott is the senior partner at the firm responsible for relationships with existing clients.

Scott is a lecturer in the Management of Private Wealth course in the MBA program at the University of Toronto's Rotman School of Management, and an Entrepreneur-in-Residence at the Ivey Business School at Western University.

Over the years, Scott has been involved in a number of charities with much of his time devoted to the Juvenile Diabetes Foundation.

CHAPTER 8

What Is the Right Balance Between Saving and Spending in Retirement?

Meir Statman

An elderly couple moving to an assisted living apartment call their son in another state for help in moving their belongings. A 92-year old widow finds it difficult to clean her home, yet refuses to hire help. Each has more than enough to pay a moving company or cleaning crew without the risk of running out of money before running out of life. Yet they resist, insisting that they cannot afford these services. *Why do people behave this way?*

I was intrigued by that question, especially given that I research and teach behavioral finance – a field that combines finance and human behavior. And I also wanted to know what we could learn about how people change – or fail to change – their attitudes about saving and spending as they go from work to retirement. So I set out to try to answer them in my book, *Finance for Normal People*, and in an article I've written for the *Wall Street Journal*. The responses have been fascinating in their own right. Here is one: "I've been a dedicated saver and investor for 40 years, always practicing self-denial to the point that it's extremely difficult to spend money. I honestly get uptight about small purchases that are insignificant. The difficulty is changing a mind-set that has gripped my thinking for four decades."

Here's a look at some basic points I've put forward in the book to answer the question: *Why do people behave this way?*, and also some stories from people who agree – or who push back.

Hard to Grasp

Let's start with the feeling of financial well-being, a feeling that we have as much money as we need. Some people with high financial well-being are wealthy, but many more are middle class people who earn adequate incomes throughout their working years, save enough, and spend their savings judicially in retirement. Low financial well-being afflicts the poor, but it also afflicts spendthrifts who spend more than they earn, and frugal people who slip into stinginess by excessive fear – depriving themselves, their families, and the needy. One wrote: "Since I retired, every withdrawal from savings has been painful. So many articles are about the fear of not having enough … This article gave me hope and the thought to pursue joy with my money, not stew in fear."

Pensions promote financial well-being. Those lucky to have them typically do not need to save much for retirement and do not fear running out of money. My parents were among the lucky. They left us their house, some mementos, precious memories, and deep gratitude. I have the menorah that held the candles my mother would light every Friday night, and a painting that hung in the kitchen since I was a small child.

Fewer have pensions these days, and more have retirement savings in tax-advantaged accounts. Many bear the difficult task of saving enough during their working years and the equally difficult task of spending the right amount in each retirement year. These tasks are difficult, because spending needs and temptations abound during working years, and fear of running out of money haunts us, including many who are wealthy, in retirement.

Many people are justifiably concerned about the cost of long-term care, reluctant to accept aid, and adamant about maintaining their dignity. My father would say, "When parents give to children, all smile. When children give to parents, all cry." One retired parent wrote to me about "maintaining a certain amount of that capital to cover the possibility of long-term care expenses. One of the 'gifts' I intend to leave my children is never to be in a position where my wife or I do not have the resources to adequately take care of ourselves. If we never need it, great, the kids/grandkids can have it and use it however they want and I won't be around to cringe."

Our Mental Toolbox

We tackle the tasks of saving and spending with the mental tools of framing, mental accounting, and self-control. We frame our money into distinct mental accounts, mainly "capital" and "income," and set self-control rules of saving and spending. Income includes salaries, pensions, interest, and dividends, among other sources. Capital includes houses, bonds, stocks, and other investments. Self-control tools include automatic transfers from income such as salary, to capital such as retirement accounts, and automatic reinvestment of interest and dividends, and the rule of "spend income but don't dip into capital."

People who are fortunate to earn good incomes during their working years – and employ these mental tools successfully – accumulate substantial savings. But these useful mental tools can turn into obstacles in retirement when income diminishes and it is time to dip into capital. One extremely wealthy man, a retired senior executive, wrote: "I've struggled with boundary issues between income and capital. I've actually taken on a couple of board of director assignments so that I feel justified spending for what I consider extravagant."

Self-Control Helps

Self-control is not easy to muster. Some fail to muster it at all. When self-control is weak, the desire to spend it today overwhelms the desire to save for tomorrow. National Football League (NFL) players enjoy very large income spikes that amount to substantial wealth, but wants for spending today often overwhelm wants for saving for tomorrow. Bankruptcy filings of many NFL players begin soon after the end of their careers.

Some people are savers by nature and nurture. The Big Five personality traits psychologists discuss are conscientiousness, neuroticism, extraversion, agreeableness, and openness. Conscientiousness is the trait most closely associated with self-control. The retired senior executive wrote: "The points on conscientious saving hit the nail on the head. I grew up as one of nine children of Depression-era parents. They always stressed education, achievement, savings, and marital happiness over satisfying urges for material things."

Excessive Self-Control

Self-control can be excessive. Indeed, *excessive* self-control is as prevalent as *insufficient* self-control. Excessive self-control is evident in the tendency to spend less today than our ideal level of spending, driving tightwads to extremes beyond frugality. The prospect of spending money inflicts emotional pain on tightwads even when it might otherwise be in their interest to spend. The interplay between emotion and understanding is evident in MRI brain images of people who see a product followed by its price and then are asked to decide whether to buy it or not. Seeing the price caused greater activation in the brain's insula among people who decided *not* to buy the product than among people who decided to buy. (The insula is the region associated with painful sensations such as social exclusion and disgusting odors.)

One person wrote: "What if the enjoyment is in the saving, and the pain is in the spending?" Another wrote: "Every so often there are articles about people who have accumulated vast wealth relative to their lifetime income, and when they pass at an old age and people find out they feel sad for them—that they lived frugally and never spent it on anything. I sometimes think they are missing the point. The total enjoyment for that person was in the saving and living miserly and frugally and well below one's means. To a certain degree, I am that person."

Moreover, excessive self-control can induce a mindset where spending is what irresponsible people do, reflected in this statement: "I'm saving now because good, admirable, upstanding people sacrifice their current standard of living to save, save, save for the future."

We Spend Less as We Age, and We Die Sooner Than We Hope

Concern about running out of money is regularly exaggerated in inflated estimates of life-expectancy. American Social Security tables indicate that, on average, only 1 in 10 of today's 65-year-old men will live to age 95. Yet one wrote: "With discoveries in biotech rolling out of labs in droves, we may have reached a technological tipping point as regards life expectancy. I think today's 60-somethings will live to be 100 easy, maybe 110 – and their children will probably make it to 150." Reality, however, is still some distance away from the labs. The oldest-in-the-world Italian woman died in April 2017 at age 117, followed by the oldest-in-the-world Israeli man, who died in August 2017 at age 113.

Moreover, older people spend less, in large part because physical limitations make them less able to spend and because they are less inclined to spend for personal reasons. Spending at age 84, adjusted for inflation, is 23% less than it was at age 62 among college-educated American couples. Spending on movies, theater, opera, and concerts declines by more than 50% between the ages of 60 and 80. Spending on hearing aids, nursing homes, and funeral expenses increases by more than 50%.

One older person wrote: "Lots of people lose a spouse and do not travel or vacation much because they are by themselves. They have enough money but just do not go anywhere or do much. They have lost their best friend and have not found a second life after losing their spouse. So they sort of mope around and just do not do much. It is really sad. I know a few people in this situation and have tried to help but there does not seem to be much you can do. We lose not only spouses, but friends ... Suddenly we're left to do things alone, or not do them at all. Balance, while we have the resources to seek balance, is important to a fulfilling retirement."

Spend Here Now

We need not feel guilty about spending our hard-earned savings on ourselves. As one wrote: "During my career I was a very conscientious saver and investor. I always maxed out my retirement fund contribution and put a large percentage of my salary and bonus into a deferred compensation program. I have had a difficult time changing my mindset from a saver to a spender. This article helped me make that mental transition. The first thing I did was to go out and get fitted for a new set of golf clubs and didn't feel guilty about it!"

Some people derive no pleasure from spending on themselves. One wrote: "If one has never derived pleasure from material things, why would that change in retirement? A cup of coffee and a walk on the beach at dawn and I'm happy. The psychic income from being over-saved has value."

I empathize with this man. I, too, like a cup of coffee and a walk on the beach, even if not at dawn. But why not share "oversaved" money with family and the needy? One who has learned the lesson wrote: "I learned from my mom that the greatest joy in life is giving to your family. She would give something to all her six children, their spouses, the grandchildren, the great grandchildren and all their spouses on their birthdays, anniversaries, St. Patrick's Day, Valentine's Day, and for no reason at all. If you want the closest thing to eternal life, try this."

Another wrote about balancing spending on himself, his family, and the needy: "I am deriving pleasure from assuming the strategy of 'I am through saving. Now I am spending.' Judiciously, to be sure, but nevertheless with a view to obtaining satisfaction. Thus, my wife and I have made some long-desired renovations to our home, schedule at least two major overseas vacations a year, supplement our children's financial needs at a time when they need it and when I can see the result. I devote more time and financial support to charitable work. I continue to spend time exercising at a local athletic club, now free thanks to Silver Sneakers. I read more, and indulge in my love of classical music. All of this gives me significant satisfaction."

Better Warm Than Cold

One reader faulted me for failing to "address preserving capital for the next generation which is a priority for some of us octogenarians." But why not give money to the next generation with a warm hand rather than with a cold one?

Some months ago I was speaking to a large group of financial advisers about the difficulties facing well-off people when transitioning from work to retirement and from saving to spending. Several advisers walked over to me as I stepped off the stage to ask questions and share experiences. One stood aside, waiting until all the others have left. "I burst out crying when you said, 'It is better to give with a warm hand than with a cold one.'" Indeed, she was crying when she spoke to me. It turned out that she lent her son some $27,000 for college tuition and now demanded that he pay her back by the agreed schedule. She reasoned that paying by schedule would benefit her son, teaching him financial responsibility. But the son was now financially squeezed, at the beginning of his career, lacking even the money to buy his girlfriend an engagement ring, and his mother's demand soured their relationship. The mother had more than enough to forgive the loan without imposing any hardship on herself, giving with a warm hand rather than with a cold one. I hope this is what she did that day.

One last story and lesson: "My husband was reared by extremely thrifty parents who survived the Great Depression and World War II, and through hard work and frugality bordering on stinginess (all Christmas gifts came from the Salvation Army) they accumulated a very comfortable nest egg. They passed on to him their fiscal philosophies and my husband absorbed them like a sponge.

"My husband handled our finances. Once he died and I took over the finances, I was amazed at how much money we had. I shall have to work very hard to spend all of it, but I plan to give it my best effort. In the two and a half years since my husband died, I have been to Africa and made three trips to Europe. I have already booked trips to see lowland gorillas in Rwanda and Uganda, snow monkeys in Japan, penguins in Antarctica, and ride a horse across the Mongolian steppes. These trips were booked after my doctor told me that based on her patients, 80 is the age at which people lose their energy and enthusiasm for traveling. I am attempting to get in as many trips as I can before hitting that mile marker.

"I have also made many donations to local charities and plan to set up a trust fund for a friend's grandchild who has Down's syndrome and would otherwise become a ward of the state when his hand-to-mouth existence parents die.

"My husband never reaped any benefits from his saving habits and received only three months of Social Security before dying. May others escape his fate."

Questions for Consideration

1. Is it hard for me to spend money? Why is that? What am I worried about? Are my fears justified?
2. Are there opportunities for me to "give with a warm hand than with a cold one"?
3. Do I get pleasure from spending or from saving?
4. Do I have insufficient self-control or excessive self-control?
5. How might I change my behavior to improve my well-being?

Additional Resources

Meir Statman, *Finance for Normal People* (New York: Oxford University Press, 2017).

Biography

Meir Statman is the Glenn Klimek Professor of Finance at Santa Clara University, where his research focuses on behavioral finance. He attempts to understand how investors and managers make financial decisions and how these decisions are reflected in financial markets. His most recent book is *Finance for Normal People: How Investors and Markets Behave*, published by Oxford University Press.

Meir's research has been published in the *Journal of Finance*, the *Journal of Financial Economics*, the *Review of Financial Studies*, the *Journal of Financial and Quantitative Analysis*, the *Financial Analysts Journal*, the *Journal of Portfolio*

Management, and many other journals. Meir is also a member of the advisory board and/or associate editor of multiple respected academic journals.

Meir was named as one of the 25 most influential people by *Investment Advisor*. He consults with many investment companies and presents his work to academics and professionals in many forums in the United States and abroad.

Meir received his PhD from Columbia University and his BA and MBA from the Hebrew University of Jerusalem.

CHAPTER 9

How Do You Start a Family Conversation About Prenuptial Arrangements?

Charles Collier

"My wife and I talked to our two daughters about a prenuptial arrangement when they were in college," says Steve Baird, president and CEO of a family business, Baird & Warner, a real estate company in Chicago. "After a number of conversations, they agreed to have a prenuptial arrangement when they get married. Our business has been good to the family for five generations, and I hope that the enterprise will survive another generation."

There are compelling arguments for having prenuptial arrangements for members of a family for whom a business is important. The company is a family asset and ongoing enterprise that may have been in place for a number of generations, and many families want to see the business continue to grow for many additional generations. A business family's financial future is interconnected in a way that is different from a financial family, whose worth may consist of houses and marketable securities that allow each member to manage his or her own financial affairs independently of the others. In contrast, having a vital business requires an interdependence among family members that is best served without competing outside interests of non-blood relatives or possible divorce disagreements.

If you have a family business or financial wealth or a vacation home that you would like to be part of your family's legacy in the future, should you consider a prenuptial arrangement for your children? Are you concerned that the dissolution of a marriage of one of the next generation heirs would jeopardize that cohesive ownership? If yes, what would make it feasible to talk with your children about a possible financial contract? Should you have *all* the children in the room? The primary question is, how do you prepare yourself for this important conversation? This can be an extremely difficult but rewarding conversation to have with your children.

Many families have had prenuptial arrangements and they often say to their children, "This is just what our family does." Other families stress that the financial wealth of the family is an important family asset and needs to be passed down for more than one generation. And the threat to that happening is worth planning for and discussing. In some cases, parents say that this takes money off the table when a young man or woman marries into your family – meaning that they are not marrying your son or daughter for their money. Some parents say to their daughter or son, "Your spouse will enjoy the benefits of our money for a long time." While these answers suffice at the start of the conversation, they do little to address the main issue and to use the opportunity to discuss an important topic with the next generation.

There is no question that timing about this conversation regarding prenuptial arrangements creates anxiety. This is an important and sensitive subject. There will be differences that provoke emotions. "Discussing them creates a lot of anxiety," says Michael Fay, a senior trusts and estates attorney in Boston. "The anxiety relates to the fact that these arrangements are intended to deal specifically with the possibility that the marriage will be terminated. Prenuptial arrangements have distrust written all over them. There is really no easy way to address this except by urging openness and honesty on both parties."

Another way of discussing a form of prenuptial arrangements can be started while talking about the trust documents and the financial legacy currently in place. Many parents have trusts for their children, and, in many cases, the parents think of the trust almost as a prenuptial arrangement. Some lawyers will say that the prenuptial arrangement is a companion document to reinforce the trust provisions for their children. Research indicates that a high percentage of what the children who are beneficiaries receive comes to them under discretionary trusts, and they have no control over the principal or the income during their lifetime.

At the root of the discussion is "the parents' fear as the driving force," says James Hughes, a retired counselor of law in Aspen and author of *Family Wealth – Keeping It in the Family*. "They are afraid of the money getting into the wrong hands, which often means their son-in-law who is not good enough. It is totally impractical to ask these young people to enter into an agreement requested by the earlier generation. The reason for doing this is the parents' fears – fears over financial assets that their children will never own." Perhaps articulating the fears in a conversation will assist in finding an agreeable solution.

James Hughes continues his thinking: "The core question is, 'Can you be a resource to this young couple?' Can you have a conversation about money and discover one another's philosophy, so that whatever agreement emerges will reflect that philosophy? The highest good that parents should keep in mind is being focused on encouraging the success and sustainability of their children's relationships."

It is my opinion that one way through this prenuptial dilemma is a series of conversations that I call "breakthrough conversations." The topic of prenuptial agreements is hard to discuss and can be uncomfortable. It takes time and courage to confront. Needless to say, I think the conversation should take place early enough so that no fiancé(e) has yet arrived at the door.

My preferred process is a two-part conversation. The first part begins with your spouse and focuses on what is important to you around your money and a prenuptial arrangement. A key goal is to create clarity about your expectations and why they are important to you. The two of you may not agree, but these differences should be discussed and respected. Indeed, you may find that there are differences where you thought there were none, and points of agreement that you did not expect.

Ask yourselves the following questions:

- What is the prenuptial arrangement meant to accomplish? For what reasons to you want a prenuptial arrangement?
- What worries you if your children get divorced?
- What history and principles inform your thinking around the prenuptial arrangement?
- Where have you seen this done well? Where have you seen it managed poorly?
- What would your parents say about asking your children to negotiate a prenuptial agreement?
- How does your faith factor into these decisions?
- What will it take to bring your children into a conversation around the idea of a prenuptial arrangement?
- What are the downsides of a prenuptial arrangement?
- Could you let the couple or the individual family member make their own decision?
- In what ways do you want to share some of your wealth with your daughter- or son-in-law?

The second part is a talk with your children about a prenuptial arrangement. You can have this talk one child at a time or all the children together. It may be helpful to have a facilitator at one of your meetings. Steve Baird had a number of conversations with his daughters, and I led one discussion for the whole family. Here are questions that you may want to ask:

- What is the purpose of the inheritance for the next generation?
- In what ways is a prenuptial arrangement important to you or not? Why?
- How do you differ from your mother or father?
- How do you differ from your siblings?
- Can you maintain separate financial resources and have a viable marriage? What would it take?

- What principles inform your thinking?
- What potential obstacles stand in the way of negotiating a prenuptial arrangement?
- How does your faith factor into these decisions?
- Could you bring your fiancé(e) into the conversation?
- What would your fiancé(e) be up against in marrying into our family?
- What are you up against in marrying into your fiancé(e)'s family?
- What is your dream for the future of your family?

So my suggestion is: *Engage all your young adult children in conversations about the distribution of your financial wealth.* Planning for a *possible* prenuptial arrangement is both a legal process and a family process. Meaningful conversations over a period of time can be an opportunity for strengthening the family and addressing difficult topics with openness and respect. In the long run, these breakthrough conversations can be enormously informative and useful all around.

Additional Resources

Charles W. Collier, *Wealth in Families,* 3rd ed. (Cambridge, MA: Harvard University Press, 2012).

Biography

Charles Collier was the senior philanthropic adviser at Harvard University, where he served for 25 years. He worked with hundreds of individuals and families to shape their philanthropy, helping them make wise gift decisions and advising them on family relationships surrounding financial wealth. He served as a speaker and consultant for many institutions and organizations ranging from universities and independent schools to private banks and community foundations. Charlie published articles in *Trusts & Estates, The ACTEC Journal, Family Business Review, Journal of Gift Planning, Advancing Philanthropy,* and *Gift Planning Today.* He has been quoted in the *Boston Globe, The New York Times, The Wall Street Journal, Financial Times,* and *Forbes.* In 2004 he was named to *The NonProfit Times* Power and Influence Top 50 and in 2014 Family Wealth Report honored him with its lifetime achievement award. From the time of his diagnosis in 2008 with early-onset Alzheimer's until his death in 2018 Charlie was an outspoken advocate for research into the disease and compassion for its sufferers. Charlie was a graduate of Phillips Academy, Andover, from which he received a distinguished service award in 2002. He held a BA from Dartmouth College and a MTS from Harvard Divinity School. He completed the postgraduate course in family systems theory at the Bowen Center for the Study of the Family. The third edition of his book, *Wealth in Families,* was published by Harvard University in 2012. That same year, he received the Harvard Medal, which honors "extraordinary service to the University."

CHAPTER 10

How Can You Preserve a Beloved Family Vacation Home or Estate?

Jamie Forbes

Legacy family properties can be a powerful grounding force. It's rare these days to have one place that remains constant throughout our lives. Many people move away for school, then to an apartment, and then to a larger house with the arrival of children. The average US citizen moves more than 11 times in their lives.[1] Americans tend to move more than residents from other countries, but the fact remains that most of us move multiple times throughout life.

Having a home to which you can return through all those transitions provides a sense of place, a connection that remains unchanged amid all the other changes in life.

Such a place can be a huge gift. As someone with a shared family property that has been in my family for eight generations, I know first-hand that sense of belonging to a place and to the people who share it with me. I feel connected across nearly two centuries to relatives who have walked the same sandy paths, learned to sail in the same wooden boats, and taught their own kids how to safely pick up turtles, frogs, and snakes.

And yet, as anyone who has ever shared a property with other family members can attest, it takes work. There can be conflict that, if unresolved, can fester and upset family relationships. For this reason, many advisors recommend selling family properties instead of passing them on to your descendants and hoping they can figure out how to make it work.

Perhaps selling is the right thing to do for your family. But before you make that decision, it's worth considering what makes the most sense. This really

[1]Mona Chalabi, "How Many Times Does the Average Person Move?" FiveThirtyEight (January 29, 2015), https://fivethirtyeight.com/features/how-many-times-the-average-person-moves.

needs to be a group discussion that includes everyone who will be responsible for the successful transition and ongoing decisions. Keeping a legacy family property while also keeping the family together requires clear communication, thoughtful planning, structure, commitment. And it takes funding.

This conversation will take time. Depending on geographic and personal constraints, it could take several months or even several years to reach a decision and create a plan.

It is useful to think of the process as three different steps or phases. Each of the steps can result in a decision to sell, or it can progress to the end with a specific plan for transitioning ownership, according to decisions made along the way.

- *Step 1.* Owner discussion – Hold the property or transition out.
- *Step 2.* Family discussion – Interest and willingness.
- *Step 3.* Family discussion – Creating a working plan.

Step 1. Owner Discussion – Hold the Property or Transition Out

This is a discussion among those who currently own, manage, and control the property, and your advisors. Often the owners are a couple who acquired the real estate. Sometimes it's more than one couple, as when the owners are siblings or even friends who decided to buy the property together. Key considerations for this discussion include:

1. Will you need the proceeds for another use?
2. Do family members have an attachment to the property?
3. Do family members enjoy the property together?
4. Have family members expressed interest in keeping the property?
5. Do you think the property would help maintain family relationships?
6. Do you have any specific concerns about whether it would work?
7. Are some family members more interested than others?
8. If so, do you have a way to make your decision seem fair for those not interested in keeping the property?
9. Would keeping the property put a financial burden on your family that may create stress?

There are likely other questions you'll want to ask yourself that relate to the property itself or to the specific dynamics of your family. The main objectives in this step are to become clear about what your vision is for the property and to understand what the major challenges are to achieve your vision for future ownership.

Step 2. Family Discussion – Interest and Willingness

Whether you plan to keep the property in the family or sell it, the next step is to meet with your family. This step begins with outlining to what you think makes sense: what is your vision for the future of the property? If you plan to sell, explain why that makes sense to you so everyone understands. If you'd like to explore the possibility of keeping the property in the family, let everyone know you want their input. The goal in this step is to understand what family members want to do and begin exploring how that might work. You may come to an agreement in Step 2 that it is time to sell. Or the discussions may lead you to create a specific plan in place for transitioning the property to family members.

***Step 3.* Family Discussion – Creating a Working Plan**

This step requires a lot of detailed discussions and generally takes the most time. The objective of Step 3 is to develop a clear understanding of what will be required for each owner/family member. You need to create a structure and process for management, usage, decision-making, and capital investments. You should discuss how family members will resolve conflict (because there will be conflict!). If there is no endowment or revenue that fully supports the annual expenses, consider how family members are to deal with financial disparity among themselves. In other words, what happens when some are more able to contribute to the property's upkeep than others? And you need to discuss how you plan to add new family members as owners (through marriage or new generations) and how ownership will transition (because of divorce, death, or for financial reasons).

Things to Consider Throughout the Process

Don't force the discussion. Being patient can be very challenging, and it's not always possible. Sometimes a death in the family or terminal illness creates a sense of urgency that is unavoidable. But ideally this conversation should begin well before any decisions are required. Planning enough time allows for everyone to process the choices at their own speed rather than feel forced into a decision before they've been able to consider all the implications. You can move the process forward by creating agendas for meetings and clarifying next steps. This process doesn't need to be overly formal, but it can be useful to make sure everyone knows what to expect and has the same understanding of decisions or action steps coming out of each meeting. Consider using a professional facilitator for larger families or more complex properties so that everyone can participate fully.

Be open. You may have a vision that you're really excited about, but if it's not shared by others, it will not be successful. The more flexible you are about the outcome, the more likely it is that everyone will feel good about the process and support the eventual decision.

Don't feel you have to go it alone. Families often find that hiring an outside facilitator is helpful. It can make the process feel a bit more formal at times, but it is generally more efficient and allows everyone to participate rather than letting family dynamics interfere with the discussion. For small properties with only several participants, having a facilitator is less critical but can still be useful.

Observe behaviors. Conversations about emotionally-charged topics such as money and cherished family properties can be very revealing. Disagreement and conflict is fine as long as it can be resolved. Use the discussion with your family as a way to anticipate how well they will work together on the property. Pay attention to how engaged everyone is in the discussion. Draw people out to make sure all challenges and concerns are expressed.

Talk about the things that might go wrong. Things *will* go wrong, whether it's from a natural disaster, mechanical failure, or accident. Some of these are easy to discuss. Others may be more difficult. You won't be able to anticipate everything, but the more you are able to talk through, the easier it will be to think in practical terms about what you will do.

Document the vision. It's useful to document why you are choosing to work with your family members to preserve the property. This does not need to be a lengthy document. In fact, it can even be a short paragraph. It simply needs to state why the property is important to you as a family. You might start this with your personal vision and have your family add their vision, so the result is collaborative. This statement can be a reference point for decisions and to resolve conflict.

Tricky Issues

The following is a list of common things that can cause conflict over time with legacy family properties. Talk through them during Step 3 and think of any others that may be more specific to your family or to the property itself. The more your family members are aware of and can discuss these factors, the easier it is to identify and talk through them when they arise.

Communication. Poor communication between family members is generally what begins to make family members disengage. The best way to maintain clear communication is to start with it in the planning process and to recognize that strong communication is an essential ingredient in keeping the property in the family. Create a process that supports consistent communication. Don't make it so time-consuming that it's not reasonable. Family members should meet at least once a year to discuss financial details, make decisions, discuss usage, and address any challenges. I suggest you meet once a year in person and, in addition, have quarterly conference calls. The quarterly discussions enable you to address any issues that came up in the previous season and address topics about future needs. It is essential to create a process for raising and resolving disagreement because conflict is inevitable in group ownership.

Financial burden. It is easy to enjoy a place that someone else is funding or has endowed. When there is no mortgage on the property, and there's actually a funding plan to support whatever is needed in the way of capital expenses, real estate taxes, and property management, there is one less major source of conflict. But these situations are extremely rare. Typically, there are at least annual expenses that need to be covered. There are too many options for a complete discussion on the different ownership structures and the implications for each. These details also vary by state and country. Find good advisors who specialize in these matters to help you understand what type of ownership structure and financial model makes sense for both your property and your family. Make sure the model is sustainable for whatever time horizon you think is reasonable for your family's ownership. Consider how to make it affordable for everyone.

Financial disparity. Sooner or later this will be an issue for family members if the property remains in the family for a long time. It first appears in discussions about upkeep or the question of whether it's time to renovate the kitchen. Then it creeps into conversations about annual fees or dues. Think about how you will handle these issues. In general, families that find ways to successfully accommodate financial disparity are also able to sustain their collective ownership longer than families that have more rigid "pay-to-play" rules. The most straightforward way to do this is by establishing an endowment or using an earned revenue stream, such as rental income, some or all of which can be set aside for current or future use. Although it may be something you want to avoid, some also find it useful to create a process for buying out family members who no longer wish to participate. Others focus more on creating a process to ensure that the property is available to all family members, regardless of their ability to pay.

Usage disparity. The more users there are, the faster this will become an issue. Some family members may live within driving distance to the property while others may require lengthy travel. Those who live close-by are more likely to be frequent visitors while those who live further afield may visit fewer times during the year and for longer stretches of time. It's important to be aware of these differences, discuss them, and find ways to accommodate them. Creating a scheduling, reservation, and time-allocation process can be a useful way of ensuring everyone understands and follows the process. If there is no process, usage disparity can turn into resentment. This resentment stems from feeling like the arrangement isn't fair for everyone.

Ownership perception. This issue can be closely tied to usage disparity. Ownership perception is different than actual ownership. It describes the perceived difference in ownership among family members. In general, your objective is to prevent differences in ownership perception within the family. And it's not easy because more frequent users are available and often participate more in property management and maintenance needs. For example, imagine you cut, split, and stack the three cords of wood needed for the fireplace each winter while other family members use their time on the property to relax and enjoy the view. Over time, recurring patterns like this can translate into some family members feeling like their hard work should give them more say when decisions need to be made. Those who spend just one week on the property may begin to sense over time that their vote doesn't count as much on decisions because they aren't as active in ongoing management details. All these challenges can be addressed and mitigated, but they need to be discussed and aired.

Management burden. The size and scope of the property will dictate how much time it takes to manage and steward the property. If a lot of hands-on work is required, consider including property management fees or other staffing costs into the annual expenses. Sometimes family members decide to rotate the management responsibilities, so every member shares the burden over time. If that's not practical, be clear about what makes the most sense and discuss whether the "manager's" time commitment should be recognized in some way, whether in a reduction of annual fees or some other gesture. If you decide to create exceptions, be mindful of how it might impact everyone's ownership perception.

House rules. House cleaning, food stocking, storage space, and even parenting styles can all come into play here. It is no fun to arrive to a house that isn't clean or has no food in the pantry when you left it fully stocked on your last visit. Establishing clear expectations for these details can go a long way towards family harmony. If there are discrepancies between family members about what it means to leave the house "clean," create a checklist and guidelines. That way, when there is conflict, you can have a specific conversation about how to address it.

There are undoubtedly other details that are specific to your property or family that need to be included in your family discussions. The intent of compiling these considerations into one document is to recognize that putting the time in before you make a decision ensures that your family will be able to consider the realities, talk through them, and use the information to make an informed decision.

Legacy family properties can build long-standing family connections, provide a lifetime of memories and create continuity through generations that establishes a unique sense of belonging and identity. When families are intentional with how they make it work, it can be magical. It's worth taking the time. That will make all the difference.

Questions for Further Reflection

1. What are you trying to preserve?
2. What are some of the things you find most meaningful about the property?
3. Do others share your vision?
4. Is your vision realistic?
5. How willing are you to let your family manage without your input?
6. How will you feel if it works?
7. How will you feel if it doesn't?

Additional Resources

James Hughes, *Family: The Compact Among Generations* (New York: Bloomberg Press, 2007).

James Hughes, Susan Massenzio, and Keith Whitaker, *Complete Family Wealth* (New York: Bloomberg Press, 2018).

Charles W. Collier, *Wealth in Families*, 3rd ed. (Cambridge, MA: Harvard University, 2012).

Roy Williams and Vic Preisser, *Preparing Heirs* (Bandon, OR: Robert D. Reed Publishers, 2011).

George Howe Colt, *The Big House* (New York: Simon & Schuster, 2004).

Biography

Jamie Forbes grew up in an old New England family imbued with a strong sense of belonging, good fortune, and a clear understanding that with privilege comes responsibility. This experience taught him the importance of family culture, tradition, mentoring, and stewardship.

As founder of Forbes Legacy Advisors, Jamie works with individuals and families on all aspects of family culture. He believes that sustaining a healthy family culture is an essential element of creating resilient families. Jamie advises clients in the areas of family culture, governance, and philanthropy.

When he is not at work, Jamie can be found with his wife and two daughters or enjoying time with friends. Jamie is a Charter Advisor of Philanthropy (CAP®), holds a BA in Economics from Connecticut College, and has also studied at The Wharton School and Babson College.

CHAPTER 11

How Can You Prepare for Longevity and Mental Incapacity Among Family Members?

Patricia Annino

With an increasing aging population how can a family prepare for both sides of competence – older family members who may live longer in good shape and older family members who may live longer with declining competence?

We are living in a global societal phase change and a non-linear world. All of us know someone who is one year old and most of us know individuals who are over 100 years old. All the generations are co-existing, entwining families emotionally, intellectually, physically, and financially in unprecedented ways. A significant and fundamentally important planning challenge is how to grapple with the concept of competence – both *sustained* competence and *diminished* competence.

Sustained Competence

Sustained competence exists when an older competent family patriarch or matriarch ("Queen Elizabeth") chooses not to leave or step aside because she does not have to, physically or mentally, and because she enjoys the position. The consequence of this can be a *lost generation member* ("Prince Charles") who waited his entire life for an event that may never happen. Although the current lost generation may be too advanced in age to remedy the situation, thinking about how to incorporate sustained competence in planning for future generations is advisable.

Practical planning steps include:

1. Intentional financial planning. As part of an annual review, families can discuss the net worth of family members to be sure that each generation is sustainable and not dependent upon the gifts/inheritances of

other generations. In the past, a family member who knows he or she is receiving a significant inheritance may not be prudent with their own financial planning because they were counting on receiving a substantial sum. With sustained competence, that expected inheritance may never arrive and the lost generation member may not have the same sustained competence to live on and enjoy the benefits of the inheritance. Early development of sustainable personal financial plans (income and assets) is fundamental and useful.

2. Understand that in a family that is economically entwined, every action causes a reaction and open communication among family members is essential. Many wealthy families have shared wealth – a family business, shared investments, trusts, and so on. It is important for the family system to understand the succession management of these common assets, who is to receive income, assets when and why.
3. Explore creative solutions, such as intrapreneurship. Encourage family members who may never get to advance to where they hoped they would because of the sustained competence of the older generation to pursue interests of meaning and purpose at earlier stages. Treading water and waiting on the sidelines for their day in the sun is not a prudent strategy.
4. Life is a movie, not a snapshot. All plans should be reviewed on an ongoing basis. As life advances, personal financial and estate planning should be reviewed and adjusted.

Diminished Competence

Diminishing competence can have a very long runway. Human nature will focus on the days that seem to be going well, and not on the days that slide into weeks, and then months, of diminishing competence. There is no single definition of competence. As Dr. James Osher of Williams James College notes, "Complicating the picture is the lack of uniform definitions of competence. Competency is very specific to a skill. For example, an older executive might be deemed competent to manage his own personal affairs and yet not to run a complex business." Dr. Sanam Herfeez adds, "There is no single test for competency, and usually several tests are required to gauge a person's fitness to manage the challenges of running a company. When it comes to determining whether a person is capable of running a Fortune 500 company, being asked to spell 'world' backwards or count backwards by seven is not enough."

In a trial concerning the competence of Sumner Redstone, his primary care physician stated that he was mentally fit. A geriatric psychiatrist found he lacked mental capacity. Perhaps both were right?

The question of whether someone is competent is a very tricky one within families. Decisions such as when to take away the keys to the car are very emotionally charged. Bringing up the issue of diminished capacity with someone who knows what the discussion means is fraught with emotional peril. It means discussing a loss of personal liberty and the beginning of a walk down a long and frightening path.

Frequently there is no clear demarcation between competence and incompetence until the day when the demarcation line is very clear, and incompetence is definite. The challenge is to handle the issue with the planning process when there is no need to. Human nature, being human nature, can be tricky. As Scarlett O'Hara said so eloquently: "I can't think about that right now. If I do, I'll go crazy. I'll think about that tomorrow."

Practical steps:

1. Plan for disability or incapacity. This planning should be as important as financial planning and traditional "what happens when I die" estate planning. Review all boilerplate clauses in estate planning documents to determine who will be in charge if you become disabled or incapacitated and what the trigger mechanism is (certified by your personal physician, two physicians, etc.). Make sure all documents are up to date and recently ratified.
2. Put checks and balances in place to deal with conflicts of interest. Is the person who will be making your medical decisions the same one who will be handling your financial decisions? Is there a conflict between those decision makers? For example, is a second spouse named to make the medical decisions but an adult child or a trustee in charge of the durable or continuing power of attorney? If so, how does the second spouse make medical decisions without having the authority to authorize payment? And how does the one named to make financial decisions understand what the medical options are? Should you set up a separate mechanism to handle any conflicts? Be sure to have updated legal documents, including a health care proxy and a durable power of attorney. Your disability or incapacity could last a long time, and those initially named may predecease you or be unable to continue to serve in those capacities. Be sure to have thought through who the backups will be and the mechanism for appointing any successor. In the durable power of attorney, you also can nominate now the person who would be your guardian or conservator if protective proceedings were commenced. This is a very important and often overlooked clause because the nominated person can have legal standing in any court proceeding concerning incompetence and must be given notice of any proceeding.
3. If you live in the United States, consider carefully who should have the right to your medical information and waive the right to HIPAA (the Health Insurance Portability and Accountability Act of 1996). Should it just be persons who are authorized to handle your medical affairs? Should it also include those who will handle your financial affairs?

4. Clarify who those you designate with the authority to handle your financial affairs if you are disabled or incapacitated are legally accountable to. Who should they have to report their actions to? Who has the right to review, approve, and object?

Our global society is facing one of its most significant challenges – an increasing aging population. We will redefine what it means to work, to be a family, to manage a company, and to pass leadership on. We will explore new ways to remain vital and active both physically and mentally for as long as we can. We will find new ways to honor the wisdom of the aging and prior generations and incorporate them more meaningfully into the fabric of the family life. We will no longer think of generations in sequence, but rather as a tapestry. An 85-year-old grandfather may work aside his 65-year-old daughter, 40-year-old granddaughter, and 20-year-old great-granddaughter. This will force increased collaboration, not hierarchy. Important family and business roles that are based on wisdom will evolve. We will become increasingly aware of the additional assistance the aging population will need and rethink family and business involvement with care – both on the financial side and on the side of the family contribution to care. Many of the decisions we face in the next decade will involve moral choices and open, honest communication among generations. The wisdom we will all gain from each other on this journey will strengthen our global society and global wisdom.

Questions for Further Reflection

1. Knowing that there will be competence challenges in the coming years what intentional financial and medical plans should family members put in place now?
2. Should "purpose" be redefined so that the role of purpose evolves and is valued as the family and/or family enterprise evolves? (For example, Prince Charles now knows that even if he becomes King it will be farther ahead in years than he most likely anticipated. He has found other ways to share wisdom and be purposeful.)
3. What steps can be taken to plan for non-hierarchical legacy?
4. What obligations do generations have to each other? To provide wisdom, to step aside? To work together in non-linear ways? To openly communicate about plans?
5. Is putting a risk management plan in place important now when there is no crisis so that the open issues of competence are on the table?
6. How important is it to evolve advisors as the issues change?

Additional Resources

Laura Ziegler, "Of Minds and Money: The Donald Sterling Case and Mental Capacity," *Bessemer Trust Newsletter*, 2014.

Keith Drewery, "Managing Declining Capacity: The Role of a Family Office," *Journal of International Family Offices*, 2017.

Biography

Patricia Annino, attorney, is a partner with Rimon P.C. She is a nationally recognized authority on estate planning and taxation, with more than 30 years of experience serving the estate planning needs of families, individuals, and owners of closely held and family-owned businesses.

Patricia has been voted by her peers as one of the Best Lawyers in America (trust and estates), a Super Lawyer, a top 50 Massachusetts Female Lawyer, Boston Estate Planning Council's Estate Planner of the Year and the initial recipient of Euromoney/Legal Media's "Best in Wealth Management – USA" award. Patricia has written five books.

Patricia is a graduate of Smith College (AB), Suffolk University School of Law (JD), and Boston University School of Law (LLM in Taxation). She is a Fellow of the American College of Trust and Estates Council (ACTEC), a member of the Board of Directors of the Family Firm Institute (FFI), the Board of Directors of Business Families Foundation (BFF), and the Advisory Board of the Indiana University Women's Philanthropy Institute.

CHAPTER 12

How Do You Prepare for a Good Goodbye?

Kathy Wiseman

As leaders, we are accustomed to addressing life's challenges with great attention to detail in the present and an eye toward possible repercussions in the future. We not only make intentional life decisions for ourselves, but often help others do the same.

The hardest and one of the most important of these life challenges, however, is most often the one left to chance or time. It is by far the most difficult one to address with any kind of openness, clarity, or creativity. And so we put it off or end up excluding the ones it will affect the most. It is our own death.

The following story is an unabashedly biased plea for planning one's end of life with the people most important to us. It advocates for the thought, attention and presence worthy of this most profound of all life's passages.

Ed is an example of one leader's commitment to bringing those qualities to his end of life. He wanted it to be intentional, and he did so by making it a family affair, adding the gift of transparency to the mix. Ed involved everyone in his family in one capacity or another: his nieces and nephews, their spouses, his stepson, his deceased daughter's husband, and his wife, grandchildren, and even his ex-wife. The result was an enriched network of family relationships and the best legacy there is – a stronger, deeply connected family prepared for the patriarch's death.

How It Happened

At the age of 87, Ed summoned two of his nieces to his home in Palm Desert. Both were the daughters of his long-deceased sisters. The last of five siblings, although the youngest, Ed had long ago made himself head of the clan. The purpose of the summons was to begin an end-of-life discussion. He wanted to talk about his concerns: contingencies for his end of life; the location of his assets and valuables; and the details for his intricately thought-out funeral.

A planner by nature, Ed was also a consummate worrier, a by-product of having lived through the Great Depression as a young man. He had built two successful import businesses, made wise investments with his earnings, and was rewarded with a more than comfortable living during his working life and throughout his retirement. Nevertheless, he worried about financial security for himself and everyone he loved. Along with his desire to be remembered and to be duly honored at his funeral – naval band and gun salute – he wanted his clan secure and if he could, leave them all better off. Family was his number-one priority.

It was at that first meeting that the nieces also learned that they were to be the executors of his estate. Although he had no natural children of his own, Ed did have a middle-aged stepson whom he had reared from the age of 12. Although there was love, their relationship had a long history of rough patches. Ed would need to inform him of the executorship as well as other decisions along the way so that there would be no surprises or animosity after his death.

That first discussion provided the groundwork for a powerful family trust-building exercise. Ed's 90th-birthday celebration onboard a cruise ship with the invited 24 family members accelerated the process. As he gathered his family around him at different times during the seven-day trip, he began to share his wishes and worries regarding his death. Family members – folks who generally liked each other but who knew each other from once-a-year holiday get-togethers only – responded well, jumping in with ideas, questions, and commitments.

An infrastructure of sorts was crafted regarding who would do what if Ed became sick or unable to manage his affairs. The doctors in the group volunteered to be of counsel and others joined informal committees of care. Everyone stepped up with a renewed sense of purpose, solidifying their connection not only to Ed but to each other.

From then on, bicoastal phone conversations ensued with greater frequency, as did coordinated short family trips to the desert, always with Ed at the helm. Plans were amended and strategy revamped as needed. By this time, he had shared his fear of dying alone. He wanted to be with family, both at the end and during the process.

When the inevitable health event occurred, it heralded a new stage of care, requiring immediate intervention by the three designated leaders, aided by the on-call support of the two doctors in the family. Not surprisingly, Ed turned out to be a difficult patient, stubbornly unwavering in his opinion, particularly regarding the cost for the additional help he needed.

With the ensuing dramas of agency firings, and change of caretakers, repeated emergency late night visits to the hospital, as well as dealing with his suspicion that the caregivers were stealing, Ed never stopped wanting to call the shots. He wanted care and attention, but always on his terms. Even in his diminished condition, he wanted to remain in control.

Outcomes

The many months of planning and open communication helped the family to better understand situations as they arose, particularly as the relationship with caretakers and professionals became strained. It allowed them to get to know one another, and comfortably share on issues such as aging; or "the help that really helps"; or imposing – or not – one's will on a dying loved one. They now understood each other's points of view, each other's strengths and weaknesses. Because of it, they were able to navigate even the most stressful circumstances. They had become an effective team, albeit living on different coasts, and working full time.

Ed died approximately three years after that first meeting. He died accompanied by beloved family members. He would say that it was a good death, not just at the last but from the very start of the process. He had addressed the most daunting life event head on, aided by the people who meant the most to him.

The small group designated with his care would agree. Ed's ability to communicate what he needed, long before it was called for, had given them time to learn to work together, to plan thoughtfully, and ultimately do right by him. And clearly, it was good for the entire family. By including everyone in his end-of-life process, Ed mitigated the deleterious emotional shock waves that come from a death in the family, shock waves that often cause divisiveness and distance.

> The "Emotional Shock Wave" is a network of underground "aftershocks" of serious life events that can occur anywhere in the extended family system in the months or years after the death of a significant family member. It is not directly related to the usual grief or mourning reactions of people close to one who died. It operates on an underground network of emotional dependence of family members on each other …
> At first, this appeared to be a coincidence. Then it was discovered that some version of this phenomenon appeared in a sufficiently high percentage of all families, and a check for the shock wave is done in all family histories. The symptoms in a shock wave can be any human problem. Symptoms can include the entire spectrum of physical illness from an increased incidence of colds to the first appearance of a chronic condition such as diabetes or allergies to acute medical and surgical illnesses. It is as if the shock wave is the stimulus that can trigger the physical process activity. The symptoms can also include the full range of emotional symptoms from mild depression to phobias to psychotic episodes. The social problems can include drinking, failures in school and business abortions and increase in accidents. Knowledge of the presence of the shock wave provides opportunity to assist in treating the condition. Without such knowledge, the sequence of events is treated as separate, unrelated events. (Bowen 1992, pp. 325–326)

Why Do This?

Life is made up of a series of nodal events: births, deaths, marriages, rites of passage, children leaving, work successes, and failures. All represent change. Both negative and positive change can be disruptive to a family, increasing anxiety, and impacting family relationships negatively. Consciously engaging with family is an opportunity to increase exponentially the odds of a positive outcome.

As Ed knew, preparing for death is about the care and attention paid to the people who will live on. It is the purpose and the gift. As the father of the protagonist says in the blockbuster film *Black Panther*, "A man who has not prepared his children for his own death has failed as a father." And so it is with a real leader.

Questions for Further Reflection

1. Beyond communicating financial and funeral arrangements, what conversations are important for you to have with your family before you die?
2. If preparing your family for your "good death" is a goal, what does "good" mean to you?
3. What are the three things that you would like your extended family to experience with regard to your death? What can you do to prepare them for it?
4. What advice would you like to give your family with regard to family relationships and what it takes to make a family "work"?

Additional Resources

Dr. Murray Bowen, *Family Therapy in Clinical Practice* (Lanham, MD: Jason Aronson, 1985).

Biography

With 40-plus years of experience learning how human families function, Kathy Wiseman advises families, family enterprise advisors, and financial and wealth managers as they strive to bring the best outcomes to the families they serve. With this knowledge, she offers motivated clients the opportunity to change the course of their own life and the trajectory of their nuclear and extended family, assisting them in the best decisions for their family, family business, and financial assets.

Kathy is a faculty member at the Bowen Center for the Study of the Family in Washington, DC and a co-founder of Navigating Systems, a course dedicated to the robust study of family, one's own and one's clients. She has co-authored three books: *Navigating the Trustscape*, with Hartley Goldstone; *Emotional Process in Organizations* and *Understanding Organizations*, both with Ruth Riley Sagar. Kathy is the oldest of four, mother of three, grandmother of five, mother-in-law of two, and a regular attendee at Burning Man.

SECTION 3

INVESTING WISELY

It is not surprising that families have questions on investments. They are notoriously difficult to forecast and are often complex, there are many self-proclaimed experts on the topic with contradictory opinions, and they are rife with misinformation and conflicts of interest.

Yet it is extremely important for families to understand their investments, because they are the engine that powers the family's financial ship and funds the family goals. When thinking about investments, the focus is frequently on expected returns. The articles in this section try to shine the light in a different way – paying special attention to the goals, the risks, and the choices implicit in the investment returns.

We start with an essay by Ashvin Chhabra that answers the question "How can you make sure your portfolio lines up with your actual goals?" Many investors set out into capital markets without understanding what they are trying to achieve. Ashvin explains why a clear path makes for happier outcomes.

Christopher Brightman proposes a thoughtful response to the question "What return should you expect from your investments?" Although it is fair to say that no one can predict investment results (particularly in the short run), Chris lays out a fact-based and time-tested formula for capital market expectations that investors and their advisors can use.

Jean Brunel addresses the very practical challenge of "What should your asset allocation be?" He marries the ideas of quantifying family goals and constraints, creating specific portfolios to meet specific goals, and aggregating the portfolios into an overall investment policy. The result is an investment program that improves the probability of meeting investor goals.

It has become almost axiomatic that to be a sophisticated investor, you need a more specialized and complex strategy. Robert Maynard hits the question "Does investing have to be complicated?" head on, and argues that a simple, transparent, and focused approach is a viable and successful alternative.

We then offer two essays on the topic of financial risk. Howard Marks responds to the question: "How should you understand and deal with investment risk?", and James Garland answers: "What is the most useful definition of 'risk' for private investors?" Each of them brings their own experience and expertise to this important topic. One issue they agree on is that the most common definition of investment risk – volatility – can be deceptive and even dangerous and may lead investors astray, and that there are better ways to quantify and apply risk.

Finally, we tackle how to determine the best approach to selecting suitable investment strategies and vehicles. Charles Ellis answers the question "Is active management still worthwhile?" with a resounding no. He argues that, given the substantial changes in the investment industry, performance-seeking investment managers can, on average, no longer outperform their benchmarks net of the fees they charge and that index investing is the way of the future. Randolph Cohen takes the other side of the argument and suggests that, with the right combination of factors, active management can deliver substantial net benefits to investors.

Investing is a challenge for all families. For some, the investments are a counterweight to their operating company assets, and for others they are the main store of wealth. Some choose to make decisions themselves, whereas others opt for advisors and investment managers. And some invest in public, liquid assets, and others seek out unique private investments. Whatever the approach a family takes, solid answers to the key questions – the goals they want to fund, the returns that are realistically achievable, the risks the family can bear, and the strategies they choose to employ – will substantially improve the likelihood of success and the comfort of the journey.

CHAPTER 13

How Can You Make Sure Your Portfolio Lines Up with Your Actual Goals?

Ashvin Chhabra

Unless you are a professional money manager, investing is not about the markets. Investing is about you. Individuals, families, and institutions use their financial assets to take on investment risk in order to achieve specific goals.

Certain goals are universal, whereas others are deeply personal. Although desired goals vary greatly from person to person, they can be organized within a formal investing framework.

The psychologist Maslow traced out a universal hierarchy of goals in his pioneering work (Figure 13.1), where he studied successful people.

Humans, he concluded, start with the requirement of fulfilling their basic needs: food and shelter for themselves and their family. Once this is accomplished, they move to becoming a bigger part of a social structure by achieving success in their jobs, businesses, and communities. Finally, they aspire to differentiate themselves through individual achievement: to leave a legacy. This basic Maslowian structure of human needs and desires also lends itself to investment goals.

In the Wealth Allocation Framework, goals are classified into one of three categories: essential, important, and aspirational. Essential goals must be achieved, or else there will be devastating consequences: food may not get on the table, a home or a business will be lost.

Next come the goals that are not essential but important. These consist of additional goals a family may want to achieve, once the essentials have been taken care of. Alternatively, they may be embellishments to essential goals. For example, an essential goal may cover the cost of basic needs but an important goal may be maintaining current lifestyle.

Figure 13.1 Maslow's hierarchy.

Aspirational goals are those that may or may not be beyond our current reach. Creating something new, starting or scaling up a business, funding a project to help a community or our planet: all these can fall into this category.

Different people may classify the same goal differently. Depending on your wealth level and your life philosophy, a goal such as "putting your kids through college" or even "creating a charitable foundation" may get labeled as essential, important, or aspirational.

Start by asking yourself: "Why are you investing – in effect, risking your wealth? What do you *hope* to achieve? What do you *need* to achieve?"

To translate each goal into an investment strategy you must begin by defining failure and success. This is accomplished by translating each specific objective into desired cash flows or, especially in the case of aspirational goals, the desired outcome. The desired outcome, for example, may be achieving a specific wealth level or transforming a community less fortunate than your own.

Certain goals may also be in the form of affirmative filters, for example making sure all of your investments reflect your values.

Institutions are usually better than most individuals at creating a formal goal-setting process. Institutions set their goals through strategic planning documents that reflect their mission statements. These goals also fit nicely into the three categories discussed earlier – relating to the financial stability of the institution, keeping up with the competition (or peer group), and the articulation and achievement of a mission statement. Institutions also have a formal investment policy that outlines the risk-return objectives of the portfolio, as well as additional guidelines that are consistent with their original goals or mission statement.

Individuals and families of all wealth levels are encouraged to do the same!

Once this all-important step of defining and categorizing goals has been accomplished, you can move over to organizing your wealth to work towards the achievement of these goals.

In doing so, you will encounter an important challenge: the uncertain world! You are forced to allocate between investments that provide the promise of safety, but little or no return, and investments that provide the promise of return, but are accompanied by considerable risk. Complicating the issue is that it is impossible to estimate what return the market will provide in the future.

So how much should you allocate to safety assets as opposed to the markets? How big a house can you buy? How big a foundation can you create?

In solving these questions, it turns out that it becomes advantageous to organize the entire balance sheet – all of one's assets (including human capital) and liabilities or obligations – into three categories, buckets, or sub-portfolios.

The three sub-portfolios can be labeled as safety, market, and aspirational (see Figure 13.2). The safety portfolio takes little risk, it provides protection, but delivers almost no market return. On the other hand, a well-diversified market portfolio will give a market return, but we do not know what that is. Not surprisingly, the value of these investments will go up and down in tandem with the financial markets.

The aspirational portfolio consists of investments that amplify your expertise (such as your business) and is usually accompanied by non-recourse leverage and asset concentration. This portfolio is optional, but it also turns out to be the engine of wealth creation. Not surprisingly, these investments are accompanied by a great deal of risk and uncertainty in their outcome.

A key part of implementing the Wealth Allocation Framework is determining the appropriate allocation of wealth to each of the three sub-portfolios. A simple way to start is to categorize your entire balance sheet (assets and liabilities) into these three categories. Then assume dire market conditions and see if your essential and important goals are compromised. That will be an indication that there is too much risk in the portfolio.

Safety Risk	Market Risk	Aspirational Risk
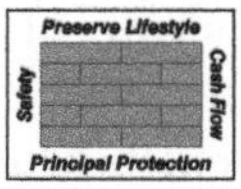	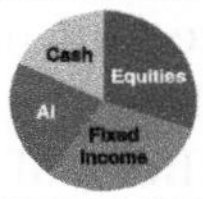	
Do Not Jeopardize Basic Standard of Living	Maintain Lifestyle	Enhance Lifestyle
• Minimize downside risk • Safety • Accept below-market returns for minimal risk	• Balance risk and return to attain market-level performance from a broadly diversified portfolio	• Maximize upside • Take measured risk to achieve significant return enhancement

Figure 13.2 The safety, market, and aspirational sub-portfolios.

On the other side of the spectrum, go through scenarios where success is achieved. Are most of your aspirational goals realized? If not, that would be an indication that you may want to allocate some of your capital towards achieving those unfulfilled goals. Repeating this process periodically, but not too often, is the key to a creating a disciplined investment process oriented towards achieving your goals.

The performance of each sub-portfolio can and should be monitored by well-defined market benchmarks. However, that process is more about the market efficiency of your portfolio, i.e. the efficient use of capital. The key overall objective is to understand and monitor your progress towards your essential, important, and aspirational goals.

I wish you a long and successful life devoid of aspirational regret!

Questions for Further Reflection

1. What are your goals for your investments?
2. Are your investments appropriately allocated to achieve those goals?
3. In a severe or prolonged market dislocation would your balance sheet suffer irreparable harm? Would any of your essential goals become compromised?
4. Are you positioned to achieve your aspirational goals? If not, would you like to reallocate some of your resources towards them?

Additional Resources

Ashvin B. Chhabra, *The Aspirational Investor: Taming the Markets to Achieve Your Life's Goals* (New York: HarperCollins), 2015.

Ashvin B. Chhabra, "Beyond Markowitz: A Comprehensive Wealth Allocation Framework for Individual Investors," *The Journal of Wealth Management*, 2005.

A.H. Maslow, "A Theory of Human Motivation," *Psychological Review*, 1943.

Biography

Ashvin Chhabra is president of Euclidean Capital, which is responsible for the management of investments for James H. Simons and Marilyn Simons and their associated foundations. The Simons Foundation is dedicated to advancing research in basic science and mathematics and is one of America's largest private funders of these areas.

Ashvin was chief investment officer of Merrill Lynch Wealth Management from 2013 to 2015. Prior to that, he was the chief investment officer at the Institute for Advanced Study from 2007 to 2013. He is also the author of *The Aspirational Investor* (2015).

He is also widely recognized as one of the founders of goals-based wealth management and for his seminal work "Beyond Markowitz," which integrates modern portfolio theory with behavioral finance and proposes a novel wealth allocation framework.

Ashvin is a member of the board of trustees and chair of the investment committee of the Stony Brook Foundation and a member of the investment committees of the Institute for Advanced Study and Rockefeller University. He has lectured at Yale University, Carnegie Mellon University, Baruch College CUNY, and the University of Chicago. He holds a PhD in applied physics from Yale University in the field of non-linear dynamics (chaos theory).

CHAPTER 14

What Return Should You Expect from Your Investments?

Christopher Brightman

Expected rates of return are a key component in any family financial plan, and they are notoriously unpredictable and uncertain, especially in the short term. In this section, we lay out a framework for developing reasonable estimates for future returns from key asset classes, using the current market environment as a case in point.

Over the long history of US capital markets (see Table 14.1), stocks have provided a 9.1% annualized return, bonds 5.0%, and a traditional mix of 60% stocks and 40% bonds 7.7%. Adjusted for inflation of about 2%, this traditional 60/40 mix has provided an annualized real (net of inflation) return of 5.5%. These long-term historical averages match the 7–8% returns planned by pension funds and the 5% sustainable spending rate traditionally assumed by foundations and endowments.

Should we follow this practice? Should we prepare our financial plans assuming that future capital market returns will be consistent with these long-term historical averages?

No – starting yields (the income returns on investments as a percent of market value) strongly influence future returns: high returns follow high yields, and low returns follow low yields. Empirical evidence and just plain common sense support this observation of a linkage between starting yield and subsequent return. Unless today's yields approximately match historical average yields, we shouldn't expect to receive historical average returns. For instance, today's lower-than-historical-average yields forecast lower future returns.

Table 14.1: US market returns, 1871–2017.

Annualized Nominal Returns				Inflation	Annualized Real Returns			
Equity	60/40	Bonds	Cash	CPI	Equity	60/40	Bonds	Cash
9.1%	7.7%	5.0%	3.5%	2.1%	6.9%	5.5%	2.9%	1.5%

Bond Returns Equal Starting Yields

For bonds (see Figure 14.1), the relationship between starting yield and subsequent return is intuitive and obvious. Our expected future return for bonds is determined by the cash flows to be paid by those bonds and the price we pay for them, simply summarized as our starting yield. When bonds yield 12%, then we expect a 12% return. When bonds yield 6%, then we expect a 6% return. When bonds yield 3%, then we expect a 3% return.

The US bond market has provided a 5% long-term historical return because its average historical price has provided a 5% yield. Should we expect future returns of 5% from our bond portfolio today? No, of course not. Today, we plan for bond market returns of 3% because today's bond market is priced at a yield of 3%.

What Return Should We Expect from the Stock Market?

Stocks are more complex than bonds, yet we observe the same relationship: higher returns follow higher yields, and lower returns follow lower yields. When

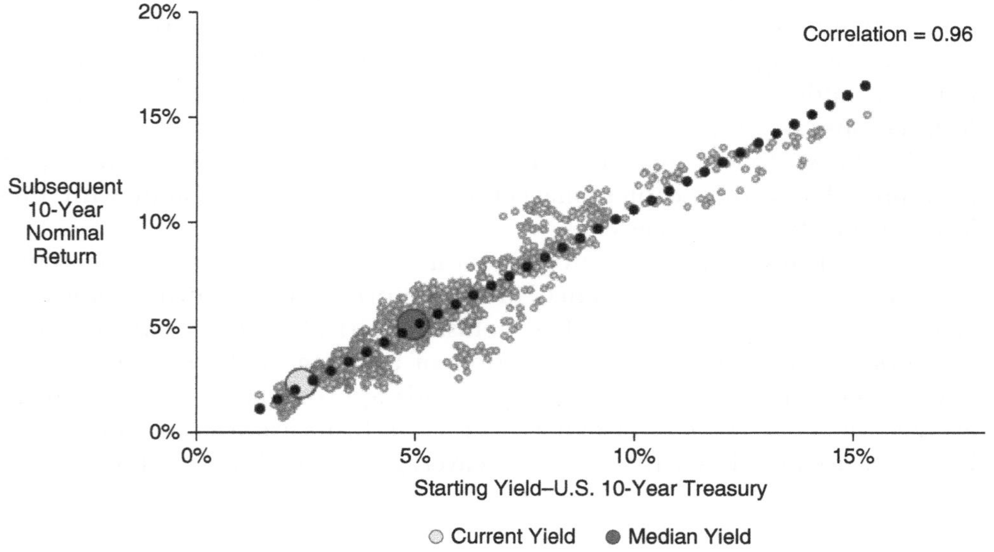

Figure 14.1 Bonds: Future returns follow starting yields (United States, 1800–2017).

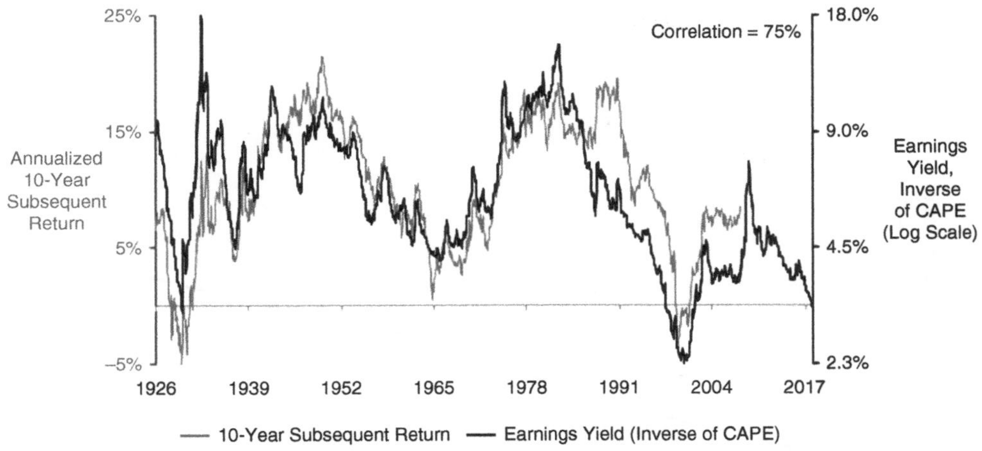

Figure 14.2 Equities: Future returns follow starting earnings yields (United States, 1926–2017).

the market prices stocks with higher prices that produce lower dividend and earnings yields, we expect lower future returns. When the market prices stocks with lower prices that produce higher dividend and earnings yields, we expect higher future returns.

Future returns of the stock market follow its cyclically adjusted earnings yield (CAEY), the 10-year average of the market's real earnings per share divided by its current price (see Figure 14.2). When forecasting returns, a 10-year average of earnings is superior to current or one-year trailing earnings because annual earnings are so volatile.[1]

The Building Blocks of Equity Returns

We can better understand stock market returns by breaking the total return down into its fundamental building blocks. The US stock market's 9.1% long-term historical annualized return can be decomposed into dividend yield, real growth, inflation, and valuation change. The historical average dividend yield has been 4.4%. Real growth in earnings per share has been 1.8%. Inflation has averaged 2.1%. Finally, rising price-to-earnings (P/E) multiples have added 0.6% to the long-term historical return of the US stock market. See Figure 14.3 and Table 14.2.

[1]When annual earnings and hence the annual yield of the market are temporarily depressed, as is common in a recession, subsequent returns are more often higher than normal during the inevitable recovery. Likewise, when earnings and the resulting yield are temporarily elevated, as is common during euphoric periods, subsequent returns are more often lower than normal during the inevitable correction. By smoothing out the volatility of annual earnings, the CAEY provides a simple and reliable forecast of the future return of the stock market.

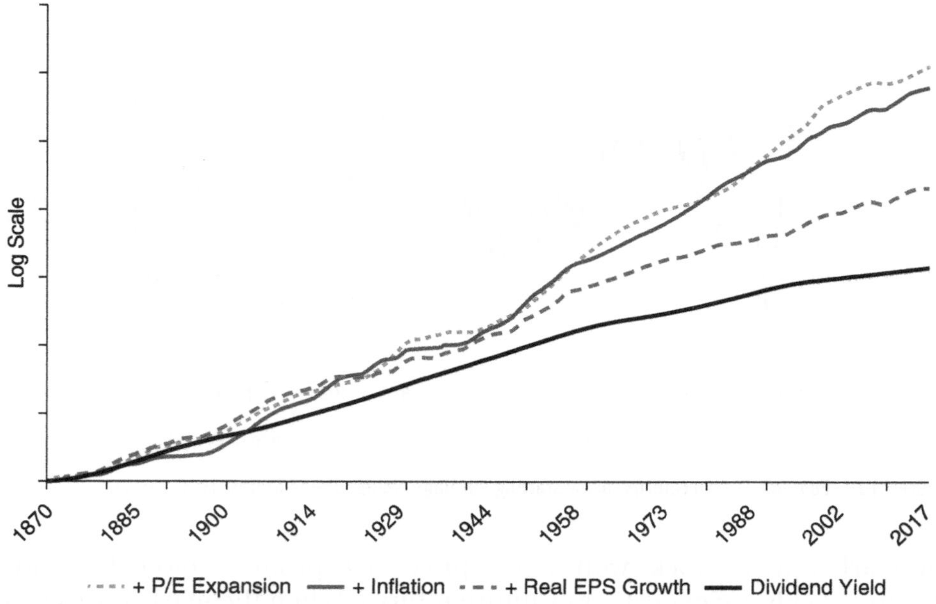

Figure 14.3 US equity return building blocks, 10-year rolling averages.

Table 14.2: US market returns, 1871 through 2017.[a]

	Annualized Return	Annual Std Dev
Total Market	9.1%	18%
P/E Expansion	0.6%	33%
Inflation	2.1%	6%
EPS Growth	1.8%	32%
Dividend Yield	4.4%	2%

[a]Return components are multiplicative, $(1+0.6\%) * (1+2.1\%) * (1+1.8\%) * (1+4.4\%) - 1 = 9.1\%$

Today, the US stock market provides a dividend yield of only 1.8%. If we assume that real earnings per share grow at their historical average of 1.8%, inflation remains stable at 2%, and valuation multiples remain at today's (high) level, then we should expect annualized returns from the stock market to be centered on 5.6% nominal (before inflation) and 3.6% real (after inflation).

Reversion to the Mean

What if a stock's valuation multiple reverts toward its historical mean? If we buy stocks at lower-than-average valuations, not only can we expect higher returns from the higher income delivered for each dollar we pay, we may also receive capital gains from rising prices.

Conversely, if we buy stocks at higher-than-average valuations, not only can we expect lower returns from the lower income delivered for each dollar we pay, we may also suffer capital losses from falling prices. See Figure 14.4.

If we expect returns from the stock market to be centered on about 6% nominal (4% real) ignoring changes in multiples, what should we expect with reversion to the mean of stock prices? Since the market is presently (2018) priced at nearly twice its historical average cyclically adjusted P/E (CAPE) multiple, we might expect a 50% decline in prices, or capital losses of 5% a year annualized over the next 10 years, thus taking our expected annualized return for the coming decade down to 1% nominal and negative in real terms.

History provides ample precedent for such meager returns from the stock market. The annualized 10-year real return for the US market was −4% from 1901 to 1920, 0% from 1971 to 1980, and −1% from 2001 to 2010.

Now, we shouldn't necessarily assume that the CAPE will revert fully back to its historical mean. Because today's economy is less volatile than in decades past, interest rates are lower, and technology has significantly reduced the cost of investing, future P/E multiples might revert to a higher mean than has historically been the case. If we assume that valuations will revert only halfway back to their respective historical means, then we should expect stock market returns centered on 3–4% nominal and 1–2% real.

Because the future is uncertain, we plan for returns within an appropriately wide range. From today's yields for a traditional mix of US stocks and bonds, a 7% nominal annualized return (5% real) lie at the very top of that range of plausible future returns. Returns near 4% nominal (2% real) are more likely. A nominal return of 0% (−2% real) is near the bottom of the range of plausible returns for a traditional mix of US stocks and bonds over the coming decade.

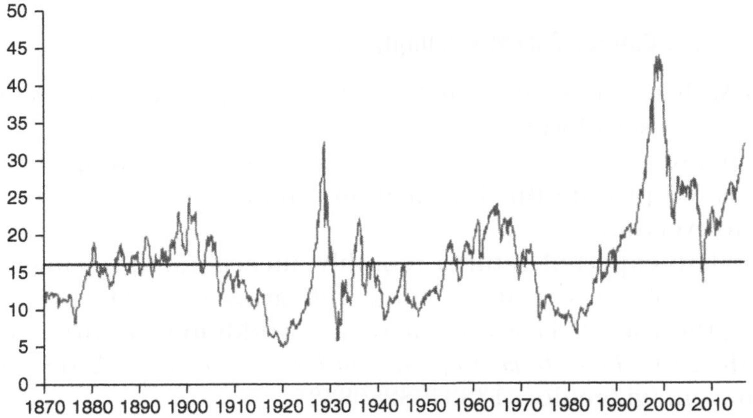

Figure 14.4 Cyclically adjusted P/E (CAPE), real price/10-year average real EPS.

Private investors, as well as institutions, should use long-term return expectations to plan income and spending. Although tempting, it is usually not wise to adapt investments to changes in expected returns. Beware of the difficulty of timing markets; few have the skill, patience, and persistence to improve upon systematically rebalancing to a broadly diversified policy portfolio.

Questions for Further Reflection

1. Which is more controllable, spending or investment returns? How should we set our family spending plans given the range of outcomes of potential investment returns?
2. Like Pascal's Wager, are the *consequences* of a bad investment outcome worse than the *probability* of a bad investment outcome? What does that mean for our investment choices and asset mix?
3. Is this time really different? Are we convincing ourselves that the logical historical framework be set aside because conditions seem to be different this time?
4. Can the same principles be applied to other asset classes?

Additional Resources

Robert Shiller, *Irrational Exuberance* (Princeton, NJ: Princeton University Press, 2000).

James Garland, "The Fecundity of Endowments and Long Duration Trusts," *Economics and Portfolio Strategy Newsletter*, 2004.

Christopher Brightman, "Expected Return," *Investments and Wealth Monitor*, 2012.

Other Sources of Capital Market Assumptions

Research Affiliates, *Asset Allocation Interactive,* 2018 (https://interactive.researchaffiliates.com/asset-allocation).

In response to repeated requests to share our expectations for capital market returns, we provide this information online. The tool is free to use and available to everyone.

We update expected returns monthly, incorporating changes in market prices. We display expectations for a full array of asset classes, portfolios combining those asset classes, and a wealth of additional information.

J.P. Morgan, *Long-Term Capital Market Assumptions,* 2018 (https://am.jpmorgan.com/gi/getdoc/1383498280832).

Blackrock Investment Institute, *Capital Market Assumptions,* 2018 (https://www.blackrockblog.com/blackrock-capital-markets-assumptions).

Biography

Christopher Brightman leads the Research and Investment Management team at Research Affiliates, LLC, where he supervises the firm's research and development activities, provision of index strategies, and management of client portfolios.

Christopher has three decades of investment management experience. He has traded securities and derivatives, managed portfolios, supervised quantitative product development, and allocated assets to alternative investment strategies. He also has extensive organizational and people management expertise.

Prior to joining Research Affiliates, Christopher served as board chair of The Investment Fund for Foundations (TIFF), vice chair of the Investment Advisory Committee for the Virginia Retirement System, CEO of the University of Virginia Investment Management Company, chief investment officer of Strategic Investment Group, director of global equity strategy at UBS Asset Management, senior portfolio manager at Brinson Partners, VP and head of asset/liability management at Maryland National Bank, and associate national bank examiner at the Comptroller of the Currency.

Christopher holds the Chartered Financial Analyst® designation and is a member of CFA Institute. He serves on the board of directors and the investment committee of the Virginia Tech Foundation.

Christopher received a BS in finance from Virginia Tech and an MBA from Loyola University, Maryland.

CHAPTER 15

What Should Your Asset Allocation Be?

Jean Brunel

Though it may not be – nor should it be – the first question families ask, it is often one of the most important ones when it comes to the management of their financial assets: *What should my asset allocation be?* Historically, when the asset management industry was simply applying tried and true institutional approaches to their private clients, asset allocation was determined by a combination of mean-variance optimization (to define an efficient frontier that would be suitable to the family's preferences and constraints) and some form of risk mapping (to answer to the old saw, *what is your risk profile?*). Identifying a client's risk profile made it possible to choose the "right" portfolio on the efficient frontier – or to pigeonhole the client into one of a few model portfolios available.

Needless to say, private clients found the process both hard to understand and often irrelevant. The main issue is its key underlying assumption: individuals are like institutions! They have a single goal, a single time horizon, and some well-understood risk profile. Since then, the wealth management industry has learned something that our clients knew all along – individuals and families have several goals, with differing time horizons and different degrees of urgency.

Although certain goals can be viewed as *needs* (which *must* be achieved), others fall somewhere on a continuum including *wants, wishes,* and *dreams* (desirable, but not absolutely necessary). In fact, one of the most important insights is this: risk, in the context of individuals or families, should not be measured in terms of volatility of return, but in relation to the degree of urgency associated with reaching the goal (or its reciprocal: the pain associated with failing to reach the goal).

A new process was needed that recognized the requirement for each goal to be provided for independently. Distinct sub-portfolios ought to be set up, each dedicated to meet a goal, over the required time horizon and with the required degree of urgency. Of course, once formulated, they can be aggregated into a single strategic family asset allocation, within the limits imposed by the nature and beneficial ownership of the holding structures created by the family, which are typically created to allow wealth transfers; asset protection; or other personal, dynastic, or philanthropic motives.

The process involves four major conceptual steps:

1. *Create a list of all the goals* the family wishes to express. These goals can be driven by a specific regular annual cash flow that needs to be met over a certain time period and with a required level of urgency (or probability of success). That level of urgency should range from as close to 100% as feasible for *absolute* needs to as low as 50% for more aspirational *dreams.* Goals can also be thought of as a terminal "bullet" amount of funds the family wants to target.
2. *Identify the constraints* that naturally apply to each portfolio designed to meet each specific goal. This, for instance, would involve excluding overly risky or illiquid assets when dealing with a high-urgency need to be met over the short- to medium-term (such as funding short-term capital needs). By contrast, one can begin to consider riskier and less-liquid assets or strategies as the time horizon lengthens and the required probability of success diminishes.
3. *Determine the amount of assets that should be dedicated to meet each goal,* by selecting the portfolio with the highest return possible, given both the time horizon and the required urgency. The so-called funding rate for each goal is the return that must be met or exceeded over that period and with the required probability of success. It is not the return expected to be earned on average over the period by a suitable portfolio. For instance, a portfolio could have an expected return of 8% over five years with 7% annual volatility. But, what if the return you could be certain of, with a 95% probability over that same period, is only 2.9%? So, cash flows should be discounted by 2.9% over the next five years to identify the amount of assets that should be set aside to meet that goal.
4. *Aggregate all the individual portfolios* into an overall investment policy to manage the assets on a continuing basis. It is interesting to note that the eventual "risk" for the overall portfolio as defined in the institutional world (i.e. the expected standard deviation or volatility of expected returns) will here be derived from the bottom up, rather than from the top down. It will be the average of the risk of each sub-portfolio, weighted by the share of assets dedicated to the goal. Is that not considerably more intuitive?

Our point here is to highlight three important elements that contribute ready benefits to families and individuals, all the while allowing wealth managers to discharge their professional duties to the best of their abilities.

1. The ultimate end goal of the process is to help families "marry their financial assets." Though this may seem like an odd statement, it is still a fact that many families know they are wealthy, but do not know how their wealth is helping them achieve their life's goals. Being able to identify the amount of assets needed to reach any goal is a wonderfully liberating exercise on two fronts. First, it allows the family – and individuals within it – to appreciate the amount of their wealth needed to achieve a particular goal; think, for instance, of how much is needed to maintain some lifestyle over some defined period of time. Second, it allows the family to initiate the process through which goals may be changed or amended (e.g. pushed out further in time or their urgency reduced) when they see conflicts. Such conflicts occur most frequently when the total assets needed to reach stated goals exceed the assets available. In short, the family is "in control" and knows why certain steps may be necessary, though they may not be pleasant. They are driving the process rather than having "something done *to* them."
2. Such a process, which must be repeated at regular intervals, such as yearly, allows the family or individual to "stay current." Indeed, though budgets may be created with the best of intentions, it is a fact of life that they may not hold. Spending may be higher – or lower – than anticipated. Similarly, particularly for goals that "mature" further down the line, capital markets may not produce the returns that were expected. Finally, goals and preferences change with time, as certain "needs" seem to recede, while others appear. Being able to revisit the goals that need to be revisited is considerably more intuitive than the former institutional approach, which required looking at an amorphous asset allocation statistic and arguing that it should be changed. Did one's risk tolerance change? Was there a structural change in capital market circumstances? The goals-based approach speaks more directly to the wealth holder with the simpler observation: "I do not have enough left to meet my goal because I am spending more than anticipated" or "capital markets have proven riskier or less generous than I expected."
3. Particularly for families with substantial non-financial assets, this process can be a useful guide to the eventual disposition of certain assets. Here we focus on assets that, though they may well appreciate in value through time, are, in the short-term at least, liability drivers. They drive liabilities because they require maintenance or insurance that adds to the family's spending needs without contributing any direct financial

return. This might apply to an expensive house that doubles as a primary or secondary residence, for instance. Families will often find it as difficult to divest such prized non-financial assets, as they might a low-basis stock, which was acquired through some original entrepreneurial activity. Psychological pressures are then too high for the family to recognize that such assets create what might become an excessive annual draw on their financial wealth. Having the ability to show exactly what is needed to maintain the family's lifestyle and to illustrate when financial assets might become insufficient to play that role is crucial in helping families overcome these psychological pressures.

It is now possible for families to develop truly customized investment policies based on their specific goals and preferences. It is useful, however, to remind ourselves of the practical limits to customization. The example of a racing bicycle might help illustrate the point. Although it is feasible for a bicycle to be built based on the specifics of each individual, it is usually not necessary to create new parts. For instance, the frame can reflect the exact physical measurements of the racer, but the elements that create the frame can be cut from standard tubes. Similarly, pedals can have various lengths but do not need to be manufactured specifically. A racing bicycle is thus more a case of mass customization than ultimate bespoke manufacturing.

The same is true for families, except when they have preferences or requirements that make them so different from some "norm" that no pre-existing solution can possibly fit. This may be where the challenge is the greatest, as true customization – such as a Savile Row suit crafted with a special fabric as opposed to a custom-tailored suit made from standard fabric – tends to be quite costly. A good advisor can help the family to understand the trade-off and find an economical and yet satisfactory solution and will act as an interpreter who is working to translate the goals and constraints of the family into the realities of capital markets.

In conclusion, the question that we asked at the outset (*What should my asset allocation be?*) is indeed daunting, but new processes that are more clearly designed with the family in mind can help transform an unpleasant experience into a satisfactory and gratifying outcome. Though the realities of capital markets cannot be changed just because we would like them to be different, they can be accommodated in a way that allows the family or individual to reach as many goals as desired, over the horizons chosen and with the appropriate urgency.

Questions for Further Reflection

1. Combining asset allocation and asset location: How does one need to modify the module construction process to encompass the various vehicles through which assets may be owned?

2. How can one use simulations to plan for the future when assets include both income generating (usually mostly financial) and expense generating (mostly real, particularly "trophy" assets)?
3. How does one manage the need to revisit the investment policy yearly as certain time horizons, actual spending, or asset return differ from expectations?
4. How does one need to change the structure of the "advisory process" to ensure the focus is appropriately placed on clarifying and specifying client goals?

Additional Resources

For those who are interested in the adequacy of the approach within classical financial theory:

Sanjiv Das, Harry Markowitz, Jonathan Scheid, and Meir Statman, "Portfolio Optimization with Mental Accounts," *The Journal of Financial and Quantitative Analysis,* 2010.

For those interested in a practical presentation of the new theoretical framework by acclaimed financial academics:

Sanjiv Das, Harry Markowitz, Jonathan Scheid, and Meir Statman, "Portfolios for Investors Who Want to Reach Their Goals While Staying on the Mean-Variance Efficient Frontier," *The Journal of Wealth Management,* 2011.

For those seeking the full details of the process introduced here:

Jean L.P. Brunel, *Goals-Based Wealth Management: An Integrated and Practical Approach to Changing the Structure of Wealth Advisory Practices* (Hoboken, NJ: Wiley, 2015).

Biography

Jean Brunel is the managing principal of Brunel Associates, a firm founded in 2001 to serve ultra-high-net-worth individuals and their advisors. Prior to this, Jean spent the bulk of his career with J.P. Morgan, becoming, in 1990, the chief investment officer of JP Morgan's global private bank and a director and executive committee member of J.P. Morgan Investment Management, Inc. He has been the editor of the *Journal of Wealth Management* since its founding in 1998 and authored two books – *Integrated Wealth Management: The New Direction for Portfolio Managers* (London: Euromoney Institutional Investor Plc, 2002, 2006), and *Goals-Based Wealth Management: An Integrated and Practical Approach to Changing the Structure of Wealth Advisory Practices* (Hoboken, NJ: Wiley, 2015), as well as many peer-reviewed articles.

In 2011, Jean received the prestigious C. Stewart Sheppard Award from the CFA Institute. In June 2012, he was named the 2012 Multi-Family Office Chief Investment Officer of the Year by *Family Office Review*. In April 2015, he was the first recipient of the J. Richard Joyner Wealth Management Impact Award newly created by IMCA.

He is a graduate of École des Hautes Études Commerciales (HEC) in France, received his MBA from the Kellogg School of Business at Northwestern University, and is a CFA charterholder.

CHAPTER 16

Does Investing Have to Be Complicated?

Robert Maynard

No, investing does not have to be complicated, for institutions or private investors.

The Public Employee Retirement System of Idaho (PERSI) is a conventional, reasonably diversified institutional investor ($17 billion) that assures the delivery of market returns through the patient use of simple, transparent, and focused investment vehicles. We believe more aggressive approaches carry greater long-term dangers than the problematic shorter-term opportunities warrant. As a result, we are committed to a "conventional investment" approach. This is in contrast to the more complex approaches taken by a number of other investment institutions that have sprung up in recent years.

Why Conventional Investing?

We believe conventional investing is the best framework for the management of our portfolio. This is due to our goals and constraints, including the size of the portfolio, the staff resources available, and the changing nature of the membership of our board over the next few years (which will include non-investment professionals).

In contrast, the endowment model and the various factor approaches require too many resources, are too opaque, are expensive, and have problematic return prospects for the vast majority of funds. We think complex portfolios are difficult to fully comprehend and control and we prefer to use well-understood concepts with a well-established literature and tradition.

Moreover, market returns are more than sufficient to meet our conservative liabilities, and there is no evidence that more complicated or complex investment strategies add to return for the great majority of investors.

Overview of Conventional Investing: Simple, Transparent, Focused, and Patient

Conventional investing as implemented in our portfolio emphasizes the values of simplicity, transparency, focus, and patience. It relies primarily on general public markets (global equities and investment-grade fixed income) with the addition of some private investments (real estate and other private equity).

Simple

The portfolio is diversified among conventional, liquid, transparent asset classes and uses long-term market returns to meet its investment goals. The investment policy is relatively simple and easy to follow and does not tactically allocate the portfolio in any significant way over short-term time periods. The strategic asset mix is:

10% TIPS (inflation-protected Treasuries)
15% Aggregate (bonds)
5% Idaho Mortgages
18% S&P 500 (US large-cap)
11% R2500 (US small-cap)
15% EAFE (Europe, Australasia, Far East)
10% Emerging Markets
8% Private Equity
8% Real Estate (4% REITs, 4% Private)

Transparent

Conventional investing relies on transparency as the primary risk control. Index funds provide the base position, primarily in the larger more liquid markets for broad basic exposures and as the primary vehicles for portfolio rebalancing and transitions (as well as cost control). We maintain around 45–50% of the portfolio in capitalization-weighted passive index funds.

The active managers we use typically have broad mandates, with a preference for managers with either clear styles or concentrated portfolios (as much if not more for risk control and transparency than clear additional return benefit). The portfolio concentrates the relationships to relatively few in number (around 20 public managers, around 20 private equity relationships, and a few real estate agents).

We avoid so-called black box investing, and we have a strong preference for public securities or funds that can be independently daily priced and private strategies that would be understandable to reasonably intelligent people who may not have extensive investment training.

Focused

Conventional investing recognizes that the benefits of diversification basically disappear after 10–11 asset types are used in the portfolio, and that the benefits of moving from four asset types to five are much greater than moving from 44 to 45. Further, we believe that a position needs to be at least 5% (and preferably at least 8–10%) of the portfolio in order to have any noticeable impact on either the risk or the return of the entire portfolio.

In addition, for diversification purposes, we have added private assets (both equity and real estate) in an attempt to capture an illiquidity premium (and to realize the annual smoothing benefits recognized by the practices of actuaries and accountants). For decades, we have also maintained a larger than typical exposure to emerging markets and small-capitalization U.S. equities due to their long-term growth prospects.

Patient

Conventional investing accepts capital market volatility and understands that it will often be greater than what many market participants expect. We look at returns over the long term and we do not use tactical asset allocation based on our short-term return expectations. Avoiding tactical moves in volatile markets is analogous to staying put in a known, sound structure during a severe earthquake rather than running around wildly. Our goal is to ensure that our liabilities can be easily met over the much longer term while being maintained at acceptable levels through short-term turbulence.

Patience is a requirement of all successful investment approaches – not just traditional investing. As Warren Buffett once said, "In the investing business, if you have an IQ of 150, you should sell 30 points to someone else. You do not need to be a genius. You need to have emotional stability, inner peace and be able to think for yourself … Emotional makeup is more important than technical skill."

Some Additional Considerations

We are also focused on surviving expected extreme short-term volatility (such as that which occurred in 2007–2009). This is accomplished by assuring that the cash needs of the organization can survive a market disruption of at least three years. This is primarily achieved through sufficient cash holdings or near-certain cash flows that can assure meeting our known near-term obligations. We have a very stable stream of diversified government contributions that cover over 90% of our ongoing cash payments for benefits, and therefore we have a stable three-year time horizon – one that easily navigated the 2007–2009 crisis. (This, of course, can be very different from many private family investors who rely primarily on returns on invested capital and cannot count on ongoing inflows into the portfolio.)

Another objective is to "Avoid the Big Mistake." Conventional investing takes as its base position that market returns with the appropriate equity/fixed mix are sufficient to meet obligations over the long term, and that any attempt to generate extra return should not jeopardize basic market returns.

As a result, major tactical asset allocation moves in anticipation of "poor" or "great" market opportunities are viewed with great suspicion and are disfavored. In order to make a major tactical asset allocation move pay off, three decisions, not just one, have to be correct: (1) when to get out of an asset type; (2) when to get back in; and (3) where to put the money in the meantime. An incorrect decision on any of these three can lead to severe losses.

Another consequence of this principle is that conventional investing never makes a major move in the middle of a crisis: instead, it "blindly" rebalances during volatile market moves, and doesn't try to time markets instead of following previously agreed upon investment policy.

Problems with Conventional Investing: Fighting Boredom and Emotional Exhaustion

The problem with conventional investing is that it requires extreme patience. An organization must be able to ride through extremely volatile markets without taking major action (except rebalancing) in anticipation of benefits over the long term. Conventional investing values inaction – keeping to a basic market posture without much alteration during both good and trying times. For many individuals and organizations, it has proven to be harder doing nothing than doing something.

There is an old saying in investing that there are three ways to make money in the markets: one is physically exhausting, one is intellectually exhausting, and one is emotionally exhausting.

The physically exhausting path is to work harder than everyone else – usually to try and find an "edge." But there are only so many hours in a day, and finding extra information legally is getting more difficult by the day with the rewards diminishing almost by the second.

The intellectually exhausting path is to be noticeably smarter than anyone else in the market, but by definition this only happens to a very few. Being smart, well-resourced, articulate, and previously successful simply gets one in the institutional investment game – winning that game consistently in the future requires much more.

The emotionally exhausting path is that advocated by conventional investing, and requires facing periods of crisis with organizational equanimity. It is easier said than done.

The Conventional Investment Framework and the PERSI Portfolio

A conventional investment framework looks at an investment portfolio with several basic questions:

What should be the basic equity/fixed income allocation?

We have chosen a 70% equity/30% fixed allocation as our base posture due to the nature of our liabilities, and a need for a real (after inflation) return of 3.75% over decades in order to meet basic statutory liabilities. Over the past two centuries, and over rolling 20- to 30-year periods, equities have relatively consistently delivered real returns in the 5–7% range, and fixed income has returned 1–3% fairly consistently. Therefore a 70/30 split would produce returns of 3.8% real at the low end (if both capital markets had 20-year returns at the low end of their historic range) to 5.7% real at the high end (if capital markets are jubilant). Thus a 70/30 split gives an excellent chance of meeting at least statutory benefits in poor capital markets (as occurred in the 2000s), while also giving a good chance of maintaining full purchasing power in good markets (as occurred in the 1990s).

What home-country bias, if any, is desired?

We hold significant home-country bias due to three factors. First, our liabilities are in US dollars, and therefore most of our assets should be held in US dollars. Second, our liabilities are linked to US inflation, and should be responsive to long-term movements in US inflation. Since US inflation is caused by higher US prices, and higher US prices are mainly charged by US corporations, US equities have been shown to respond to US inflation quite well over longer periods of time (10–25 years). Finally, the US equity capital market has historically been one of the best performing (and stable) equity capital markets in the world, and there is some reason to believe that outperformance and additional safety over long periods of time are not just a historical accident.

How is diversification maintained or has there been drift because of rebalancing (or lack thereof) and/or tactical asset allocation?

We follow standard institutional practice and occasionally rebalance our portfolio. Having said that, there is no universally accepted rebalancing procedure, with some arguing that standard rebalancing practices are not appropriate at all. Rebalancing essentially relies on the idea of mean reversion in markets, which can take a few years to occur. And, the practical impact is somewhat limited – at most about 40 basis points a year over a decade, but not in each and every year.

How much active management will be used, and with what firms?

The focus – too often lost – should be on those decisions that drive over 95% of portfolio results – the portfolio construction and maintenance. Unfortunately, most analysis often concentrates on the other 5% – how active management individually or collectively may or may not have beaten the relevant benchmarks for those managers over recent periods of time.

We normally have about 50% of our assets in capitalization-weighted index funds, and around 20 private equity relationships. We have also historically maintained about 20 public security relationships, allocating about 3–4% of the portfolio to each manager.

Conventional Investing – Summary

A conventional investing approach works for our fund and may be appropriate for other private and institutional investors as well, depending on their specific needs. It relies on the basic components of simplicity, transparency, focus, and patience, which, while easier said than done, can allow markets to do their work and deliver the required results over time.

This article was adapted from "The PERSI Investment Portfolio," a detailed description of the PERSI investment approach and reasons for choosing it. It is available on the fund's website, https://www.persi.idaho.gov/Documents/Investments/Portfolio Narrative/persi_investment_portfolio_narrative_12-29-2017.pdf.

Questions for Consideration

1. What rate of return do you need to meet your goals/liabilities?
2. Do you need complex or illiquid assets to meet those goals, or will simple, liquid, transparent assets do the job?
3. Do you understand and are you comfortable with all of the components of your current portfolio?
4. Do you have the emotional strength and patience to withstand the inevitable volatility of public equity markets?

Additional Resources

Ben Carlson, *A Wealth of Common Sense: Why Simplicity Trumps Complexity in Any Investment Plan* (New York: Bloomberg Press, 2015).

David Swensen, *Unconventional Success* (New York: Free Press, 2005).

Burton G. Malkiel, *A Random Walk Down Wall Street* (New York: W.W. Norton, 2012).

Charles Ellis, *Winning the Loser's Game* (New York: McGraw-Hill, 2009).

John Bogle, *John Bogle on Investing: The First 50 Years* (Hoboken, NJ: Wiley, 2012).

Charles Ellis and Burton G. Malkiel, *The Elements of Investing* (Hoboken, NJ: Wiley, 2010).

Larry E. Swedroe, *The Quest for Alpha: The Holy Grail of Investing* (New York: Bloomberg Press, 2011).

Biography

Robert Maynard is chief investment officer for the $17 billion Public Employee Retirement System of Idaho, where he is responsible for all investment activities of the organization. He has served in that position since 1992. Previously he served as deputy executive director of the Alaska Permanent Fund Corporation, and as assistant attorney general for the State of Alaska.

In addition to his duties for the Idaho Retirement System, Robert participates or has participated as an advisor, board member, or chair of a number of investment-related and charitable organizations and has lectured frequently on investment topics at numerous conferences and institutions. He has also written a number of investment articles for various publications.

Robert has been recognized for his investment activities on a number of occasions, including being named Chief Investment Officer of the Year by the Institute for Fiduciary Education (2006), receiving the Richard L. Stoddard Award for outstanding contributions to the investment of public funds (awarded by other state CIOs) (2006), and also receiving the Lifetime Achievement Award for Public Fund Investing (collectively awarded by Institutional Investor Press, Information Management Network, and the Money Management Letter) (2010). Robert has also been named as one of the 100 most influential global investors by *Asset International CIO* magazine, as one of the Sovereign Wealth Fund Institute's global 100 "most significant and impactful public investor executives," and as one of the top 30 public fund CIOs by Trusted Insight.

Robert graduated from Claremont Men's (now Claremont McKenna) College and received his JD from the University of California, Davis School of Law.

CHAPTER 17

How Should You Understand and Deal with Investment Risk?

Howard Marks

The act of investing can be defined as forgoing consumption today to make money in uncertain ventures in the hope of increasing one's ability to consume tomorrow. *Thus, investing entails making decisions regarding the future, even though the future can't be known with confidence. It boils down to the conscious acceptance of risk in pursuit of return.*

Most people think about investing primarily in terms of the return they might make, but clearly there are not one but two important elements: return and risk – in other words, the amount of money made and the risk borne to make it. Both must be considered by any intelligent investor.

It's easy to make money in the stock market, especially in the good years, and most of the years are good. If you look at historical returns, they've been good most of the time, and good on average over the long term.

After roughly 50 years in the business, I'm convinced that risk is the more important, intriguing and difficult part of investing. Risk, not return, is what distinguishes the superior investor: whatever the return may be, I'm convinced the superior investor achieves it with less risk than others.

In order to determine whether an investor did a good job, we have to look at something called "risk-adjusted return," which considers both the return that was achieved and the risk that was taken in the process. But whereas return is easily measured and stated, risk is not.

In an attempt to quantify risk, finance academics and theoreticians in the early 1960s chose volatility as the measure of risk. Volatility – or how much an asset price or a stream of returns fluctuates over time – is easy to quantify. For me, that is volatility's greatest advantage. The problem is that, in my opinion and in the eyes of most investors, volatility is not the real risk (although it might be viewed as a symptom or product of risk).

Therein lies the problem: historic volatility can be measured, but for me it isn't really risk. Risk, the way I define it – the probability of future loss – is something that can't be quantified. In general, the probability of a future event can't be measured; it's just a matter of opinion. And although the probability of future loss obviously can't be measured, I find it interesting (and somewhat surprising) that the probability of loss can't be measured even after the fact. For instance, if you buy something for $100 and sell it for $200, was it risky or not? How much risk was there at the time the investment was made? Where do you look to find that number? Was it a risky asset that produced a lucky gain, or was a smart (and safe) investment that was sure to produce a profit? You can't tell from the outcome.

Because of my doubts about the relevance of volatility, the formulas that calculate risk-adjusted return using volatility as the measure of risk are easy to apply but not completely appropriate. Thus, the question of how much risk of loss was borne can only be a matter of subjective opinion. For this reason, although important, adjusting for risk isn't easy.

Risk is something that the intelligent investor either (a) avoids if it's intolerable in the absolute or (b) demands compensation to bear. I've never heard anyone say, "I'm not going to make that investment: it might be volatile." What they say is, "I'm not going to make that investment: I might lose money." Thus I reject defining risk as volatility. For me, risk is mainly the probability of losing money.

An aside: I say "mainly" because there are many forms of risk, and they should all be considered to varying degrees. For someone who needs a certain return from his investments to live on, the risk of earning too low a return might have serious consequences. Likewise, an investment manager whose return falls below that achieved by a market index or by his competitors might lose his clients. In both these cases, the investor doesn't lose money; he makes it ... just not enough. That's a risk. There's also the risk that, in the case of an investment that ultimately proves to be profitable, an interim price decline or frightening environment might cause an investor to sell at a low and miss out on the subsequent rebound. These are all forms of risk, but in general, I think the possibility of permanent loss is the one that matters most.

Where does risk come from? As the late investment sage Peter Bernstein wrote, risk arises from uncertainty. "There's a range of outcomes, and we don't know where [the outcome] is going to fall within that range. Often we don't even know what the range is." Or as Elroy Dimson of the London Business School put it, "Risk means more things can happen than will happen."

The future isn't known or knowable. In fact I don't think the future has been determined yet, so how can it be known today? It can only be guessed at, but investors can try to add value by enumerating the possible outcomes and estimating their probabilities. Thus we have to think about the future in terms of a probability distribution. What's most likely to happen? What other outcomes are nearly as likely? What are the improbable possibilities, or "tail events"? How likely are they and what would be their consequences? These are things we can estimate but not know.

And it's essential to remember that even if we're right about the possible outcomes and their respective probabilities, we still don't know which one is going to happen. Thus, uncertainty – risk – is generally inescapable. We can decide on an optimal course of action: one that would be successful under the likely outcomes and not too bad if one of the less likely outcomes comes to pass. But we can still get one of those less likely negative outcomes for which we're not ideally prepared. (We can't prepare for all possibilities at once; rather, we generally prepare well only for outcomes that are among the ones we consider likely.)

So, in other words:

- Many outcomes are possible.
- We can't know which of them will happen.
- At best we can list them and assign them probabilities.
- Even if we do so correctly, the actual outcome will still be in doubt.
- Invariably some of the outcomes that materialize will be unpleasant.
- The uncertainty surrounding which outcome will materialize and the possibility that it will be a bad one are the source of risk.

Many people think "riskier investments produce higher returns" and "if you want to make more money, the way to do so is to take more risk." I consider both of these formulations potentially disastrous. In short, if riskier investments could be counted on for higher returns, they wouldn't be riskier. Rather, I think the way to think about the relationship between risk and return is that "investments that *appear* riskier have to *appear* to offer higher returns, or else no one will invest in them. *But they don't have to deliver.*" There you have it: the possibility of disappointing outcomes (including permanent loss) from "risky" investments.

So rather than saying "increasing risk increases return," I think the right way to view it is that "increasing risk increases an investment's expected return; it expands the range of possible outcomes; and it causes the range of outcomes to include some that are unfavorable." That's the way investors should think about risk. Only that view will enable them to handle it wisely.

How should risk be dealt with? The answer is "thorough questioning." Do you understand the risks involved? How realistic are your expectations regarding return and the possibility of loss? Have they been estimated using conservative assumptions? Is it possible to estimate the downside risk under negative scenarios? Does the probable return compensate sufficiently for the risk involved? Can the risk borne be reduced through diversification? Is the downside risk under unfavorable outcomes bearable?

This last question is really a key one. You mustn't let the attraction of big potential returns blind you to the possibility of losses that exceed your ability to bear them. That's what Warren Buffett means when he says, "It's insane to risk what you have and need to get what you don't have and don't need." Risk is a serious matter, and everyone who wants to be a successful investor should work extra-hard to deal with it maturely.

Questions for Further Reflection

1. How realistic (but hopefully still conservative) are your expectations regarding return and the possibility of loss?
2. Does the probable return compensate sufficiently for the risk involved?
3. Is the downside risk under unfavorable outcomes bearable?

Additional Resources

Howard Marks, *Risk*, Oaktree Capital Insights, 2006, https://www.oaktreecapital.com/insights/howard-marks-memos.

Howard Marks, *Risk Revisited Again*, Oaktree Capital Insights, 2015, https://www.oaktreecapital.com/insights/howard-marks-memos.

Peter Bernstein, *Against the Gods: The Remarkable Story of Risk* (New York: Wiley, 1996).

Seth Klarman, *Margin of Safety* (Philadelphia: Beard Books, Inc., 1991).

Nassim Nicholas Taleb, *Fooled by Randomness* (New York: Random House Trade, 2001).

Biography

Howard Marks, CFA®, is co-founder and co-chairman of Oaktree Capital Management, where he spends most of his time determining and communicating regarding the firm's strategic posture. In addition to leading Oaktree, he is well known for the memos to Oaktree clients he has written over the past 28 years, and for his 2011 book, *The Most Important Thing*. Howard holds a BSEc degree cum laude in finance from the Wharton School and an MBA in accounting and marketing from the Booth School of Business of the University of Chicago. He is a CFA charterholder; vice chairman of the Investment Committee of the Metropolitan Museum of Art; chairman of the board and the investment committee of the Royal Drawing School in London; and a member of the investment committee of the Edmond J. Safra Foundation.

CHAPTER 18

What Is the Most Useful Definition of Risk for Family Investors?

James Garland

In an investment context, *risk* means the possibility of not having available the money you need at the time when you need it.

This definition requires two elaborations. First of all, "need" is subjective. Some people may feel that they need a Rolls Royce, or a condo in Palm Beach, or a private jet. Others can lead happy lives without such luxuries. What do you *really* need?

In addition, the *probability* of a shortfall is less important than the *consequences* of that shortfall. Suppose that your twin children are about to enter college, that they've been accepted to elite schools ("elite" meaning you'll pay over $65,000 a year), and that you've accumulated an equity portfolio whose current value is roughly the amount needed to pay their expenses for the next four years. The portfolio is invested in just a few companies, and furthermore it's leveraged with margin debt.

The consequences of your hanging on to those securities are lopsided; if the stocks continue to rise, you'll make a few more dollars, but if they decline, the kids may be headed for community college. The serious potential consequences of continuing to hold these stocks makes this a very risky bet. But if the consequences were minor – if this were play money, so to speak – then the risk would be far less. Bill Gates doesn't have to worry about his grandchildren's college tuitions. You may have to.

Volatility as a Proxy for Risk

The market values of financial assets are volatile. Investors understand that stocks are more volatile than bonds and that real estate lies somewhere in between. Therefore, in the most widely accepted hierarchy of risk, stocks are at the top, followed by real estate, with bonds near the bottom.

Volatility can be a good proxy for risk, particularly in the short term, as illustrated by the college tuition story just told. However, volatility is only one dimension of risk, and sometimes volatility doesn't even matter. If the stock market goes down a lot this year, for example, that's not at all a risk for you, except if you're intending to sell stocks soon to make a significant purchase. Price declines matter only when people are selling. But because volatility can be quantified, whereas other risks cannot be, economists and investment firms have latched onto volatility as the sole proxy for risk. That's an incomplete view of the world.

Investment Models

To navigate through the fog of finance, academics use mathematical models. Academics love models because they reduce very messy real-world living to simple formulae that can fit on a classroom blackboard. Some models are highly respected. One, the capital asset pricing model, won its creators a Nobel Prize.

Use models, but don't believe them. Models can be useful, but in only a limited way.

First, the good news: some models (including the capital asset pricing model) describe how markets are supposed to behave, and such descriptions are useful in understanding basic principles, such as the virtue of diversification, the equity risk premium, and so on.

But the bad news is that models fail in at least two important regards.

First, models fail to account for human nature. They describe how markets are supposed to behave, but real-life markets – not knowing the expectations with which economists have burdened them – don't behave that way. A whole new field called behavioral finance has arisen to explain how investors actually behave. Because real-life behavior cannot be described mathematically, economists' models are incomplete.

Second, many models assume that outcomes are normally distributed. In lay terms, they assume that outcomes fit within what are known as bell curves. Bell curves are good at describing normal circumstances, but circumstances are not always normal, and abnormal circumstances are the dangerous ones. A simple bell curve appears in Figure 18.1.

The black line plots investment returns on the horizontal axis, and the probability of earning those returns on the vertical axis. This bell curve is derived from a commonly used theoretical model. The most likely outcomes are clustered near the center (around the average); extremely low returns (at the left) and extremely high returns (at the right) are quite rare.

But real life looks more like the gray line. In many situations, including in financial markets, extreme events happen more often than the models predict.

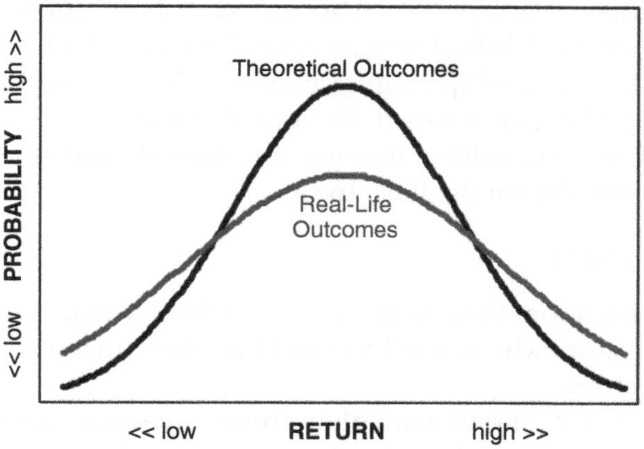

Figure 18.1 Theoretical outcomes versus real-life outcomes.

This is known as a "fat-tail" problem, because events at the left and right ends of the curves – at the tails – are more common than expected and are often quite consequential. The fat-tail events with which we're most familiar involve the weather. Hundred-year floods seem to happen not every hundred years, as models would suggest, but rather once every decade or two.

The most extreme financial event in my lifetime was the October 1987 US stock market crash, when the S&P 500 Index declined by 23% in just one day. According to standard stock market models, that 23% single-day decline should happen only once in every three trillion years.[1] *That* was a fat-tail event!

Investing for Income

A small number of investors have very long time horizons and have enough capital that they can afford to live off the income that their capital generates. This is a game changer. So-called "income investors" don't have to worry about market values at all. For them, all that matters is the stability and security of their income sources.

In the United States, at least, dividends from equities (in particular, from the S&P 500 Composite Stock Index) have been far more stable than the market values of those equities. For example, there has been only one peak-to-trough decline in S&P 500 dividends of more than 5% since 1950 (i.e. a 21% drop in 2008–2009), and dividends recovered from that particular decline in just three years. There are simple ways to self-insure against such a decline – for example, by holding some bonds that can be cannibalized to fill in any dividend "potholes."

[1]This number comes from David F. Swensen, *Unconventional Success* (New York: Free Press, 2005), p. 186.

Most investors – e.g., people who are saving for their retirements, and families who have established private foundations – do have to worry about market values though, and managing market values is a difficult task. Income investors inhabit a lower-risk world. Because the rest of the investment universe is obsessed with market values, income investors should ignore most of what other investors and the media have to say.

Primary Sources of Risk

For investors with short time horizons, *volatility* is a risk. This is true also for longer-term investors who intend to liquidate their investment assets, such as retirement investors.

However, it's not always true that these investors need to fear market declines. Younger investors should welcome bear markets, because bear markets will enable them to accumulate shares and bonds at favorable prices. It's only *dissaving* investors, such as retirees, for whom bear markets are a worry.

For investors with long-term horizons, however, the risks are different. The primary source of returns for long-term equity investors is the profits that their corporations earn. As a result, the primary risks for long-term investors are risks that threaten corporate profits. Some of them are the following.

- *Economic risks* include such events as recessions and depressions.
- *Business risks* matter particularly for families who are undiversified, i.e. that still own one or more operating businesses.
- *Governmental risks* are threats from things such as poor governmental policies or weak property rights, or from blatant actions such as expropriation of assets.
- *Hyperinflation* is self-explanatory. Modest inflation generally is not a problem, at least for equity investors, because profits and dividends tend to keep pace with increases in the cost of living.
- *Environmental risks* may be important in the future if some predicted effects of climate change come to pass.

Well-to-do investors have a moral obligation to try to improve the communities and nations in which they live. A happy paradox is that fulfilling this obligation, in the long run, may benefit these investors as well as the world at large.

But for investors who are reading this book, no matter what your time horizon, the biggest risk may be *you*. Have you made a long-term investment plan? Is it any good? Have you stuck by it? Were you caught up in the Internet Bubble? Did you panic during the Great Recession of 2008–2009? Do you pay attention to mundane but potentially corrosive issues such as costs? Do you trade or change managers too often? Do you search hungrily for self-proclaimed "experts" to guide you on your way? Have you inoculated yourself and your family members against common behavioral errors such as overconfidence, trend following, anchoring, and so forth?

Contrary to any claims it may make, your brain is not always your best friend. If you fail to understand the errors that your mind can make, your mind will make them.

How to Reduce Risk

Set clear, achievable, and meaningful objectives. Risk can only be defined in terms of your particular objectives. For example, if you seek income, then market value fluctuations will matter very little or perhaps not at all.

Prepare. Study history. (As Jack Bogle of The Vanguard Group once said, "Learn from the experience of others – it's cheaper.") Educate your family members. Help them understand (among other things) how markets work, the industry's potential conflicts of interest, why minimizing costs is important, and the traps that lurk along the way.

Understand yourself. Study behavioral finance.

Diversify. The way to make a fortune is to invest in just one company – the right company. The way to preserve that fortune is to diversify.

And finally, *save more and spend less.* Spending less than one earns is a magical way to lessen the risk of running out of money.

One Final Word

To boil all of this down to its core, the fundamental objective of investing is *to survive.* There are no guarantees in investing. Diversify your life as well as your investments. Get a good education, find a good job, and make good friends.

Questions for Further Reflection

1. If we have to choose between higher potential returns and lower price volatility, how do we choose?
2. Can't hedge funds protect us from market downturns? What about absolute-return funds?
3. How can we protect ourselves against fat-tail events?
4. How broadly should we diversify?
5. How can I keep our family from panicking during bear markets? From jumping onto fads?

Additional Resources

Charles Ellis, *Winning the Loser's Game* (New York: McGraw-Hill, 2017).

There are two messages in this book: first, that markets are efficient, and therefore investors should not shoot for better-than-market returns; and second, that investors need to take charge of the entire investment process.

Burton G. Malkiel, *A Random Walk Down Wall Street* (New York: W.W. Norton, 2016).

The classic all-in-one investment manual.

James Montier, *The Little Book of Behavioral Investing* (Hoboken, NJ: Wiley, 2010).

The best short guide to the many ways that smart investors can (and will!) make foolish errors.

Elroy Dimson, Paul Marsh, and Mike Staunton, *Triumph of the Optimists* (Princeton, NJ: Princeton University Press, 2002).

This is a history of national stock and bond market returns during the twentieth century. The best such source around. One lesson from the book is that North American investors have been fortunate – US and Canadian stock market returns since 1900 have been among the best in the world. Will that good fortune continue?

None of these are light reading, but if you care about your family's investments, make the effort. Keep an eye out for occasional good articles in the media or on the Internet. For starters, almost any articles by Charles Ellis, or Burton Malkiel, or Meir Statman (a specialist in behavioral finance) will be worth reading. And watch for articles by the dean of financial columnists, Jason Zweig, whose work resides these days at the *Wall Street Journal*.

Biography

James Garland is former president of The Jeffrey Company, a family investment company based in Columbus, Ohio. A Maine native, he graduated from Bowdoin College in 1969 with a degree in music history. He worked for seven years at NASA's Goddard Space Flight Center in Greenbelt, Maryland, then returned to Maine in 1976 to join an investment advisory firm as a securities analyst and portfolio manager. He then moved to Ohio in 1995 to work for The Jeffrey Company. He is the author of papers dealing with personal trusts, endowment spending, and taxable investing that have appeared in the *Financial Analysts Journal*, *The Journal of Portfolio Management*, and *The Journal of Investing*.

CHAPTER 19

Is Active Management Still Worthwhile? – I

Charles Ellis

Active "performance" investment managers today are so attached to their work, stature, and income that most do not yet recognize the impact of multiple seismic changes in their profession. The dynamics that produced the rise of active investing to prominence also carried the seeds of its inevitable peaking, which is now being followed by an increasingly recognizable decline in benefits to clients.

As we all know – but without always understanding the ominous long-term consequences – over the past 50 years, increasing numbers of highly talented young investment professionals have entered the competition for a faster and more accurate discovery of pricing errors ("price discovery"), the key to achieving the holy grail of superior investment performance. They have more advanced training than their predecessors, better analytical tools, and faster access to more information. Thus, the skill and effectiveness of active managers as a group have risen continuously for more than half a century, producing an increasingly expert and successful price discovery market mechanism.

Because all have ready access to almost all the same information, the probabilities continue to rise that any mispricing – particularly for the 500 largest capitalization stocks that necessarily dominate major managers' portfolios and so are closely covered by experienced portfolio managers and expert analysts – will be quickly discovered and swiftly arbitraged away. The increasing efficiency of modern stock markets makes it harder to match them and much harder to beat them – particularly after covering costs and fees.

Fifty years ago, beating the market (i.e. beating the competition: part-time individual amateurs and overstructured, conservative institutions) was not just possible – it was probable for well-informed, boldly active professionals. Institutions did less than 10% of total NYSE trading, and individuals did more than 90%. Those individual investors made their decisions – fewer than one a year – primarily for such *outside*-the-market reasons. Today, full-time professionals who are constantly comparison-shopping *inside* the market for any competitive advantage are executing more than 98% of trades in listed stocks, and nearly 100% of derivative transactions. All investment professionals now have access to more market information than they can possibly use. And with Regulation Fair Disclosure (Reg. FD), the SEC insists all information be disclosed to all investors at the same time.[1] The compounding change of all the many changing factors over the past 50 years has been astounding.

Although clients put up all the capital and accept all the market risks, "performance" for clients – incremental returns above the market index – has been failing. Over 80% of mutual funds fall short of their chosen benchmarks. Meanwhile, active investing has become one of the most financially rewarding service businesses in history.

A Brief History of Performance Investing

The key to understanding the profound forces for change in active investing – particularly the dismal results produced for investors – is to study major trends over the long term. Early practitioners of performance investing experienced significant impediments and costs that would be strange to today's participants. Block trading was just beginning and daily NYSE trading volume was only one-third of 1% of today's volume; thus, trades of 10,000 shares could take hours to execute. Brokerage commissions were fixed at an average of more than 40 cents a share. In-depth research from new firms on Wall Street had barely begun. Computers were confined to the "cage" or back office.

The opportunities for superior price discovery were so good in the 1970s and 1980s that the leading active managers were able to attract substantial assets and – not always, but often – deliver superior performance. But as the collective search for mispricing opportunities attracted more and more skilful competitors – aided by a surging increase in Bloomberg machines, e-mail, and other extraordinary new data-gathering and data-processing tools – price discovery got increasingly swift and effective, and active investors got more and more equal and less and less able to do better than their equally superb competitors.

With all these changes, the core question is not whether the markets are *perfectly* efficient but rather, whether they are *sufficiently* efficient that active managers, after fees and costs of operations, are unlikely to be able to get ahead of the price discovery consensus of the experts. As asked earlier, do clients have sufficient reason to accept all the risks, costs, and uncertainties – and fees – of active management?

During the glory days of active investing – compared with the magnitude of the predicted superior performance – the fees for active investment simply

---

[1]Facebook and Twitter were recently approved as vehicles for fair disclosure.

did not seem to matter; any quibbling about fees was dismissed with such comments as, "You wouldn't choose your child's brain surgeon on the basis of price, would you?"

As assets of mutual funds and pension funds multiplied, fee schedules for active investment management went up, not down, as might be expected in economic theory. With this combination, the investment *business* grew increasingly profitable. High pay and interesting work attracted increasing numbers of highly capable MBAs and PhDs, who became analysts and portfolio managers *and*, collectively, more competition for each other.

Fees for equity management are typically described with one four-letter word and a single number. The four-letter word is *only*, as in "only 1%" for mutual funds or "only half of 1%" for institutions. If you accept the 1%, you will easily accept the "only." But is that not a self-deception?[2] "Only 1%" *is* the ratio of fees to *assets*, but the investor already *has* the assets, and so active investment managers must be offering to deliver something else: *returns*. If annual future equity returns are, as the consensus expectation now holds, 7–8%, then for what is being delivered to investors, 1% of *assets* quickly balloons to nearly 12–15% of *returns*. But that is not the end of it.

A rigorous definition of costs for active management would begin by recognizing the wide availability of low-cost indexing. Because indexing consistently delivers the market return at no more than the market level of risk, the informed realist's definition of the fee for active management is the *incremental* fee as a percentage of *incremental* returns after adjusting for risk. *That* fee is high – very high.

If a mutual fund charging 1.25% of assets also charged a 12b-1 fee (an annual marketing or distribution fee in the United States) of 0.25% and produced a net return of 0.5% above the benchmark index each year – an eye-popping performance – the true fee would be very nearly 75% of the incremental return before fees! Because a majority of active managers now underperform the market, their incremental fees are actually over 100% of long-term incremental, risk-adjusted returns. This grim reality has largely gone unnoticed by clients – so far. But "not yet caught" is certainly not the strong, protective moat that Warren Buffett wants around every business.

Fees for investment management are remarkable in a significant way: Nobody actually pays the fees by writing a check for an explicit amount. Instead, fees are quietly and automatically deducted by the investment managers and, by custom, are stated not in dollars but as a percentage of assets.

---

[2]The impact of "only 1%" can accumulate over time into a very large number. In one example, two investors each start with $100,000 and add $14,000 each year for 25 years. One of the investors selects a manager who charges 1.25%, whereas the other investor pays only 0.25% – a difference of "only 1%." After 25 years, both have more than $1 million, but the difference between them is $255,423: Over a quarter-million dollars separates $1,400,666 from $1,145,243.

Seen correctly – incremental fees compared to incremental results, not simply as a percent of assets – fees have become surprisingly important. This view can best be seen by contrasting conventional perceptions with reality.

The Investor's Challenge

The challenge that clients accept when selecting an active manager is *not* to find talented, hardworking, highly disciplined investment managers. That is easy. The challenge is to select a manager sufficiently *more* hardworking, *more* highly disciplined, and *more* creative than the other managers – managers that equally aspirational investors have already chosen – and *more* by at least enough to cover the manager's fees and compensate for risks taken.

As the information resources, computing power, and skills of competitors converge, luck becomes increasingly important in determining the increasingly meaningless performance rankings of investment managers.[3] Although firms continue to advertise performance rankings and investors continue to rely on them when selecting managers, rankings have virtually zero predictive power.

As price discovery becomes increasingly effective, and security markets become increasingly efficient, any deviations from equilibrium prices – which are based on experts' consensus expectations of returns based on analyzing all accessible information – become merely unpredictable, random noise.

Investment professionals know that any long-term performance record must be interpreted with great care. Behind every long-term record are many, many changes in important factors: Markets change, portfolio managers change, assets managed by a firm change, managers age, their incomes and interests change, whole organizations change. Meanwhile, the fundamentals of the companies they invest in also change. Forecasting the future of any one variable is difficult, forecasting the interacting futures of many changing variables is more difficult, and estimating how other expert investors will interpret such complex changes is extraordinarily difficult, and estimating changes in all their competitors' changing estimates across portfolios of 60–80 different positions is exponentially difficult – even if we don't admit the reality.

A Clear Alternative

For many years, the persistent and increasing drumbeat of underperformance by active managers was endured because there were no clear alternatives to trying harder and hoping for the best. However, with the proliferation of low-cost index funds and exchange-traded funds (ETFs) as plain "commodity" products,

---

[3]Stephen Gould described the "paradox of risk": As people become more skilled, luck ironically becomes more important in determining outcomes because although absolute skill rises, relative skills decline.

there are proven alternatives to active investing. Meanwhile, active managers, on average, continue to underperform.[4]

After a slow beginning, some clients are increasingly recognizing that reality and taking action. Yet, many clients continue to believe that their managers can and will outperform. (The triumph of hope over experience is clearly not confined to repetitive matrimony.)

Eugene Fama summarized his study of the performance of all domestic mutual funds with at least 10 years of results: "After costs, only the top 3% of managers produce a return that indicates they have sufficient skill to just cover their costs, which means that going forward, and despite extraordinary past returns, even the top performers are expected to be only about as good as a low-cost passive index fund. The other 97% can be expected to do worse."

Quantitative observers might point out that only 3% of active managers' beating their chosen markets is not far from what would be expected in a purely random distribution. But *qualitative* observers would caution that odds of 97 to 3 are, frankly, terrible – particularly when risking real money. The long-term data repeatedly document that investors would benefit by switching from active "performance" investing to low-cost indexing.[5] This rational change, however, has been exceedingly slow to develop, raising the obvious question: Why?

Members of the establishment in any field have much to lose in institutional stature, their reputations as experts, and their earning power. They depend on the status quo – *their* status quo, so they defend against the new. In his scholarly book *Diffusion of Innovations*,[6] Everett M. Rogers established the classic paradigm by which innovations reach a "tipping point" and then spread exponentially through a social system.

Most members of a social system rely on observing the decisions of others when making their own decisions and repeatedly follow a five-step process:

1. Become aware of the innovation.
2. Form a favorable opinion of the innovation.

---

[4]For international developed- and emerging-market managers, the failure to match or exceed benchmarks has been 85% and 86%, respectively. For bond managers, failure rates have averaged 78% (including 93% for high-yield bonds and 86% for mortgage bonds).

[5]An intriguing question: What if all investors indexed? Because that is unlikely, ask instead, "At what level of indexing would price discovery – which serves important societal purposes – become sufficiently imperfect that active management would once again be successful?" Assuming that NYSE daily turnover continues at over 100% of listed shares and index funds average 5% annual turnover, if indexing rose to represent 50% of total equity assets (from about 10% today), the trading activities of index funds would involve less than 3% of total trading. Even if 80% of assets were indexed, indexing would represent less than 5% of total trading. It is hard to believe that even this large hypothetical change would make a substantial difference to the price discovery success of active managers, who would still be doing well over 90% of trading volume.

[6]Free Press (1962).

3. Decide whether to adopt the innovation.
4. Adopt the innovation.
5. Evaluate the results of the innovation

Successful innovations steadily overcome resistance and gain acceptance through a process that is remarkably consistent, but the pace of change differs markedly from one innovation to another. Demand for indexing has been retarded by several factors that still encourage investors to stay with active management: the human desire to do better by trying harder; the "yes, you can" encouragement of fund managers and investment consultants; and the tax cost of switching from one strategy to another.

However, little is said about the numbing consistency with which a majority of active managers fall short of the index or how seldom the past years' winners are winners again in subsequent years. Glossed over, too, is how hard it is to identify future winners when many investment committees and fund executives apparently believe they can somehow beat the odds by switching from manager to manager.[7] Other than choosing managers with low fees, no method has been found to identify in advance which actively managed funds will beat the market.

Of course, recognition of the ever-increasing difficulty of outperforming the expert consensus after substantial fees has not come quickly or easily, particularly from the active managers themselves. We cannot reasonably expect them to say "We, the emperors, have no clothes" and to give up on performance investing when they are so committed to active management as a career, work so hard to achieve superior performance for clients, and are so admired for continuously striving.

Nobel Laureate Daniel Kahneman, author of *Thinking, Fast and Slow,*[8] described the socializing power of a culture like the one that pervades active investment management: "We know that people can maintain an unshakable faith in any proposition, however absurd, when they are sustained by a community of like-minded believers. Given the competitive culture of the financial community, it is not surprising that large numbers of individuals in that world believe themselves to be among the chosen few who can do what they believe others cannot."

Many puzzling examples of less-than-rational human behaviour can be explained by turning to behavioral economics, where studies have shown, with remarkable consistency, that the 80/20 rule applies to most people when asked to rate themselves "above average" or "below average." Over and over again,

[7]Extensive data show that in the years after the decision to change, the recently fired managers typically outperform the newly hired managers.

[8]Farrar, Straus and Giroux (2011).

about 80% of us rate ourselves "above average" on most virtues – including being good investors or good evaluators of investment managers.[9] This finding may be the key to explaining why indexing has not been pursued even more boldly.

The ironic triumph of active performance investors, who are so capable of price discovery, is that they have reduced the opportunity to achieve superior price discovery so much that the "money game" of outperformance after fees is, for clients, no longer a game worth playing. The obvious central question for our profession – for each individual and for each firm in active investment management – is, When will we recognize and accept that most of us can no longer expect to outperform the expert consensus by enough to cover costs and management fees and offer good risk-adjusted value to our clients? When will investors decide that continuing to take all the risks and pay all the costs with so little success is no longer a good deal?

Ideally, investment management has always been "two hands clapping": one hand based on skills of price discovery and the other hand based on values discovery. Price discovery is the skilful process of identifying pricing errors not yet recognized by other investors. Values discovery is the process of determining each client's realistic objectives with respect to various factors – wealth, income, time horizon, age, obligations and responsibilities, investment knowledge, personal financial history, etc. – and designing the appropriate long-term investing strategy.

One way to test our thinking would be to ask the question in reverse: Given that your index manager reliably delivers the full market return with no more than market risk for a fee of just 5 bps, would you be willing to switch to active performance managers who incur greater costs, charge many multiples more, and not only produce unpredictably varying results but also fall short of their chosen benchmarks nearly twice as often as they outperform, and when they fall short, lose much more than they gain when they outperform? The question answers itself. And that is the question each investor should be asking – and more and more apparently are asking.

Questions for Further Reflection

1. Do you know what your after-fee investment manager performance is relative to passive alternatives? Is it worth it?
2. How reasonable is it to assume that you will be able to choose one of the 15% of investment managers that outperform their benchmarks over 10 years?
3. If you are resisting passive investing, what are your main reasons?

[9]In a recent survey, 87% of respondents also confided that they deserved to go to heaven – well above their estimates for Mother Teresa and Martin Luther King.

Additional Resources

For institutional investing, the best book ever written is:

David Swensen, *Pioneering Portfolio Management* (New York: Free Press, 2000).

For personal investing please try the following books:

Charles D. Ellis, *Winning the Loser's Game* (New York: McGraw-Hill, 1998).

Charles D. Ellis, *Index Revolution* (Hoboken, NJ: Wiley, 2016).

Burton G. Malkiel, *The Elements of Investing* (New York: Gildan Media, LLC, 2009).

Biography

Charles D. Ellis's professional career has centered on Greenwich Associates, the international strategy consulting firm he founded in 1972. It grew in the 30 years he was managing partner to serve the leading firms in over 130 professional financial markets around the world. He now serves as a consultant on investing to several of the world's largest institutional investors, government organizations, and wealthy families.

Charley chairs the Whitehead Institute for Biomedical Research. He also chaired the governing board and the investment committee and sat on the investment board for King Abdullah University in Saudi Arabia. He served as a successor trustee of Yale University, where he chaired the investment committee.

A graduate of Exeter and Yale College, Charley earned an MBA at Harvard Business School and a PhD at New York University. He is the author of 16 books, including *Falling Short, What it Takes, The Partnership: The Making of Goldman Sachs, CAPITAL, Winning the Loser's Game,* and, with Burt Malkiel, *Elements of Investing.* He has taught advanced courses in investment management at both Yale and Harvard Business School, and is one of 14 individuals honored for lifetime contributions to the investment profession.

CHAPTER 20

Is Active Management Still Worthwhile? – II

Randolph Cohen

The failure of investment managers to outperform the market is a financial puzzle. Charley Ellis cites research suggesting that 97% of equity mutual funds underperformed their benchmark (see the chapter by Charles Ellis in this book). You take remarkably talented, intensively trained young people and provide the powerful incentive that if they play an incredibly fun video game called "Beat the Stock Market" and win, they'll be paid millions to continue playing, but if they lose, they'll be kicked out of the business and forced to earn a living doing real work! How is it that with exceptional talent, training, and incentives, we're nevertheless getting results worse than a monkey throwing at a dartboard?

We aren't! Research by Russell Wermers and others shows the average stock mutual fund managers pick actually outperforms – by around 1–1.5% per year.[1] The reason funds underperform is that trading costs eat into the returns, leaving the typical manager with less than 1% advantage; and then management fees take another bite, driving median-fund net returns below the benchmark.

But the finding that even average professional stock-pickers can and do outperform the market (i.e. produce "alpha") has important implications:

- We should compare fund performance not to benchmarks, but, rather, to passive alternatives, a comparison in which active managers fare better. However lower, passive funds have fees and costs, too!
- Active managers do add value with their stock picking, but they charge high fees to cover the costs of salaries, customer service, and owner profits. Institutional investors can obtain better net returns than passive funds

[1]Russ Wermers, "Mutual Fund Performance: An Empirical Decomposition into Stock-Picking Talent, Style, Transactions Costs, and Expenses," *Journal of Finance* 55, no. 4 (August 2000).

because larger accounts are more efficient, and massive clients can negotiate lower fees. But typical net outperformance is still modest; as little as 50–100 basis points (0.5–1.0%) annually is considered successful.

- Since stock picking does produce alpha, if managers achieve a better balance between their skill, their risk, and their fees, they can outperform the market.

To summarize:

- Do active managers pick stocks well on average? Yes, but after fees and costs, investors in typical institutional funds usually beat passive benchmarks by less than 1% per year, and retail-focused mutual funds do even worse, falling short of the benchmark on average.
- Is it possible to find diversified managers who will consistently net outperform by 2–3%? I suspect the answer is yes, but such performance is unusual.
- Is it possible for managers to outperform the market by more, say 4–8%? I believe that diversified, liquid, unlevered long-only funds cannot. Only managers employing extraordinary approaches can outperform by such a margin.

Framework: The Lot-Little, Little-Lot World

Liquid-asset investors live in a lot-little, little-lot (LLLL) world. Among liquid securities, a lot are mispriced by a little, and a little are mispriced by a lot. Considering the relative pricing of the 2000 largest US stocks on any given day, hundreds differ from fair value by a small amount (1% or 2%), and perhaps only dozens are mispriced to a larger extent (5–10%). Research hasn't yet answered whether any are mispriced by, say, 20–30%.

No one research paper proves the LLLL framework, but it is consistent with the overwhelming totality of finance research showing the real-but-imperfect efficiency of markets. A manager will probably hold large numbers of modestly underpriced stocks, plenty of fairly priced positions, inevitably a few overpriced stocks, and a few true bargains bought 5–10% below their value. Before costs, such a mix will outperform the market by 1–2%, based on the aforementioned study. After costs, they will fail to match the benchmark, but may perform as well as passive funds, like those of real-world managers. Thus, the lot-little, little-lot framework describes the investment manager performance we observe.

Successful Active Management in the LLLL World

If the typical manager holds an LLLL portfolio, can you find exceptional active managers who do better? Investing in unlevered, long-only liquid assets, you should expect very small, if any, net outperformance. Only the very best funds of this type consistently outperform by 2–3% per year, and even these funds push the envelope of what is possible. A manager who can deliver such returns is doing a superb job, and should be greatly appreciated!

Many investors long for the high returns they enjoyed in the 1990s, but with interest rates so low, such results may be out of reach. However, some managers may be able to obtain high-single-digit returns, even given the challenges of LLLL, if they employ the following strategies: illiquidity, leverage, velocity, and concentration.

Illiquidity

The LLLL framework applies to liquid securities such as stocks, bonds, currencies, and commodities. Different rules apply outside the liquid world. For example, a student once pitched me on investments in Bulgarian farmland, which he claimed would triple in price if Bulgaria became an EU member and had access to lucrative Western markets. Though I could not tell whether this was a great investment opportunity, I couldn't reject it out of hand, unlike, say, Ford Motor, which is definitely not trading at one-third of its fair value! Even the smartest investor knows less than the combined wisdom of millions of investors who daily trade in a stock. But that rule doesn't apply to the "dark little corners" of the market, where transactions are rare and information is scarce.

Assets like private companies, tiny stocks, rarely traded bonds, oddball derivatives, frontier markets, and cryptocurrencies may be mispriced. It doesn't necessarily mean they are underpriced – this is not an argument for an "illiquidity premium" in which illiquids as a group trade cheaper than similar liquid investments. Illiquid assets can be either greatly overpriced or greatly underpriced, creating opportunities for the shrewd investor that don't exist in the LLLL zone. It is important to preserve sufficient liquidity in your portfolio as a whole, but carefully allocating a portion to illiquid investments may add substantially to returns.

Furthermore, as established markets grow more efficient, emergent asset classes may remain quite inefficient. In 1980, no true market for convertible bonds existed; by 1990, many wise investors realized convertibles were an inefficient market offering great opportunity; now, convertibles are probably pretty accurately priced. Since 2000, Chinese stocks have likewise progressed from impossible, to inefficient, heading toward efficient. And the wild-west world of cryptocurrencies has similar potential for evolution. Old markets may grow more efficient, but new markets and new tools to analyze them will always provide opportunities for performance above traditional returns.

Leverage

Levering an investment can turn small mispricings into large returns. Take the classic "carry trade" in which a fund buys long-term US bonds yielding 3%. Without leverage, the returns on a $10 million investment are modest. But if the fund invests $10 million of its own capital alongside $90 million of capital borrowed at 1% interest (for a total of $100 million), then returns can be impressive, because the leverage multiplies any outperformance of the 1% borrowing rate by 10.

Of course, leverage entails risk. As with mortgages and other forms of borrowing, this kind of leverage creates volatility – if the US bonds fall 1% in value, the $1 MM loss (1% of $100 MM) means a –10% equity return (10% of $10 MM).

But worse, leverage makes temporary losses permanent. Suppose US bonds drop 7%, crushing the fund with a $7 million, or 70%, loss. Warren Buffett is said to "not mind the bumpy ride, as long as he gets there in the end." If you can wait, the market may return to its previous level. But if you own a levered fund and have a 70% loss, you would likely be forced to sell your holdings at the bottom, since the $3 million that remains of your equity will not support a $100 million position. Even if the bonds quickly return to 100, investors will lose half their money. And such events usually occur during a crisis, meaning that the fund may take several permanent losses all at once. So, while levered strategies can offer opportunities, they require substantial caution as well.

Velocity

Increasing the turnover or velocity of trades is another way to deliver high returns on slightly mispriced securities without employing leverage. Buying stocks 1.5% cheap and selling them a month later at 0.5% below fair may make only 1%, but does so quickly. Replicating that monthly would yield a 12% annualized pre-fee return. There are two problems with velocity trading. Some underpriced stocks may require more than one month to return to fair value. And typical round-trip trading costs, including price impact, often approach 1%, which could erase the profits in many short-term trades.

One solution is to be a middleman or "market maker" receiving the trading costs, rather than paying them. Profits of half a percent or a full percent on a trade are common. An active market can enable the portfolio to turn over 10 or 20 times a year, resulting in significant profits with modest volatility. Financial institutions have traditionally employed these elite traders, paying them so much that outside investors cannot hire them away. But the Volcker Rule in the Dodd-Frank law has prompted some of these traders to create their own funds, offering their skills to a broader group of investors.

Concentration, Specialization, and Active Share

When you ask fund managers about their portfolios, they will likely tell you a compelling story of a particular holding that demonstrates their deep knowledge of the stock and intense passion and conviction about the opportunity. When you realize the managers hold 100 positions, you might ask whether they have similar feelings about all their investments – how could one brain contain that much knowledge and passion? Managers will likely explain that they have only four or five such high-conviction bets and the remaining 95% of investments are there to round out the fund.

You might well ask: "Can I just have the good ones?" If the fund is very large, the answer is usually that you can't. It's exceptionally difficult to manage billions in assets with just a few holdings, since this necessitates taking enormous positions in individual securities, with concomitant impact on the price. And the desire for fees encourages the manager to build a fund worth billions, not millions.

Investors can benefit by picking funds focusing only on the best holdings. Considerable empirical evidence, including my own research paper entitled "Best Ideas," suggests that a manager's 10 best ideas usually outperform his 50 or 100 best.[2] By holding a highly concentrated portfolio, a stock picking manager can select only the stocks they believe are greatly mispriced. This circumvents the principle of LLLL, which says a manager might find half a dozen "a-lot-mispriced" positions, but will not discover 100.

Closely related is the idea of specialization – choosing investments in an area in which the manager has true expertise. Just as it's impractical to expect a manager to have 100 brilliant ideas, it's also unrealistic to presume a manager can know every kind of asset. So research, unsurprisingly, shows that specialized sector funds do indeed outperform. Other kinds of specialization include region, security, or trade.

In the paper "How Active Is Your Fund Manager?," Cremers and Petajisto argue that the higher a fund's "active share" – the higher a percentage of the fund's volatility comes from active trading rather than mere movements of the index – the better they do.[3] Concentration creates a high active share because a fund with a small number of stocks will have performance that differs greatly from the index. And the same goes for specialization; even if a manager holds 100 stocks, if they are all biotechs, then his returns will not correlate that highly with the market. Concentration and specialization both work, and together they work even better than either one alone.

A Word on Fees

Fees deserve their own essay, but a single point suffices for now: fees should be measured not as a fraction of assets under management, but rather in relation to the amount and quality of active management. In a world where a passive S&P 500 fund might charge 10 basis points, 50 basis points a year may seem a modest fee for long-only stock picking. It certainly seems far lower than "2-and-20" hedge fund fees, which give the manager not just 2% of assets but also 20% of profit.

---

[2]Randolph B. Cohen, Christopher Polk, and Miguel Anton, "Best Ideas," working paper, 2018.

[3]Martijn Cremers, and Antti Petajisto, "How Active Is Your Fund Manager?," *Review of Financial Studies* 22, no. 9 (2009).

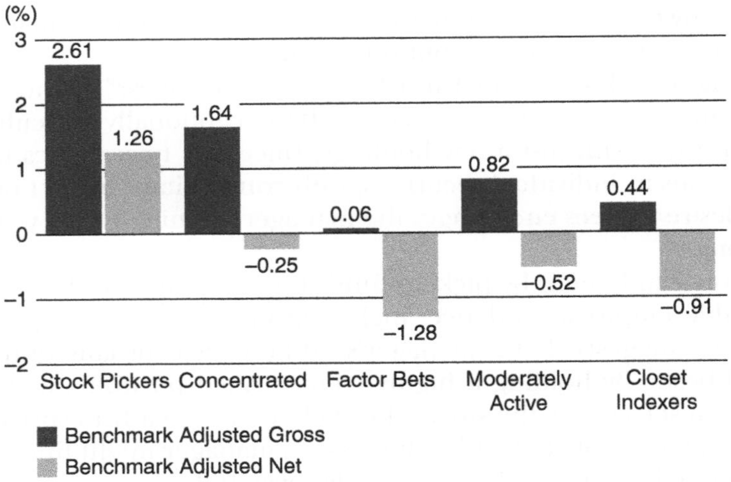

Figure 20.1 Annualized performance by active management categories.

But consider the long-only manager whose fund is 99% correlated with the S&P, which is more common than you might imagine! If that manager charges 50 basis points, he or she has very little chance to outperform the passive alternative in any year. Even if he gets a high percentage of his "bets" right, they won't impact results sufficiently to cover the fees. In a 2017 paper for Lazard, Khusainova and Mier show how large this effect truly is: once we take out these so-called closet indexers,[4] the performance of the remaining, "true" active managers looks far better than what is typically reported, i.e. 1.26% excess return by stock pickers versus –0.91% from closet indexers (after fees).[5] See Figure 20.1.

Even a hedge fund charging 2-and-20 that invests $2 long and $2 short for every dollar in the fund may actually have fairly modest fees when properly measured, since that manager is doing so much stock-picking per dollar managed that it may justify the fee rate. Conversely, a 2-and-20 manager who has modest gross exposure may offer the worst of both worlds, high fees per dollar under management and low active share. One of the best ways to find active managers who will deliver strong net performance is to find those whose fees, properly measured, are low compared to peers of equal ability.

---

[4]Closet indexers are investment managers who purport to be active managers but end up with a portfolio that is not much different than the overall index, usually because they don't want to risk losing their jobs or fund assets under management by lagging too far behind the benchmark.

[5]Erianna Khusainova and Juan Mier, "Taking a Closer Look at Active Share," Lazard September 2017. The definition of *stock picking* and *concentrated managers* can vary quite a bit. The study shows that even the modest concentration and active share leads to returns superior to average managers.

Putting It All Together

If investors don't embrace all these approaches, it's likely because they appear to involve risk. But some of these risks can be effectively managed. A diversified portfolio of volatile funds may well produce higher returns, but also be less dangerous than a portfolio of low-volatility generalists. Suppose that there are 10 major sectors and 10 key regions of the world. Further, suppose we were to identify and allocate to a great concentrated manager/stock picker who specializes in that particular sector and region. Such a portfolio, once aggregated, would consist of perhaps a thousand stocks, across all countries and sectors, so it would assume similar risk to a fully-diversified world market index.

But because there would only be a small number of positions in each country and sector, we would not face the problem of overdiversification in which a portfolio of managers merely equals the index, cancelling out all the outperformance. Further diversification with managers in unusual, low-correlation, non-equity strategies would make it possible to have a low-risk portfolio of managers overall, despite many of them being quite volatile individually.

Of course, a manager who meets our high standards doesn't necessarily exist for every niche. A well-designed portfolio will employ passive strategies in markets and sectors where no stellar manager can be found. This could include both far-flung areas with few resident asset managers, and highly efficient sectors of the market like US large-cap. Passive investing is an attractive choice, and in order for active managers to justify their higher fees, they need to offer a combination of positive characteristics, including:

- Exceptional skill
- Boldness to deviate substantially from the benchmark
- Modest fees, when properly measured
- One or more of the skill-intensifying factors: illiquidity, leverage, velocity, and concentration
- Size appropriate to the strategy, since many of the approaches described earlier have limited capacity

With the right combination of these attributes, active management can deliver substantial net benefits to investors. Thus, there is an important role for both active and passive managers in a well-constructed portfolio.

Questions for Further Reflection

1. Where are you employing illiquidity, leverage, velocity, or concentration in your portfolio now? How might you add these strategies in the future?
2. Given your own knowledge, goals for your portfolio, and tolerance for volatility, what part of your portfolio could you imagine devoting to active strategies? What part to passive?

3. When you consider active managers you are using, are they "closet indexers"? How are they employing the strategies described earlier? How would you quantify the value you're getting for the fees you are paying?

Additional Resources

Randolph B. Cohen, Christopher Polk, and Bernhard Silli, "Best Ideas," 2010, https://personal.lse.ac.uk/POLK/research/bestideas.pdf.

This is my co-authored paper that presents evidence that even average managers would deliver substantial outperformance if they offered a concentrated portfolio of only their best ideas.

Martijn Cremers, "Active Share and the Three Pillars of Active Management: Skill, Conviction, and Opportunity," *Financial Analysts Journal* 73, no. 2 (second quarter, 2017): 61–79, https://papers.ssrn.com/sol3/papers.cfm?abstract_id=2860356.

Bruce C.N. Greenwald, Judd Kahn, Paul D. Sonkin, and Michael van Biema, *Value Investing: From Graham to Buffett and Beyond* (Hoboken, NJ: Wiley, 2004), https://www.amazon.com/Value-Investing-Graham-Buffett-Beyond/dp/0471463396.

This book wins universal praise as by far the best and most practical book on beating the market via value investing.

Erianna Khusainova and Juan Mier, "Taking a Closer Look at Active Share," Lazard, September 2017.

Biography

Randolph Cohen is MBA Class of 1975 senior lecturer of Entrepreneurial Management at Harvard Business School and Partner at Alignvest Investment Management; previously he was associate professor at HBS and visiting associate professor at MIT Sloan. He teaches finance and entrepreneurship.

Randolph's main research interests are the identification of money managers who will outperform, and the interface between institutional-investor behavior and asset-price levels. Randolph has helped start and grow a number of investment firms, and has served as a consultant to many other companies.

Randolph holds an AB in mathematics from Harvard College and a PhD in finance and economics from the University of Chicago.

SECTION 4

RAISING THE RISING GENERATION

Most people believe that their children are among the greatest goods in life, and they would do anything for them. This love for our children sets up one of the greatest paradoxes of family wealth: Many parents work day in and day out to amass wealth for their families, and at the same time they fear that their financial success will ruin their children or grandchildren.

In the light of this paradox, it is not surprising that some of the wealthiest people at present are pledging to leave their descendants only a relatively small percentage of their financial assets. We have generations of evidence that a financial inheritance can inflict great harm on its recipients, including a poor sense of self-worth, difficulty establishing healthy relationships with others, substance abuse or addiction, or a general sense of airy insubstantiality.

Yet, as real as these dangers are, "giving it all away" is not the only solution.

The chapters in this section take on some of the thorniest questions on how to make sure that money benefits rather than harms those we love most.

Suniya Luthar and Nina Kumar point out some of the troubling behaviors that an environment of success can encourage in young people, as well as specific practices parents can adopt to address those dangers.

Beyond not falling prey to dysfunction, independence is what all parents want for their children. Although children from poor or even middle-class families are forced by necessity to make their own ways in life, wealth can easily encourage dependency. Jill Shipley offers concrete practices parents can use to promote independence. Coventry Edwards-Pitt shares key considerations in promoting financial literacy, which importantly begins with personal values, not the knowledge of financial terms.

Financial literacy is a theme that runs through several of these essays. Lee Hausner raises it along with very practical considerations around when to share money with children or grandchildren, how to manage the use of trusts in making such gifts, and what to do when your recipients themselves are unequal in their abilities to make (or keep) money. Peter Evans takes on similar questions, with a focus on ways that family members can learn about how they learn – to make this exercise of helping children integrate wealth into their lives all the more productive.

Although independence is perhaps the highest goal of parenting, parents also hope that their children find strength and joy in being interdependent with the rest of their family. Two other essays explore this delicate balance. Kelin Gersick takes it up in the context of family governance, explaining how the family landscape often looks so different to parents and to children and how to bridge that gap. Charles Collier offers clear and engaging questions that can spark a family conversation between parents and children about a financial inheritance. While doing so may feel like "letting the genie out of the bottle," Charles's questions provide a framework that can make all generations approach shared deliberation with comfort and respect.

Finally, a word on the title of this section: within the world of family wealth, many advisors use the term *next generation* to identify the children or grandchildren of their clients. We and our contributors have tried to nudge gently against this term, in favor of the "rising" generation. We have heard from many family members that the word "next" makes them feel less important, compared with the impressive wealth-creators who, presumably, came "first." In contrast, "rising" honors the opportunity that every generation has to grow, define itself, and flourish. That is a hope that all parents share.

CHAPTER 21

How Do You Raise Responsible, Independent, and Productive Children (versus Entitled Trust Fund Babies)?

Jill Shipley

The rags-to-riches story is core to the modern mindset. Hard work, risk-taking, and financial success are what make nations strong. Although this dream is a powerful one, and inspirational success stories are powerful motivations, they are incomplete. The challenge that awaits when you've scaled that summit is perhaps equally daunting and with a far less-clear scorecard: how do I raise my kids to flourish in this land of wealth[1] (one that I may not be 100% comfortable living in myself)?

The real question is *How do I ensure the money does not mess up my kids' lives?*

Many parents with means worry about their children becoming stereotypical trust-fund babies – lazy, wasteful, and spoiled. There are also reasonable concerns that inherited wealth can foster isolation, addiction, delayed emotional development, and depression.[2] It is scary to think that after achieving a dream of providing a better life for your family, the assets could do the opposite and have a negative effect on the family relationships and development and happiness of your children.

There are no guarantees, no matter what we do as parents. There is no magic solution that ensures you raise children that are grounded, independent, and responsible. But I have found the following practices that help individuals and families flourish across generations.

[1]James Grubman, PhD, *Strangers in Paradise: How Families Adapt to Wealth Across Generations* (Boston: Family Wealth Consulting, 2013).

[2]John Levy, *Coping with Inherited Wealth: Opportunities and Dilemmas* (North Charleston, SC: BookSurge Publishing, 2008).

Start With a Mirror

To really answer the question posed in this essay, start with yourself. Dig deep to gain greater self-awareness around your own values, money history, fears, hopes, and biases. You can't help others grow and develop until you are aware of what you need to work on, so seek out more awareness, be it by feedback from others, coaching, or self-reflection.

It is also helpful to reflect on your habits and behaviors. *Do as I say not as I do* will not lead to success. What do you want your children to be like? Kind, giving, financially responsible, positive, accountable, full of joy? Consider what you can do to model these traits. If you only fly on private jets, your kids will expect to always fly private (and they certainly will not be prepared for what a security line pat-down entails). If they do not see you engaging in activities that have meaning – like work, volunteering, or active childcare – they may not value these activities either. I am not suggesting you live like a pauper. As Ellen Perry suggests, provide your kids experiences in both the bleachers and the box seats.[3]

Look inward to enhance self-awareness and role-model the behaviors you strive to see in your children.

Foster a Reason to Get off the Couch

Growing up with extraordinarily financially successful parents or grandparents can cast a shadow on the rising generation.[4] It can be paralyzing and is likely impossible for them to be able to live up to that standard. Foster and celebrate your child's interests and dreams,[5] no matter if they correlate to your own (or the potential you see in them, which is likely driven by your definition of success rather than theirs).

When people dream of winning the lottery, often the first thing they say they will do is quit their job. Receiving an inheritance (even a modest one) can reduce the need to work to put food on the table and it can be tempting to quit when a task or job gets hard. In all my years, I have yet to meet someone who is happy and well adjusted who does not have a reason to get off the couch. We all need purpose and meaning. This can be a commitment to being a stay-at-home dad, giving your time and talents to those in need through volunteering, or working at a traditional job. Positive psychology agrees that the keys to living a fulfilling life include engagement in a project or task, meaningful connections, serving others, focus on gratitude, and accomplishment or achievement.[6]

---

[3]Ellen Perry, *A Wealth of Possibilities* (Washington, DC: Egremont Press, 2012).

[4]James Hughes Jr, Susan Massenzio, and Keith Whitaker, *Complete Family Wealth* (New York: Bloomberg Press, 2017).

[5]James Hughes Jr, Susan Massenzio and Keith Whitaker, *The Voice of the Rising Generation* (New York: Bloomberg Press, 2015).

[6]Martin E.P. Seligman, *Flourish* (New York: Free Press, 2011).

Encourage independence and devote time and resources to helping children uncover what brings them joy.

Talk about the Tough Stuff

There is no substitute for open, honest, and transparent communication, especially when it is hard.

Some parents ask when and how to talk to their kids about their wealth transfer plans – to share the specifics about what they will inherit and when. Some are too uncomfortable even to broach the subject and figure their children will find out once they are gone. I have heard parents in their 70s and 80s say that their 50- to 60-year-old children are still "too young" to be told about what they will inherit.

I do not believe there is one right answer about when and how to talk about your financial wealth. There are many factors that impact the answer including age, life stage, maturity, experience, personality, and learning style. I rarely have heard someone say they were told too early, and many inheritors have expressed sadness or disappointed they did not have knowledge or access until it was "too late" to be able to ask questions, to feel prepared to manage it, or to benefit from the resources. The time to tell them is not the day assets are transferred into an account or the day a trust distribution or financial statement is received, because there is no time to become emotionally prepared or financially responsible.

In my experience, no matter when you decide to share the information, your children already know they are different than other kids, by way of intuition or Google! It is perhaps more important to foster an environment in which it is okay to ask questions, to have and talk about insecurities, and to be afraid. As noted by Brené Brown, there is no substitute for courage, connection, and compassion (for ourselves and each other).[7] Relationships and true connection takes work. Create a safe space where vulnerability and authenticity are encouraged early on as this practice will last a lifetime. Being able to talk openly and honestly about achievements, setbacks, money, expectations, and emotions is as great a legacy as you can hope to give your children.

Invest in Learning

In addition to role modeling, create a culture of learning in your family. Consider developing a plan to prepare the rising generation for their roles and responsibilities today and in the future, addressing the qualitative and quantitative implications of being an inheritor, a trust beneficiary, a shareholder in a family business, or a foundation board member. The approach to

---

[7]Brené Brown, *The Art of Imperfection* (Center City, MN: Hazelden, 2010).

this preparation will look different for each family member, based on who that individual is and how he or she best learns, while also being grounded in the values of the family. Developmental opportunities could span from learning effective communication and conflict-management techniques to becoming more financially savvy, to leadership and character building,[8] to estate planning and philanthropy. In addition, seek out opportunities for inheritors to learn how to navigate being heirs, including the stigma that comes from being perceived as rich or trust-fund babies.

How much do you spend on the custody, management, preservation, and transition of your financial capital? Imagine spending as much or more time and resources on the development of the human, intellectual, social, and spiritual capitals of your family.

Let Go

Hodding Carter said, "There are only two lasting bequests we can give our children. One is roots and the other is wings." What most deters parents from achieving the objective of this essay is the issue of control. Children need to be told no, and they need boundaries, rules, and structure to feel safe during their formative years. Roots are solidified by modeling your values, showing love and compassion, and creating a safe space where children can truly be themselves.

As children develop into young adults, they need to differentiate. They need space and encouragement to chart their own course, to fall down and pick themselves back up. Wings. Significant resources can be used to stunt this growth – used as a shelter from consequences, to offer undeserved opportunity, and to foster dependence.

To put it simply – do not parent with your wallet. Pause before having your maid clean up after your child, before asking your financial advisor to remove the overdraft fees from your college student's bank account, before using your connections or resources to get your child a job, or before putting cash in your child's purse or wallet when he or she brings your grandchild over to visit. Pause before stopping your annual gift when your child misses the family or foundation meeting. Pause before finalizing a strict incentive trust for generations today and generations you will never know that gives you influence and control *from the grave.*

There is value in the struggle, lessons in failure, and character forged in the journey, so support and equip them but don't overprotect or control them. All the money in the world can't give your child (internal and external) credibility – they need to earn it themselves.

---

[8]Greg McCann, *Who Do You Think You Are? Aligning Your Character and Reputation* (CreateSpace, 2012).

Conclusion

The blessing of abundance that you and your family worked hard to achieve brings a new set of benefits, opportunities and challenges. Significant resources can remove the stress of ensuring your family's basic needs are met and often provide children, grandchildren, and future generations the freedom and financial security to explore their passions.

To raise productive, independent, generous and grounded kids first look inside yourself to gain clarity on your values and goals and role-model the behaviors you hope to see in your children. Support their dreams, recognizing their definition of success may be different than your own. Talk openly and honestly with your children. Be vulnerable. Share your fears and failures in addition to your successes. Do not wait until it is *too late* to talk about money and prepare your heirs for its impact. Finally, money can be used as a tool to support connection, development, and independence. Be careful not to use it as a carrot or a stick tied to power, control, and dependence.

Questions for Further Reflection

1. What might help you increase your self-awareness and empathy?
2. What might be an important discussion to start (that you have been avoiding)?
3. How can you help your child cultivate their sense of self and purpose?
4. What people, resources, and support can help you?

Additional Resources

Ellen Perry, *A Wealth of Possibilities* (Washington, DC: Egremont Press, 2012).

Jessie H. O'Neill, *Golden Ghetto* (Delray Beach, FL: The Affluenza Project, 1997).

James Hughes, Susan Massenzio, and Keith Whitaker, *The Voice of the Rising Generation: Family Wealth and Wisdom* (New York: Bloomberg Press, 2014).

Biography

Jill Shipley is dedicated to helping families sustain their wealth and ensure it has a positive impact on the family, on individual family members, and on the community. As Senior Managing Director and Partner at Cresset Family Office, she works to help families clarify values, enhance communication, plan for transitions, engage in shared philanthropy, and prepare heirs.

Prior to joining Cresset, Jill was a Managing Director in Abbot Downing's Institute of Family Culture where she pioneered the creation of experiential development programs and facilitated multi-generational family meetings. Jill started her career as assistant director of Stetson University's Family Enterprise Center and was an adjunct professor in the program.

Jill was awarded the 2014 Family Wealth Report Award for being the Rising Star in the family wealth management industry. She is a noted speaker on the topic of family wealth and has been quoted in such publications as the *Wall Street Journal,* Barron's *Penta, Trust & Estate Magazine,* and *Financial Advisor Magazine.*

CHAPTER 22

How Can You Help Children Thrive in a World Focused on Success?

Suniya Luthar and Nina Kumar

What Are Challenges of Growing up in Affluence?

Children in affluent families are often seen as "having it all." However, students who grow up in high-achieving families or schools often deal with several challenges, above all the high and ongoing pressure to excel themselves.

Growing up surrounded by parents who are financially well off and peers who are experiencing the same pressures to succeed can build a highly pressured environment for youth. From a very young age, these students face demands from their parents, coaches, and teachers. As soon as they are old enough, many parents sign them up for the most competitive schools, sports leagues, and arts classes. Sometimes, even before a child is born, parents put their children on waiting lists for highly competitive preschools. These children may be pressured to begin compiling and enhancing their resumes as early as junior high school. The unrelenting emphasis on success fosters a highly stressed environment that engenders adjustment problems in these students, including higher rates of substance abuse, rule-breaking, depression, and anxiety as compared to the average teen. Research at the local school and community levels, as well as studies of large national samples in the United States and Norway, all points to the challenges that success can pose to children growing up in its midst.

What Should You Be on the Lookout For?

A first sign to be mindful of is a child's preoccupation with success and status, and this can be reflected in many aspects of his or her everyday behaviors. The most obvious sign is pronounced anxiety and stress about falling short, as in not getting the highest grades in every class or being the best at everything.

Students intensely focused on achievement often try to attain perfection in too many activities at once to build up a resume. Although striving to succeed in various sports and activities can be commended, this desire for perfection can quickly spiral out of control.

Excessive envy of peers is another sign that a child is feeling too much stress and pressure. When children's self-worth depends on the impressiveness of their accomplishments, they can become highly envious of peers whom they see as doing better than them academically, in perceived attractiveness, or in popularity at school. This envy, in turn, is linked with depression, anxiety, and withdrawal from activities that they used to enjoy.

Additionally, rule-breaking and substance use should be cautiously monitored. Some children may feel that they need to cheat or steal to reach their goals (such as getting exceptionally high grades at school) and gain acceptance and approval from peers (with display of expensive clothing and accessories, for example). With regard to drug and alcohol abuse, it is important for parents not only to be vigilant but also, importantly, not to dismiss it as "something all kids do" as this perceived tolerance in parents is linked with increasing risks for substance abuse among teens. Additionally, many students report using substances as self-medication to relieve pressure, and stimulants, such as Adderall and Ritalin, are abused both as study aids and as recreational drugs.

These problems tend to emerge around seventh grade, when children are almost 13, for a number of reasons. Around this age, children start to seek independence from their parents; they are often left unsupervised, as their parents believe that they are safe in "good neighborhoods and schools." During this time, students also experience, more than ever, a strong desire to be accepted by peer groups. This desire for acceptance often involves rebellious behaviors, such as stealing and experimenting with alcohol and drugs. Finally, around age 13, teens must also deal with the hormonal changes of puberty.

Are There Different Types of Problems Seen Among Girls as Opposed to Boys?

Boys and girls have been found to reflect slightly different patterns of problems, and there are some variations in factors that tend to exacerbate their respective difficulties. For example, among boys, high self-reported levels of substance abuse have been significantly linked with being "liked most" by their classmates; in other words, their peer group actively supports and reinforces their use of drugs and alcohol (more so than among youth in less affluent settings). Girls with high levels of substance abuse are similarly liked most by their peers, but substance use among girls has also been linked with being liked least, indicating gender-based double standards in peers' perceptions of substance abuse. Double standards are also applied to "hooking up" with multiple sexual partners; whereas peers admire boys for this, girls tend to be viewed negatively.

Girls also show additional problems with peers' admiration of relational aggression and physical attractiveness. In affluent school communities, girls who are viewed by peers as being aggressive towards others are admired; "mean girls" are generally socially dominant. These young women also receive high admiration scores from peers if they are seen as attractive. It's not surprising, therefore, that many young women are excessively preoccupied with their physical attractiveness. Girls also face high, often competing demands from peers as well as adults. Although these girls are expected to do just as well as boys in academics and sports, they are also expected to be kind and caring. These young women feel pressured to be "exceptional" across multiple areas and are prone to envy other girls whom they see as doing much better than they are.

Because of a fear of failure, some of these young women shy away from taking chances in their lives. They might be wary of intimacy in relationships that is critical for bringing them comfort, support, and affirmation of their true selves. This ultimately results in an underlying sense of anxiety, self-criticism, and a conviction that no matter how hard they try, they will never be successful enough, attractive enough, popular enough, or admired enough. This mask of perfection often prevents these students from seeking the help they need.

Boys can be highly preoccupied with good looks, athletic prowess, being sexually desired by many girls, and the "cool factor" of frequent substance abuse, as these are associated with high peer status. Again, these preoccupations may lead to low capacity for true intimacy with others, as well as overly high investment in power and status.

Though there are some differences between the problems faced by girls and boys, all groups constantly face images of effortless perfection from their peers, both in real life and in social media. These deceptive portrayals create impossible standards for upward comparisons. Effectively, students are comparing themselves to the misleading narrative presented by peers who seem to have the ideal life.

What Can You Do to Prevent Problems?

Parents must care for themselves first, if they are to provide good care for their children. As parents, the single most important thing you can do to prevent problems in children is first to ensure that you are psychologically stable and healthy, as opposed to being chronically stressed, overextended, exhausted, and anxious. Being a "good enough parent" across decades is a challenging task, and this is particularly true in highly pressured environments. You cannot be effective first-responders to your child's stress and pressure unless you are psychologically "refueled." Children can tell when you are struggling, and they are affected by these struggles. Therefore, it is essential that you deliberately prioritize taking care of yourself.

In high-income families, the nature of parents' jobs may lead to high levels of stress. Stakes tend to be high, with mistakes costly; work hours are long and demanding, often requiring a great deal of time away from families.

Large amounts of time away from families, in turn, can leave a parent out of the family circle, exacerbating his or her feelings of alienation. If you are in such a position, you need to be especially cognizant of the time that you spend away from your family, and must make concerted, deliberate efforts at connecting authentically with family members, maintaining open communication with – and among – all of them. You must also acknowledge the need for supportive, authentic relationships in your own lives, and deliberately prioritize the development and maintenance of these close relationships.

Modeling Good Behaviors and Values

Children tend to model behaviors that they observe in their parents, particularly those of the same gender; therefore, it's important for you to be cognizant of the behavior that you are modeling for your children and the values you exhibit. In affluent communities, both young women and their mothers tend to hold themselves to excessively high, unreasonable standards of perfectionism. Well-educated mothers are expected to be, simultaneously, independent and ambitious, as professionally successful as men and yet appealing to them, nurturing and sensitive to children's emotional needs while efficiently coordinating family schedules, and of course, beautiful and well put-together. Mothers can struggle at least as much as their daughters in this quest for perfectionism, and this becomes exhausting and depleting for their personal well-being. Thus, mothers must be mindful of displaying this type of unachievable perfection for their daughters.

In many families, fathers are primary breadwinners and work long hours; however, the quality of children's relationships with their fathers certainly does matter. Even though children spend more time with mothers than with fathers on average, relationships with fathers have their own unique effects. For example, boys in their late teens seem to react particularly strongly to perceived depression in their fathers. Girls' academic grades are often linked with high levels of closeness to their fathers.

As parents, you need to be particularly mindful of overemphasizing achievements versus personal decency or integrity. Our research has shown that when students were asked to rank order the top three values out of six that their parents would want for them, students who felt that their parents disproportionately prioritized achievement dimensions were at significantly greater risk than others for various adjustment difficulties. Contrastingly, the healthiest profiles were seen among students who reported that both parents had middle to low emphasis on achievements relative to integrity, compassion, or decency. Thus, you need to ensure that there is not an overwhelming emphasis on extrinsic values at home, and you must be vigilant about keeping your children firmly grounded in intrinsic values. Children need to be reminded that there are things that must not be compromised in the pursuit of top-ranked colleges or the most lucrative jobs, including kindness to others, doing for the greater good, and maintaining close, mutually supportive personal relationships.

Fostering a Safe and Caring Environment

In parenting (as well as other activities, such as management), "bad is stronger than good," that is, disparaging words can have as much as three times more of an effect than words of praise or affection. Thus, as parents, you should make every effort to minimize critical, negative communications to your children, while increasing those that are affectionate, affirming, and directly conveying to your children that they truly "matter." Also, it is important to remember that your disappointment or criticism can be conveyed non-verbally; your children will be sensitive to your raised eyebrow or change of tone when they come home with the report that they did not make the honor roll list or the lead in the school play.

A key consideration is that, though all of us are naturally inclined to protect our children from failure, our children need to be allowed to fail in life to learn. Although it can be difficult to watch your child struggle, you need to be mindful of solving all your child's problems. Keeping in mind age-appropriate challenges (for example, a three-year-old should not be expected to have the same task perseverance as an eleven-year-old), it is important to give children the chance to work at acquiring and practicing everyday life and coping skills.

Be vigilant for signs of distress among your children and quickly seek professional help if needed. In general, parents seek outside help only when children get poor academic grades or are consistently disruptive. However, resilience is not an across-the-board phenomenon – children under stress can do exceptionally well in some areas while struggling silently with others – such that all-around academic and extracurricular achievements can in fact co-exist with high levels of depression and anxiety. Left unattended, this high internalized unhappiness can snowball to dangerous levels over time.

Setting Firm Limits

Parents in affluent communities should be particularly mindful of how children perceive their reactions to discovering the child's use of drugs and alcohol. Low levels of parental "containment" of substance abuse have been shown to be related to high levels of self-reported substance abuse among teens in the United States. Firm and consistent setting of limits on this topic is vital. At the same time, it is important to recognize that some experimentation with substances is developmentally normative for teens, so that "zero tolerance" parental attitudes with overly harsh punishments can backfire, as teens will simply hide use while still in high school and will gravitate towards substances that are more easily hidden but are also more dangerous, such as ecstasy and cocaine. Once in college, high schoolers from "zero tolerance households" may be more likely to engage in binge drinking. Thus, giving some a little leeway by no means implies that you should be laissez-faire on this topic; you must strive to maintain honest and open conversations with your children on substance use along with clear, mutually agreed upon consequences for repeated or egregious violations of these household rules and parameters.

Summary

Though children growing up amid affluence can experience difficulties stemming from an emphasis on achievement and success, you, as parents, can take actions to limit the negative effects of pressure on your children. First, ensure that you yourself are physically and psychologically well. To facilitate this, work to foster authentic relationships with others whom you can rely on. Second, model good behaviors and deemphasize the importance of achievements by fostering a safe environment for failure. Finally, set firm limits to deter excessive alcohol and drug use.

Further Questions for Reflection

1. Where can you find help or support in facing these challenges of parenting amid affluence?
2. Who at your children's schools can you work with in trying to decrease unhealthy pressure on students?
3. In what ways do policies at your children's schools help or hurt your efforts as a parent to provide your children with a safe environment?

Additional Resources

Suniya S. Luthar, *Mothering Mothers* (New York: Routledge, 2018).

Suniya S. Luthar and Nina L. Kumar, "Youth in High-Achieving Schools: Challenges to Mental Health and Directions for Evidence-Based Interventions," in *Handbook of School-Based Mental Health Promotion: An Evidence-Informed Framework*, eds. A.W. Leschied, D.H. Saklofske, and G.L. Flett (New York: Springer, 2018).

Suniya S. Luthar, Samuel H. Barkin, and Elizabeth J. Crossman, "'I can, therefore I must': Fragility in the Upper-middle Classes," *Development and Psychopathology* 25 (2013): 1529–1549.

Suniya S. Luthar, Phillip J. Small, and Lucia Ciciolla, "Adolescents from Upper Middle Class Communities: Substance Misuse and Addiction across Early Adulthood," *Development and Psychopathology* 30, no. 1 (2018): 315–335.

Biographies

Dr. Suniya Luthar is Foundation professor of Psychology at Arizona State University, professor emerita at Columbia University's Teachers College, and Founder and Executive Director of *Authentic Connections,* a science-based, non-profit group committed to maximizing individuals' personal well-being and resilience in their communities, schools, and work settings. Her research involves vulnerability and resilience among various populations including youth in poverty, teens in upper-middle class families, and parents (especially mothers) in high-achieving, stressful communities. Suniya's work is frequently cited in major news outlets in the United States including the *New York Times,* the *Washington Post,* the *Wall Street Journal,* the *Atlantic,* NPR, PBS, and CNN, as well as overseas, in Europe, Asia, and Australia. Suniya is a fellow of the American Association for Psychological Science and is also fellow of the American Psychological Associations (APA) Divisions 7 and 37.

Nina Kumar is a product manager at IBM Watson Health in Cambridge, Massachusetts and Vice President of Operations at Authentic Connections, a science-based, non-profit group committed to maximizing individuals' personal well-being in their communities, schools, and work settings. She graduated from Williams College with a BA in Computer Science and Psychology, and a concentration with Honors in Cognitive Science.

CHAPTER 23

How Much Money Should You Leave Your Children, and When?

Peter Evans

The question I most often hear from parents and grandparents is "What do I need to do to ensure the likelihood that money will amplify the good in my family members, not the bad?" It is amazing the amount of anxiety behind this question. I've yet to meet a parent who wants to support entitlement in their children or grandchildren. Nobody wants to look back on their choices and realize they have created an atmosphere conducive to *affluenza.* We all want our family members to be self-actualized, happy, productive, contributive members of society. We want them to have relationships that flourish and a life of meaning and aliveness.

But so often, well-meaning parents and grandparents undermine the chances of their offspring leading fulfilling lives of purpose and meaning by unconsciously perpetuating family and cultural patterns that no longer serve. The opportunity of wealth is to enhance the lives of its beneficiaries and the world around them. The best answer I've ever heard is frustratingly akin to a koan from a wise Zen Master: How much money should I leave my children? – "As much as they are prepared for."

Invariably, the next question is: "Okay, how do I prepare my kids?" What is the curriculum? What do I focus on at each age and stage? Here is where the Zen Master sits back with a wry smile and awaits the dawning of recognition on the face of the student. The answer is both complex and simple.

I remember those early days as a new parent and realizing that this little being didn't pop out with an instruction manual! I was both eager and afraid to step into this new role of being a parent, and without the manual, defaulted to either repeating how I was raised or resolving *never* to do what my parents did, at the same time trying to reconcile my impulses with my wife's impulses. I had no idea this would be so complicated and nuanced. How could I take the best of the values and example my parents gave me and leave the parts that didn't serve? As Yoda said: "You must unlearn what you have learned."

So begins the journey. We begin focusing on manners and how to play fair ... then comes contributing to the family chores. In some families there is a significant focus on spiritual practice or more down-to-earth matters: "Stand up straight, make eye contact, and offer a strong handshake!" We work at teaching responsibility, reliability, dependability, morality, and work to transfer our values.

But so often, practices around money are left behind. Yes, there is the attempt at allowances, and perhaps some compensation for extra jobs around the house. But so often, the parental desire to help gets in the way. For example, the classic gift of a new car upon achieving a driver's license is, at first glance a wonderful way to celebrate a step on the path to adulthood. But what message does this gift send to the 16-year-old? Many families choose a slightly different path: they give *half* of the first car, inviting the young family member the opportunity to *earn* the other half. There is nothing like achieving a goal by earning it yourself.

A tried and true course begins as early as age 5 with an allowance, then a conversation encouraging savings. Of course the child will eventually desire something for which they haven't saved enough – capitalize on this learning opportunity to teach about budgeting. Helping the child with their struggle to solve this problem is one of the best ways for them to learn. Eventually, lessons include keeping a "financial journal," learning how to invest in stocks, and how to give philanthropically.

As the child becomes a young adult, perhaps attends college, and has more complex financial needs, a simple and reliable formula for how much money to give them and when is that parents (or trustees) should cover all educational expenses, healthcare, and provide a safe place to live. Perhaps under certain circumstances, help with a down-payment for a house or capital to start a business can be very useful. But beyond that, I've come to believe strongly that no significant inheritance should be received until 35–40 years of age – after the family member has *earned* their way into adulthood. There is nothing like love and work to build healthy self-esteem.

Whoever is the gatekeeper of the money, whether parents or trustees, they must have enough of a relationship with the emerging adult to understand their motivations, goals, aspirations, and tendencies in order to make sound decisions around finances. We all know our kids show up as individuals, different from birth in their learning styles, needs, capacities and ambitions, ways of thinking, introverted or extraverted, artist or a math whiz. Call it Karma, or God's way of making things interesting, but the simple truth is we all have different challenges, opportunities, biases, and ways of expressing our creativity.

I strongly recommend a variety of assessments to help family members know themselves first, know each member of the family, and for the parent/trustee to understand more clearly how they are hardwired. Although there are many excellent assessments, some of the classic and useful assessments are the Myers-Briggs Type Indicator (MBTI), the Enneagram, and the Structure of Intellect (SOI). A place to start might be the MBTI. Groups that experience the MBTI for the first time often gain significant constructive insight into their relationships. It identifies personality types based on four basic preferences and provides a framework to explain how different types interact.

For those who want to invest significant time and energy, the Enneagram is one of the most subtle, useful tools for personal and family development. The Enneagram shows how we are the same, how we are different, and most importantly, how we relate to each other. Each of the nine personality types maps patterns of thinking, feeling, and behaving. The SOI profile is most useful to help individuals discover their learning style, strengths, and how they can work to improve.

With assessments as a start, the family and each individual can begin to create a bias toward lifelong learning. I strongly recommend that each family member creates an individual development plan. These plans can be as simple as an annual list of six to eight goals, or a strategic roadmap for the future. Often it is useful to work with a life coach or mentor to create traction and accountability around the goals.

Some families even ritualize sharing of the goals in order to create an environment of support for each person's aspirations. One of the benefits of sharing the plans is that it often yields themes for the whole family. Thus a family can create a comprehensive family development plan that incorporates goals of each family member. For instance, if several rising generation members express interest in learning how to be a board member, a family-wide discussion or educational session on family governance, process, roles, and responsibilities may be right and timely. As family members begin their journeys of self-awareness, and grow through myriad ups and downs, they gain self-efficacy from their experiences.

Money is agnostic. It doesn't have an opinion, it only has a role to *amplify* whatever it is serving at the moment. Money will surely amplify *good* just as effortlessly as it amplifies *bad*. Thus, it is incumbent upon the stewards of money, the holders of wealth, the child with her first $10 in a piggy bank, to learn to be conscious of its power and their relationship to it. The prepared heir will more often make choices toward amplifying good and chalk up the fewer bad choices as learning opportunities.

Questions for Further Reflection

1. What was your experience learning about money?
2. What was your experience with work and making mistakes?

3. What from your experiences do you want to bring forward in your family, and what do you want to do differently?

Additional Resources

Joline Godfrey, *Raising Financially Fit Kids* (New York: Ten Speed Press, 2013).

Lee Hausner, *Children of Paradise* (Los Angeles: Jeremy P. Tarcher, 1990).

John de Graaf, *Affluenza: The All-Consuming Epidemic* (Oakland, CA: Berrett-Koehler Publishers, 2001).

Roy Williams & Vic Preisser, *Preparing Heirs: Five Steps to a Successful Transition of Family Wealth and Values* (Bandon, OR: Robert D. Reed Publishers, 2003).

Biography

Peter Evans is the principal of aFgo (a Family growth opportunity) Associates, a consultancy focused on helping affluent families flourish. His work is as a *personne de confiance,* a long-term, most-trusted advisor helping to build cohesion, vitality, and meaning in multi-generational family systems.

CHAPTER 24

How Do You Start a Family Conversation About Financial Inheritance?

Charles Collier

"I used to think I was up against more than I actually am regarding our daughters' inheritances," says Bill Collatos, founding managing partner of Spectrum Equity Investors in Boston. "The dialogue between my wife and me has taken an interesting turn. For some time, we had differences about how much to give our three daughters, but, after a few years and numerous conversations, we came up with the principles and the strategy, and then the dollar amounts came into sharper focus."

Several key questions illuminate decisions regarding a financial inheritance:

- What amount of financial inheritance will you leave for your children and grandchildren?
- What, if anything, will you tell your children about your estate plan and their inheritance? And, if you do tell them about this, how much detail will you provide?
- Will you actively help this next generation learn about finance and investments?
- Should you include sons- and daughters-in-law in these conversations?
- What do you think is the purpose of a financial inheritance for your children? For example, is it to be used to provide a safety net, to purchase a vacation home, to fund financial or social entrepreneurial initiatives, to enable a choice of career without regard for the economics of that choice, or for anything your children choose?

Because I believe that the true wealth of your family is not financial, I think that you should first discuss the *principles* that will guide your decision about how much to give your children. It makes sense to have these conversations *before* implementing various estate planning strategies. Remember, money is important, but not all-important. The best thing you can do for your family is to invest in their human, intellectual, and social capital.

"The most important truths, I believe," says James Hughes, a retired counselor of law in Aspen, Colorado, and the author of *Family Wealth – Keeping It in the Family*, "are whether the gifts will permit the recipient to bring his or her own dream to life and enable him or her the choice of a vocation. The priority is to help this person whom you love and invest in their journey. Another truth is that, if the recipient receives a greater sum than they need to live a liberated life, that extra sum will require them to act as a steward of those funds – for someone or something other than themselves. Those excess funds will impose a responsibility upon them that will restrict the experience of enhancement of freedom that the gift was designed to achieve."

What Is the Best Way to Proceed?

"Where should a parent begin?" asks Kathy Wiseman, a family facilitator and the CEO of Working Systems, Inc. "Should you begin with your spouse or your adult children? As with any discussion about a sensitive topic, it is important that all conversations about family assets be planned, factual and detail-based, open, and inviting of questions. Difficult conversations are always challenging, but the benefits are significant. Planning and thinking through what you want to achieve are a first step, while at the same time remembering that questions are a good start to knowing what it is that the next generation wants to learn."

My recommended process is a three-part conversation, starting with your spouse and then your children. One way through those questions listed previously is a series of "breakthrough conversations," which are critical to the success of the family in the future. The conversations start small and evolve over time.

The first part begins with a conversation with your spouse and focuses on exploring all your options. How much to give, through which vehicles – that is, outright or via trusts – and so on.

From that conversation, a key goal is to create clarity about what the inheritance should achieve and generally how much to leave the children. You may not agree, but differences are critically important and should be discussed and respected. Indeed, you may find that there are differences where you thought there were none, and points of agreement that you did not expect.

Ask yourselves the following questions:

- What principles guide our decisions regarding our children's inheritances? What factors might make it difficult to follow our principles?
- Do we treat our children equally or fairly? What are the challenges and solutions for both scenarios?
- At what stage do we tell them about their financial inheritance?

- What would our parents say about the financial inheritance we plan to leave our children?
- What worries us most about our children's use of their inheritances?
- What are our hopes for the next and then future generations?
- What amount of inheritance would be life-giving to our children?
- Could we give them a *say* in their financial inheritance?

The second part of the conversation is talking with your children about what you have decided in part one. You can have this talk with one child at a time or all the children together. Sometimes, families need only one conversation. Other families have a number of conversations, often over a number of years.

You may want to begin with the following general questions, with the option of adding others that are more specific to your own family:

- What is the meaning and purpose of a financial inheritance for you?
- How much money do you need to live a worthwhile life?
- What do you think about the purpose of inheritance for your generation?
- Do you want to bring your husband/wife/partner into this conversation?
- What is the best financial decision you have made? The worst?
- Is it important to you to work together with your siblings around inheritances?
- What are the challenges that your parents' estate presents for you and your family?
- What kind of guidance/consultation would assist you in the management of your parents' estate?

The third part of the conversation should be a discussion of the principles that guided your decisions, the general nature of the estate plan, and then the amounts that your children will receive. Also, you can explain how you have integrated some of their ideas into your planning. You can also discuss any next steps and other issues that focus on the future.

My primary message is this:

Think carefully about the purpose of the financial inheritance. Engage all your children in conversations about your financial wealth and their inheritances. Planning for a financial inheritance is both a legal process and a family process. It is an opportunity for connection, education, and openness. It also can be an opportunity for strengthening the family as you address difficult issues with candor and respect.

"My wife and I are both comfortable with our decisions to date," says Bill Collatos, "but we view this as an iterative process. We have not told our daughters what we have done yet, but we will have a conversation when the last one graduates from college."

Further Reading

Charles W. Collier, *Wealth in Families,* 3rd ed. (Cambridge, MA: Harvard University, 2012).

Biography

Charles Collier was the senior philanthropic adviser at Harvard University, where he served for 25 years. He worked with hundreds of individuals and families to shape their philanthropy, helping them make wise gift decisions and advising them on family relationships surrounding financial wealth. He served as a speaker and consultant for many institutions and organizations ranging from universities and independent schools to private banks and community foundations. Charles published articles in *Trusts & Estates, The ACTEC Journal, Family Business Review, Journal of Gift Planning, Advancing Philanthropy,* and *Gift Planning Today.* He has been quoted in the *Boston Globe, The New York Times, The Wall Street Journal, Financial Times,* and *Forbes.* In 2004 he was named to *The NonProfit Times* Power and Influence Top 50 and in 2014 Family Wealth Report honored him with its lifetime achievement award. From the time of his diagnosis in 2008 with early-onset Alzheimer's until his death in 2018 Charles was an outspoken advocate for research into the disease and compassion for its sufferers. Charles was a graduate of Phillips Academy, Andover, from which he received a distinguished service award in 2002. He held a BA from Dartmouth College and a MTS from Harvard Divinity School. He completed the postgraduate course in family systems theory at the Bowen Center for the Study of the Family. The third edition of his book, *Wealth in Families,* was published by Harvard University in 2012. That same year, he received the Harvard Medal, which honors "extraordinary service to the University."

CHAPTER 25

How Can You Avoid the Negative Impacts of Giving Money to Family Members?

Lee Hausner

For lottery players, the dream of "hitting the jackpot" creates a fantasy of happily-ever-after. However studies of instant lottery winners often reveal just the opposite. Lives are upended, relationships fall apart and the "fortune" rapidly disappears, leaving the recipient in a state of despair. What might affluent families learn from instant money winners that can help create positive and productive wealth transfers? What are the challenges to the gifting process and why might a gift of wealth to children, grandchildren, or other descendants create discomfort and dysfunction for the recipient?

The success or failure of instant wealth recipients appears to depend on factors such as the maturity of the recipient, the degree of preparation for the prize, and what emotions have been attached to wealth in general.

Money is merely a means of exchange for goods or services. However, our unique money histories create various emotional connections. The first step in giving wisely is to face honestly the money beliefs that you have inherited and that hold sway in your family. Did you grow up believing that the love of money is the root of all evil, as the Bible admonishes us? Was money in your family used as a substitute for love and emotional support? Was it a method of controlling behavior and exerting power? When money is used as a reward for "good" behavior but withheld as punishment for unacceptable actions, the development of positive self-esteem may become compromised, leaving the recipient feeling unworthy of the financial gift.

Many financially successful families always worry about being taken advantage of, and they pass on the message to the next generation not to trust others. Have you or other members of your family grown up with the concern over whether friends really like you or instead want what your financial resources can provide? Was money in the family thought to be the key to happiness rather than emphasizing the development of internal resources? Was it viewed as a means to an end or as the end itself? Has money been handled primarily by the men in the family, leaving female beneficiaries overwhelmed by the responsibility of stewardship? These are but a few of the varied emotional responses a financial success or a financial gift can create.

The next thing to consider, if you are to give effectively, is timing. Timing of the gift appears to be an important determinant regarding the positive or negative effects of passive income. Unlike the random timing of instant lottery winners, affluent families have choices regarding wealth transfers. Experience suggests that giving significant financial gifts during that period of time when the recipient is developing his or her own sense of identity and self-worth through education and career building can impede this important developmental period. Passive wealth may enable the individual to avoid overcoming the necessary challenges and discipline in life that leads to personal accomplishments and self-esteem.

A key point in preparation is financial literacy. Fostering financial literacy in your recipients can also help make sure that when the gift is received the recipient is not overwhelmed with its management. When a family has little or limited money, there are ongoing discussions regarding its usage involving all family members. Significant purchases may be delayed because other priority needs arise. Family members are required to begin working at early ages in order to contribute to their daily expenses and/or their education. Budgeting is a daily activity. However, as families become more affluent, stuff just seems to appear with little conversation about cost, budgeting, or attitudes of stewardship. Responsibility without preparation is a disastrous combination.

Even the process of selecting appropriate advisors can be traumatic. Without knowledge in this area, the individual may make very poor choices as everyone vies for his or her piece of the financial pie. There are many excellent programs and books available (including some referenced later) to help families with this educational process, which should begin in the early elementary school years. This is an important ongoing learning process. Additionally, children pick up many of their money habits from observing how their parents deal with money, so it is important for Mom and Dad to honestly look at what lessons regarding money their actions may be demonstrating. How are your words and deeds preparing the next generation to deal responsibly with assets they may inherit?

Another topic to face squarely is trusts. Often, money is transferred through trusts with little explanation or understanding on the part of the beneficiary about the rationale for the trust, leaving the recipient to wonder, "Why didn't you 'trust' me?" To avoid this result, you need to explain to your beneficiaries, either in person or in a letter of intent, why you set up the trust in the way you did. This way of gifting also requires careful selection of the appropriate type of trustees. Will the individual(s) chosen have the necessary fiduciary ability to manage the assets, the time to devote to the task, and, equally important, the ability to serve as a coach/mentor to the beneficiary? (On these points, see also Hartley Goldstone's essay in this collection.) Beneficiaries need sufficient education to be able to understand the rationale and the terms of the trust, as well as the rights and responsibilities of both trustees and beneficiary. This will enable the beneficiary to appreciate rather than resent the trust structure as well as utilize the trustee as a trusted advisor.

A perennial concern is whether to give to recipients equally. For example, I have often been asked the following question: "My children have achieved different degrees of financial success in their individual lives. Should I correct this difference in my estate planning, by giving more to those who have made less and less to those who have made more?" Generally, giving unequal amounts of money to sibling heirs without giving them a clear understanding of the reasons for these differences will create estrangements in the relationships between the siblings. If your estate plan attempts to correct the imbalance by allocating distribution based on need, the conscientious achiever may feel "punished" for his or her hard work, while seeing siblings who earned or saved less seemingly rewarded. If, however, the more financially successful siblings initiate or agree in a conversation with parents about allocating greater funds to less affluent siblings, relationships can remain intact. Thoughtful, extended communication is crucial here. It is not a "one and done" matter.

Challenges may also occur when one sibling in a family has created considerable wealth and wants to share the good fortune with the rest of the family. Buying a home for mom and dad may create resentment and jealousy as the "financier" gains a favored position with parents, whereas indulging brothers and sisters can create discomfort for everyone's spouses. This situation, too, needs frank and honest communication between the family members and the potential giver if a positive outcome is to occur. However, there are some types of gifting that can minimize any negative consequences of the generosity. Actions might include:

1. Creation of an educational trust to be used by nieces and nephews or siblings to help them complete their education.
2. Funding a family foundation that provides an opportunity for the family to work together on philanthropic projects.
3. Funding an annual family retreat, permitting the planning to be done by a family committee not dominated by the wealth creator.

It may seems that a gift – particularly a gift of significant wealth – should be seen as a completely joyful, welcome occurrence. A more sober analysis of the power of money suggests that careful thought and consideration is necessary if a financial gift is to have the positive impact that the grantor envisioned.

Questions for Further Reflection

1. What are the most powerful beliefs about money that you learned as part of your money history?
2. How have you prepared the rising generation to receive well? What more would you like to do?
3. What are your thoughts with regard to giving "equally" versus giving "fairly"?

Additional Resources

Dr. Lee Hausner, *Children of Paradise* (Los Angeles: Jeremy P. Tarcher), 1990.

Dr. Lee Hausner and Douglas K. Freeman, *The Legacy Family: The Definitive Guide to Creating a Successful Multi-Generational Family* (New York: Palgrave Macmillan, 2009).

Ernest A. Doud and Dr. Lee Hausner, *Hats Off to You: Finding Success in Family Business Succession* (Glendale, CA: Doud/Hausner and Associates, 2000).

Biography

Dr. Lee Hausner is an internationally recognized clinical psychologist and business consultant. She served as the senior psychologist for the Beverly Hills Unified School District for 17 years, in addition to establishing a reputation as a sought-after keynote speaker, seminar leader, and highly rated resource for Young President's Organization, World President's Organization, and the CEO organization.

An acknowledged expert on psychological issues involving wealth and wealth transfer, she was a presenter at the World Economic Forum in Davos, and is a frequent presenter for the high wealth/private client conferences for major financial institutions as well as national wealth management conferences.

Most recently she assisted the University of Southern California in creating their Family Business Center and serves as the senior advisor to the program.

Lee resides in Los Angeles with her husband, two married children, and five grandchildren.

CHAPTER 26

How Can Your Family Encourage Financial Literacy in Every Member?

Coventry Edwards-Pitt

You hear a lot about financial literacy in the world of wealth advising. Programs abound that teach family members, especially younger ones, the nuts and bolts of our complex financial world – the power of compounding, the difference between a stock and a bond, the importance of a credit score, to name a few. And the hope is that by taking and mastering these courses, family members will be better prepared to go out into the world and make decisions that are financially sound.

But it's worth asking what we really mean by financial literacy. Usually, what families mean is that an individual will be equipped with financial wisdom – that they will understand the value of a dollar, that they will know not to spend more than they earn or have available to them, and that they will understand that money has a place and that materialistic acquisition, although fun at times, is not a foundation for true happiness.

In other words, families hope their members will hold certain values with regard to money. And there's the rub. Values cannot be taught in a course. Values have to be modeled and lived with, usually for many years before they take root and become second nature.

Values

My view on this topic was heavily influenced by what I heard in the interviews I conducted for my book *Raised Healthy, Wealthy & Wise* (2014). I talked with children raised with wealth who grew up to be productive, self-motivated, and content, and I asked them what messages they had heard from their parents that helped them get that way.

Somewhat surprisingly to me, I learned that very few of them attributed their sound money values to a textbook education in financial literacy. Instead, they had learned by watching their parents – how they lived, what they talked about, what they bought and didn't buy, and what they valued and didn't value. The stories I heard of how parents modeled values were all about the day-to-day – the "no" at the cash register, the offer to match what a child would save for a car, the conversations and family stories that showed money has a place, but that it does not determine a person's character or happiness and that it can be gone as easily as it came.

What's even more interesting is that many of the interviewees I spoke with, as a result of being raised amid sound financial *values*, sought out financial *knowledge* (the nuts and bolts) for themselves. Because they had already been equipped with financial wisdom, they were motivated to make good financial decisions, so they found ways to educate themselves when faced with a financial choice – for instance, what type of credit card to get, how much to save in their company's 401K at their first job, or what type of apartment they would be able to afford when they were first on their own.

So, if values are key, which values are most important to model? Of course, values are personal, and this isn't meant to be a one-size-fits-all prescription. That said, through numerous interviews, certain messages emerged again and again as being the most helpful for young family members to hear:

- *There is joy and freedom in financial self-sufficiency.* It means being able to earn your own money, in being able to buy things with money you've earned, and in being able to solve your own problems.
- *Fulfilling work is a lifelong gift.* Work is about contribution and purpose; work you are passionate about is a goal, but this can take a while to discover, and in the meantime, no job is too small and all work is a learning opportunity.
- *Just because we have money doesn't mean we have to spend it.* That material possessions don't make a life, that there is a difference between needs and wants, and that money should be respected as the tool it is (to ensure security, to bring about the change you hope to see in the world, etc.) rather than as an end unto itself.
- *If we do spend it, let's spend it well.* There is joy in saving up for quality and in using money for experiences that contribute to family togetherness, learning new things, or other meaningful goals.
- *We should cultivate gratitude for the opportunities money affords us and maintain perspective.* We should keep in mind how fortunate we are to have these resources and not lose sight of (or the ability to be satisfied with) the average experience and what it is like for those with less.
- *And, regardless of how much money we have, we shouldn't squander it.* It's important to keep track of where it's going, make sure we are getting value for price, and do what we need to do to responsibly steward it.

How do parents model these values? In little moments, day in and day out. There is the story of David, who remembers spending time with his father on Sunday mornings while his dad outlined the family budget and expenses on Quicken. As one of three children, David valued this time alone with his dad, but he also told me how much those mornings impressed upon him the importance of having a budget and knowing how every dollar was spent. And there is the story of Taylor, whose wealthy parents prioritized family and togetherness and now finds herself passing this same value on to her children. During a recent trip to the store, confronted with her children crying over something they wanted her to buy for them, she responded, "Why are you crying? You have everything you could ever need – you have parents who love you, and grandparents who love you!"

Nuts and Bolts

Once you have established the foundation with modeled values, by all means, add on those lessons in the nuts and bolts. But do it as much as possible as part of the day-to-day, so family members can practice their skills in the here-and-now, in the context of a financial decision that is meaningful to them. For instance, expect a teenager to earn a growing percentage of their clothing budget as they advance through their teens and manage the shopping decisions within that budget. Or, rather than just providing a young adult with a credit card, have them research the various card options and make a proposal to you. Lay out some basic parameters for them to cover, such as which option will best allow them to build their credit history, what the various rates and penalties are, what the fees are, and how they plan to pay off the costs each month – and then let them surprise you with how much they discover on the topic.

The bottom line with all these day-to-day experiences is to provide as much "ownership" as possible. This holds true at any age. Even family members who have become accustomed to being financially dependent or financially illiterate can be weaned off of this dependence over time or can be educated in taking more ownership over aspects of their financial life (for instance, establishing their own budgets and then making a proposal to their trustees).

In fact, emphasizing ownership is one of the ways in which more "typical" financial literacy education can work well if it's done right. An underlying assumption of most financial literacy sessions is a presumption of agency – that the individual will need to know this information because their decisions will matter. This emphasis on a family member's agency, the concept that they are in charge and accountable, both for their successes and failures, can lay the groundwork for true financial literacy, especially if it is borne out by a subsequent reality of practicing actually being in charge of a financial life and all the decisions and responsibilities it entails – from supporting themselves, to saving for the future, to investing what they've saved.

Any lover of literature knows that there is a world of difference between reading a classic and truly comprehending it. Often, true comprehension is elusive until the reader has lived enough of life to grasp the significance, import, and poignancy of the message. It's the same with financial literacy. A grounding in values is the life that needs to be lived before the lessons can take root.

Questions for Further Reflection

1. Think about how you learned about money in your own life (the importance of earning money, and how to save, spend, and invest it). Which of those experiences were the most valuable to you?
2. Would the family member whose financial literacy skills you hope to develop be able to point to similar experiences in his or her own life?
3. If not, are there opportunities for you to create similar experiences for them?

Additional Resources

Coventry Edwards-Pitt, *Raised Healthy, Wealthy & Wise: Lessons From Successful and Grounded Inheritors on How They Got That Way* (Waltham, MA: BP Books, 2014).

Joline Godfrey, *Raising Financially Fit Kids* (Berkeley, CA: Ten Speed Press, 2003).

Ron Lieber, *The Opposite of Spoiled: Raising Kids Who Are Grounded, Generous, and Smart About Money.* (New York: HarperCollins, 2015).

Biography

Coventry Edwards-Pitt is the Chief Wealth Advisory Officer of Ballentine Partners, a Boston-area based investment and wealth advisory firm. She was pre-med in college, and was drawn to the wealth management industry by her desire to help people – to help them navigate a complex, noisy, often-conflicted financial world to implement strategies that are not just financially sophisticated but also emotionally relevant. Covie is the author of the *Healthy, Wealthy & Wise Collection,* a two-book series based on interviews highlighting success stories, from the very young to the young at heart. She has been a featured speaker on the lessons in the books at over 80 events for wealth-owning families and their advisors and consults with individuals about how to implement the books' best practices in their own lives and within their own families.

CHAPTER 27

How Can Families Support Both Individuality and a Shared Dream?

Kelin Gersick

Parenting is a uniquely difficult job. From the day that your child is born, his or her welfare – security, health, and happiness – is the most important thing in your life. But there are pitfalls on every side, and the safe pathway between the threats feels razor thin. How do you protect without smothering or "helicoptering?" How do you model strategies that have worked well for you without compelling imitation? How do you create intimate connection without fostering overdependency?

Furthermore, parents get no time off, and no final resolutions. In fact, parenting would look like a bad bargain, full of costs, risks, and anxieties, if it didn't simultaneously provide such compelling and joyful meaning. Despite the demands, it seems that most people are hard-wired to draw sustenance from loving and being loved by a child.

Although all parents face childrearing challenges, parents in enterprise families have to deal with additional levels of complexity. Family business owners, and stewards of collective family wealth, need intergenerational relationships to be successful not only in family terms, but also as partnerships. The enterprise goals of economic and organizational success interact with the family goals of individual development and family harmony. The result is the *core challenge of parenting* in enterprise families: *balancing the centrifugal force toward individuation with the centripetal force toward common purpose and collaboration.*

The first impetus is the basic dream of parents: to foster their children's development into competent, self-aware, and self-confident *individuals,* who have a sense of who they are, how they are unique, what they are good at, what they enjoy and what they dislike, and how to grow into their own authentic space in the family and in the world.

The second need is to create a strong sense of *we* – the common history, identity, and vision that bind the family together, and can sustain governance in a collectively owned enterprise. Without some appreciation of a shared purpose, mutual commitment wanes and the benefits of belonging evaporate.

Parents who manage the balance between these centrifugal and centripetal forces, and launch their children into the adult world able to honor both the *I* and the *we* of their identity, have done all they can to nourish the future, both as parents and as owners.

Easier said than done, particularly in families who not only want to be together but also to own and run things together. Expanding the focus from the nuclear family to the extended family highlights the implications of this parenting challenge for governance. Family units and branches face the same dilemma as individual parents: honoring the particular resources and agendas of distinct sub-families while building an adequate common ground of shared goals and overlapping priorities.

For most senior-generation leaders, this requires a fundamental transformation in their concept of what makes them a family. Most seniors, especially founders, initially see the family as a pyramid of human capital. Each generation adds an expanding layer to the bottom of the pyramid. The culture, history, traditions, and accumulated wisdom of the family percolate down through the pyramid like water through layers of limestone, picking up minerals as it goes. The boundary around the pyramid is meaningful – it defines "who we are," "what we own," and "how we do things." Marriages import individuals across the boundary, either deep into an undifferentiated generational heart, or just over the line into a special compartment for in-laws, but definitely inside, because the children of those marriages are the essential next layer (see Figure 27.1).

But in most cases that is not how the younger generations picture the family. Each younger generation, as they move into adulthood, begins to create a pyramid of their own (at least in Western cultures). See Figure 27.2.

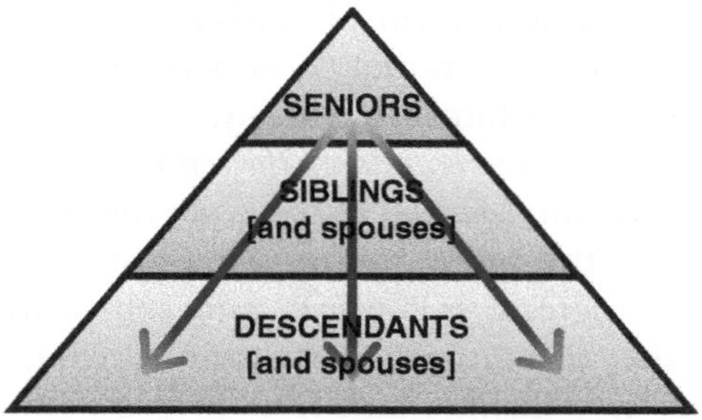

Figure 27.1 The Seniors' "Pyramid" View of the Family

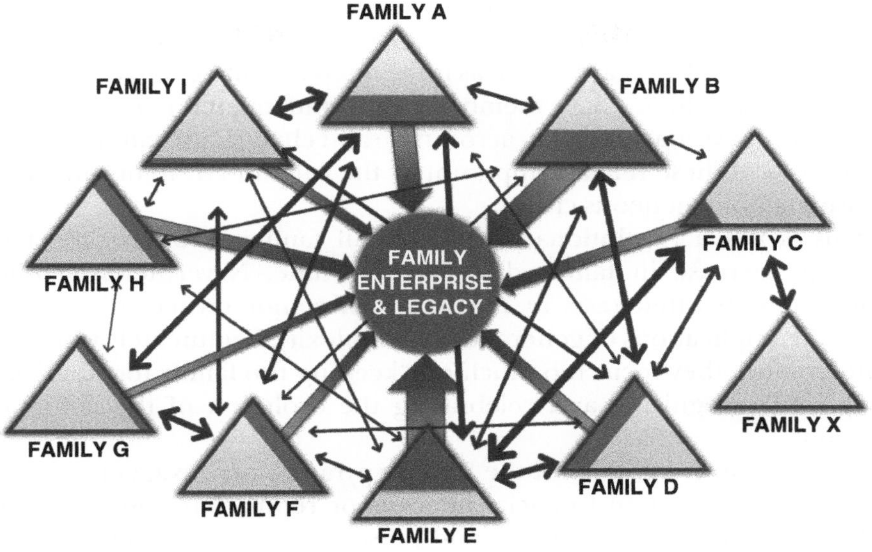

Figure 27.2 The Complex Family Network

Education, work, finding a partner, and having children, enact the "centrifugal" force toward differentiation, as offspring grow up and create a "self" as a more independent adult. Some portion of their new pyramid will be connected to the original structure (the thicker arrows) – more if they work in the company, or live near their parents and foster close ties between grandparents and grandchildren; less if they move away, geographically or psychologically, and have little to do with the operations and financial benefits of enterprise ownership. But in all cases, the link to the home pyramid is only part of their lives (especially since their spouse is connected to her or his own "pyramid of origin" as well, closely or loosely). Very importantly, the new sub-families are also connected to each other directly, not through their parents, with varying degrees of closeness (the thinner arrows). As families move through the third and later generations, the number of sibling and cousin pyramids can get very large, working outward in concentric circles of engagement, as the thinner arrows come to greatly outnumber the thicker ones.

The most important consequence of this natural development is that the governing family is no longer a unified pyramid, but a *network* of units, constantly adjusting their links in the overall system. The idea that "this is who we are and this is how we do things" gives way to a woven array of unit-to-unit relationships – some tight and close, some stretched and weak, some units closely embedded in connection with many others, and some only attached to one or two, with little connection to the core. The emotional tone of individual relationships can range from constant active hostility to indifference to lifetime intimacy, each link contributing to the pattern of interdependence and distance that is the unique "footprint" of every particular family network. Furthermore, that footprint evolves year by year, as individuals age and change, and their personal pyramids add and lose members. The fundamental perspective that has meaning for governance is that, across time and change, the family is defined by the network of these relationships, not by the rules of an "in or out" boundary enclosing a homogeneous crowd.

This is not a revolutionary concept. All family theorists reflect on the inevitable increase in family diversity over time. Nevertheless, family governance design often rests in the hands of senior owners who may try to ignore the implications of generational complexity. Legitimately worried about disintegration, they focus too much on "keeping the family together" and not enough on recognizing and celebrating the evolution of the family in new directions.

Parents who try to defend the unitary pyramid may exaggerate the threat to the family's common financial interests or reputation posed by variability in lifestyle, politics, expenditures, and personal choices like religion and marriage. Even well-intentioned and valuable tools such as family constitutions, mission statements, family councils, rules of engagement, conservative trusts that postpone self-determination well into midlife, and estate plans that are constraining and secretive can all be overused to try to reinforce orthodoxy and compliance.

If the parents go too far in trying to prevent divergence from the original pyramid, those offspring and extended family members who do not feel seen or accepted lose motivation and build either resentment or apathy. It feels less and less like *their* family. The very goal of continuity leads to policies that work in exactly the opposite direction, and the glue that holds the family together dissolves.

What is the alternative? How can parents and senior leaders balance their support of *both* individuation and collaboration, and build a governance system that can succeed across generations? Just seeing the dilemma – understanding the tension between the centrifugal and centripetal forces that keeps the enterprise in orbit, connected to the legacy while discovering its own path – is the most important step.

Beyond that, there are four fundamental approaches that parents can adopt as they consider governance architecture and process, all of them with a bias toward openness. They are not meant to be absolutes; some children become substance-addicted, or naively manipulated, or truly impaired in a way that requires lifetime caretaking. But cautious parents in typical families may tend to exaggerate "un-readiness," underestimating the next generation's deep (if unspoken) gratitude and commitment to the family, and undervaluing their adult children's ability to self-manage and learn from their experience. The best path to nurturing good judgment and the ability to govern is to treat offspring as legitimate participants from an early age, capable of responsibly balancing their individual desires with the common good.

1. In distributing resources and opportunities, *recognize that fair is not the same thing as equal, and equal is not the same thing as identical.* Make the effort to understand the unique needs and capacity of each child. Trust that differentiation will not automatically fire up sibling rivalry and resentment if it is based on good reasons, openly shared. Your kids are hurt by unequal access to you and evidence of unequal caring, but not necessarily by a customized and non-identical distribution of things. In fact, opportunities to be unjealously generous to each other are valued by siblings. Later generations are much more inclined than parents realize to want a "best-fit solution," matching what the enterprise needs with the individuals who are most capable of leading, for the benefit of all.
2. *Provide lots of opportunity to exercise the muscle of problem-solving.* Avoid the impulse to protect offspring from all failures. Dealing with disappointment and frustration strengthens the immune system, building self-confidence, and a sense of self-worth that are the best antidotes for entitlement, presumption, triviality, and vulnerability to exploitation. For children, confidence does not come from your parents telling you how wonderful you are, but from your observations of your own behavior, dealing with challenges and setbacks, and accomplishing things.
3. *For all kinds of planning – succession, financial, strategic – don't do it* for *your kids, but* with *your kids.* Define the challenges and decisions to be made as *family* dilemmas instead of problems that parents must solve. Be transparent about the realities of your situation – financial and organizational in particular – from an early age, and respect the younger generation's input, even if it is grounded in much less experience than your own.[1] Ultimately, let them not only participate, but lead.

---

[1]Parents are always eager for guidelines on what to share at what ages. It is very difficult to generalize across the huge variations of personality and maturity in children, but consider: (1) Preteens need to have honest answers to their questions about their family's business, and even "Are we rich?" (answers such as "We have lots more than most people, less than some, and here is how we need to act to be responsible friends and neighbours"); (2) adolescents (12–18) may eagerly embrace conversations about the meaning of work, volunteerism and citizenship, budgeting and managing money, and opportunities to work in the family enterprise; (3) young adults (18–30) should have gradually increasing access to all or nearly all data on family wealth, trusts, enterprise governance, and career opportunities, and should have some degree of self-determination over a portion of capital; (4) adults (age 30 and above) should be partners, invited into decision-making in line with their proven capabilities and interests.

Many parents worry that providing awareness of wealth to young adult offspring will be demotivating and overwhelming. They underestimate that their children are already aware of the family's wealth from an early age. They see their parents' lifestyle. They understand what it takes to own companies, take these kinds of vacations, and have so many luxuries. If they are denied access to the facts of their family's finances, they will fill in with fantasy about how much there is and where it comes from. What is the advantage of assumptions and choices based on guessing rather than truth?

Parents can pose to themselves the following "what if?" "What would I have done if, as a young adult, I were made aware of the level of wealth and ownership that my parents had reached, and if I had been given early responsibility to determine my own use of some of those resources? What impact would it have had on my education, worklife, expenditures, and lifestyle?" Almost invariably, thoughtful seniors imagine that they would have done some foolish things, but not many; that they would have learned from their experience; that they would have been more conservative than necessary about expenditures and risk-taking; and that they would have worked just as hard, aspired just as high, but with less anxiety. Nevertheless, they are reluctant to assume that their own offspring would exhibit the same moderation, unaware of the subtle insult that is conveyed by their secrecy and the protective constraints they build into their governance designs.

4. *Invite spouses into full participation in the enterprise.* Even senior couples who built their businesses together in the early days by working shoulder to shoulder may embrace policies that bar future spouses from employment, board service, or even information about the enterprise. The cost of these policies is high. Half the human capital in a later-generation family is the result of marrying in. Of course, a realistic concern about divorce is legitimate. Dealing with a vengeful "ex" can be painful, and more so if the divorcing spouse is a shareholder or an important manager. But is it sensible to reject a priori the ambition of a whole class of potential dedicated contributors because of the *possibility* that some of them may not remain forever?

   There are special cases, and qualification by merit is essential (as it should be for blood descendants as well). Many spouses are not interested in being inside the enterprise. In fact they may work hard to defend a boundary between the core business and the world they are creating for their children. But other in-laws can be the most highly motivated members of each generation, eager to be contributors rather than just beneficiaries of the family's work. And they are half the parents of the next generation – the children whose support is essential for continuity, and who are watching how each parent is being treated. Nothing demonstrates an understanding and embracing of the "network" model more than respecting the talent of a chosen spouse, and allowing her or him to play a role that is earned by merit and appreciated as helping the family to meet its responsibilities.

Family networks are challenging systems. They are hard to control. But they also have incredible potential to harness human capital and create chain-reactions of creativity, commitment, and adaptability. With all the best intentions of protecting and nurturing their offspring and the generations that follow, parents can get trapped in trying to preserve the singular family identity that defined their own life history. Embracing the emergence of new and different worldviews can be the secret to lifelong intimacy with their adult descendants, and to adaptive continuity in their enterprises, sustaining their evolving family for generations.

Questions for Further Reflection

1. How can siblings and extended families negotiate common goals and strategies without enhancing competition, conflict, and the feeling that there are winners and losers?
2. How can parents decide on the amount and timing of the information their children should receive about the family and the company?
3. What do you do with a relative who is consistently disruptive and uncooperative?

Additional Resources

Intergenerational Relationships in Business Continuity

Kelin E. Gersick, John A. Davis, Marion McCollom Hampton, and Ivan Lansberg, *Generation to Generation: Life Cycles of the Family Business* (Boston: Harvard Business Review Press, 1997).

Ivan Lansberg, *Succeeding Generations: Realizing the Dream of Families in Business* (Boston: Harvard Business Review Press, 1999).

Parenting and Wealth

Madeline Levine, PhD, *The Price of Privilege: How Parental Pressure and Material Advantage Are Creating a Generation of Disconnected and Unhappy Kids* (New York: HarperCollins, 2006).

Madeline Levine, PhD, *Teach Your Children Well: Why Values and Coping Skills Matter More Than Grades, Trophies, or Fat Envelopes* (New York: Harper Perennial, 2012).

Also:

Lee Hausner, *Children of Paradise: Successful Parenting for Prosperous Families* (Los Angeles, CA: Jeremy P. Tarcher, 1990).

James Grubman, *Strangers in Paradise: How Families Adapt to Wealth Across Generations* (Boston: Family Wealth Consulting, 2013).

Biography

Kelin Gersick is a lecturer in psychiatry at the Yale School of Medicine and professor emeritus of organizational psychology at the California School of Professional Psychology. He is also co-founder of Lansberg, Gersick & Associates, a research and consulting firm in New Haven, Connecticut, that serves family businesses, family offices, and family foundations around the world.

Kelin's work as a researcher, consultant, writer, and teacher focuses on the impact of family relationships – marriage, parenting, siblings, cousins, and multiple generations – on governance and continuity in family enterprise and philanthropy. He is the lead author of *Generation to Generation: Life Cycles of the Family Business* (1997) and *Generations of Giving: Leadership and Continuity in Family Foundations* (2004), and many articles, cases, and columns.

Kelin holds a PhD from Harvard University and a BA from Yale University, where he also served on the faculty. His consulting, lecturing, and research on family business and family foundations have taken him throughout North America and to more than 35 countries in Central and South America, Europe, Asia, Australia, the Middle East, and Africa.

SECTION 5

MAKING SHARED DECISIONS

There is a reason that families with wealth or family businesses sometimes speak about *family governance* but never about *family government.* Government implies an authority: a group that rules and another group that is ruled; it implies laws, that is, rules that are backed up by force. At least in Western families, which place great importance on individualism, family "government" would never fly.[1]

As a result, *family governance* can become something of a squishy term; what does it really mean? Is every family a democracy? Hardly. Nor does every family have to be.

Rather than talking about governance, we prefer focusing on the question, "How do we make shared decisions?" Who shares in what decisions may change from time to time, decision to decision. But of course the first and most fundamental decision is, "How do we decide?"

That fundamental decision is the one that all the essays in this section approach, in one way or another.

Barbara Hauser begins by highlighting principles and practices from the Organisation of Economic Co-operation and Development. These include transparency and the sharing of financial information, principles often captured in the form of a Family Constitution.

But how can you get to the point of designing and agreeing on a family constitution? The next two essays take up this challenge. Jennifer East offers practical, concrete steps for improving family communication, which come down to good planning, structure, and the courage to take action. Christian Stewart then offers an actual curriculum that families can implement – focused

[1]Other cultures may accept a more "governmental" approach to family decision-making. For this reason, in this section alone (not to mention other sections of this book) we have included, authors with broad geographic experience outside the United States: Barbara Hauser in Europe and the Middle East, Jennifer East in Canada and the Middle East, Christian Stewart in the Far East and Australia, Katherine Grady and Ivan Lansberg in Europe and South America, and Mary Duke in Asia and Europe.

on strengths, stories, difficult conversations, and trust – to build healthy relationships. These are the foundation for the very ability to make shared decisions that last.

For many families, the process of making shared decisions intersects with the structures that organize their material assets, such as business entities or trusts. In the next essay, Katherine Grady and Ivan Lansberg describe the proper use of a business board of directors and a family owners council – and, very importantly, their points of intersection. They also include advice on how to prepare family members to contribute effectively to these deliberative bodies.

A fundamental tool for making decisions amid family wealth or business is the family meeting. These come in all sorts of shapes and sizes, and families who succeed over time use family meetings regularly. Mary Duke offers practical guidance in the what, where, who, and how of family meetings.

Finally, conflict is a natural part of family life, because different members have different interests and, sometimes, different values. Blair Trippe outlines ways that families can better define and manage their natural conflicts, with a particular attention to development – of the family as a structure and the individuals within it – as a means to manage and resolve conflict. Doug Baumoel then considers the crucial question, "Should you stay together as a family or go your separate ways?" Though it is deeply challenging to consider going your separate ways, the family that faces this question and then decides to continue together has made the most fundamental shared decision.

CHAPTER 28

What Are the Best Ways for a Family to Make Decisions Together?

Barbara Hauser

"Why are people talking about family governance?" "What do they mean and why is it important?" "Does family governance mean I need a family council? A family constitution?"

The word *governance* often sounds intimidating. I recommend replacing it with the term *decision-making*.

Every family is always making decisions. The question is whether the way they are making decisions is a way that seems fair to everyone involved. When the decisions are not seen as fair, the likely result is resentment, and eventually rebellion – sometimes including dramatic press coverage.

From countries to businesses to families, each group has made an agreement – explicit or implicit – about who has the power to make which decisions for the group. In my book *International Family Governance*, I compare six countries for their governance system: United States, Japan, India, Saudi Arabia, France, and the Navajo Nation. Each group has given decision-making authority to a smaller delegation. We see a Congress, a Diet, Parliaments, a monarchy, and a Council of Elders.

Each system has some advantages and disadvantages. Strict monarchies seem the hardest to survive for long periods. We can compare monarchies to families that are ruled by an autocratic patriarch – a common feature in so many families. This form of governance reminds us of the French Revolution, and the American revolt against taxation without representation.

I have found that many families gain a better understanding about how their family works when they look at other social groups. On a grand scale, we have the countries to think about. If the goal of good governance is to make the people free, safe, and able to engage in their own pursuit of happiness, some systems work better than others. In my extensive work in Saudi Arabia with substantial family businesses, I would often address the patriarch with, "Imagine that your family is a small country – how would you like decisions to be made?"

On the business level, a lot of work has been done in the area of good governance. We can adapt much of that learning to family groups. The OECD (Organisation for Economic Co-operation and Development) has developed standards for good governance that can apply easily to families. For example, the OECD Principle Five focuses on the importance of complete and correct information:

> *The corporate governance framework should ensure that timely and accurate disclosure is made on all material matters regarding the corporation, including the financial situation, performance, ownership, and governance of the company.*

In my experience, the lack of sharing of information in a family is the most common cause of distrust among the members, and the buildup of conflict. Another term for the same principle is to have transparency as a strong family value.

Sharing financial information is particularly important. I worked with one Pakistani family where the patriarch had taken this advice to heart. He had a loose-leaf notebook with a section for each family member's net worth and investments, and he left the book in the study – available for all family members to see. This was a family that held transparency at unusually high value.

The other key principle from the OECD that I think applies very aptly to families is Principle Six, part of which states the importance of "the board's accountability to the company and the shareholders." But these two are not enough. Over the years, I have learned how important *participation* is in the family governance system. So I argue that there are three so-called universal principles of good governance for families to follow: transparency, accountability, and participation.

Let's assume a family agrees with this advice so far. What next?

Most groups begin with a foundational agreement. At the country level, this is usually a constitution – England being an exception with no written constitution – which spells out who has the power to make which type of decision. At the business level, most jurisdictions provide a basic governance framework, specifying the need for Articles of Incorporation and accompanying by-laws. In those documents, a board of directors is chosen. To simplify the governance, we have a group of shareholders (which may or may not encompass all the adult family members) who vote on the election (and removal) of the board of directors, who in turn hire (and fire) the top management of the company.

At a family level, you might have a board or, more often, a family council, which acts like a board. The larger family (usually meaning all adult family members) will elect the family council, whether or not they are shareholders or wealthholders, just as shareholders elect a board. The same issues come up: Who is qualified to be a board member? Is there a minimum age? How often does voting take place? Can someone vote by proxy? And so on. In the family setting there are often additional considerations addressing "branches" in the family. Should representation be along branch lines, or along generational lines? That is, should each branch of the family – no matter how many members it has – have the same number of seats on the family council? Likewise, should every generation have some representation?

There is no one-size-fits-all answer to these questions. The key is to ask and discuss what answers feel right. I really enjoy helping a family choose the system that fits them, as there is so much flexibility of choices. It is always interesting to learn as much as possible about what other families do, and what they think works well.

Now we come to the family constitution. When the work has been done to agree on who makes which decisions, it helps to have it all written down. Sometimes it's called a family charter or a family compact or even family mission/values. I think it is most helpful to call it a family constitution, to keep its role familiar. Many families slowly get used to the idea of having a family constitution, and by the end of the discussions and drafting, they feel a proud sense of ownership.

I worked with one ethnic Chinese family that began the governance-process with a fair amount of skepticism. We went through all the decision areas they had: a family business, family charities, family collections, family home compounds, oversight of trusts and investments, agreement on distributions, and so on. The only two provisions I prompted them to include were the preamble, in which they would record their family statement about why they were doing this – in this case it was to honor their ancestors – and a provision at the end on how it could be amended, to allow future generations to make changes. At the end of this process of creating the family constitution, family members were proudly, with some surprise, telling each other, "This is ours, and this is who we are."

John Ward taught me a lesson that I find families reinforce each time I work with them on governance – namely, the process of going through all these issues and reaching agreement is the most valuable result, more than the actual document. By doing this work, the family learns how to discuss and resolve tough issues. When those discussions are not encouraged, or even forbidden, the resulting conflicts are inevitable.

The bottom line is that developing good governance in your family can promote pride and happiness to be a part of your family.

Questions for Further Reflection

1. How would you describe the way in which your family makes decisions?
2. Do you think each family member would confirm that he or she feels fairly included in the process?
3. Can you think of issues that are not to be discussed in your family?
4. Is the younger generation included, as appropriate for their ages?

Additional Resources

I recommend reading the whole OECD document on Corporate Governance:

G20/OECD Principles of Corporate Governance, OECD Report to G20 Finance Ministers and Central Bank Governors, 2015 (https://www.oecd.org/daf/ca/Corporate-Governance-Principles-ENG.pdf).

I recommend reading *The World Happiness Report* on which countries have the happiest subjects; you can apply the findings to families: *The World Happiness Report,* 2018 (https://s3.amazonaws.com/happiness-report/2018/WHR_web.pdf).

Barbara Hauser, *International Family Governance* (Rochester, MN: Mesatop Press, 2009).

Mihaly Csikszentmihalyi, *Flow: The Psychology of Optimal Experience* (New York: Harper & Row, 1990). My favorite book about the meaning of a happy/good life.

Jay Hughes, Susan Massenzio, and Keith Whitaker, *Complete Family Wealth* (New York: Bloomberg Press, 2017).

Biography

Barbara Hauser began as a private-client lawyer (Wellesley, University of Pennsylvania Law, clerk at U.S. Supreme Court, partner in law firms) working with international wealthy families. In her traditional role, she helped implement the wishes of the Patriarch only. Eventually she realized that those unilateral plans often led to litigation. She began working with the whole family instead, as an advisor to the whole family. This worked. Barbara wrote a book about it: *International Family Governance.* For the past 15 years, she has enjoyed helping families create their own good governance and in many cases develop their own family constitution.

CHAPTER 29

How Can You Improve Family Communication?

Jennifer East

Ernesto Sinclair[1] had a problem. Having sold his manufacturing business two years ago, he thought he'd have considerably more time to talk to his wife and children about their newfound wealth, his plans for the future, and their philanthropic goals. Instead, each time he broached what he thought was an "important" conversation, his family seemed to brush him aside.

The worst part was he had always been so busy working that he didn't have much experience talking to his family about sensitive issues. His teenage daughter and two 20-something sons didn't seem that interested in communicating with anyone, except through their smartphones. Everyone was incredibly busy and overscheduled. He'd never really talked to his wife in detail about his business affairs. And so he found himself feeling rather isolated ... in his own family. It was all beginning to weigh on him, and he wasn't sure where to turn. What should he do?

Make It a Priority

Often considered one of the soft issues, poor family communication underlies every tragic tale you hear about affluent families. Family leaders – and their advisors – often prioritize the hard issues like tax planning at the expense of a family's emotional and relational health. It's a simple equation: if you're concerned that your family needs more or better communication, you must make a commitment to improve it. This involves allocating time (yours and your family's), resources (yes, this costs money), and a willingness to roll up your emotional sleeves and do some hard work together. Naturally, not every family is willing or able to make this type of commitment.

[1]Ernesto is a fictional character.

Designate Time to Set Goals

Until Ernesto closed his office door one day and started to think seriously about what his goals were for his family, and why he was concerned about their lack of communication, he didn't have any clear sense of direction. After asking his wife to join him for a working lunch to discuss some simple questions about her goals and concerns about their children, he realized he had absolutely no idea what others in the family were thinking. It turned out their daughter was angry with him because their newfound wealth had affected her relationship with some of her friends. He'd been aware something had changed with his daughter, but he assumed it was just teenage hormones. This was more serious than he thought.

Seek Outside Advice and Support

Wealth creators are typically resourceful people who overestimate their ability to fix a family problem. There is also a natural reluctance to reveal family troubles to outsiders. If a family leader does trust someone enough to share an intimate family struggle, it's usually a long-time advisor. Your current team of advisors can be a useful resource, but they're rarely the solution to poor family communication. If your family communication needs work, identify the right professional to assist. These advisors come from a variety of backgrounds, but typically have some combination of training in communication, coaching, facilitation, therapy, or mediation.

Working with a neutral third party helps level the playing field in the family, so all members feel they have a voice at the table. Difficult issues can be unearthed in a sensitive way, as a family advisor can be a confidential sounding board for each family member. A good advisor will also incorporate education into the process, so your family will learn new skills together.

Engage Your Children in the Planning

Although Ernesto struggled to talk meaningfully with those closest to him, he'd always been good at seeking input and ideas from his employees. Therefore, he readily agreed when the two family facilitators he met with suggested involving as many family members as possible in the decision about whom to hire. This changed the conversation from yet another project Dad wanted his children to work on, to a process the whole family was part of. The children also had a chance to connect with each advisor to determine the right chemistry.

This collaborative approach continued throughout the process. What Ernesto found was that by engaging his wife and children in the planning stages as his "partners," they became more open to what he was proposing and were more willing to accept decisions he or the family made collectively.

Obviously, he didn't agree with everything his children suggested, but they were able to include some of their key priorities: no meetings at home; a third party to teach better communication skills; the next generation must be able to speak their minds without Dad criticizing them so much. The last one Ernesto struggled with, but he did his best.

Put Structure Around It

Once a family contracts with a family advisor to improve their communication, the patriarch or matriarch often struggles with how to define success. Business people are accustomed to tangible, measurable results. How can progress be measured?

Ernesto's family identified a specific time horizon of 18 months, with a series of individual and group meetings. All family members participated in setting project milestones, so they could measure their progress. These included:

- A commitment that family members will raise issues with each other when they arise so they can be dealt with immediately. This avoids stockpiling complaints that could lead to more significant arguments.
- Ernesto will spend time one-on-one with each of his children every month, to strengthen their relationship and open the lines of communication.
- Family meetings will be held every other month, with a goal of each child chairing the meeting on a rotating basis. This will help to build leadership skills, and get the family into a routine of regular communication.

Ernesto was struck by how much of what they were doing was simply common sense. He realized that without the accountability structure provided by the process and the family's advisor, it would have been very difficult for them to make progress on their own.

Work and Play

How do you keep family members engaged, especially when the going gets tough? Improving communication, especially when there are difficult issues to address, can be hard work. Families do best when they find a good balance between work and play. Going off-site can help set the right tone, whether you meet in a local boardroom or find a weekend retreat you travel to. Find educational topics that interest different family members to ensure everyone gets something out of the process.

Balance your "working" time with fun activities you can enjoy together. Ernesto and his family rekindled their love of the outdoors by choosing locations where they could hike together after meetings were completed. This was something they did when the children were younger but had lost touch with as the family grew up. Their collective passion helped energize the experience, and tip the balance from something they *had* to do to an event they all *looked forward* to.

Build Community

Affluence, although it has many benefits, can often feel isolating. This applies to the business owner or founder, his/her spouse and the next generation. As a family embarks on the road to better communication, it's important to connect with peers and mentors who have been in your shoes. Ernesto rebuilt relationships that had fallen away during the busy years of growing his business, and he learned valuable insights about how to get past family roadblocks. Through Ernesto's YPO (Young Presidents' Organization) network, his wife put together a forum-style group of spouses who had been through the sale of a business.

Ernesto and his wife encouraged their children to attend programs at leading universities designed specifically for next-generation wealth inheritors, as well as leadership development workshops. These venues gave their children confidence, enhanced communication skills, and gave them a newfound awareness that they weren't the only ones struggling with family issues. Ultimately, each family member developed a peer group they could consult with, and that inspired them.

Be Brave

Nothing good comes easily. As you open the lines of communication in your family, you may find yourself challenged in ways you haven't experienced before. Your family needs you to lead through the tough times, just as you did with your employees, suppliers, and customers in turbulent times. Take stock of your own leadership strengths and find ways to apply them here.

One of Ernesto's strengths in business was a knack for understanding when his company needed different expertise. When Ernesto's family became comfortable enough with the communication process to share some long-standing frustrations with him, he was devastated. His wife and children explained they had been hurt by his abrupt communication style, and found him a distant husband and father because of his frequent business trips. Ernesto worked with the family's advisor to set up an additional support structure for him. Although he couldn't have imagined it a few weeks prior, he began working on a weekly basis with a therapist who specialized in family conflict. Ernesto also encouraged other family members to seek similar support. Between their individual work and the family sessions with their advisor, they worked through the pain they had all experienced and built a stronger foundation for their relationships.

Families are complicated. Wealth adds an additional layer of complexity that can cripple a family without the proper communication skills. Like so many things in life, you get out what you put in, and communication is no different. The families who invest time, money, effort, and their love for each other will receive dividends for generations to come.

Questions for Further Consideration

1. How have I contributed to poor communication in our family?
2. Am I willing to improve our family communication, knowing it will be emotionally exhausting?
3. Wouldn't it be better to let my children deal with their relationships and communication issues after I'm gone?

Additional Resources

For videos on family communication: *Business Families Foundation* (https://www.businessfamilies.org).

For an article library: *The Family Business Consulting Group* (https://www.thefbcg.com).

David Lansky and Kent Rhodes, *Managing Conflict in the Family Business: Understanding Challenges at the Intersection of Family and Business* (New York: Palgrave Macmillan, 2013).

Craig Aronoff and John Ward, *Family Meetings: How to Build a Stronger Family and a Stronger Business* (New York: Palgrave Macmillan, 1992).

Biography

Jennifer East grew up in an entrepreneurial family in Canada. She is the founder of ONIDA Family Advisors Inc., a firm focused exclusively on family business and family offices since 2006. As a trained executive coach and family business facilitator, Jennifer specializes in continuity planning, governance policies and structures, family team building and communication, succession and next-generation leadership development. She has consulted to family owned or controlled enterprises in Canada, the United States, and the Middle East. Jennifer is a fellow of the Family Firm Institute, and holds the FFI GEN Advanced Certificate in Family Business Advising (ACFBA). She is a frequent speaker at family enterprise conferences and a faculty member of the Family Firm Institute's Global Education Network.

CHAPTER 30

What Are Practical Tools for Building Healthy Families?

Christian Stewart[1]

If your family is going to succeed over time, it needs to make itself into a learning organization. But what should you learn and how will you learn together?

As an individual with significant financial capital, you are in a special, advantaged situation. You can deploy financial capital to help grow your family human, intellectual, social, and spiritual capital. If you have not been doing this to date, you and your family can start a learning journey together of figuring out how to invest financial capital to grow the other forms of capital. Improving trust and communication and helping family members acquire related skills is a critical part of this investment, and a key topic for family learning and development. This chapter summarizes specific skills, practices, and resources that can be included in your learning and development curriculum.

Work on Yourself

There are two perspectives to consider as you read this chapter. The first is your individual perspective.

What can you do as an individual to improve the way you communicate, and to become more adept at working with trust? The best lever for change within a family is to change the one person you can control – yourself. As a family leader, if you put a focus on your change efforts, you will also provide a role model for everyone.

[1]The assistance of Mary K. Duke, Hartley Goldstone, and James E. Hughes Jr. is gratefully acknowledged.

What would best support you in your own learning and development efforts? Options include reading, enrolling in external learning programs, engaging a communication coach or a counselor who can teach you (and your spouse/partner) new skills and provide ongoing support on your interactions with others.

Family Leadership

The second perspective is the family perspective. You should start to think of your family as a learning organization requiring its own leadership, administrative support and learning curriculum.

What leadership will be required? Often a critical element of success is a family champion, a family member who is passionate and committed to raising the skill levels of the family, and if applicable, seeing family relationships healed.

What support will the family need? Individuals with wealth typically have an advisory team that can help with technical and quantitative issues. Who on your advisory team will provide professional advice on qualitative issues? You can also consider a chief learning officer inside your family office who has responsibility for all aspects of learning and development.

How can your family learn new skills? Options include a family book club; hiring external coaches, counselors and/or trainers to teach new concepts and skills; or providing funding for family members to seek personal or couples coaching or counseling or to attend externally run programs.

Curriculum

The following curriculum differentiates between individual and family learning; however, this is not a hard and fast division. A key to delivering family learning and development, both individual and family, will be family meetings (discussed in other essays in this book).

Curriculum Part A: Individual Skills

Learning Forgiveness Are you holding onto grievances toward your family members? Are you holding onto any grievances toward persons outside your family? If so, are there reasons that stop you from considering forgiveness as one of your options?

Holding onto a grievance ties up emotional energy. Forgiving frees up that energy by improving relationships. Forgiveness is a practical tool to improve relationships, trust, and communication. Where there has been a breach of trust, forgiveness is the way to repair that breach.

According to Dr. Fred Luskin in *Forgive for Good,*[2] forgiveness is a learnable skill. Many people fail to forgive simply because they have not learned the right

---

[2]*Forgive for Good, A Proven Prescription for Health and Happiness* (New York: HarperCollins, 2002).

skills. A second obstacle is that people do not understand that forgiveness is for oneself; it is to provide peace of mind, health, and well-being. Forgiveness is not the same as condoning or reconciling. You can forgive a person without them knowing.

Using Positive Emotion to Change Perspective When was the last time you experienced a positive emotion? What were you doing? How long did the positive experience last? Can you replicate that positive emotion? Do you know what kinds of activities bring you a positive emotional experience?

Positive emotion expands our perspective from "me to we," making us more open, flexible, and creative. Bringing positive emotion into our life, being mindful of it, being able to prolong the effect, helps us to flourish. Shifting our perspective from "me to we," to be more open to other family members, is a key part of improving family communication.

Barbara Fredrickson's book *Positivity*[3] summarizes specific strategies for reducing gratuitous negative emotions and increasing positive emotions. One effective practice is to keep a gratitude journal, to list everything you are grateful for every couple of days. Another powerful practice is doing a Loving Kindness Meditation (LKM) on a regular basis.

Regularly practicing gratitude journaling and/or LKM literally rewires your brain. These are practices that you can do yourself, as part of working on yourself that can have a positive impact on your relationships. However, Fredrickson explains, bringing more positive emotion into your own life is like moving a river. It is possible to change the river's course, but it takes sustained long-term effort.

Gratitude exercises and LKM can bring a more open and flexible mindset into family meetings making the atmosphere more positive.

Working with Strengths Do you know what your strengths are? Do you know activities that allow you to experience a state of flow (where we feel and perform our best)?

Martin Seligman in *Authentic Happiness*[4] writes about the importance of identifying your top five character strengths (or signature strengths) using the Values in Action (VIA) Character Strengths Assessment.[5] The assessment helps you identify which of the 24 character strengths are your signature strengths.

Engaging your signature strengths is another way to bring positive emotion into your life. According to Seligman, identifying and engaging our signature

[3]Barbara L. Fredrickson, *Positivity, Top-Notch Research Reveals the Upward Spiral That Will Change Your Life* (New York: Random House, 2009).

[4]Martin Seligman, *Authentic Happiness: Using the New Positive Psychology to Realize Your Potential for Lasting Fulfilment* (New York: Simon & Schuster, 2002).

[5]You can take the assessment at https://www.viacharacter.org/www/Character-Strengths-Survey.

strengths leads to an *engaged* life; engaging them in service of something greater than ourselves leads to a *meaningful* life. Although character strengths are about individual flourishing, engaging them will contribute to family flourishing.

Once you are familiar with your signature strengths, the next question to work on is whether you can recognize strengths in other family members.

A powerful exercise for a family meeting is the Your Partner's Strengths Exercise,[6] which is conducted by pairs intentionally reflecting on and giving feedback to their partner about their strengths. *What would it be like if, in your family, recognition and affirmation of each other's strengths became the norm?*

Investing in Your Relationships Can you recollect a time when one of your family members shared news with you of a positive experience? How did you respond? Was your response typical of you?

Research has shown that a key element of satisfying relationships is how we react to positive events in the other person's life. The way a person responds to good news is classified based on two aspects, whether the response is active or passive, and whether it is constructive or destructive.[7] This means there are four basic ways of responding: active-constructive, active-destructive, passive-constructive, and passive-destructive. Of these four ways of responding, only one – active-constructive responding (ACR) – builds relationships. ACR means responding in a way that amplifies the positive news being shared with you.

ACR is a skill that you can learn. It can also be taught as a skill at your family meetings. For more on ACR see *Flourish*, by Martin Seligman.[8]

The book *Family Trusts, a Guide for Beneficiaries, Trustees, Trust Protectors and Trust Creators*[9] discusses how to use Character Strengths[10] and ACR[11] to create a positive relationship between trustees and beneficiaries.

Curriculum Part B: Family Skills

Where Is Your Family Today? When you think about your family and all its relationships, what is the overall trend? Is the trend toward growth or entropy (gradual decline), fission (conflict), or fusion (synergy)?

As a family leader, you need to think about the big picture and consider the direction of your family system.

---

[6]Seligman, *Authentic Happiness*, pp. 198 and 199.

[7]Margarita Tarragona, *Positive Identities: Narrative Practices and Positive Psychology* (Milwaukee, OR: Positive Acorn, 2015), who in turn quotes the work of Dr. Shelly Gable and team.

[8]Published by Free Press, 2011, pp. 48–51.

[9]Hartley Goldstone, James E. Hughes Jr., and Keith Whitaker (Hoboken, NJ: Wiley, 2016).

[10]Ibid., pp. 121–122.

[11]Ibid., pp. 119–120.

The following exercise is taken from *Family, The Compact Among Generations* by James E. Hughes Jr.[12]

- On a white board draw a large circle. Write the names of each of your key family members spaced equally around the perimeter.
- Draw a line connecting each person to every other person.
- Label each relationship as trending toward entropy, fission, or fusion.
- Stand back and look at the whole.

What is the overall trend you can see in the system of family relationships? This is your starting point as a family.

Next, consider: *What would be one small change within the system that would have the biggest positive impact on the whole system?*

When you look at yourself and your relationships, which should you be working on to help improve the whole?

Family Stories When you think about your family's past, what kind of narrative do you have? Is it:

- A descending narrative, e.g. "in the past we were a special family in some way, but then we lost it."
- An ascending narrative, e.g. "look at where we are today when you compare to where we came from."
- An oscillating narrative, e.g. "we have had times when we were up and times when we were down, but we always managed to make it through the hard times"?

The healthiest family narrative is the oscillating narrative, because it does not sugarcoat the past and it teaches resilience through examples of overcoming hardship.[13] *Another question to think about is whether the story of any of your relatives or ancestors is a story from which you can draw strength.*

Sharing family stories of the past, going back as far as you can, is a powerful source of family connection and bonding. Including time for family storytelling should be an ongoing element of your family meetings.

A Thinking Environment How good are you at helping other people think for themselves, especially members of your own family? If someone comes to you with an issue, do you give them attention, do you hear them out, are you curious to see where their thinking will take them?

---

[12]New York: Bloomberg Press, 2007.

[13]Bruce Feiler, "The Stories that Bind Us." *New York Times*, March 17, 2013.

According to Nancy Kline in *Time to Think,*[14] the quality of the attention that you give a person determines the quality of another's thinking. "The most important factor in whether or not a person can think well for themselves is how they are being treated by the people with them."

The environment a person is in also affects their thinking. Your family meetings can be designed using Kline's Ten Components of a Thinking Environment. Kline's recommendations include:

- When someone has a turn to speak, no one is allowed to interrupt.
- Remind everyone to keep their eyes on the speaker and let their faces communicate respect for the speaker.
- It is okay to think out loud. You do not have to complete your thinking before you talk.
- Treat every person as your thinking equal.
- Give each person encouragement to do their very best thinking.
- Listeners should not compete with the thinker.
- Relax. Don't rush. Put the thinker at ease.

Kline's books also offer a process for conducting a Thinking Session in pairs (a "Thinking Partnership"). According to Kline, even with excellent attention thinkers can face blocks to their thinking. These blocks, called limiting assumptions, are beliefs that the thinker is unaware of that seem like the truth to the thinker. Kline's thinking-environment and thinking-partnerships processes include incisive questions designed to remove limiting assumptions.

Difficult Conversations In a family enterprise, there will always be conflicts and difficult conversations. The book *Difficult Conversations, How to Discuss What Matters Most*[15] offers a process for preparing for and conducting difficult conversations, including worksheets. It teaches how to move from a "battle of messages" to a "learning conversation."

In any difficult conversation, there are always three underlying conversations going on:

- *The "what happened" conversation.* Each party will have their own story of events; each party will have made a contribution; you need to separate intentions (you can never know what their intentions really were) from the impact of what happened.
- *The "feelings" conversation.* There are always feelings present in such conversations and these need to be brought into your awareness; and

---

[14] *Time to Think, Listening to Ignite the Human Mind* (London: Ward Lock Cassell Illustrated, 1999).

[15] Douglas Stone, Bruce Patton, and Sheila Heen (New York: Penguin Books, 1999).

- *The "identity" conversation.* It is very easy to be knocked off balance if your identity is challenged during a conversation. The key is to reflect in advance on how the conversation might impact on your identity so you can remain grounded.

The process includes thinking through and choosing your purpose in planning to have a difficult conversation, in choosing whether to raise the issue or not.

The Trust Matrix You also want your family to become adept with the topic of trust. Include the elements of trust, how to build trust, and what to do when trust has been broken, in the curriculum.

Is there anyone in your family that you would say you don't trust?

To say that you don't trust a person is a very broad statement. It is important to be able to narrow down what you mean when you think you don't trust someone. A useful practical tool for being more precise is the Trust Matrix.[16]

Trust Matrix				
(Name)	Individual	Team	Family	Company
Honesty				
Intentions				
Skills and abilities				
Communication				

The Trust Matrix shows the need to be specific about both the different elements of trust and the context that you are referring to.

"Honesty" refers to being truthful. "Intentions" refer to whether the other person has their own interests at heart or the interests of others. "Skills and Abilities" means they have the skills and abilities to do their job or function effectively in the relevant group they are in. "Communication" means they tell you what you need to know when you need to know it. Your family can learn about the Trust Matrix together and use it to skillfully provide each other with constructive feedback.

The focus of this chapter has been on the family as a learning organization, intentionally investing in developing the trust and communication skills of its members. Families with shared ownership of financial capital are more complex than other families. Conflicts are an inherent part of such a complex system. Intentionally working to increase trust and to communicate more effectively

[16]Joseph Astrachan and Kristi McMillan, *Conflict and Communication in the Family Business*, Family Business Leadership Series No. 16 (Marietta, GA: Family Enterprise Publishers).

is critical to ensure sustainability. In addition, the curriculum outlined in this chapter can also represent an investment by the family in enhancing family human and intellectual capital, teaching individual family members valuable life skills.

Questions for Further Reflection

1. What does your family think about the curriculum?
   - What else could be added?
   - What do you already have?
   - How might you measure signs of progress?
2. Who in your family would make a good champion to implement the curriculum? Should there be a family committee?
3. What kind of professional support might help you and your family work through the curriculum?
4. What if you created a small study group of peers who are committed and interested in the curriculum that you share your learning experiences with?
5. What is the easiest part of the curriculum for you to put into action? What would be the first small step that you could take to get started?

Additional Resources

Ian A. Marsh, *If It Is So Good to Talk, Why Is It So Hard? Rediscovering the Power of Communication* (Leicester, UK: Troubador Publishing, 2018).

Andrew Bernstein, *The Myth of Stress: Where Stress Really Comes From and How to Live a Happier and Healthier Life* (New York: Simon & Schuster, 2015).

Fred Luskin, *Forgive for Good: A Proven Prescription for Health and Happiness* (New York: HarperOne, 2002).

Barbara L. Fredrickson, *Positivity: Top-Notch Research Reveals the Upward Spiral That Will Change Your Life* (New York: Three Rivers Press, 2009).

Martin Seligman, *Authentic Happiness: Using the New Positive Psychology to Realize Your Potential for Lasting Fulfilment* (New York: Simon & Schuster), 2002.

Hartley Goldstone, James E. Hughes Jr., and Keith Whitaker, *Family Trusts: A Guide for Beneficiaries, Trustees, Trust Protectors and Trust Creators* (Hoboken, NJ: Wiley, 2016).

Nancy Kline, *Time to Think: Listening to Ignite the Human Mind* (London: Cassell & Co., 1999).

Douglas Stone, Bruce Patton, and Sheila Heen, *Difficult Conversations: How to Discuss What Matters Most* (New York: Penguin Books, 1999).

Biography

Christian Stewart is the managing director of the Hong Kong-based process consulting firm Family Legacy Asia (HK) Limited. He is also an associate of the Boston-based think tank and consultancy Wise Counsel Research Associates. He consults to significant enterprising families and family offices around family governance. Christian received the award for leading individual (advisor) at the WealthBriefingAsia 2017 Awards, Singapore.

CHAPTER 31

What Is the Point of Family Enterprise Governance?

Katherine Grady and Ivan Lansberg

If you are asking this question it is likely that you are a first-generation founder wondering why you would want to bother with a "real" board or a family council. You are probably asking, "Why complicate things? Why involve people unnecessarily in decisions that are beyond their expertise? Doesn't everyone understand that the main thing is to continue growing and developing the business?"

Or you may be a second-generation sibling partnership and just beginning to see that you might need some more meetings to cope with issues that the first generation did not need to debate, such things as: how do we work together as a sibling team? How do we deal with owners who do not work in the business? And, how do we plan our estates so that the business is protected? As a second-generation family business, you begin to understand that the business, ownership, and family issues are intertwined in a way that is going to get very complicated, but often these issues are still not as compelling as the immediate needs of the business. Why have any more meetings than are absolutely necessary? Why involve others? Doesn't everyone understand that we need to focus on managing the transition from our parents while running the business and making sure we have money for some dividends?

But unless you are going to prune back the ownership of the business and return to a model that concentrates ownership in a single owner (or in a very small group of owners), you have a growing group of stakeholders that want, expect, and need a voice regarding the family enterprise. The question now becomes: How much voice should they have, in what decisions, and where do these decisions get made? Family members working in the business will expect a say in major business decisions, though, of course, a family member who is a mid-level manager should not expect to have the same voice as his or her CEO cousin. Family shareholders not working in the business may expect to be able to influence business and ownership decisions, but they are not necessarily in a position to understand all the factors that are involved in these decisions. As family shareholders begin to understand how the family business decisions affect their and their children's finances, careers, and family relationships, their voices get louder over time. It is then that business, ownership, and family issues can erupt into heated and rather chaotic discussions resulting in ineffective decisions and complicated personal reactions. Sometimes such discussions create scars that last years.

This is when you need an effective family governance system with the purpose of appropriately channeling the voice and involvement of all the stakeholders into decision-making forums that demarcate their legitimate spheres of influence. In thinking about how best to organize their involvement, it can be helpful for family business owners to imagine that the company they own is a large jetliner. As with any investment, the shareholders have a very legitimate right to expect a certain level of return, define an overall risk–reward ratio, to require that the plane be used in accordance to their fundamental values, and to insist that pilots flying the plane be competent. Even though they own the plane, owners do not have a right to enter the cockpit and fly the plane themselves – unless of course they are competent, licensed pilots, selected to do so. In the first generation, the owners are almost always the pilots and there is no need to separate out the issues into separate decision-making forums. As the enterprise moves into later generations, however, it is the time to decouple governance and management roles. Yes, you can still have owners in the cockpit if they are qualified and there is room, but other owners should be directed into governing entities where owners both can, and should, be involved.

The place to start as you transition to more complex forms of ownership is the development of a board of directors that goes beyond the rubber-stamp version typical of the founding generation stage, and the creation of a family owners council that goes beyond the kitchen-table discussions typical of first- and second-generation businesses. It is helpful to develop both of these in tandem, so that you can begin to triage questions and concerns to the right group. Over time, you can consider other governance structures such as a family or shareholders assembly for all family members, a career committee for family members entering the business, and a family management team for those working in the business. Depending on how your enterprise develops, you may want to consider other structures such as a family foundation, a family office or a private trust company. These additional governing bodies usually link into the council and the board, which continue to serve as the pillars of the evolving governance structure.

The Board ...

Serves at the discretion of the shareholders, to oversee the performance of management in leading the company toward the goals identified by the shareholders.

Reviews and approves the strategic plan.

Provides oversight of the performance of the CEO and senior management.

Monitors financial performance and reporting.

Approves the compensation of top executives.

Sets the dividends and oversees redemption plan.

Manages the board committees.

The Council ...

Serves at the discretion of the family shareholders as a whole, to manage activities that provide continuity in family values.

Gives guidance to the family directors about the family's interest in policies of the enterprise.

Provides information to the board and management regarding the family's perspective and concerns.

Helps to maintain family unity and harmony.

Develops and educates family owners.

Advises on selection of family directors for the board.

Assists in planning family shareholder assemblies.

The board needs to become the forum for overseeing the growth and performance of the business, and its members are those who address the fundamental strategic issues facing the company. Management proposes the strategy, but it is the board's role to test the underlying assumptions and ensure that management has thought it through. Once the strategy is duly vetted and approved, the board oversees the effective implementation and holds management accountable. Boards usually develop over time to match the needs of the business and the family owners, often moving from the pro forma, on-paper board, to a board of family directors who are selected for their knowledge and experience, to an advisory board of family directors and independent directors, and ultimately to a fiduciary board with a majority of independent directors. Effective boards move to meeting four to six times a year and develop the professional structure of business review and strategic planning. Family directors, as elected or selected representatives, should bring the values and views of the family shareholders as a whole to the board meetings. This structure provides a way to have family shareholders have a voice in critical decisions such as growth aspirations, risk, debt, dividends and major acquisitions, without board members getting bogged down with family issues or family members dipping too far into the business. The board also serves to formalize oversight and accountability for the enterprise, which is always critical, but particularly when the CEO is a family member.

The family owners council becomes the forum for discussing ownership and family matters and guides the development of the family shareholder group. An effective council provides guidance to the board regarding ownership and family interests, as well as concerns, and manages activities that provide continuity in family values, identity, and education. A council might typically meet three or four times a year and take on such activities as periodic reviews with the chairman, discussions with family shareholders, resolution of family ownership concerns, development of ownership policies, educational events for family members, and assistance with the annual meetings.

These two fundamental governing bodies can be mapped onto the familiar three-circle model, which shows the interlocking stakeholder groups of business, owners, and family. The board of directors, which serves the shareholders, rightly belongs in the boundary between the ownership and business circles. The council, which serves the family and the shareholders, finds its place on the boundary of the owners and family circles. Later on, as the business grows and becomes even more formalized, it may be necessary to separate the family and the ownership forums by creating a family council to address the family's evolving needs and a formal shareholders' assembly to attend to the owners' concerns. See Figure 31.1.

The family enterprise is like a home with four separate rooms: strong family businesses need to separate decision-making into the owner, board, management, and family rooms (see the *Harvard Business Review* article by

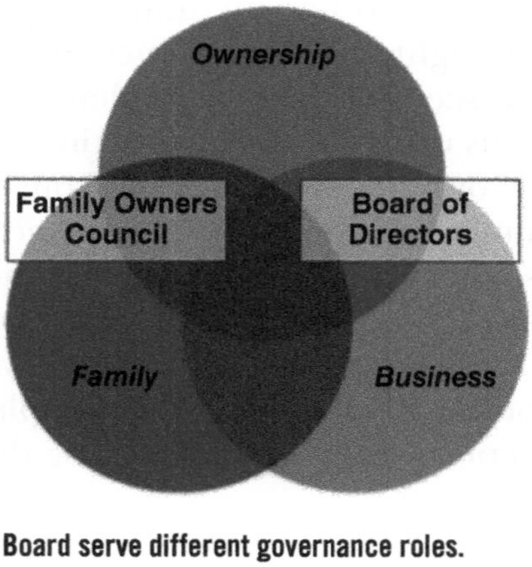

Figure 31.1 The Council and the Board serve different governance roles.

Josh Baron, Rob Lachenauer, and Sebastian Ehrensberger). Effective family businesses become skilled at directing the decisions to the appropriate rooms. These rooms are not just empty boxes – they must be filled with the right people, who can effectively make the decisions for that area of the enterprise. For many families, once the boxes are set up, it becomes easier to define the skill sets that are needed for each room and the selection process needed to select the right people. If done well, family owners understand that they have a legitimate voice regarding the family and ownership decisions, and a place to discuss these matters responsibly. And, business leaders, in turn, also have the appropriate forums to tackle the fundamental strategic, financial, and operational issues impacting the enterprise.

Designing Governance Structure . . .

Just like designing a new house for a growing family, designing the architecture of governance for a family enterprise calls for those in the leadership to ask themselves a number of fundamental questions:

On education. Does our family understand the need for governance? Do they understand the roles they will be called upon to play?

On values. What are our fundamental values? How can we best sustain these values in both the family and business?

On vision. Do we know what we want for the future of our family, our business and ourselves? Do we understand what the options for continuity are?

On structure. What forums will we need? What will be their purpose? And, how will they interrelate and communicate among each other to be most effective?

On process. How will these forums make decisions? How will we select, replenish, and retire the members of each forum?

On policies. What policies ought to guide the employment of family members or their service on the board? How do we manage conflicts of interests? What if an owner wants to sell their stake?

On leadership. What skills will our leaders need to manage our enterprise in the future? What processes do we have in place to attract, develop, select, motivate, and eventually retire our leaders? How will we manage succession in key roles?

How, when, and of whom these questions are asked matters tremendously. The key is to involve the current and – especially – future owners in a carefully designed and managed exploration of possibilities for the family and enterprise. In smaller families, the design process is often highly inclusive and participatory. In more complex ones, a design committee may need to be set up to shepherd the process forward while checking with key stakeholders along the way.

While the architecture of governance matters hugely, any governing structures need the right processes and people to make them work. The information sharing channel between the board and the family owners council is of particular importance, along with additional communication lines between any of the evolving governing bodies. Effective boards and councils find ways of letting all the stakeholders know what is being discussed and decided. For example, one highly successful enterprise sends out quarterly letters from the board and the council after every quarterly meeting letting shareholders know what was discussed in the quarterly meetings. These letters are complemented by reports and summaries in their annual meeting along with periodic phone calls and surveys with family shareholders. At the same company, the chairs of the board and the council meet regularly to coordinate their efforts and to ensure that the issues are being channeled appropriately to the right forums.

A founder might scratch his or her head at all these meetings and letters, but the siblings and the cousins who follow know that they are building a structure that will give them the best chance of succeeding for generations. The key is to keep in mind that, as ownership fragments with the passing of the generations, *someone* will be making decisions on all these fundamental issues. Your choice is not whether things will change or not with the passage of time – *they will.* Your *only* choice is whether you want to manage the transition to the future or not. Experience and a growing body of research show that if the design of governance is not attended to responsibly, the likelihood of continuity will be seriously compromised.

Questions for Further Reflection

1. What stage is your family business at now – founder, sibling partnership, or cousin consortium? Do you have the right governance structure for this stage?
2. How effective are your two core governing bodies: your board of directors and your family owners council? What needs to be done to make them more effective?

Additional Resources

Ivan Lansberg, *Succeeding Generations: Realizing the Dream of Families in Business* (Boston: Harvard Business Review Press, 1999).

Josh Baron, Rob Lachenauer, and Sebastian Ehrensberger, "Making Better Decisions in Your Family Business," *Harvard Business Review,* September 8, 2015.

Biographies

Katherine Grady, PhD is a partner at Lansberg, Gersick and Associates in New Haven, Connecticut. Formerly on the faculty at Yale University and the Center for Creative Leadership, she has been a family business consultant for over 25 years. A licensed psychologist, Katherine's expertise as both a family business advisor and an executive coach has allowed her to focus on individual and organizational development within different family and organizational contexts. She also lectures and publishes on continuity planning, leadership, career development, personality differences, team building, and family dynamics.

Ivan Lansberg, PhD is a senior partner at Lansberg, Gersick and Associates. He is also an adjunct professor of family enterprise and co-director of Family Enterprise Programs at Northwestern University's Kellogg School of Management. Prior to joining the faculty at Kellogg, Ivan was on the faculty at the Yale School of Management. He was one of the founders of the Family Firm Institute (FFI) and the first editor of its professional journal, the *Family Business Review.* His research and consulting work deals with governance, succession, and continuity in complex multi-generational family enterprises.

CHAPTER 32

Should You Have a Family Meeting?

Mary Duke

The most consequential regimen a family can adopt to build hope for a sustainable future together is a practice of convening regular family meetings. But how does one start such a practice?

Family meetings are the one habit every family should form – especially families with significant wealth. Why? Because families with wealth are caught between two very dramatic forces – one is complexity, and the other is change. Families are supremely complex systems to begin with. Add money, and powerful new forces of economic complexity come into play.

Likewise, change creates stresses on families. Some changes in families come predictably with the passage of time: marriages, divorces, births, deaths, economic successes and failures, to name a few. Today, families are also called on to navigate a new age of change, including a vastly expanding definition of family and the increasingly global spread of family members. These introduce new cultural dynamics to families and also challenge traditional concepts of togetherness.

All these forces of change are accelerating rapidly, leaving families unprepared for their implications. The cost of failing to address complexity and change can be exceptionally high for families of wealth and the ecosystems they influence.

Why Family Meetings?

Money has its own gravitational force, generating an inexorable pull on a family's attention to attend to it. Managing money is complex. There are many advisors seeking "air time" to discuss, review and plan for the money. And yet, the biggest challenge to sustaining wealth from generation to generation does not lie in managing the money; it lies in the space where a family's dynamics intersect with their wealth. The key factors cited as causing the failure of families to make successful wealth transitions are:

1. The lack of trust among family members.
2. The inability of family members to communicate effectively.
3. The failure to prepare the rising generation for their roles ahead.[1]

A simple antidote to these factors and the first step a family can take to empower its members to manage all this change and complexity is to meet regularly as a family to address the challenges they face. Families who are successful in sustaining their wealth across generations adopt a practice of family meetings.[2] Family meetings are neither glorified holiday dinners, nor are they typical business meetings that focus on all things financial. At their best, family meetings provide a place where the family does the vital work needed to address its total wealth – the human wealth as well as the financial. Family meetings are where the generations come together to touch on the intangible aspects of their wealth – express their dreams, grow their capacity and knowledge, share their concerns and explore common goals. It's where family members reframe troubling aspects of their pasts and form a collective vision for their future.

The Mechanics of a Family Meeting

What

Not all family meetings are the same. Some might have a very specific objective, such as a decision that needs to be made (to accept or reject an offer made for the family business), or information that needs to be communicated (reviewing the estate plan in the wake of a founder's death). But there is great value in holding regular meetings where there are no pressing issues and the family can focus on growing its human capital. In fact, there is no better time to start this practice than when the seas are calm. The trust, communication, and decision-making skills developed through regular meetings equip a family to navigate challenges and transitions as they arise.

Where

Location and duration are often driven by the purpose of the meeting. A meeting with a decision-making focus may be held over a few hours in a conference room. But the kind of family meeting that provides the rich forum for family bonding and growth is different. To get optimum benefit, the meeting should

[1]Roy Williams and Vic Preisser, *Preparing Heirs* (Bandon, OR: Robert D. Reed Publishers, 2010).

[2]Dennis Jaffe, *Resilience of 100-Year Family Enterprises* (Milton, MA: Wise Counsel Research, 2018).

be held in a neutral place with no ties to any family member. I have heard younger generations say they don't want to feel that they are being called to the elders' power base. So the company headquarters or a family home is generally not a good choice. Often family meetings are held at a destination resort, so a combination of more formal gatherings can be balanced with fun, team building activities, and leisure. Consider that family meetings often become part of a family's collective memory, and the location can take on special meaning. The room layout can help to disrupt the usual power dynamics that occur around a large boardroom table with a head position. A living room style – or soft seating arranged in a circle – helps set the scene for peer-to-peer engagement.

Who

What seems like a straightforward question about how many people to invite, the "who" question actually touches on an essential consideration for the family – namely, who is family. The answer to this will evolve as the family begins to consider the implications of exclusion. In-laws may be new members, but are they lesser members? Can the family see the benefits of taking a wide and inclusive approach? Can the skills, energies, and experiences of new members be leveraged for the benefit of the whole? Could it be beneficial for potentially marginalized members to be brought into the fold – both informed and heard?

The number of family members who participate in a family meeting often starts small and expands over time. Attendance at a first meeting might be limited to adult members of the nuclear family, with or without spouses. It is inevitable that participation will expand; and it is often very beneficial to broaden the scope of members invited to attend. Depending on the ages of family members, consider including children for a portion of the meeting, or conducting break-out sessions for groups with common interests or challenges. Depending on the content of the meeting, guests with expertise or knowledge may be invited to present during some or all of the meeting.

Facilitation

A Korean proverb holds that "even a monk cannot shave his own head." There are some things we cannot do for ourselves. A family is almost always well served to bring a facilitator in to help plan and manage the flow of their meetings. A masterful facilitator will create a forum where family members build trust, express their innermost desires and concerns, and increase their capacity to understand and navigate the complexity and change ahead. Facilitators work to balance the push to move through delicate conversations with the need to hold back and give full consideration to differing views. Helping the silent find their voices and containing or quieting those accustomed to commanding the floor is another important role facilitators play.

But the work a family does together cannot be delegated to a facilitator. Unlike hiring a lawyer or architect, where the professional is given an assignment and then goes away to create a work product, in family meetings, family members actually do the work. The facilitator helps maintain the safe harbor where that family work can take place, figuratively running alongside the family, with coaching and encouragement and shining a light on the path ahead. But the family must run the course and navigate the obstacles.

A good facilitator is an alchemist, helping to nurture family alignment, inspire learning, heal and reframe past hurts, and provide space for a flourishing future to emerge.

Costs

Embracing a practice of regular family meetings is expensive and involves significant time and preparation. If we accept the premise that these meetings provide the greatest opportunity for the family to grow its human capital and adopt practices that will ensure its members flourish as the family navigates complexity and change, I believe that there is no more important investment a family can make.

By way of comparison, when considering budgets for these meetings, it helps to take a look at the amounts the family pays for custody of its financial assets, or investment advice or legal fees. These professional services are focused exclusively on the financial capital of the family. Where in the budget is the family's investment in its human capital? Is that not at least equally as important as managing the money? In my experience, successful families create a source of funding for family togetherness (including meetings) in their budgets and their estate plans so that future generations will not have to grapple with whether they can afford to come together or who pays.[3]

Three Key Spheres of Activity in a Family Meeting

Communications

Family members often develop communications skills through their work together in family meetings. Among these skills are:

- Active listening, to really hear what others are saying, rather than to build a case in response.
- Being able to express feelings, motivations, and desired goals to help the family make better collective decisions.

---

[3]Family branches often grow at very different rates and there can be tensions between those with few offspring and those with many when it comes to funding this type of activity.

- Empathy – the ability to truly understand and share the feelings of others.
- Flexibility of both perspective and action.
- Patience and the ability to tolerate ambiguity.

Conflict occurs naturally in families, and yet may be suppressed because it is seen as impolite. Families can learn how to manage conflict, thereby opening opportunities to deepen understanding between members. A facilitator can play an important role in navigating conflict and sharing practices that can help the family manage its levels of conflict.

A family meeting also provides a forum for different generations to come together as peers. Such a meeting might be the first time family members engage as equals, stepping away from the traditional narratives of parent/child relationships. This is an important step in the evolution of a family toward learning and acting together – as peers.

Collaborative Decision-making

Significant wealth often involves collective decision-making. This is the natural effect of a wealth creator leaving a fortune to descendants who often hold this wealth collectively in trusts, foundations, holding and operating companies, and real estate. Suddenly a group of peers (e.g. siblings or cousins) find themselves in economic relationships with each other, with no role model or experience with collaborative decision-making. Family meetings are a powerful forum for learning and practicing the skills of collaboration: advocacy, compromise, problem solving, agreeing on goals, assuming responsibility, and managing conflict.

The skills and knowledge required for effective collaboration among family members take time and practice to master. These are life-long learning skills that are invaluable when navigating the complex problems families face.

Learning Together as a Family

In addition to learning a wide variety of technical skills, such as financial stewardship, the roles and responsibilities of beneficiaries, and understanding business strategy, some of the most powerful learning that can occur in a family meeting has to do with a journey of self-discovery.

Families often use meetings to explore each member's values and goals, as well as to gain understanding of personal perceptions and potential biases. Assessment tools are useful to provide insights into personality types, preferred learning and leadership styles, and to survey members on perspectives toward the family and its interactions.

Being equipped with a new understanding of what makes each member tick contributes to a family learning more effective ways of working together. Importantly, a family comes to embrace their differences as essential assets for effective collaboration.

Ground Rules

An important element of a family meeting is a set of ground rules. These are often codified by a family in their first meeting and then reviewed at the start of each meeting to help set the scene. These rules help differentiate a family meeting from any other family gathering, and they create a space for the important work ahead. Ground rules offer a framework for respectful interactions (not interrupting and eliminating distractions from technology), encourage teamwork, and provide guidance for managing communications and emotion.

Advanced Considerations

There are additional practices that successful families adopt as they advance in their work together. They formalize governance structures by creating bodies such as a family forum, a family council, and committees to address specific areas such as planning family meetings and opportunities for life-long learning. They may form committees that empower the rising generations, as well as committees made up of elders who are invited to provide wisdom and help resolve impasses. Some successful families memorialize their values, principles, and practices in writing, sometimes in the form of a formal family constitution. Family members may seek training in facilitation and family systems so that they can act more effectively. The possibilities are vast.

The Closing Case

There are so many ways a family can break – and it does not always start with high drama or an epic battle. Sometimes the quiet erosion of connections and the challenges of living far apart simply wear bonds away. These broken ties rob a family of the opportunity to discover the many ways that their members have evolved and grown and matured. Adopting a practice of family meetings helps sustain family connections and deepen relations – all of which give hope to the family for sustaining itself into the future.

Families with wealth know that money can buy many things, but it does not ensure a family will thrive. The challenges these families must navigate require them to grapple with the economic *and* emotional dimensions. This requires each member to invest time and intention into a process together. The place where this work can occur is in regular family meetings.

Examples of Ground Rules

One of the activities a family should undertake in its first family meeting is agreeing on a set of ground rules by which they will be governed. I highly encourage each family to start with a blank sheet of paper and really grapple with the important values they want to bring into their meeting space. Generally, by starting with the four primary categories – communications, managing self, interacting with others and leadership, and teamwork – participants will generally arrive organically at most of the following points. Here are some of my favorites:

Communication

- *Embrace constructive debate.* Encourage the exploration of all sides of an issue.
- *Over-communicate.* Do not assume others know what you think – or that you know what others are thinking.
- *Engage in real conversation.* Be specific and speak only for yourself.
- *Be kind.* Constrain public criticism, restrain private criticism.

Managing self

- *Be present.* Focused mentally and physically.
- *Be proactive.* Recognize problems and work toward solutions.
- *Be a team player.* No silos or finger pointing.
- *Be accountable,* be on time, do what you say, be available.
- *Be open to change.* Don't settle for "we have always done it like that."

Interacting with others

- Have good intentions toward all.
- Hold a common legacy or agreed goals as bond.
- Honor the confidentiality of discussions. Do not replay with non-participants.
- *Listen with respect* – especially to the quietest voices.

Leadership and Teamwork

- *Foster courageous conversations.* Feedback should be constructive and honest
- *Treat others with respect* – always!
- *Ensure equality.* No family member is more important than another.
- *Be open and honest.* No beating around the bush or hidden agendas.

Have fun!

Questions for Further Reflection

1. What are the predictable challenges that lie ahead for our family? Are we equipped to navigate them? What about the unpredictable challenges?
2. Could we productively build on our family's strengths and work together on shifting our weaknesses? If so, how?
3. Can our family be resilient in the face of setbacks – picking up and starting again with lessons learned in the process?

4. Does our family have a place where we are able to discuss our thoughts and concerns about how we will manage – openly and honestly – together?
5. What are our unexplored opportunities for individual growth and family flourishing? Is there anything hindering our growth and development?

Additional Resources

Craig E. Aronoff and John L. Ward, *Family Meetings – How to Build a Stronger Family and a Stronger Business* (New York: Palgrave Macmillan, 1992).

Jay Hughes, Susan Massenzio, and Keith Whitaker, "Family Meetings," Chapter 16 in *Complete Family Wealth* (New York: Bloomberg Press, 2018).

Biography

Mary Duke is an internationally recognized advisor to families navigating the complexities of substantial wealth. She is known for her expertise in generational transition in family businesses and the impact of trusts on families.

Mary's work is typically anchored in the facilitation of family meetings, mentoring of family members, and strategic planning for family owned businesses.

She focuses on empowering rising generations and helps families leverage governance to enhance their decision-making and collaboration. With a background in law, business and finance, and training in family systems and managing family conflict, she has an excellent track record helping families conceive and achieve positive outcomes.

CHAPTER 33

How Can You Best Manage Conflict in Your Family?

Blair Trippe

Everyone fights over the things that matter to them. When unrelated people fight, they can choose to walk away and completely sever their relationships. When family members fight, it's not that easy. It's more difficult to entirely cut ties, as family relationships often continue even if affinity does not. What's more, when family members fight, beyond the substantive issues at the core of their disagreement, they often are fighting over deeper, more personal concerns. They are also trying to figure out how they will continue as family in the future.

Given that conflict is likely unavoidable, how can you think through options to manage it well?

Defining Conflict in Families

First, it is important to distinguish conflict from dispute. Disputes are isolated disagreements that generally involve a limited number of people, can be traced to a specific time or event, and can often be logically articulated. As such, disputes can be negotiated or mediated and resolved.

Conflict, in contrast, is systemic, evolves over time, and can entangle many people either directly or tangentially. It typically involves a series of interconnected issues on which individuals disagree as their perceptions of the situation differ. For example, an argument over distribution of inheritance quickly expands to include in-laws, and becomes a challenge of values about wealth and property, beliefs about fairness, questions of love and loyalty, and opportunities to assert one's identity. Conflict cannot be "resolved"; it must be managed.

Conflict can be active (fighting) or passive (feeling stuck). Everyone knows how active conflict feels and sounds. Passive conflict, or the fear of conflict, can be just as damaging and more insidious. Fear of conflict causes people to avoid making decisions together, leaving families and their enterprises stuck. When families know that tensions and differences exist, rather than fighting they may simply avoid doing anything that could trigger active conflict. Although this may seem like everyone getting along, it can be just as damaging to families as active conflict.

The Causes of Conflict in Families

Differences always exist between individuals; any time individuals interact, they will be doing so in the context of those differences. Family members are interdependent with each other – some families more than others – increasing opportunities for individuals with different values and goals to interact. The larger and more connected the family is, the greater the complexity, which makes conflict management more challenging.

Add a family business or shared family wealth and property to this mix, and the level of interdependence skyrockets, adding further complexity. When families share assets, family members often juggle several roles at the same time, which not only makes it challenging for them to manage their own motivations and concerns but also those of their siblings, parents, and cousins. Conflict arises when those differences impact decision making. When this is not managed well, conflict can be easily triggered.

In any complex machine with many interconnected, moving parts, something can go wrong. A machine will break down or perform poorly when things go awry. In a family – especially an enterprising family – conflict indicates that something is going wrong. I am not implying any judgment when we say something is going "wrong." I am suggesting that something is happening in the system for which it is unprepared. Even in the most well-developed families with governance, constitutions and councils, unanticipated conflicts can occur.

Conflict is simply woven into the fabric of any highly interdependent system, and families – especially enterprising families – are no exception.

Sometimes affluent families are at a disadvantage when conflict strikes. When family members grow up with wealth, they may grow up with independence rather than interdependence. Siblings who never had to fight over use of the family car in their youth, for example, may not have had the invaluable experience of managing conflict together. In later life, they may find that they are more interdependent than they were when they were younger. They may be co-beneficiaries, employees of their family enterprise, or they may share ownership of real estate. Although independence in their youth helped them avoid conflict, it may also have kept them from building an important skill.

Managing Conflict in Families

The role of the peacemaker in a family is fraught. Despite best intentions and, often, great skill, every family member has a stake in the outcome of a conflict. This compromises their ability to be truly neutral and unbiased. Of course there are exceptions, but as a rule, it is very difficult to manage conflict when you are, or can be thought of by some as, one of the participants/part of the problem itself.

This does not mean that all conflicts require outside facilitation. Family members in conflict can educate themselves on dispute resolution techniques, communication practice, family-systems theory, and the substantive issues at play, and they can engage directly in negotiation and solution building. Although there are certainly benefits to having a trained, outside professional conflict manager, engaging directly in a thoughtful manner can be very effective.

Understanding what aspects of conflict respond to dispute resolution techniques such as negotiation, voting, or arbitration is crucial to avoid missteps in the conflict management process. Some aspects of a systemic conflict can be negotiated or mediated if, for example, a disagreement is unconnected to other issues and confined to a few people.

It is rare, however, that a family fight is a simple dispute. More likely, there are identity issues involving values, beliefs, personal experiences, and personalities at play. These are not negotiable issues and therefore don't respond to force or bargaining. You cannot negotiate with a person to be more risk tolerant or to like you more. You cannot vote to make someone believe an outcome is fair. When you try to do so, you will simply increase tension and likely make matters worse.

Development as a Conflict-Management Strategy

The best solution for family conflicts that transcend mere dispute and involve deeply held identity issues such as values, beliefs, and character, is what we call "development." This can be broken into two categories: structural and personal development. Structural development addresses issues related to the enterprise or family governance system such as clear role definitions, policies, and procedures. Personal development attends to the human capital in the equation. For example, educating family members about the substantive issues at play can expand potential solutions and soften positions that were taken without full understanding of the topic. Similarly, family members getting to know and value each other through shared experience increases empathy and improves communication. When you know your fellow family members well, and truly care about their welfare, compromise is easier to achieve.

Learning some of the various frameworks and methods that have been developed for both resolving dispute and managing systemic, identity-based conflict will provide additional help for families struggling in the trenches. An example of this is the Thomas Kilmann model (and the Baumoel-Trippe extension to it), which helps family members understand how the importance of an issue at hand as compared to the relationship with other stakeholders will impact their decision-making approach in any given situation. Similarly, unpacking a person's intent versus his or her impact in a charged encounter sheds light on what is going on, which provides perspective and helps all participants engage in a measured and thoughtful manner.

Engaging conflict-management professionals who are able to deconstruct the situation to attend to the true tensions can be transformative for a family and can turn a conflict into an opportunity for personal growth, improved family functioning, and even harmony.

Remember that conflict is normal, because it is built into the family enterprise system. Conflict tells you that the system you have built needs some work. Either something unexpected happened for which the system wasn't ready, or the system needs additional capability to support a family with expanding opportunity and complexity. Avoiding conflict gets families stuck in the same position until their relationships atrophy. How you and your family deal with conflict can make all the difference in how your relationships continue into the future.

Questions for Further Reflection

1. Is your family in the process of managing (or avoiding) a conflict that goes beyond a mere "dispute"?
2. When conflict strikes, how strong is your desire to remain committed to being family?
3. Do your family members have a high level of understanding and competence regarding the financial, legal, and social apparatus that connects them?
4. Do you have a shared identity as a connected family that matters – and how well do you know and accept one another as individuals?
5. Does your family have a process for achieving genuine forgiveness?
6. Have you reached the point at which change is necessary, but the road ahead is daunting?

Additional Resources

Doug Baumoel and Blair Trippe, *Deconstructing Conflict: Understanding Family Business, Shared Wealth, and Power* (St. Louis, MO: Continuity Media, 2016).

Roger Fisher, William Ury, and Bruce Patton, *Getting to Yes: Negotiating Agreement Without Giving In* (New York: Penguin Books, 1981).

Don Miguel Ruiz, *The Four Agreements: A Practical Guide to Personal Freedom* (San Rafael, CA: Amber-Allen Publishing, 1997).

Janis A. Spring, *How Can I Forgive You? The Courage to Forgive, the Freedom Not To* (New York: HarperCollins, 2004).

Douglas Stone, Bruce Patton, and Sheila Heen, *Difficult Conversations: How to Discuss What Matters Most* (New York: Penguin Books, 1999).

Biography

Blair Trippe is managing partner of Continuity Family Business Consulting, where she works with enterprising families on issues related to succession planning, governance development, and conflict management. An experienced negotiator, mediator, and family-business consultant, Blair's background includes executive posts on Wall Street and in other corporate settings.

Blair is a nationally recognized speaker and has presented at the Program on Negotiation at Harvard Law School, the NYU Schack Institute of Real Estate, Cornell University, the Family Firm Institute, American Bar Association, and Attorneys for Family Held Enterprises (AFHE), among others.

Blair co-authored the book *Deconstructing Conflict: Understanding Family Business, Shared Wealth and Power,* which helps families that share business and other assets become better decision-makers, negotiators, and communicators. She also co-authored the book *Mom Always Liked You Best: A Guide for Resolving Family Feuds, Inheritance Battles & Eldercare Crises.*

Blair earned an MBA from Northwestern's Kellogg School, a BA in psychology from Connecticut College, and certificates in negotiation and mediation from the Program on Negotiation at Harvard University. She serves on the boards of the Boston Symphony Orchestra, DeCordova Museum, and Attorneys for Family Held Enterprises.

CHAPTER 34

Should You Stay Together as a Family or Go Your Separate Ways?

Doug Baumoel

Should we manage our wealth, business, or philanthropy together as a family or go our separate ways? This is a question that is at the back of the minds of many members of families who share significant assets. Too rarely do they face it, until a conflict or crisis arises.

One key challenge with legacy assets is that the group that ends up sharing these assets with each other, unlike a non-family partnership, often did not purposefully chose to do so. They may have aligned goals, compatible values, and may even truly like each other. Or, they may not. This uncertainty increases the risks associated with sharing. The rewards, however, of being able to share assets and opportunity together as a connected family in a productive and purposeful way can be extraordinarily meaningful and impactful. It is this risk-versus-reward context that brings us to two key questions: "Does sharing assets enhance or detract from being family?" and "Are we still family without shared assets?" This section will explore these questions and provide a framework for evaluating the impact of family-ness on these questions.

Legacy can be positive, giving us a powerful sense of identity and of being a tribe, or it can be negative, interfering with our personal agendas and generating unwanted conflict. For families who share significant assets, the term "family" often brings with it certain expectations and responsibilities: expectations of behavior, attendance, and participation in events, compromise of individual interests for the sake of family, and a host of legal and fiduciary responsibilities. Families of true affinity find it easier to embrace these complications to help one another navigate through life together.

But when family devolves to being about obligation and frustration over differences, family members may begin to question if it is only their shared assets that make them family. The benefits of being a "100-year connected family"[1] may seem elusive or not important anymore.

A Pragmatic Test for Family Affinity

Evaluating your family's level of "family-ness" can provide useful insights to help you productively work with existing differences, or to determine if it could be more beneficial to separate. We call this "family-ness" the family factor, and you can begin to examine it by asking:

> *Is our family bond strong enough to leverage compromise, forgiveness, and commitment to change?*

This question describes the key elements required for family members to manage conflict. If they can manage conflict well, they have more choices available to them to figure out how to be family together and how to successfully share and manage important assets together.

The framework of the family factor lets families gauge their family glue. When that glue is strong, families can derive great benefit from navigating the challenges of shared wealth together; the shared journey can become an opportunity for growth and enrichment. When the glue is weak, clashing over shared assets and competing interests without resolution can erode connections, or worse, and it can interfere with what remains of the vision of family. Understanding the family factor gives clarity to discussions about what boundaries and bridges need to be built for the shared family enterprise to succeed.

Exploring Your Family Factor

In order to better understand the family factor, break it down into three key components:

- Shared history
- Shared vision
- Trust

Shared History: Does Your Family Have a Distinct and Meaningful Shared History?

Shared history does not necessarily mean a positive history – it simply means shared experience. Even when families argue, disagree, and take sides against one another, shared history can be strong. When families value their traditions and stories, take pride in their shared lineage, communicate with or see

---

[1]Intergenerational families who sustain shared family values and identity, along with partnership over successful financial ventures, over three or more generations.

each other regularly, shared experience trumps harmony. Even if that shared experience was lived separately from each other – such as a shared experience of ethnicity or family reputation that each has dealt with in a meaningful way – that forms the basis of a family bond.

If your family has a meaningful shared history, you all will have something to *lose* if you disband and cease to identify as a family group. Some family members may need reminders of that shared history and its meaning. Sometimes the shared history is co-mingled with negative experiences and emotions. But even negative experiences can provide valuable lessons and build connections. When your family can construct a shared narrative that provides meaning and value – even out of difficulty – you can build on shared history, which can lead to finding "family" within.

Shared Vision: Does Your Family Have a Shared Vision of Being Family in the Future?

Do family members see value in identifying as family in the future? Will holding shared family events be something they choose to do? Or, when the patriarch or matriarch passes, will the sense of family-ness quickly dissolve? If your family sees value in defining itself as a connected family in the future, and in maintaining connectedness and shared experience through subsequent generations, then family members have something to *gain* by compromising, forgiving, or learning/changing to secure that future. The challenging work of sharing assets can play a role in strengthening these relationships. This vision of future connectedness is a powerful motivation for working things out and overcoming differences to make decisions together.

When anger, incompatible values, and conflict damage relationships, it's sometimes difficult to see value in maintaining a family bond. When family members or branches of the family have significantly different interests and values, exacerbated by disagreements and distance, it can be easy to assume that splitting up the assets, and their associated family ties, is the logical next step. Reframing the question to the broader or generational question of family vision can often help families to see beyond current relationship challenges and determine whether their family factor is strong enough to benefit from sharing assets or whether separating assets actually protects their vision of family for the future.

Trust: Do Your Family Members Know Each Other Well?

Erik Erikson, in his work on life stages, defined trust as predictability. An infant passes the first developmental stage when he or she figures out that the world is predictable – that when he cries, he gets picked up and comforted. This sense of predictability is the key component of trust that factors into our evaluation of whether a family can benefit from defining as family either with or without the added complexity of shared assets.

Families can create difficult environments – especially when there are shared assets, shared decision-making, and power hierarchies. Interests and values collide and often set individuals against each other. But, rather than defining trust as we commonly do – as aligned interests or affinity (i.e. I like you, you like me, we want the same things, so I trust you) – consider trust as Erikson did – as predictability. In this context, if I know you are competitive and will relentlessly pursue your goals, I know that even if you "love" me, you will do what you can to "win." If I know you want something in opposition to what I want, I can "trust" that you will pursue your interest. In addition, if we both know how our system of engagement works, (i.e. we are financially literate and understand the companies, industries, and legal documents that connect us) we can predict how we each might pursue our goals.

When family members know each other well and know how things work in the family, including how shared assets are structured, family members won't be surprised or suspicious of each other's behavior. When you can each anticipate how others will behave in their own decision-making efforts, this enables each of you to make decisions for the greater good of the group, beyond your individual self-interest. Although predictability may enable compromise and selflessness, it does not ensure it.

When family members don't know each other well and don't have insight into each other's values, interests, and concerns, then this type of trust (i.e. predictability) breaks down. Having different interests, values, and concerns is not the enemy of trust. Not knowing someone well is the enemy of trust, because they seem unpredictable. Additionally, when family members understand how the systems that connect them work – when they are financially literate, knowledgeable about the family enterprise, understand the agreements and trusts that connect family, and understand how things get done among members of their group, trust is increased because predictability is increased.

When Splitting Up Makes Sense

Family meetings, family retreats, family websites, and newsletters can serve to build the shared history and trust components of the family factor. Sharing stories and experiences, getting to know each other well, and building trust help define families and improve family functioning. Families that choose to stay connected, whether or not they continue to share assets, can benefit from activities and structures that build their family factor. However, when assets are shared, building a strong family factor can be the best investment of time and resources for reducing risk.

Sometimes a break is unavoidable. The family factor framework can provide some clarity regarding the reasons for a split. It can also define a process for measured approach to the question of a split. Laying out a time frame for trying to build the components of the family factor can offer a family an objective process that either results in a split for clear reason or rebuilds a family's ability to compromise, change, and forgive so they can reclaim their legacy together with renewed purpose.

Families consider separating interests for a variety of very legitimate reasons:

1. You do not feel affinity for the others and want little or nothing to do with them.
2. You may feel affinity for the others but do not like the way they manage shared assets and/or you have a different risk tolerance or values regarding investment targets.
3. You simply want more autonomy or control for yourself or your family branch.

Sharing assets with a low family factor increases the investment risk for all. Building the family factor reduces risk and can be its own reward. Knowing your family factor, however, is essential for understanding and managing risk in sharing assets among family.

Splitting shared family assets can be extraordinarily difficult. Exiting shareholders are often forced to take discounted payouts over time at significant loss of value. The no-confidence vote this sends to other family members may exacerbate family rifts in addition to the financial break. And, often, not all family members within an exiting branch agree with their majority, sometimes causing fractures within the exiting branch or group.

Separating Efficiently

When a split is necessary, consider that some family members (possibly all) may want to maintain family relationships with those with whom they are parting ways financially.[2] Seek to create a shared narrative for the economic split that supports continuing family relationships among future generations.

Splitting some of the assets may be a matter of negotiation, supported by creative thinking and the advice of valuation experts and attorneys skilled in trusts, real estate, and corporate law. When businesses are involved, spinning out real estate from operations and using insurance to provide liquidity for shareholder exits may provide options. Exploring options for splitting or decanting trusts can add to these options for separation.

Some assets may carry with them significant emotional attachment or family identity and may be more difficult to split. Consider if these assets might be jointly retained – perhaps through more formal family or corporate governance. If this is untenable, be aware that separating such assets is not a simple

[2]See "Beyond the Thomas-Kilmann Model: Into Extreme Conflict" in *Negotiation Journal.*

negotiation of value. When identity and emotion are involved *and* when continued family connection is valued, separating these assets will take more time and patience. This is especially true when family members are employed in an executive capacity that may be threatened by a split, because one's professional identity is a difficult thing to negotiate.

Questions for Further Reflection

1. Imagine your family in 10 years. What does it look like? How does that vision feel? Now imagine a different picture, with your family more narrowly defined. How does that change your life in 10 years?
2. To what lengths are you willing to go to keep your extended family connected? Are you willing to forgive? Learn? Compromise?
3. How has shared wealth contributed to differences and conflict among family members?
4. Do you think that a positive shared narrative can be crafted from a significant family conflict your family has experienced?
5. Consider trust from the perspective of predictability. Think of three things you can do to be more predictable to others, to improve your ability to predict the behaviors of others, and to better understand the system in which you are connected.
6. Think of three things you can do to build your family's family factor.

Additional Resources

Doug Baumoel and Blair Trippe, *Deconstructing Conflict: Understanding Family Business, Shared Wealth, and Power* (St. Louis, MO: Continuity Media), 2016.

James Grubman, PhD, *Strangers in Paradise* (Boston: Family Wealth Consulting, 2013).

James E. Hughes, Jr., *Family: The Compact Among Generations* (New York: Bloomberg Press, 2007).

Blair Trippe and Doug Baumoel, "Beyond the Thomas-Kilmann Model: Into Extreme Conflict," *Negotiation Journal* 31, no. 2 (April 2015).

Dennis Jaffe, PhD, "Succeeding Against All Odds: Lessons Learned from 100-Year Business Families," dennisjaffe.com, 2017.

Biography

Doug Baumoel is the founder of Continuity Family Business Consulting. He has applied more than 25 years of business experience to developing a process for analyzing key variables of conflict in family enterprise. He co-authored, with Continuity Managing Partner Blair Trippe, *Deconstructing Conflict: Understanding Family Business, Shared Wealth and Power.*

Doug has presented at the Program on Negotiation at Harvard Law School, Cornell University's Smith Family Business Initiative, National Association of Corporate Directors (NACD), the Family Firm Institute (FFI), American Bar Association, Attorneys for Family-Held Enterprises, and the International Academy of Collaborative Professionals (IACP), among others.

Doug earned an MBA from the Wharton School at the University of Pennsylvania, and a BS in Electrical Engineering from Cornell University. He has been awarded Fellow status with FFI, the NACD and is a practitioner scholar for Cornell Smith Family Business Initiative. He holds a certificate in Civil Mediation from Massachusetts Continuing Legal Education and is a graduate of the Director Professionalism program of NACD. Doug also served as president of the New England chapter of the Family Firm Institute.

SECTION 6

COMBINING FAMILY AND BUSINESS

In a unique study of families that have managed, against the odds, to preserve a major family enterprise into or beyond at least the third generation of family control, Wise Counsel Research found that 77% of the families in the study continue to own or manage operating businesses together – on average 114 years after the founding of the original enterprise! By itself, this result suggests that the presence of an operating business – with its sense of identity, commitment, collaboration, and impact – may play a large part in long-term family success.[1]

Of course, combining family and business is also fraught with financial, managerial, and emotional pitfalls. There are strong forces against family business continuity. The essays in this section take on those challenges and offer ways to increase the probability of continuing an operating family enterprise.

No family enterprise lasts unless future generations want it to continue. So every enterprise must find ways to engage the rising generation, ways that Dennis Jaffe takes up in the first essay in this section. He particularly focuses on increasing connection, transparency, capability, and commitment. Because the use of family meetings is so crucial to family businesses, he also emphasizes some of the best practices around designing and holding effective family meetings.

The next two essays then consider the question of how to turn engaged rising generation family members into leaders in the family enterprise. Greg McCann considers the different types of leadership needed in different situations, and then offers a model of "vertical leadership" development that focuses on potential family leaders' ability to be aware of themselves, empathize, effectively frame issues, and inspire others to create change. Dean Fowler then offers seven habits that families and their members can engage in to ensure that their successors succeed, not just in business but in life: all the way from achieving

[1]See Dennis Jaffe, *Resilience of 100-Year Family Enterprises* (Milton, MA: Wise Counsel Research, 2018).

psychological and financial independence to committing their own funds to the family enterprise.

The next two essays in this section step back to consider the relation between family unity and family business. Andrew Hier and John Davis frame the issue by highlighting the dangers of disunity and then offering specific practices for building family unity, ranging from organizational changes to changes in ownership of shared assets. Josh Baron and Rob Lachenauer then describe specific warning signs to look for that indicate that you may be losing control of your family business; many of these problems arise merely from habit or a mistaken sense of efficiency, making it all the more important to watch out for them.

Finally, Alex Scott, a descendant of the founder of the Provincial Insurance Company (UK), considers the crucial question, "Can a family stay together after the operating business is sold?" His answer is a resounding, "Yes" – but of course that result does not come about without considerable intentionality and effort. He describes some of the practices that worked for his family, concluding with the importance of cultivating an attitude of stewardship and the desire to be valuable citizens. With this conclusion, he takes us full-circle to some of the first essays in this book, hinting that family success may depend not only on commitment to shared business (which involves doing good for customers and workers) but also and perhaps most importantly on citizenship, a sense of contribution to the nations that provide our families a home.

CHAPTER 35

How Can You Engage Your Children in the Management of Your Family Wealth or Business?

Dennis Jaffe

After building a successful business, founders often shift to concern about passing it on to their "rising" generation heirs. How will the family wealth affect them? Will it derail them from becoming productive and fulfilled individuals, creating their own families and their own success? Since the wealth creators generally did not grow up with such family wealth, they often fear the worst, perhaps with a twinge of envy for their children's good fortune.

Their concerns usually focus on how to prepare their children for wealth. They ask:

- How much should I give them, and when?
- How can I prevent them from feeling entitled and unproductive?
- When should I tell them about how much wealth we have?

These questions do not have answers, but if they did, the answers would not help you with the core problem – how to use your family resources that you have so proudly acquired in wise and useful ways? These are questions of values that must be explored, rather than technical queries that a professional can answer for a family.

To deal with these concerns, you must first look at the assumptions you are making about your children. You may *assume* that, as parents, wealth distribution is something you can and should decide, and, if you created the wealth, you may conclude that it is *your* money to give. But you should consider how these assumptions will affect your children. Your children, growing up in the world of wealth, might be shocked to learn that the family wealth is separate from them. The potential for miscommunication about what is fair and reasonable is significant.

Another issue is who actually makes these decisions. It is perfectly appropriate for parents to make decisions for young children, but as they reach adulthood, when do you stop acting unilaterally and start exploring possibilities and choices with them? You might then reconsider some of your assumptions and consider that the future of the family's wealth and resources, which your children have now grown up with, is a shared dilemma for everyone to consider. That is not to say that everyone has an equal vote, but nevertheless, everyone should have some input.

As a family advisor, when a parent asks me these questions about "How much?" and "When?," my first response is, "What do your children have to say about all this?" What sort of discussions has the family had together and what have you already said or hinted at? Some families have never talked about any of these things! As a result, these parents have no idea what their children know, expect, or assume about the family wealth. Parents' anxiety about listening to their children leads them to avoid the conversation entirely. Such parents are in for some surprises when they begin to open this for discussion.

Although the parents fear the worst – that their children expect to inherit enough wealth so that they don't have to do anything – they may find that their children are also concerned about the future and have responsible and thoughtful ideas about what they want and what would be helpful to them. Your children can be partners in the inquiry, rather than passive spectators about things that affect their future choices and opportunities.

Paul Schervish, who has been researching the effects of wealth on families for many years (and who has an essay in this collection), defines the dilemma this way:

> Especially for the entrepreneurially wealthy – but for those with family wealth as well – the quandary is how to teach their children the responsibilities of wealth while also providing for their needs. Having gone through hard times, they do not want their children to face the same insecurities ... they furnish a life of affluence for their children while at the same time attempting to instill frugality, humility, and responsibility ... the problem is that once he chose an affluent neighborhood in which to live, his children automatically became exposed to an environment that threatens to make them materialistic.

Wisdom of 100-Year Families of Wealth

Over the past five years I have been interviewing "generative" families around the world who have sustained family wealth or a family enterprise across more than three generations.[1] One major finding is that these families have made a

[1] Wise Counsel Research has published several working papers based on this research. They include "Good Fortune" (2014), "Releasing the Potential of the Rising Generation" (2016), "Governing the Family Enterprise" (2017), and "Resilience of 100-Year Families" (2018).

clear decision that in order to develop a successful rising generation, they have to *invest* family resources not just in sustaining their financial wealth, but in developing the skills and capability of each new generation. It is too important; they can't leave it to chance. All these families have some form of regular family meetings, and actively engage members of the new generation, from early in their lives, in discussions of expectations, values, and responsibilities for what is important to the family.

Members of each generation may have different assumptions about what is fair and reasonable about the future of family wealth, but each generation may also fear upsetting or challenging the other, leading to a state of mutual avoidance. In many cases, the younger generation has grown up with family wealth. They are concerned with what they can expect for the future and how to discover and pursue their life paths. They often live in the shadow of highly successful and famous parents and wonder what they can do that is significant. Their parents, who have humble roots and often struggled, do not really understand their children's concerns. How can this communication gap be bridged?

Different family members grow up with strong and deeply held notions of what would be fair and reasonable. These views are held and often do not surface until someone does something that goes against their sense of fairness. The generative families in our study, in contrast, found ways to define for each generation what they feel is fair about family resources. The family defines, sometimes when children are very young, rules and policies about fairness that the rising generation are expected to live by. The two generations then trust each other because they know what they can expect and depend upon from each other.

From the example of families that have succeeded in passing their wealth along with responsibility to their children for two generations or more, we learned that "generative" families worked together to develop and prepare their new generations in four ways, as shown in Figure 35.1.

Connection

They set regular times to engage their children about the challenges of the future. These meetings and discussions often begin when children are very young. These families set aside times for discussions about what it means to be a family with significant wealth and resources. The elders share the hopes, dreams, values, and principles they expect, but they were also willing to listen to the concerns, ideas, and needs of their children. Each generation learns to listen to the other and learns that family policies and practices are to be developed together.

Transparency

They were transparent in sharing the nature of the family business and family wealth, teaching their children about what they did. They talked about their

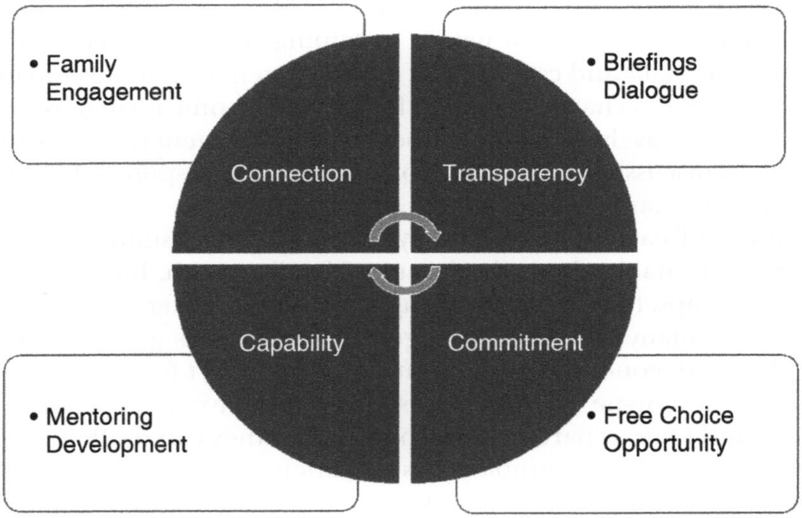

Figure 35.1 Preparing the Next Generation

business (in appropriate detail for the ages of their children) and what was needed for the future. They fostered an atmosphere of openness. Family "enterprises," even if they are a family investment office or a family foundation, are talked about, visited, and explained to the rising generation. Questions are entertained, and family members are able, even expected, to be familiar with what the family does.

Capability

They offered resources for their children to be mentored and develop financial and business skills, no matter what they wanted to do with their lives. They realized that having significant wealth meant that their children had to have skills to oversee and manage what they would inherit and encouraged them to seek help and develop themselves. They want all their children, and their new spouses, to be informed and responsible for sustaining the family resources. To be responsible, however, means that family members must learn financial stewardship skills that other young people do not. They offered opportunities for family members to learn about family enterprise and meet and learn from other families. They have formal and informal educational and learning opportunities for young family members to learn together.

Commitment

They offered their children the choice to become involved in family enterprises in many ways. Although a small number of rising generation family members might become operational leaders of family enterprises, all of the next generation could expect to share ownership and there were many ways that they could become involved in supporting the family. They realize that roles in the family enterprise are not all or nothing, nor are they one-time choices. A family member can pursue a professional career, or be an artist, and still participate in family governance or board roles. Ownership is a responsibility, not an entitlement, and they educate and develop family members to become active in overseeing the family enterprises.

Convening a Family Meeting to Initiate Family Engagement

How does a family get started along this path? What if you have not taken the initiative to open the discussion, but your children want to talk and realize how important this is? Our research found that in many families, the initiative came from the younger generation themselves, who initiated communication with their parents about expectations. They say to their parents, who may be avoiding it, "We need to talk." Of course, they bring this topic up with sensitivity and respect. In other families, advisors introduce cross-generational communication, and they help them set up the initial family meeting.

Families hear about family councils and governance documents like a family constitution. At the most basic level, the engagement of the rising generation often begins with a cross-generational family meeting about family wealth and the future. A single successful meeting can lead the family to decide that they should meet regularly, maybe twice a year. These regular meetings form an embryonic family council. Whether you meet regularly as your children grow up or begin when the rising generation is reaching adulthood and is concerned about the future, engagement begins when the family sets up a family meeting.

A family meeting is not just a regular family dinner or a Sunday visit. A family meeting is an organized discussion about a difficult topic. It is never easy for a family to talk about money. So the family meeting has to respect that this is not an ordinary conversation. A good family conversation across generations must feel comfortable and safe for everyone to speak up and be honest with each other.

Good Family Meetings Have Several Elements

Shared Agreement to Hold a Family Meeting

To hold a meeting, you need agreement from the elders of the family, who may be anxious or concerned, and dealing with their concerns by making them comfortable. You must decide what you will talk about and who should be invited. For example, would it be just blood family or include spouses; how old does a family member have to be to attend; what is expected of people who attend?

Design the Meeting and Create Clear Expectations for Everyone

The most important part of a family meeting is how you set it up and plan it. A small group (two or three people) representing each generation should be the planners. They should reach out to talk with family members about what they want, and then define a theme or big task, and craft an *agenda* so people know the purpose and what will be discussed. Sometimes it is agreed beforehand that there will be no decisions made in the meeting, so people can feel comfortable exploring ideas and being there as learners.

There may be discussion about who to invite – in-laws, and children of a certain age. Select a time and place where people can come and talk freely. The agenda should be written and given to everyone before the meeting. *(If your family is large or there are a lot of difficult issues that might come up, you might want to work with an outside facilitator.)*

Create a Safe Environment with Clear Ground Rules for Participation

A safe environment is one in which individuals feel *comfortable* being authentic, open, and taking risks to bring up conflicting or controversial perspectives. This is usually a place outside the homes and office.

The convener invites participation and openness to others' perspectives as well as his or her own perspectives, feelings, and reactions. In moving toward a safe environment, recognize that willingness to openly participate will increase as others believe that they will be supported for such behavior, rather than criticized, ridiculed, or otherwise censured. Safety is needed for people to build trust and meet.

At the start of a meeting, the group should define how they need to act to create a safe space for everyone to participate. Typical ground rules include:

- Listen respectfully: don't interrupt.
- Focus on issues, not people or personalities.
- Leave titles outside the door: address each other as peers.
- Share feedback with consideration and kindness: avoid attacks.
- Use "I" statements, not "You" statements (for example, "I feel irritated and hurt when people interrupt me" rather than "You are being so nasty, interrupting me all the time").

Take Notes and Follow-up

The meeting is important for the family, and what was said should be remembered. It is important to keep notes. Notes can be made on flipcharts in the front of the room, so that people can keep track of ideas. After the meeting, the notes from the charts can be transcribed. If decisions are made or agreements are made, they should be carefully written down.

A list of action steps and who is responsible for them is also needed. *This reinforces this is an ongoing process, and that the meeting has impact.* Send notes and make sure action steps are carried out. Also plan for the next meeting and keep the process moving forward.

There are many steps along the path to create engagement across generations. Setting up dialogue across generations is an essential part of that path, and a first step to other activities that ensure that both generations are working together for a wonderful future for the family.

Questions for Further Reflection

1. What are some of the reasons a family avoids talking directly to members of the next generation about the future?
2. How can you create a positive motivation for family members to attend and participate in a family meeting?
3. What does each generation offer the other generation, and what does each generation want from the other? How can the family learn about these areas?

Additional Resources

James Grubman, *Strangers in Paradise* (Boston: Family Wealth Consulting, 2013).

Dennis Jaffe, *Releasing the Potential of the Rising Generation: How Long-Lasting Family Enterprises Prepare Their Successors* (Milton, MA: Wise Counsel Research, 2016).

Dennis Jaffe, *Stewardship in Your Family Enterprise: Developing Responsible Family Leadership Across Generations* (Maui, HI: Pioneer Imprints, 2010).

Biography

Dr. Dennis Jaffe, a San Francisco-based advisor to families about family business, governance, wealth, and philanthropy, recently completed the working papers published by Wise Counsel Research, based on his current research with global multi-generational family enterprises, including "Governing the Family Enterprise: Evolution of Family Councils, Assemblies and Constitutions," "Releasing the Potential of the Rising Generation," and "Good Fortune: Building a Hundred Year Family Enterprise."

Dennis is author (or co-author) of *Cross Cultures: How Global Families Negotiate Change Across Generations*; *Stewardship in your Family Enterprise: Developing Responsible Family Leadership Across Generations*; and *Working with the Ones You Love*, as well as management books *Rekindling Commitment, Getting Your Organization to Change* and *Take this Work and Love It.* His global insights have led to teaching or consulting engagements in Asia, Europe, the Middle East, and Latin America. The Family Firm Institute recently awarded him the 2017 International Award for service, and in 2005 he received the Beckhard Award for service to the field. He has a BA degree in philosophy, an MA in management, and a PhD in sociology, all from Yale University, and he is professor emeritus of organizational systems and psychology at Saybrook University in San Francisco.

CHAPTER 36

How Can Your Family Develop Leaders Ready to Face the Many Challenges of Business and Family?

Greg McCann

The world is more challenging and complex than it has ever been, and this trend will only continue to increase. Nowhere is this truer than in the inherent complexity of a family enterprise. Given this turbulence, how do we develop leaders who have the agility and the capacity to help our families survive and thrive in this new normal?

What Is the New Normal?

Many people use the term, VUCA (Volatile, Uncertain, Complex, and Ambiguous) to describe this world. My one concern with this description is that it may imply that this is a temporary phase and that we will return to normal. I don't believe that will ever happen.

In 2011, a landmark study (*From Longevity of Firms to Transgenerational Entrepreneurship of Families: Introducing Family Entrepreneurial Orientation,* or the FFI-Goodman study) looked at how family businesses are changing. This research studied second-generation (and older) family businesses across the United States and across industries: The average respondent owned more than three businesses (20% owned five or more!) and had changed their core business more than *two times.* The study concluded that the key wealth creation vehicle is not the firm but the *family.*

The question that this insight poses is this: In the face of constant changes in business and in family, how can you make your family a strong and resilient force for continued growth?

How Do We Develop Leaders with the Agility and Capacity for this World?

A crucial part of the answer lies in developing family leadership. Families need leaders with great capacity, including:

- *A broad perspective.* The ability to create both a strategy and a culture.
- *Agility.* The ability to shift approaches relative to the circumstance (e.g. command and control, coaching, or teamwork).
- *Resilience.* The ability to be flexible, adaptable, and manage stress.

Everything tells us that all the players in the world – such as government, NGOs, businesses, educational institutions – need to build a greater capacity for being effective, being more resilient, and looking more holistically at how they define success. (See *Thank You for Being Late: An Optimist's Guide to Thriving in the Age of Accelerations* by Thomas L. Friedman for an excellent book addressing this situation.) Nowhere is that more important and true than in a family enterprise, where there are two different systems (business and family) with often seemingly conflicting cultures. Experience and research bears this out: *when done well*, the family involvement is a strategic advantage.

Vertical Leadership Development and Character

How can you develop this more capable leadership in your family? The number one trend in leadership development today is vertical leadership development. Whereas *horizontal* leadership development focuses on putting more *in the container* (e.g. skills, knowledge, and credentials), *vertical* leadership development is about developing capacity, or *transforming the container* (or transforming the leaders themselves). The term *horizontal* relates to expanding the leader's resume, whereas *vertical* relates to elevating the perspective and capacities. Think of vertical development a bit like Russian nesting dolls, in the sense that each stage of development includes the capacities of the previous stage. The two practices are intertwined, but until recently little work has been done to focus specifically on the vertical development to increase the capacity.

Capacity can be increased through developing the four areas of:

1. Greater self-awareness.
2. Deeper empathy.
3. More effective framing of issues.
4. Ability to lead others to create value from change (i.e. innovate).

I would also add the notion of character to this work. The simplest definition of character I know of is how you would act when you believed no one was watching or if there are no consequences. It is the other side of the coin from competence of a leader. Character involves asking yourself, as a leader, if your behavior is creating a reputation that aligns with how you perceive (and want to perceive) your character. This reflection can be expanded to your entire family and its collective character, especially the character of its leaders. Character offers a powerful way to talk about the culture of your family. To paraphrase a leadership guru: the capacity of a family cannot evolve beyond the capacity (and character) of its leaders.

For your family, vertical leadership development can provide the opportunity to take advantage of your values-based decision-making, long-term relationships, and investment in the whole person to:

- Develop greater capacity in leaders, as people.
- Help family members move from a perspective of me, to we, to them.
- Be a leader who is willing and able to let go of their current role (which is vital because everything is changing more rapidly and the older generation is staying involved longer).
- Develop each family member's character to align with their intended reputation. To help shape not only the strategy but also the culture of the family to be an advantage to all of its enterprises.

How can you develop such capacities in your family leaders or potential leaders? One way is to think of stages of leadership development, such as the stages offered in the Leadership Agility model developed by Bill Joiner and William Josephs, which distinguishes six stages of leadership development (as outlined by the authors: Pre-Expert [~10%], Expert [~45%], Achiever [~35%], Catalyst [~5%], Co-Creator [~4%] and Synergist [~1%]). Of the leaders that they studied in developing their model, approximately 85% have three of the stages as their home base (i.e. where they tend to be most of the time). These stages are Expert, Achiever, and Catalyst. Since these are the most common starting points, I will focus on these stages to convey an idea of how your family members could broaden their perspectives, increase their agility, and increase their resilience by working from these stages. These stages are progressive (i.e. you have to go through them) and inclusive (i.e. you retain the capacities of the earlier stage(s) as you progress).

Expert

The Expert focuses on "me." Experts tend to have a narrower perspective; their identity is very linked to their knowledge and it is important that they be right about their areas of expertise. Thus, they tend to see issues as problems and they are the person best qualified to solve the problem. A leader at this stage is apt to just have the four agilities emerging (of self-awareness, empathy, framing, and innovation), view pivotal conversations as a contest of right and wrong, and view teams more as the leader telling individuals what to do (i.e. a spoke and wheel model). Organizational change is incremental and overall efficiency (i.e. incremental improvement to the existing system) can be valued at the cost of effectiveness.

For example, imagine Lily, the head of a family enterprise, being asked by phone by her sibling if she could hire her niece. If it is a problem for her to solve, she might decide on the call. Very efficient: problem solved in one call.

Achiever

The Achiever focuses on "we." Here, one can step back from the problem and look at the overall system and see if a systemic or strategic solution is called for. If Lily is an Achiever, she might well say, "There are several siblings and cousins to take into consideration; perhaps we need a more systematic approach. Let's have us, the siblings, craft a Family Employment Policy." This approach is less efficient – it can't be completed on the phone call with one sibling, but it may prove to be far more effective. At this level, there is a greater need for buy-in for the leader's strategy and accordingly the leader must further develop the four agilities self-awareness, empathy, framing, and innovation. Conversations are more balanced between advocacy and accommodation, others' perspectives are seen as legitimate (i.e. shades of grey versus black and white), and teams are more empowered. Being effective is now important – not merely being efficient. Organizational change is apt to follow the best practices in the industry or field.

Catalyst

The Catalyst shifts the focus to "they." The leader is no longer attached, no longer has their identity linked to being the "hero" or the person in charge. They can play that role, but they don't *have* to. Their four agilities are integrating closer to the present moment. Going back to our call with Lily, she might say, "We have several cousins interested in the family enterprise and now that they are old enough, let's frame this to have them engage with us as young professionals (as opposed to compliant family members). In other words, let's work on the culture of the family." As the leadership guru, Peter Drucker famously said, "culture eats strategy for breakfast."

In line with this last point, ask yourself, "Who is responsible for the culture in our family?" If your answer is "everyone" or "no one," you may want to think more deeply about this point.

In summary, this offers some proven ways to develop as a leader "vertically." Additionally, top leaders tend to have a daily workout regimen, a daily reflective or meditative practice, and a creative practice outside of work.

How to Cultivate Highly Conscious Leadership

1. Consistently immerse yourself in complex environments (interpersonal, work, educational).
2. Consciously engage in life's problems (e.g. inquiry, deep dialogue).
3. Become increasingly aware of and consistently explore your inner states.
4. Hold a strong desire and commitment to grow.
5. Be open and willing to construct a new frame of reference when difficulties arise.
6. Cultivate a personality, which is open and agreeable (interpersonally warm).
7. Consistently engage in dialogue and interaction with others committed to self-development.
8. Cultivate an open-minded personality that seeks novelty, is experimental, questions the status quo, and explores the unconventional.

Source: Barrett C. Brown, "The Future of Leadership for Conscious Capitalism," MetaIntegral Associates, 2015.

Conclusion

Our world is changing and is going to demand great capacity from us all, in particular families that are connected through the enterprises they are engaged in. To help us adapt and thrive in this new world, we are going to need new models, mindsets, and leaders with an ever-increasing capacity that aligns character, culture, and purpose. As the family becomes the system of greater focus, the anchor of the values, and often the author of the family enterprise's purpose, the need for developing the capacity of the family becomes essential and no longer a casual option.[1]

Questions for Further Reflection

1. Who are the leaders in your family? How would you describe their style(s) of leadership?
2. What elements of vertical leadership has your family developed? Which ones require further development?
3. What is one step your family can take today to begin developing more agile leaders?

Additional Resources

Greg McCann, *Who Do You Think You Are? Aligning Your Character and Reputation* (North Charleston, SC: CreateSpace, 2012).

Greg McCann, *When Your Parents Sign the Paychecks: Finding Success Inside or Outside the Family Enterprise,* 2nd ed. (North Charleston, SC: CreateSpace, 2013).

[1]The author would like to thank Jill Shipley and Audra Jolliffe for their help with this essay.

Biography

Greg McCann is the founder, principal, and leader of McCann & Associates, a national family-enterprise consulting firm that creates workshops, consults, publishes, and generally innovates on issues of importance to family enterprises, with a focus on vertical leadership development. Greg has coached leaders and executives for nearly 20 years and is certified in Leadership Agility and Myers-Briggs Type Indicator.

Greg collaborates with families to help them with transitions, leadership development, and communication. He helps cultivate the commitment to family, the greater trust, values-based decision-making, and longer-term thinking that are vital strengths in well-run family enterprises.

He is also the founder of the Family Enterprise Center at Stetson University, where he led the effort to develop the first undergraduate major in Family Enterprise. Greg wrote *When Your Parents Sign the Paychecks,* which is a part of the Family Enterprise curriculum at Stetson University, and *Who Do You Think You Are? Aligning Your Character and Reputation.*

CHAPTER 37

How Can You Ensure the Success of Your Successors?

Dean Fowler

How can a mentor help to ensure the success of a family business successor? One effective way is by encouraging successors to emulate behavior that fosters continuity of the business from one generation to the next. In consulting with numerous family businesses over the past 35 years, I have identified seven habits of highly successful successors (with apologies to Stephen R. Covey, author of *The 7 Habits of Highly Effective People*). Good mentors promote these best practices and guide their protégés in adopting them.

These seven habits encompass the three distinct roles of successors in family businesses: family membership, company management, and business ownership. The first two – establishing independence and reshaping communication dynamics – nurture healthy family relationships and typically develop during the protégé's 20s. The next three – demonstrating competency, participating in strategic decisions, and clarifying boundaries – provide the framework for management responsibilities and growth during the protégé's 30s. Finally, by developing liquidity strategies and assuming financial risk, successors are transformed from passive shareholders into proactive participants in ownership of the business. This final stage of mastery typically occurs during the protégé's late 30s and 40s.

Establishing Independence

The first habit – establishing adult independence – serves as the foundation for the other six by transforming the relationship between the two generations. Mentors should encourage their protégés to establish their own adult lives, separate from and independent of their family and its business. In many cases, this means working outside the family firm. Outside experience helps a young adult to gain technical competency and business experience. More important, this experience helps next-generation members to overcome emotional dependence on their parents and to prove to themselves that they can function independently of their parents' financial resources.

As an alternative to working outside the family business, mentors can help their protégés to identify key projects over which the protégé may exert leadership. Taking charge of a project enables young people to succeed in their own independent efforts. For example, one successor identified an opportunity to provide additional services to customers of the family business. Under the tutelage of the chief financial officer, she developed a formal business plan that outlined the financial viability of her business proposal. Using family venture capital, this successor started a separate business. As president of this venture, she had full authority and responsibility for future success.

Reshaping Family Communication

It's the successor's responsibility to reshape communication dynamics within the family and to break the patterns of childhood. Two skills are critical to achieving this new pattern of interaction. The first is the ability to avoid what's known as triangulation. This unhealthy communication pattern often occurs when conflict, anger, resentment, or frustration has built up between two people. To alleviate this build-up, one of the people "downloads" the negative feelings by sharing them with a third person instead of discussing the conflict directly with the other party. For example, if a daughter disagrees with a decision made by her father, she might complain about the situation to her mother, although the issue would be best resolved if she raised the issue with her father.

Non-family employees and managers are often caught in the dangerous pull of triangulation. Rather than be drawn into this scenario, a mentor can impart a valuable lesson by refusing to participate as a triangulated party. Instead, the mentor should encourage the two people in conflict to address their issues in an open and straightforward manner.

The second communication skill is active (or empathic) listening. The power of this skill rests in the listener's ability to really understand the perspective of another person. Family members must recognize that everyone needs assurance that he or she has been understood. Mentors must master active listening in order to really understand the needs of their protégés. For example, one daughter was frustrated because she felt that her father didn't really listen to her. Her mentor, the vice president of human resources, helped her to develop her own listening skills. Building on the communication principles the VP taught her, she created a code – A or O – and presented it to her father. When she wanted his acceptance, she told him the conversation was an A; when she wanted his opinion, she told him it was an O. With the help of her mentor, she took the responsibility to reshape communication dynamics with her entrepreneurial father.

Demonstrating Competency

The third habit to teach your protégé concerns competency. This habit has two dimensions: technical competency in some area of the business and demonstrated leadership capability.

Training and development programs for successors are often designed to give them limited exposure to several different aspects of a company. Although this broad-based exposure is helpful, it doesn't enable the successor to develop any detailed technical expertise. More significantly, the successor isn't given the opportunity to develop as a leader by managing direct reports.

To become competent, successors should assume long-term responsibilities that require leadership. Initially, this may involve the responsibility of overseeing a significant project and heading the project team. As experience grows and develops, successors should take on departmental leadership roles or divisional responsibilities, where profit and loss results may be measured and evaluated. In one family firm, the vice president of operations was asked to develop a comprehensive training program for the family successor. The president of the company considered mentoring to be an important part of the VP's responsibilities. These duties became part of the VP's primary goals and objectives and were measured as part of his annual performance review. Working closely with his protégé, the VP developed a four-year program that culminated in the protégé's ascent to management responsibility for a major division of this international business.

In addition to financial measures, a "360-degree" leadership performance review is an effective tool to identify strengths and weaknesses as protégés develop their leadership capabilities. In this review process, managers, peers, and direct reports of the protégé all complete a questionnaire that evaluates the next-generation member on several key dimensions of effective leadership. The questionnaires are compiled anonymously in order to ensure frankness and pinpoint areas of leadership development where the protégé needs additional mentoring.

Participating in Strategic Decisions

The fourth habit mentors teach their protégés relates to the development of business strategy. Successors are frequently involved in day-to-day operational issues without participating in strategic decisions. They must learn about strategy early in their careers by defining how their own projects fit into the broader strategy of the business. Typically, one of the senior executives who participates in the corporate strategic planning process helps the successor to develop project management skills. The mentor guides the protégé in determining how best to align the successor's projects with the strategic goals of the business, rather than simply to develop day-to-day tactics in reaction to business circumstances.

Successful successors take the strategic process one step further; they partner with the senior generation to define future strategies that fit the passions and competency of the successor generation. In one family business that specialized in long-haul trucking, a successor recognized that the company's communication technology and logistics expertise could also serve other businesses in managing their own private fleets. The vice president of operations helped him to prepare a strategic plan that outlined how these core competencies could be leveraged to create a separate profit center for the business.

In another situation, a family business founded by a mechanical engineer grew through its proprietary products that had been designed and patented by the founder. The son, who had expertise in computer systems, was not sure how he would fit into the mechanical engineering focus of the business that had been developed by his father. A long-term trusted adviser who served on the company's board of directors worked with the son to identify the son's career goals and ambitions. Together, the board member and the successor recognized that the son's expertise in computer systems could be used to serve the customers' hardware and software needs. As a result, the strategy of the business was transformed not only to meet the strengths of the senior generation, but also to build upon the competency and expertise of the successor generation. Family businesses can redefine their strategy so that the business becomes the "home" for the passions of the successor.

Clarifying Boundaries

Perhaps one of the greatest challenges facing business successors involves clarifying the boundaries separating operational responsibilities, the development of strategy, and corporate financial decisions. Effective mentors help their protégés negotiate these boundaries, which are typically complicated by role confusion between family membership and company management. Parents, as the primary shareholders of the business, usually maintain control of the major strategic and financial issues that affect the company while delegating operational responsibilities and accountability to their direct reports, including their children with management positions in the company.

Conflicts between the generations are often rooted in two distinct issues. First, the senior generation will delegate operational responsibilities without defining clear expectations and performance measures and then will step back in to take control when the outcomes don't meet their undefined expectations. Second, the senior generation is often risk-averse, whereas the successor generation wants to implement strategies to grow the business for the next 20 years.

When conflict and tension exist between parents and their children working in the business, mentors play a very important role as mediators between the two generations. One non-family president was given the challenge of balancing two alternative strategic solutions to a current business situation. With sales declining, the father wanted to reduce overhead expenses in order to bring the company back to profitability. The son, on the other hand, wanted to hire a sales manager to build future business opportunities. The mentor worked with both the father and the son to objectively evaluate the pros and cons of each alternative. The alternatives were then presented during the formal strategic planning process, so that the entire executive team could determine the best strategy to pursue.

Developing Liquidity Strategies

The first five habits that protégés must master define key characteristics of any successful manager (family or non-family) who may be considered for executive responsibilities and leadership of a company. The next two habits – developing liquidity strategies and assuming financial risk – involve areas where family membership, management expertise, and ownership dynamics intersect.

Although most family businesses have an estate plan that addresses financial issues in the event of the death of the majority owner(s), very few develop liquidity strategies to restructure the capital of the business while the senior generation is still alive. With life expectancy now in the late 80s to early 90s, more successors are recognizing the need to design a mechanism for buying the business from their inactive siblings or cousins, as well as from the senior generation.

Mentors must discuss with their protégés various approaches to financing a smooth intergenerational transition. Successors should take a proactive role in learning about effective strategies for recapitalization of the business. For example, one family is wrestling with the question, "Should we sell our business to a strategic buyer?" A non-family president manages the day-to-day responsibilities of the business and has explicit instructions from the board of directors to serve in a mentoring capacity to the successor generation. As part of their quarterly board meetings, the successors have been investigating several alternative scenarios. Under the guidance and direction of the non-family president, they have explored an employee stock ownership plan (ESOP) to create diversification and liquidity for the senior generation, new buy/sell agreements among siblings to structure future redemptions, funded non-qualified retirement programs for the senior generation, and finally, the pros and cons of selling the business to a strategic buyer. Guided by the non-family president, the successors have been given the responsibility of meeting with their parents' advisers, and other experts to identify the best possible options and then make their recommendations to the board of directors. The board will take the successors' recommendations under advisement and make a decision about the future ownership of the business.

Assuming Financial Risk

In most family businesses, successors are owners by virtue of being gifted non-voting stock. In this respect, the successors are essentially participating in estate planning tactics, rather than assuming the responsibilities of ownership. Mentors must encourage their protégés to become involved in the financial aspects of the business as a way of transforming themselves into responsible owners. Early in a protégé's career, this involves teaching the young person how to read financial statements and explaining the impact of this financial information on business decisions. Mentors should introduce successors to bankers and other trusted advisers and should explain that developing a relationship with these key people will help establish successors' credibility.

To move from being passive recipients of a gift to active owners of stock, successors must be willing to take their own financial risk. For example, in one family business that acquired a competitor, the bank asked all family members to personally guarantee the loans. Some family managers were unwilling to co-sign such a document, thereby demonstrating their lack of commitment to taking financial risk. The willingness to take on personal financial liability demarcates the difference between management and ownership roles.

Financial risk is often linked with the development of liquidity strategies. For example, when one of my young clients was ready to assume the risk of buying the company from his family, he took a proactive role. He requested his father's permission to meet with attorneys, accountants, and other advisers. With their help, he developed a proposal to purchase the business and presented it to his father. The father worked side by side with his son to present this liquidity strategy to the rest of the family, in order to promote a smooth transition of ownership from one generation to the next during the father's lifetime. The process of developing intergenerational buyouts is facilitated most effectively when the company operates with a formal board of directors. Members of the board are normally the best mentors in helping successors design ownership transition plans. To structure such transitions and to take on financial risk, protégés must learn in detail the financial aspects of the business and alternative funding strategies that can be pursued to finance these buyouts.

Liquidity strategies and corresponding financial issues are rarely addressed in family-owned businesses. Most mentoring activities focus on the first five habits. Patience is a virtue. These seven habits of successful successors can't be developed all at once; they represent a gradual process, with each habit building on the previous one, over a time span of about two decades. As family members, successors must first take the initiative in developing adult independence and reshaping family communication patterns. In their roles as managers, they must develop technical competency and demonstrate leadership; they must also help to shape the business's strategic plan and must clarify the boundaries that distinguish operational, strategic, and financial roles. As owners, successors must be proactive in designing liquidity strategies and then be willing to assume financial risk to consolidate ownership for their generation.

Successors must be patient as they navigate their way through these seven steps. Mentors must demonstrate patience themselves by embodying this virtue in their interactions with their protégés. Mastery of these seven habits is a challenging process. The senior generation and other family members must be willing to accept and encourage the transition of the business from generation to generation.

Rate Family Business for Succession Success (1 = Poor, 5 = Excellent)

Habit One: Establish adult independence – psychological and financial.
Habit Two: Reshape family communication.
Habit Three: Develop competency.
Habit Four: Design strategy.
Habit Five: Clarify boundaries.
Habit Six: Coordinate liquidity strategies.
Habit Seven: Take financial risks.

TOTAL
31–35, Excellent. 24–30, More Work Needed. Below 24, Danger Zone.

Questions for Further Reflection

1. Have family members achieved their own psychological and financial independence separate from the extended family?
2. Has the family developed effective patterns of communication based on trust and respect?
3. Do family members have the necessary competency to be effective in their current roles in the family business, and is there a career-development plan to develop additional competencies for advancement in the organization?
4. Is there alignment within the family concerning corporate strategy, and do members of the rising generation participate in designing the strategy for the future?
5. Between the generations as well as among siblings and cousins are the boundaries, roles, and responsibilities clearly defined?
6. In addition to the estate plan for the transition of ownership at death, is there a plan to transfer ownership and control from the senior to the successor generation during the lifetime of the senior generation?
7. Is the next generation willing to take on the financial risks of ownership?

Additional Resources

Dean Fowler and Peg Masterson Edquist, *Love, Power and Money: Family Business Between Generations* (Brookfield, WI: Glengrove Publishing, 2002).

Dean Fowler and Peg Masterson Edquist, *Family Business Matters* (Brookfield, WI: Glengrove Publishing, 2017).

Dean Fowler, *Proactive Family Business Successors* (Brookfield, WI: Glengrove Publishing, 2011).

Biography

Dean Fowler, PhD, is president of Dean Fowler Associates, a Brookfield, Wisconsin, management consulting firm specializing in family, management, business, and shareholder development issues facing families in business.

CHAPTER 38

Why Is Family Unity So Important and How Can You Achieve It?

Andrew Hier and John Davis

Few would dispute that family unity is important to sustain a family enterprise over generations. There are too many examples of family conflict helping to bring a family down to dispute its importance. We would go further: we believe family unity is vital for the long-term success of a family or its enterprise. It's true that some families that are fractured and unaligned are kept orderly and without overt conflict – for a time – through hefty dividends, heavy handed leadership, or sentimental appeals to tradition. But when big decisions come up or dividends run out, the serious fractures and disputes within the family become visible and these divisions hobble and sometimes scuttle the family's enterprise.

The effects of disunity are many. It can cause abrasive friction and slowness in group decisions and in day to day activities. Sometimes, because of disunity, a family group decides to just stand still to try to keep a peace that doesn't really exist. Disunity generally leads to mistrust and guardedness, the blocking of even simple actions that need to be taken, political maneuvering to seek advantages for one's side, and if prolonged, to decline for the entire group. Even mild disunity can fester and grow into a serious problem and should be addressed.

Unity About Ends and Means

Unity for any group has to do with members' authentic agreement about what the group exists to do (its mission or purpose) and how the group will do this work and treat its stakeholders (its approach). For a family, such alignment creates a solid foundation for effective work by the family, whether in its operating business, investments, philanthropy, or other activities.

Unity in a family on mission and approach doesn't mean that every family member is socially close to each other or in lockstep on all issues. A united family can have disagreements on tactics and strategies – should we discard one management practice in favor of another, is now the right time to exit a certain line of business, etc. Some debate and challenging on strategy and tactics is actually essential to being effective as a group. Strong unity accepts that members of a group will disagree on some issues and debate strongly on others, and that some members won't like each other. But unity means that members of the group are committed to the same fundamental ends and means. This commitment builds trust, reduces defensiveness, and unleashes a lot of positive energy.

Agreement by members of a group on where they are going, why they are going there, and how they are supposed to do their work and treat each other (which often goes by the labels of mission, vision, and values), enables decisiveness, innovation, boldness, and persistence in group efforts. Unity also motivates caring and support for one another in the group because "this individual wants the same things as I do." A united enterprising family can better grow the assets it needs to finance its enterprise and the family. Such alignment also clarifies the kinds of family and non-family talent the family enterprise needs in order to stay successful. Growth, talent, and unity are, we have found, the main ingredients of long-term sustainability for a family and its enterprise. Family unity deserves to be celebrated and protected.

Adapting to Change

Unfortunately, unity is not the natural order of groups, including families. Without active countermeasures, over time, entropy or disunity within families usually prevails. As families age and grow over time, they become diverse in many ways, and family complexity needs to be both embraced and managed. Failure to manage family complexity usually leads to fracturing of the family into smaller, more naturally coherent units.

In addition, conflicts among group members can occur for many reasons and these can breed resentments and create lasting wounds that spread like a virus to involve large numbers of members. Families are particularly gifted at transmitting conflicts down through generations. Conflicts among members need to be healed or at least managed, and leadership and governance need to be nurtured and adapted to current family circumstances. Without these and other measures, families grow apart and divide into smaller groups.

Unity around mission and approach is vital to maintain but mission and approach, themselves, need to evolve. Over time and certainly over generations, a family's mission and approach needs to adapt to the changing interests, talents, resources, and circumstances of a family. The same is true of the mission and approach of a family organization. Mission and approach needn't change much over time for a group to stay effective but they probably need to change some.

Periodically (and more often than in previous generations), a family needs to reflect on and renew its "vows" – what do we stand for and want to achieve, and how will we do our work together and treat our stakeholders. By evolving a family's mission and approach to be compelling to current members, the family can better maintain the focus, energy, and discipline needed to work through its many challenges and sustain its success.

Building Family Unity

We have found that family unity is built through several mutually supportive ingredients:

1. A compelling and achievable family mission, vision, and values.
2. An engaging family enterprise organization that encourages broad family involvement and contributions.
3. Family enterprise organizations and activities (family company, family investments, family philanthropy, etc.) that perform well (including representing the family well), and maintain positive momentum toward key family goals.
4. Pride in one's family and its contributions to its organizations and key activities (we have been and currently are capable, creative, decisive, brave, responsible, etc.).
5. Strong levels of trust within the family achieved through: strong family and organization performance, trustworthy leadership and governance, adequate transparency and inclusion in key discussions, fair and respectful treatment of members, and demonstrated caring for family members and key stakeholders.
6. Managed expectations of owners and family members.
7. Affordable rewards and earned opportunities going to family owners and family members.
8. Timely conflict management.
9. The ability to change the ownership group to maintain unity.

It is possible to have adequate family unity without being good at all these ingredients but these items are a helpful checklist to understand where a system can improve. Although most of the ingredients to building unity listed earlier speak for themselves, some (particularly 2, 3, 4, 8, and 9) need some elaboration.

Contribution

As much as commitment to an organization inspires an individual's contribution to it, the inverse also seems true: the more a person contributes to an organization, the greater his or her commitment to the organization grows. This principle is central to building unity in any group. If you want someone to feel committed to what a family is doing, its mission and approach, give the person opportunities to contribute to the family and the family's enterprise.

Most family members want to contribute to their family and to be regarded as adding value to the family's efforts. An important reason that some family members disengage from the family is that they feel that their contributions are not valued in their family and that the family has little commitment to their interests. The family enterprise organization needs to reflect the family's important interests and give family members an opportunity to help the family pursue its mission. As a family grows, becomes more diverse, and develops a broader set of interests, the mission of the family and the family enterprise organization should reflect the key common interests. In fact, it is rare for families to stay very united when there is only a family company to support, where only a minority of family members can contribute to the family's mission.

Organization

To achieve a family's mission, the family needs organized efforts as well as funds to support these efforts. If a family's mission were simply to support its family company, raise good children to be responsible well-educated adults, and have family members get along well, the family would need a family company, useful parenting and family activities, perhaps an education fund, and definitely some useful mechanisms (perhaps grandparents, maybe a family council) to keep the family aligned.

Some families could have the aforementioned mission *plus* want to contribute to society beyond having a socially responsible business, need a way to manage the family's financial assets, and have a desire to maintain the family's religious faith. These families would need to add organizations or activities to support their mission, such as a philanthropic foundation, perhaps a family office, etc. The point is that families need to have appropriate organizations to help support their interests and pursue their missions. Having a well-designed family enterprise organization is critical to effectively pursue the family's mission. The right family enterprise organization also helps to build unity in a family.

Pride

Of course, family unity is strengthened when the family is proud of its organizations and activities, and even further when the family can point to its members' contributions for this good performance. This requires that family talent is developed to be able to contribute strongly to the family enterprise.

Managing Conflict

Building family unity often requires some corrective actions in family relationships. When we see strains and fragmentation in a family, we address it, trying to move family members beyond past misunderstandings, hurts, and differences, and when important, we reunify the family around a compelling mission and approach that can bind them.

Changing Ownership

But we recognize that family unity can't always be maintained with the current family members. When parts of an enterprising family resist reunification and they are seriously undermining the sustainability of the family, the family needs to either divide their assets and activities or buy out members who are no longer aligned. Family unity is that important for the success of a family and its enterprise. A family is more assured of success if it has a smaller asset base and a more united family, than with the converse situation.

Questions for Further Reflection

1. What is the difference between *consensus* and *unanimity*; why is consensus the key to family unity, not unanimity?
2. How can the family and the family enterprise system change over time in order to adapt to the changing factors that affect family unity?
3. How can you help your family understand that conflict is inevitable, that it is impossible to eliminate it, that accepting some conflict, managing it, taking advantage of it, and functioning despite conflict is the goal?
4. What would a family conflict resolution policy look like?

Additional Resources

Courtney Collette and Dr. John A. Davis, *Growing Together, Not Apart, Part I: Understanding Conflict in the Family Business* (Cambridge, MA: Cambridge Institute for Family Enterprise, 2016), https://www.cfeg.com/library/understanding-conflict-in-the-family-business.asp?n=320.

Dr. John A. Davis, *Growing Together, Not Apart, Part II: Building the Family Ownership Team* (Cambridge, MA: Cambridge Institute for Family Enterprise, 2016), https://www.cfeg.com/library/building-the-family-ownership-team-part-two.asp?n=185.

Biographies

Andrew Hier is a senior advisor and partner at Cambridge Advisors to Family Enterprise, a highly specialized international advisory firm serving family enterprises.

His areas of focus include ownership issues; family and business governance; succession planning; performance evaluations of family employees; and family communication. He is a globally recognized expert on the ownership dimension of family enterprises, which encompasses ownership strategies, trust, and estate planning, shareholder agreements, the owners' council, shareholder unity, and preparing the next generation to serve as effective owners.

Andrew frequently teaches around the world at conferences, education programs, and private family meetings. For several years, he has served as a facilitator and guest lecturer at Harvard Business School's *Families in Business* program on key issues facing family enterprises.

Andrew has authored a number of important works on the unique ownership challenges of family enterprises. He earned his JD from Harvard Law School and his BA in Philosophy and Economics from Harvard College.

Professor John Davis is founder and chairman of Cambridge Family Enterprise Group, a global organization he created in 1989 that is devoted to helping families achieve long-term and lasting success for their families, enterprises, and financial wealth.

John is a globally recognized pioneer and authority on issues related to the family enterprise, family wealth, and the family office. Since the 1970s, he has been a leading researcher, author, advisor, and speaker on family enterprise, and is the creator of some the field's most impactful conceptual frameworks. He co-created the Three-Circle Model of the Family Business System, the fundamental paradigm in the field.

His insights help to build shareholder value, develop leaders, strengthen families, professionalize businesses and family offices, and pass sustainable enterprises to the next generation.

John has advised multi-generational family enterprises in more than 65 countries, including a number of the world's leading business families.

A renowned academic and shaper of the family enterprise field, John leads the family enterprise portfolio of programs at the MIT Sloan School of Management. During his 21 years on the faculty of Harvard Business School, he founded and led Harvard's family business management area and was founding faculty chair of the *Families in Business* program.

John earned his Doctorate in Business Administration from Harvard Business School, his MA in Economics from the University of Wisconsin, and his AB in Economics from Kenyon College.

CHAPTER 39

What Are the Signs You're Losing Control of Your Family Business?

Josh Baron and Rob Lachenauer

When the non-family chairman/CEO unexpectedly told family business owners that they had to live without dividends or sell the business, Tommy leaned over and whispered in his cousin's ear: "Do you get what's going on? The numbers have always been terrific."[1]

Despite their shock, Tommy and other family owners shared responsibility for this painful situation. For years, they'd been detached and unengaged owners. No family member worked in the company, and those who sat on the board rubber-stamped management's decisions. The owners sat passively until faced with the reality that they were at risk of losing the business that had been in the family for three generations.

Although the details vary, stories of family owners losing control of their businesses are common. Consider what happened when a relatively young patriarch died unexpectedly, leaving no succession plan in place. The children were unprepared to take over, and the widow had no business experience. She brought in a non-family CEO who treated the business as his personal fiefdom. Eventually he tried to buy the business himself at a deflated price. The experience broke the family, emotionally and financially.

Although sometimes a non-family CEO plays the role of villain in these situations, the blame lies more often with the owners, who created a power vacuum for others to fill. Lacking substantive direction from the owners, these executives follow their own self-interests. But even when families are fortunate enough to find that selfless, protective non-family leader – and we have seen many – owners still need to speak with a single voice about what they

[1]Some of the identifying details in this article have been changed to protect confidentiality.

want. Otherwise, there is no way to ensure that their ownership interests are being served.

Are there warning signs that you may be on the path to losing control of your family business? We primarily see five red flags:

1. *Dividends never change.* If you receive stable dividends year after year, then you should grow concerned. Dividend targets are fine, but the dividends of a well-run company are always uncertain and should vary depending on the company's performance and its future opportunities. Every year there should be some discussion about the company's profits and what to do with them. If you grow accustomed to receiving annual dividends – in the worst cases, treating them as a birthright – then you forfeit an essential mechanism for controlling the business – namely, deciding how much of your money should be reinvested annually.
2. *Board meetings are a formality.* A board of directors (or advisors) is essential for ensuring that the business is pursuing the owners' objectives. At their best, independent directors bring wisdom, expertise, and a willingness to challenge management. As owners, you must see to it that the board is properly formed and empowered. Do you have a "paper board" that rarely meets or essentially rubber-stamps the recommendations of management? Is the board filled with family friends, or with the CEO and his allies? Is the board's role murky and undefined? If you answer "yes" to any of these questions, then you're giving away a key lever for maintaining control.
3. *Too much or too little information is provided.* As an equity owner, you should receive information about business performance in a timely and appropriate way. Either 15-minute updates ("The business is great!" "Enjoy your dividend!") or 200-page "summaries" should set off alarm bells. If you don't work in the company, you are already at a disadvantage, lacking first-hand knowledge of what's happening. When management either skimps or drowns you in details, it's very difficult to understand your business's performance and potential.
4. *The CEO seems irreplaceable.* There are business leaders who can run your business and deliver outstanding results, while also cultivating proper family engagement. Do what you can to keep these people. Watch out, however, if you (and they) talk and behave as if they are irreplaceable. Respect and appreciation for a job well done are healthy. Fear and dependency are not. "Irreplaceable" executives can begin to make decisions independently, believing they know better than you do. They may even refer to you as "the kids." If your family ownership group walks on eggshells around your non-family CEO, your behavior may signal a dangerous imbalance of power.

5. *Family members are shut out of the business.* Sometimes family owners lose control of the business because the previous generation has shut the door to them during the succession process. There is either a real or perceived lack of talent among the next generation – or fear about the dangers of family conflict – and employment policies are put in place that either prevent or make it very difficult for family members to work in the business. There are times when this "professionalization" of the family business may make sense. But be aware that the family's direct link to the operations of the company will be severed. You don't need to run the business. But having owners employed there helps the family to keep a finger on the company's pulse.

When you realize that you've lost some or most of the control over your company, then it's time to ask yourselves whether you wish to continue to own your family business. You may decide it's time to sell. But if you choose instead to become an active owner, then you must first reclaim active ownership. This decision doesn't mean that you suddenly have to start micromanaging executives or meddling in operational decisions.

What *does* active ownership mean? To grapple with this and other important questions, the first step is to create a place where you and other owners can meet (without non-family executives or board members) to talk about your role and your aspirations for the business. We often call this place an owner council. It's a forum where you can decide your priorities as owners and discuss how to speak to the board and management about these priorities in a united voice.

After creating an owner council, you can then begin to set your objectives for the company. It's the owners' responsibility to put in place clear financial policies for dividends and debt levels, as well as to set financial and non-financial guardrails, such as setting a return on investment target or banning investments in, say, tobacco. One of your most important jobs is to manage the process of selecting board members. You may, of course, solicit advice from others, such as a nominating committee, but the ultimate decision rests within the ownership group. It's then up to you as owners to hold the board accountable for choosing a high performing CEO who supports your owner agenda.

Keeping control of your family business isn't easy. For a start, ownership is not typically a full-time job, but is rather peripheral to your everyday work and lives. You can also feel ill-equipped to exercise your rights thoughtfully when the financials of the business can seem impenetrable. You may never become an expert on, say, return on invested capital, which only underscores the importance of structures that let you rely on the knowledge of people who appreciate your values and follow your agenda. By becoming more active and effective owners, you can let go of many decisions without losing control of your family business.

Questions for Further Reflection

1. Do you feel like things are being hidden from you? Are answers to tough questions hard to come by?
2. Do the owners of your business or other shared assets have a private forum to discuss their issues and concerns as owners?
3. Are there enough independent voices – independent board members or auditors – in your business to provide checks and balances to management? And do you have access to them? Do they view you as their "clients"?

Additional Resources

Josh Baron, Rob Lachenauer, and Sebastian Ehrlensberger, "Making Better Decisions in Your Family Business," *Harvard Business Review*, September 8, 2015.

Josh Baron and Rob Lachenauer, "Can an Outside CEO Run a Family-Owned Business?," *Harvard Business Review*, August 15, 2014.

Biographies

Dr. Josh Baron is a co-founder and Partner at Banyan Global Family Business Advisors. For the past decade, he has worked closely with families who own assets together, such as operating companies, family foundations, and family offices, helping these families to define their purpose as owners and to establish the structures, strategies, and skills they need to accomplish their goals. During his career, Josh has worked with clients in North America, South America, Africa, Australia, and Asia. He began his career at Bain & Company, consulting to Fortune 500 companies, before helping to build a new organization called The Bridgespan Group, which has become America's leading consulting firm for the philanthropic sector. He moved on to found his own firm advising family philanthropists before joining Banyan Global.

Josh publishes and speaks frequently on subjects concerning family enterprises. He has a particular interest in how ownership creates a competitive advantage, how families can escape major conflicts, and how philanthropy can help families achieve their broader goals. He teaches a course at Columbia Business School on managing conflict in family businesses and is a frequent contributor to *Harvard Business Review*. He is the author of a book about international relations titled *Great Power Peace and American Primacy: The Origins and Future of a New International Order*.

Rob Lachenauer, a co-founder, Partner and CEO of Banyan Global Family Business Advisors, has been an advisor, business leader, and writer throughout his career. He was vice president and director of The Boston Consulting Group from 1995 to 2004, where he helped leading multi-national companies, including several family-controlled businesses, set and implement growth strategies. He has experience with industrial, distribution, consumer goods, financial, technology, and automotive firms. He has consulted for clients in North America, Europe, Asia, and Australia. While at BCG, he co-authored *Hardball: Are You Playing to Play or Playing to Win?* with George Stalk. Published by Harvard Business School Press in 2004, *Hardball* was subsequently translated into six languages.

As the founding CEO of Banyan, Rob has worked closely with scores of family businesses throughout the world, helping them navigate the decisions they face as owners, while still building family relationships. He is an expert in governance for such transitions. A graduate of Harvard Business School, Rob is also a frequent contributor to *Harvard Business Review.*

CHAPTER 40

Can a Family Stay Together After the Operating Business Is Sold?

Alex Scott

In 1903, my great-grandfather and his brother started The Provincial Insurance Company, which went on to become one of the leaders in property casualty (P&C) insurance in the northern United Kingdom. In 1994, the family sold the business, and since then has continued to manage much of our wealth together. I was reflecting on the lessons learned in our family over the past 115 years and particularly over the past almost 25 years since our liquidity event. The lessons coalesced around eight points and I suspect some of them will be relevant for other families.

The Business Marketplace Changes and You Need to Stay Vigilant

The commercial insurance business was a good one for a very long time. But in the early 1990s, our non-family directors and the company's management (both of which were professional and independent) advised us that the competitive environment was changing significantly, European Union rules on cross-border insurance were in flux, new market practices were emerging, and the risk/reward ratio in the business was under threat. At that point, The Provincial was the last remaining sizable independent P&C insurer in the country. Management recommended that the family should seriously consider selling the business.

The family leadership group (including myself, who had recently been installed as chairman of the company at the ripe old age of 34) underwent a lengthy process of evaluating the various recommendations and options, including full sale, partial sale, initial price offering (IPO) and others. We also took into account many other factors at play, such as our responsibilities to the broader shareholder group and to employees, since the company was a large employer in the local town. We did finally make the decision to sell 100% of the business to capture the control premium.

My point is that, over the years, businesses change and the environment they operate in evolves. Ownership families need to stay current and vigilant, keep all their options open, and evaluate them on a regular basis. What was once a great business may not be so in the future.

Good Independent Advisors Are Worth Their Weight in Gold

In the previous section, you will note that professional managers ran Provincial Insurance, and they were independent and not members of the family. There were about 60 family members who were owners of the business at that time and we saw ourselves as inheritors and owners, not business managers. It was the independent managers and directors who brought the idea of selling the company for strategic business reasons to us. It was not the family who was looking for an exit, per se. In fact, their recommendation to sell was a surprise to us.

I was reflecting on how important objective, independent managers and advisors have been to us over the life of our family. They provided expert management of a complex business for many years, and when it came to a strategic sale decision, they initiated the conversation with us. They were able to hold a mirror up to us and lay out the risks of continued ownership. We felt they operated in a very professional, non-conflicted manner that sought to serve the interests of the owners.

We have always had non-family, non-executive, independent directors on the board as well. They pushed us as a fourth generation family to seriously consider the sale option.

We have also benefited from excellent outside professional advisors (tax, legal, investment, etc.) over the years, who brought their expertise to bear on our behalf. That has continued as we have engaged professional management teams to run the other businesses that we have started and/or bought since 1994.

It Is Important to Delegate the Evaluation of Complex Decisions to a Small Group of Owners

In our case, in the early 1990s, we had 60 owners of the business, many of whom were non-financial and not particularly engaged in the business. For us it would have been counterproductive to have a serious, in-depth discussion of the potential sale of the business as an entire group of owners. Instead, we agreed in principle as a large group to investigate the sale options and then empowered a small group of us to come back with some proposed courses of action. Non-family directors also provided input. This was a very helpful model and yielded an excellent result, both financially and from a family relationship perspective.

Similarly, in new businesses we have started, we have had the support, goodwill, and tolerance of the broader family and their understanding that new enterprises require consistency and persistence. At the same time, the family directors, for their part, have been conscious that they are working on behalf of a large group of owners and family members.

Although it is important to have leaders within the family, there is real purpose and distinction in being good followers. Good followers need the appropriate recognition, honor and information. At the end of the day, ongoing compromise and goodwill within our family group has been key.

You Can Still Stay Together as a Family Even after the Core Family Business Is Sold

We sold our family business for business reasons, not because we reached the end of the road as a family group. We have origins as inheritors (descendants of extraordinary people) and have long thought about the stewardship of the business and the associated wealth. When the operating business was sold, we thought there would be better endurance of the wealth if we managed it in a collective pool. That isn't always right for every family, but it was for us. The liquidity event also allowed people to take their capital out if they wanted to, and some did. But the rest of us decided to stick together and recommit to each other, and almost 25 years later, we are still together.

The downside of staying together is that you have to compromise. For instance, some family members with higher personal income might want to take more risk with the communal assets than those who do not work for pay and who live off the dividends. But in our case, it has been worth it.

Of course, nothing is forever. But we have been doing the same thing, being owners together, for almost 25 years, and we still like it. It's a nice outcome.

Good Governance Is Not Sexy, but Immensely Valuable

I think of governance as a forum (or multiple forums) where owners can be included in the discussion, education, and decisions of the family and business interests, to the extent that it is appropriate and welcome.

Our family had no governance structures to speak of for the first 90 years. The oversight of the business was delegated to boards. The chair of the family company board ended up as the de facto family leader. When the business was sold in 1994, we decided to set up a family council (FC) as a place of "family conversation." It is the place where we communicate and socialize, and it is open to all. We also hold a full family gathering every two years.

We also have a shareholder advisory committee (SAC) that represents "80% of the equity in the room." One of my cousins chairs the SAC. Another family member chairs the FC. Interestingly enough, the constitution of the FC has been changed three times over the past 20 years.

No one will ever thank you for putting governance in place but it is a vital underpinning, especially for families that decide to stay together and invest together.

Shared Family Values Are an Important Anchor for all Family and Business Decisions

Few families have a unique special sauce. And I'm also always conscious that it is difficult to talk about your values without being trite. Probably for that reason we have never actually written our values down. But upon reflection for this chapter, I realize that our family, as large, diverse, and complicated as it is, does have shared values.

- We have always been very conscious that an insurance business like ours traded on probity and trustworthiness, so words like responsibility and *reputation* were ever-present in the family psyche.
- One of the founding brothers was a real entrepreneur and actively managed the business. There wasn't really space for the rest of the family to be involved, so the family has a history of being relatively hands-off. People were encouraged to get on with their own lives and pursue their own interests.
- There has always been a strong element of humility and a shared spirit of wonder – "How did we get here?".
- We also have a deep sense of fairness. My grandfather once said to me, "One day you may sell a company. If you do, be sure to leave a profit for the next man."
- We don't socialize a lot with each other, but we genuinely like being together. And I think it is fair to say that we don't take ourselves too seriously!
- We have also been very consultative and have had a willingness to surround ourselves with smart people. If a family thinks they know all the answers, they will fail.
- Stewardship is also a core value of our family. Our aim is to preserve, protect, and grow our family wealth and to continue to be worthy of the family reputation. We always want to leave the family better than we inherited it.

It Is Important to Be Proactive and Patient in Bringing the Next Generation into Family Involvement or Roles of Responsibility

It has been gratifying to see the emergence and development of each new generation in the family. The task of leadership is to find meaningful ways to engage and educate them. We need to find forums where we can get them involved. These forums also allow the family leaders to spot those who want to be involved more actively and those who don't.

We have learned to be patient to let them develop their own interests, lives, and careers. We also have learned not to expect them to engage in the family too early. They need to be given space to be involved if and when they want to. On the other hand, we have very few executive roles within our family, so we need to think creatively about how to create meaningful roles for talented people who want to be involved.

When I was a younger leader in the family, we were lucky that the older generation had an attitude that empowered us to move forward without undue deference to them. I hope we can maintain that attitude over time.

We have also maintained an attitude of inclusivity with regard to spouses and in-laws. We see them as family members and they are welcome to attend the FC.

Families of Wealth Need to Think about Their Roles in the Years Ahead

The traditional challenges and opportunities within families of wealth will continue. And new ones will emerge, particularly in an era of increased transparency and rising populism.

I think it has always been the case that business-owning and wealthy families need to plan to be (and be seen to be) valuable citizens, but the need is all the greater now. We need to fulfill worthwhile roles in society, to be positive contributors, and to stand up and be counted. We can't disengage from society. We have to embrace it and make a positive difference.

Philanthropy and volunteer activities are obvious and common examples of opportunities for families to engage constructively. But there are certainly others, such as founding businesses, impact investing, standing for political office, and other aspects of public service. I believe that families should be proactive in their positive contribution to their local communities. It will benefit the families themselves as well as the societies in which they live.

Questions for Further Reflection

1. Ask yourself, if you had to persuade a stranger to invest into your company, could you make a convincing case? And could you convince them to invest their children's inheritance into it? If you can't do this or would feel compromised, think about the reasons very carefully.
2. At what age were you ready to take the reins? Should you ensure that your children are ready and empowered at that age too?
3. What sort of people do you have as trusted advisers? Do they hold a mirror up to you as a critical friend?

Additional Resources

Philip Marcovici's book is instructional:

Philip Marcovici, *The Destructive Power of Family Wealth* (Chichester, UK: Wiley, 2016), https://sandaire.com/our-views/book-review-destructive-power-family-wealth.

This is thought-provoking:

Robert Frank, *Success and Luck: Good Fortune and the Myth of Meritocracy* (Princeton, NJ: Princeton University Press, 2016), https://sandaire.com/our-views/success-luck-good-fortune-myth-meritocracy-robert-h-frank.

And this one's a good read for successors of "mythological" leaders:

Andrew Keyt, *Myths and Mortals: Family Business Leadership and Succession Planning* (Hoboken, NJ: Wiley, 2015), https://sandaire.com/our-views/myths-mortals-family-business-leadership-succession-planning.

Biography

Alex Scott is chairman of Applerigg Limited. Following the sale of his family's financial services group in 1994, he founded Sandaire, now an international multi-family investment office serving wealthy families and not-for-profit institutions in London and Singapore. Alex has facilitated the creation of Yealand Administration, a funds administration company; Mount Kendal, a real estate investment advisor; and Horizons, a contemporary network and learning environment for the leaders of tomorrow. He is a non-executive director of his family's investment holding company, as well as of several private companies.

Alex co-founded and is a life president of the Institute for Family Business (UK), serves as a director of the Family Business Network International (FBN-i) and is a past director of the Family Firm Institute.

He is a trustee of the Grosvenor Estate (a leading UK family business), and chairs the Grosvenor Pension Plan, as well as Wheatsheaf Group.

He is a trustee of the Francis C Scott Charitable Trust, a Fellow of the Royal Society of Arts and a Patron of Tomorrow's Company.

Alex graduated from Exeter College, Oxford with an MA in philosophy, politics, and economics and holds an MBA from IMD, Lausanne, Switzerland.

SECTION 7

GIVING WELL

Philanthropy – the love (*philo*) of humanity (*anthropos*) – has been a part of the lives of wealthy families for millennia. With their dollars and time, they have helped the poor, built libraries and hospitals, become patrons of the arts, and advocated for human and political causes. Societies, locally and around the world, have benefited from these gifts.

But wealthy families themselves have also benefited from philanthropy. They have experienced the joy of giving to others and seeing progress. Through giving, they have helped to cultivate a spirit of generosity among their family members. And they have seen how a common external cause can knit their clan together and build powerful enduring cross-generation values, counteracting the natural entropy families face over time.

In some ways, we are now in a golden age of philanthropy as mega-wealthy donors – Bill Gates and Warren Buffett come to mind – commit large portions of their wealth to charitable endeavors. At all levels of wealth, families are wrestling with many of the same philanthropic questions and issues. How much of our wealth should go to our heirs and how much to charity? What is a good investment of time and money? What are the right vehicles? How do we make wise decisions? How do we involve others?

Our contributing authors will shed some light on some of these issues and give you some food for thought along the journey of family philanthropy.

There is a whole vocabulary about philanthropy these days, which can be confusing. Ellen Remmer answers those questions directly: "What is the difference between charity, philanthropy, strategic philanthropy, and impact investing?" She also provides many examples and tips to help families decide how they want to approach their giving and charitable investing.

When we think of our wishes for our children, most of us would include among them an attitude of authentic generosity, which often displays itself as gratitude, kindness, and a sense of community. Alasdair Halliday and Anne McClintock answer the question "How can you encourage generosity in your family?" and show how philanthropy can be an important tool in developing that spirit among all members of the family.

The problem is that it is often difficult to interest and involve younger generations in family philanthropy. Sometimes, based on their stage of development, they may have other interests and priorities; in other cases, philanthropy has been built into the culture and practice of the family. Lisa Parker's essay answers the question "How do you engage children and grandchildren in philanthropy?" with some highly practical advice and suggestions that are sure to encourage engagement.

Good philanthropy requires planning and forethought, but it also has a strong emotional side, often driven by passion, vision, and calling. Barnaby Marsh knits these threads together and looks at how you can wisely develop a long-term strategy for your philanthropy. He helps us think about why we give, how our giving might shift in the future as the world changes, and how we stay focused yet flexible on our philanthropic mission.

Those families who embrace and nurture their philanthropic urgings will give gifts, but are likely to receive significant gifts as well. Philanthropy allows families to face *outward* together. It encourages them to reach beyond the immediate and dream big. It provides purpose and meaning to life. And it encourages humanity and character in its members. Enjoy the journey.

CHAPTER 41

What Is the Difference Between Charity, Philanthropy, Strategic Philanthropy, and Impact Investing?

Ellen Remmer

What's the best way to make a positive impact on the world?

Charity, philanthropy, strategic philanthropy, and impact investing – these are all important ways for you and your family to contribute to society and the public good. Other approaches you could add to this list include political giving, patronage, advocacy, volunteering, and inspiring others to step into the ring. As scholar and self-described philanthropy wonk Lucy Bernholtz said in her report, *Philanthropy and Digital Civil Society: Blueprint 2018*, "All are tools with different shapes and different uses, like the (different components of the) … Swiss Army Knife."

But which of these do you want to deploy? And how do they differ from each other? Acknowledging that these terms may have overlapping meanings, I'll share with you some definitions and distinctions I've observed in years consulting to individuals, families, and corporations. I'll begin with charity, philanthropy, and strategic philanthropy. Given the skyrocketing interest in impact investing, I've devoted special attention to this market-based approach to social change. Finally, I conclude with a framework and list of considerations to help you think about what tools to use in what situations.

Charity. The term *charity* typically refers to providing resources directly to individuals (or via organizations that serve individuals) in response to their short-term needs, often for rescue or relief. Providing coats, food, or shelter for the homeless is an act of charity, as are funds to help those whose lives have been up-ended by a natural disaster. The stimulus for charity may be quite emotional and triggered by deep compassion. For some of us, charitable acts can be spurred by the sense that "there, but for good fortune, go I." For many, it comes from deeply held religious beliefs and moral upbringing.

Philanthropy. Philanthropy and, even more so, strategic philanthropy describes a form of giving that moves beyond the short term to focus on improving longer-term outcomes, often targeted at a population, problem, and/or place. In contrast to strategic philanthropy, many people use terms such as "checkbook philanthropy" or "responsive philanthropy" to refer to the practice of writing checks to a number of organizations, without a preconceived plan or specific goals. The checkbook philanthropist likely helps many worthy organizations with important annual operating needs. However, perhaps because these donors lack the time, interest, or commitment to dive deeper into their philanthropy, they do not weave their annual giving into a strategy with an underlying rationale and set of objectives. Much of their giving may be in response to requests from friends or family.

Strategic philanthropy. Strategic philanthropists focus on the root causes of societal issues and think about problems within the context of systems (e.g. homelessness may actually be rooted in the brokenness of the mental health system). They are often described as problem solvers.

In my practice at The Philanthropic Initiative, I use TPI's Philanthropic Curve™ to illustrate the path that donors may take and some of the elements they can incorporate in their quest to become strategic – from getting organized, to focusing on results, to finding leverage, and ultimately to amplifying their impact. See Figure 41.1.

Figure 41.1 TPI Philanthropic Curve™

What does it take to get to the top of the curve? Shared qualities of the most strategic donors typically include:

- A focus on one or a few areas, such as an issue, place, and/or population.
- Clarity on desired outcomes (quantitative and/or qualitative).
- Ongoing and deep learning about what works (or doesn't), including understanding and learning from failures.
- Development of a philosophy or "theory of change" about your giving (e.g. support new approaches to identify breakthrough solutions to a problem or support proven programs or strategies).
- A willingness to play active roles to increase the impact of your grants (e.g. recruit other donors, write op-eds, or connect a grantee to a public/ private partner).

Categorize Your Giving

All these giving approaches – charity, responsive philanthropy, and strategic philanthropy – provide value to civil society. Many donors employ all of them concurrently, sometimes with great intention about the contribution of each to the whole pie of giving. If you want to become more strategic in your philanthropy, one helpful exercise is to categorize how you currently allocate your time and resources, and then plan adjustments for the future to reach your desired breakdown. The example shown in Figure 41.2 also includes an "experimental" category to refer to early stage granting that might become "strategic."

Your allocation choices at any given time will depend on a variety of factors, including: (a) your personality, experience, ambition, and capacity (time and resources); and (b) context such as your position/expectations in the community, or current needs in the event of a disaster. Strategic giving requires an investment of donor time, which may only become available once a donor slows down in his/her professional or family life or makes a decision to invest in staffing or consultants.

Impact investing. Finally, there is impact investing, an exciting, fast-growing but still-emerging approach to making a difference in society through your money. Defined as investments made in companies, organizations, and funds with the intention to generate social and environmental impact alongside a financial return, it includes everything from socially responsible public equity funds, to cash flow loans to help a non-profit organization that has an uneven revenue flow, to direct investment in a local, organic farm in order to preserve land, create jobs, and provide nourishing, low-carbon footprint food. The financial return from impact investing can be below market rate (sometimes called "concessionary"), risk-adjusted market rate, or simply return of capital.

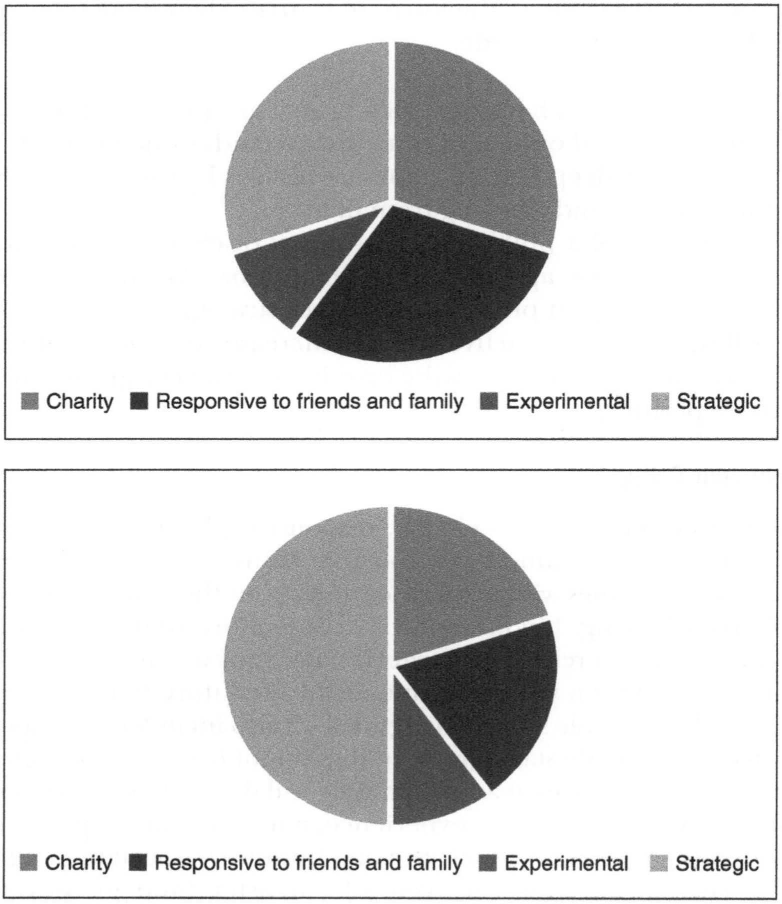

Figure 41.2 Current allocation adjusted to reach desired allocation

The investee can be a non-profit or for-profit enterprise or fund. The source of capital can be an investment portfolio, a foundation endowment, a pension fund, or a donor-advised fund.

Why is there skyrocketing interest in impact investing and how might it relate to your charity and philanthropy? Several of the principal reasons to consider adopting these practices include the following:

- *You can deploy more resources in support of your social goals.* Donors with foundations typically deploy only 5% of their philanthropic assets (the required minimum payout) toward grant-making. With an impact-investing lens, you may invest some or all of the other 95% for social benefit. Moreover, these funds can be recycled over and over again as the financial capital is returned.

- *You can expand your portfolio of tools for social good.* Most people agree that philanthropy is not big or powerful enough to solve most social problems. Impact investing uses the power of the marketplace for sustainable solutions. For example, you can seek to improve the environment through investing in a company that has produced new ways to capture methane gas for energy use.
- *You can get leverage and pursue scale.* If a sustainable, market-based solution to a problem can be found, it will ultimately attract the enormous reservoir of market-based capital.
- *You can bring integrity to your balance sheet.* At a minimum, you can gain confidence that your financial investments are not undermining your social investments; at a maximum, you can align both sets of investments towards specific social goals.

At present, a relatively small number of philanthropists and foundations are strategically seeking to leverage their giving with impact investing, but this situation is changing quickly. Early pioneers in below-market-return investing (known as program-related investments when made from foundations) focused on low-income housing, conservation finance (e.g. bridge loans to preserve conservation land), and micro-finance (e.g. small loans for developing country entrepreneurs). Today, we are seeing a wide range of investors and philanthropists craft investment strategies to achieve specific social goals in concert with their philanthropic giving. In addition, the variety and number of investable opportunities is growing exponentially. A donor interested in making more fisheries sustainable in the world can invest in eco-friendly aquaculture. Someone who wants to improve access to high quality primary education can invest in technology-based personalized learning products. Conservationists can help to preserve more wetlands by investing in highly efficient mitigation banks.

Bring It All Together

Now that you understand the differences in these types of social investments, how can you bring it all together and determine which approach to use, how often, and when?

An integrated approach requires some thoughtful identification of your goals. What do you want to accomplish in terms of social impact? These may be very specific or broad, but should include both an active verb and an articulation of the positive outcomes you seek. Examples of goals might include improving access to high quality education in our community, reducing the world's dependence on fossil fuels, or helping disadvantaged girls rise out of poverty.

Next, consider what tools can be effectively deployed to help you work toward these goals. Recognize that philanthropy and impact investing can complement or augment each other. Philanthropic donations may help an organization build the capacity to take on impact investments and reduce the risk for an investor who seeks market returns. Your responsive giving to friends and family may help you build a network of trusting relationships that are valuable social capital when you embark on something more ambitious in your strategic giving.

The following framework may provide a useful starting point for your integrated plan and give you a flavor of some of the options you can pursue in each category.

Your Goals	Philanthropy Examples		Investing Examples	
	Responsive Giving	Strategic Giving	Concessionary Returns	Market Rate Returns
Improve access to high quality education in my community	Annual gift to local school's foundation	Launch/join an initiative to improve teacher training	Provide financing for a new charter school	Invest in a tech-based solution to provide AP courses
Reduce the world's dependence on fossil fuels	Annual gifts or memberships to a range of environmental non-profits	Support multiple policy advocacy groups seeking to alter fuel standards	Provide low-cost financing for experimental technology development	Invest in clean energy funds with scalable solutions
Help disadvantaged girls rise out of poverty	Annual gifts to a range of after-school and enrichment groups	Launch and support girls education in sub-Saharan Africa	Invest in local companies making low-cost menstrual pads that allow girls to stay at school	Invest in a micro-enterprise or small/medium enterprise (SME) fund focused on women-owned businesses

Your choice of tools and vehicles is practically unlimited. Choosing the right tool for the right situation will depend on a variety of factors, both internal and external.

Internal considerations include

- How much time do you (or staff/consultants) have to spend?
- How ambitious are you?
- What is your appetite for risk? Return? Liquidity?
- What do you find most meaningful?

External considerations include

- What other high-quality opportunities are available?
- Are there sufficient resources and partners for success?
- Are there realistic metrics for success/learning?

The opportunities to contribute to a better world at home or abroad are becoming more and more plentiful. All donors can become strategic philanthropists with an investment of time and resources, and/or joining with others who share similar goals. Younger generations, in particular, are expressing high interest in impact investing and investable opportunities are becoming more varied and accessible. A philanthropic family has many choices. The ones that will find most meaning are those who are thoughtful about their goals, open to creative solutions, and disciplined about learning from others and their own experiences.

Questions for Further Reflection

1. How would you categorize your current giving along the lines of
   - Charity
   - Checkbook or responsive philanthropy
   - Strategic philanthropy
   - Impact investing?
2. Would you like to do more in any of these categories? Why and where?
3. What steps do you need to take in your own planning and learning in order to move forward?

Additional Resources

"Strategic Planning: Potential Roles and Strategies" (Boston: The Philanthropic Initiative, 2015). Accessed at https://www.tpi.org/sites/default/files/pdf/tpi_strategic_philanthropy_primer.pdf.

"Navigating the Territory: A Guide to Impact Investing for Donors," white paper (Boston: The Philanthropic Initiative, 2014). Accessed at https://www.tpi.org/sites/default/files/pdf/tpi_impact_investing_primer.pdf.

"10-Minute Impact Assessment: Explore How to Make the Most of Your Giving," white paper (Washington, DC: Exponent Philanthropy, 2013). Accessed at https://community.exponentphilanthropy.org/ProductDetail?id=01t150000059msRAAQ.

Laura Arrillaga-Andreessen, *Giving 2.0: Transform Your Giving and Our World* (San Francisco: Jossey-Bass, 2011).

Thomas Tierney and Joel Fleishman, *Give Smart: Philanthropy That Gets Results* (New York: Public Affairs, 2011).

https://www.givingcompass.org.

Biography

Ellen Remmer is senior partner at The Philanthropic Initiative (TPI), a philanthropic consulting group that helps individuals, families, foundations, and companies attain new levels of philanthropic impact. TPI is a distinct operating unit of the Boston Foundation and works with donors locally, nationally, and globally. Ellen has been with TPI since 1993 and served as president and CEO from 2007 to 2012.

She has worked directly with dozens of family, corporate, and community foundations, helping them develop powerful strategies for social impact and strong governance structures and practices. She has designed several donor education initiatives and programs to build the capacity of community foundations and professional advisors to better donors. Ellen writes and speaks on the subjects of strategic giving, family philanthropy, women donors, and impact investing. She is president of the Remmer Family Foundation and serves on a number of non-profit boards.

CHAPTER 42

How Can You Encourage Generosity in Your Family?

Alasdair Halliday and Anne McClintock

Take a bowl, fill it with water, and place it on a table. Tap the table with your hand and watch what happens. The water ripples – inward. And so it is with family philanthropy. Although philanthropy is practiced first for its *outward* ripples – the healing and hope it brings to others – the effects of philanthropy can also ripple *inward* in ways that promote family harmony and prosperity today and down through the generations.

This chapter focuses on those inward ripples that include the opportunity to create a sense of legacy within the family; to foster the binding institutions of collaboration and compromise among family members; to teach younger generations about gratitude and commitment; and to enspirit the family with principles of community and kindness.

There is much evidence confirming that family philanthropy *can* contribute powerfully to all these objectives; *whether* it will do so is a separate matter. Our conversations with philanthropists and faculty in the Harvard community have taught us that realizing the beneficial inward ripples of family philanthropy depends on the details, and further, that philanthropy's *most* beneficial inward ripple is simply this: that giving makes us more generous, and generosity makes us better in so many ways, including our ability to manage the dynamics of family wealth. In contrast, if the generosity of family members extends outward to others but not inward to kin, the formal infrastructures of philanthropy may become little more than additional forums for internecine battle.

> *I have seen the most elegant, expensive, family enterprise structures crumble overnight because the family members never got to know each other.*
>
> —Kathy Wiseman, President, Working Systems, Inc.

Kathy Wiseman reminds us that relationships outrank structure; that foundations are stages, and the grandest stage is only as good as the actors that tread its boards. Families who aspire to collaborate philanthropically across and through the generations must first learn to be generous to one another. Why? Because such collaboration occurs across overlapping territories – territories of financial worth and family hierarchy, of tribal role and philanthropic identity. In the absence of generosity, territorial skirmishes can easily become zero-sum (i.e. if they win, I lose). However, authentic generosity – which makes their success your own – can reframe those engagements and make them less contentious and more productive.

Can family philanthropy, itself, help to make family members more generous? One of the people we've discussed this with in our work for Harvard grew up in a wealthy banking family in the southern United States. He once told us that his parents' frequent encouragement to be generous outside the family looms large in his memory. We asked if that ethos had an effect on relationships *inside* the family and he said, "Of course! How could it not? It would have seemed odd to be generous to strangers and not to our own flesh and blood." We have heard some version of this story often enough to be convinced that generosity ripples inward to families, even when the initial practice is outward.

All of this begs the question of *how* to cultivate a spirit of generosity in the family.

Harvard Business School professor Michael Norton, who has studied generosity in collaboration with Professor Elizabeth Dunn at the University of British Columbia, explains that the best way to encourage a culture of generosity is to help individuals practice it regularly and in ways that provide immediate feedback. This creates what Norton, Dunn, and others describe as a "positive feedback loop of kindness and happiness": I did something nice; it felt good; I want to do it again.

As with other traits, it's best (though not essential) to start cultivating generosity early, and Professor Norton emphasizes that seeding it in children doesn't require "big philanthropy" – that small acts of kindness and generosity are just as effective. Norton suggests regularly encouraging a child to, for example, help with a younger sibling's birthday party, or sit at lunch with a classmate who may be feeling left out. For more traditional types of charity at scales that are relevant to children, Norton referred us to organizations, some online, that offer opportunities for what Warren Buffett has called retail philanthropy – gifts directed toward individual organizations and often particular purposes, such as "$43 to purchase art supplies for a third-grade classroom in Kentwood, Michigan."

Norton also notes that generosity feedback loops may be most powerful when givers engage in what social scientists call "costly giving" – that is, giving from one's own resources. Several years ago, an intriguing study was conducted at the University of British Columbia by Lara Aknin, J. Kiley Hamlin, and

Professor Dunn. Trained observers measured the reactions of children under the age of two through a variety of experiences, including being introduced to a monkey puppet; watching as a researcher gave the monkey a treat; giving the monkey a treat themselves; and finally, giving the monkey one of their *own* treats. Of those four experiences, the one that reliably elicited the greatest happiness from the children was the last – the only one involving costly giving.

In sum, the message we wish to share about family philanthropy is this: Make generosity your starting point and your end goal. In between, and as your philanthropy grows, think carefully about your structures and protocols around participation, management, and giving priorities – there is a wealth of literature to help you craft these in ways that reflect your family's principles. But start and end with generosity, and trust that the rest will be easier and better because you did so.

We close with a story we once heard from Walter Isaacson, a Harvard College alumnus, former head of the Aspen Institute, and a best-selling biographer of Einstein, Steve Jobs, Leonardo da Vinci, and others. When Walter was a child, his parents encouraged his siblings and him to each make an annual donation during the fall to a charity of their choice. Later in the year, when the thank you letters from those charities arrived in the mail they would be tied with a ribbon and placed under the Christmas tree to be opened Christmas morning by the child who had chosen that charity. It's a tradition that Walter continues in his own family today, and which he remembers fondly as one of the ways his parents regularly reminded him that "giving to others is really a gift to ourselves."

That sentiment – which re-casts generosity to include an element of self-care – is the most essential ingredient of successful family philanthropy. It produces multiplying ripples that spread outward to the world, and inward to the family. The realization that our happiness depends as much on what we *give to* the universe as what we *get from* it is enormously liberating and adds to our sense of control over the vicissitudes of life. It awakens instincts within us: to listen without judgment; to be genuinely interested in understanding another family member's point of view; to be grateful for all that is good in our piece of this shared world. And last, it helps us to appreciate Mark Twain's reflection in his later years that "There isn't time, so brief is life, for bickerings, apologies, heartburnings, callings to account. There is only time for loving, and but an instant, so to speak, for that."

Questions for Further Reflection

1. What's the purpose of our family's money? Who or what should it serve, and how?
2. What gets in the way of our fostering healthy generosity in ourselves and in our families?
3. How does it feel to help someone?
4. Are gifts to others actually gifts to ourselves?

5. What can I do to encourage my children to perform small acts of kindness and generosity?
6. Can generosity outside the family lead to generosity inside the family?
7. How can I help someone today?

Additional Resources

Charles W. Collier, *Wealth in Families*, 3rd ed. (Cambridge, MA: Harvard University Press, 2012).

Adam Grant, *Give and Take: Why Helping Others Drives Our Success* (New York: Penguin Books, 2013).

Richard Weissbourd, *The Parents We Mean to Be* (New York: Houghton Mifflin Harcourt, 2010).

Elizabeth Dunn and Michael Norton, *Happy Money* (New York: Simon & Schuster, 2013).

Robert Kegan and Lisa Lahey, *Immunity to Change* (Boston: Harvard Business Press, 2009).

Mo Willems, *Should I Share My Ice Cream?* (White Plains, NY: Disney Publishing, 2011).

Biographies

As Harvard University's philanthropic advisor, Alasdair Halliday helps Harvard families shape their philanthropy and think through the challenges and opportunities of family wealth. Alasdair speaks frequently on the subject of family dynamics, with a particular emphasis on family conversations about wealth. He has trained extensively in family systems theory, and worked closely for many years with Charles Collier, a pioneer in the field of philanthropic advising. Before joining Harvard's Alumni Affairs and Development office in 2004, Alasdair was a management consultant with the global strategy firm, Monitor Group, where he worked with Fortune 500 clients on matters of corporate strategy, mergers and acquisitions, and finance, and led equities analysis in the Internet and telecom sectors for Monitor's Asset Management Group. Alasdair has served on a number of non-profit boards in the arts, education, and financial planning sectors. He holds a BA in economics from Harvard College.

Anne McClintock is executive director of University Planned Giving at Harvard. As a charitable gift planning specialist for over 30 years, Anne has helped donors establish optimal gift arrangements for themselves, family members, Harvard and other organizations. She has trained in family systems theory and enjoys the privilege of helping individuals grapple with the complexities associated with wealth, family, and legacy. Prior to joining the University, Anne developed financing packages for corporations as a loan officer at Bank of Boston (now part of Bank of America). She is a past president of the executive board of the Planned Giving Group of New England and has served as a consultant to several non-profit organizations. Anne currently serves on the board of Lexington Montessori School. She holds an AB in economics from Smith College.

CHAPTER 43

How Do You Engage Children and Grandchildren in Philanthropy?

Lisa Parker

The idea of including children and grandchildren in philanthropy is captivating, and for good reason. In its full promise, giving as a family calls forth the most noble and generous parts of ourselves and cocoons us in a shared sense of purpose while affecting critical issues and our communities. The legal and financial expertise needed to structure a giving vehicle (Foundation, Donor Advised Fund, Charitable Trust, LLC) and accompanying investment strategy is readily available.

However, a 2009 survey of donors released by the National Center for Family Philanthropy revealed that the vast majority of founders were on their own to figure out how to engage family, particularly children, in their giving. In some cases, they were bewildered, even bitterly disappointed, that their children were uninterested in participating. These "children" ranged in age from their late 30s to mid 50s. So, what accounts for the successful engagement of children and grandchildren in family giving? Although there are many ways to prepare them to be wise and compassionate givers, the odds that they will embrace philanthropy dramatically increase when the philanthropic impulse is intentionally cultivated, often from an early age.

My Story

The most common reasons cited for establishing a family foundation (or other vehicle) include making a difference in the community, creating a shared sense of purpose, nurturing family relationships, and perpetuating the family's legacy. The mission of the foundation is built on the values forged from the founder's life circumstances and experiences of triumph and challenge. These values are the material from which to establish the mission of your giving. Articulating those values and the stories that have shaped you gives your children and grandchildren a greater understanding of the family's essential mores.

My grandfather, television personality and bandleader, Lawrence Welk, walked off the family farm in North Dakota on his 21st birthday with a dream, an accordion, and the clothes on his back. The experiences that ensued gave him a profound sense of compassion for those who struggle and seeded his passion for giving "young folks" real opportunities to do meaningful work. Above all, he valued family, even referring to his performers as his "musical family." The mission of the Lawrence Welk Family Foundation, to support grass-roots organizations providing a long-term commitment to children and families living in poverty, stems naturally from these values. These are essential tenets of our family culture and we are united in our connection to this story. Simply inviting family members to reflect on their shared values often gives meaning to your philanthropic goals as a family.

Site Visits

Including children in philanthropy gives them a wider window into the issues of need that are your focus. The most effective way of sparking interest in children and grandchildren is to include them in visits to organizations you are considering for funding. My mother took me, then aged 14, on a "site visit" to a small parish in East Los Angeles where a young priest, new to the community, was opening the doors of the church at night to homeless men – the destitute, the working poor, and migrant workers. His description of the fundamental dignity of giving a man a place to rest his head and the profound consequences for that life deeply affected me. Later he applied to our foundation for a grant to establish Homeboy Bakery in East Los Angeles, where rival gang members now stand side-by-side baking bread.

Witnessing the work non-profit leaders undertake is powerful. It can reframe the relationship to money in a culture of excess and increase children's likelihood of being givers in the future. Some donors do not want to flaunt their wealth or call attention to their giving, but when you discuss your giving and bring children with you to organizations you support you give them a gift. In fact, a poll of teen givers (defined as teens who volunteer once a week or more and actively raise funds), 84% of respondents cited their parents' example of donating and volunteering as the most influential factor in their own giving.

Start Young

Parents and grandparents universally want to pass on philanthropic values and nurture the giving instinct but often wonder when to start this process. The right time is as soon as possible! Children as young as four can explore giving and this can be as simple as setting up a Dinner Table Foundation. A Mason jar decorated as they like, becomes a "giving jar" to collect spare change (or a portion of allowance for older children) that they can donate to the cause of their choice.

Giving the proceeds in an age-appropriate and meaningful way starts with asking the young child, "What makes you happy?" Almost universally animals are children's first cause. Our daughter chose to give her giving-jar change to Arthur, the elderly deer she had befriended at the local petting zoo. Our son especially loved watching the lizards dart by on the nature path near our house. He brought his jar to the office on site so they could continue to protect the lizards. The concept works with older children too as long as the cause is relevant to them.

The most important element when a young person gives is the *processing* of that experience. How did you feel after giving that money? How did you help the animal? The "helper's high" is especially intoxicating for a little one discovering that they can make a difference. Noticing these feelings is required at this processing stage and allows the powerful feelings associated with giving to take root. Naturally they will want to replicate these feelings. As children grow, their awareness of causes expands to include their school community and the needs in the larger community (particularly homelessness). All children go through a stage of fervent concern for fairness and justice. The Dinner Table Foundation can evolve as they do.

Junior Boards

Junior Boards or Advisory Boards familiarize and prepare teens and young adults to be wise stewards of philanthropic dollars. The way in which this invitation is extended, however, can either compel or repel them. Familiar phrases like "To whom much is given, much is expected," or "You have a duty and obligation to give back," although valid, can sound couched in guilt. These sayings may diminish what can be a joyful experience.

In our case, the 10 members of the third generation were invited to become a Junior Board when we ranged in age from 12 to 24. We participated in the foundation board meetings taking a seat at the board table with our parents. We were encouraged to ask questions when we didn't understand the board jargon and were invited to share our opinions fully on the organizations seeking grants. We had a voice, even though we did not have a formal vote.

In addition, we held our own meeting and were given 10% of the gifting budget to allocate as we saw fit. With the freedom to explore what was meaningful to us as individuals and as a generation, facing issues our granddad could never have envisioned, we began to think of ourselves as having agency on critical issues of our day. Our parents were doing what came naturally but by inviting us into the experience, encouraging us to contribute, respecting our opinions, and empowering us to make our own giving decisions, they hooked us.

Whether a family's philanthropy is intended to last for a few years or in perpetuity, founders commonly have high hopes for multi-generational participation in the giving. It is important to recognize, however, that there are phases of life when it is more challenging to engage the next generation. As we became young adults, my generation was automatically promoted to the board of the Lawrence Welk Family Foundation, but the timing was off. As young adults we were defining our own paths, pursuing graduate studies, launching careers, and starting families. The obligation to be responsible, engaged, and prepared board members, and to travel across the United States to attend meetings was onerous and guilt set in.

Families I have interviewed are understandably discouraged when their children show the same lack of interest and resentment of the expectation. This is not only a disappointment, but also a real threat to the integrity of the foundation. The duty implicit with a foundation is that it will act in the best interest of the public good. Reluctant stewards are not equipped to meet this obligation. We worked around this road-block by making involvement a choice and not an edict. Most importantly, it truly was okay *not* to be interested. Now family members can opt in for three-year board terms when they wish. Family foundations that have made it to the fourth, fifth, and sixth generations expect and plan for the waxing and waning of interest. Planning a family foundation meeting around a family reunion often enhances both celebrations and shows that those who cannot participate in the foundation work are still cherished for their presence.

We have a fundamental human need to connect. Philanthropy connects us to issues and people we otherwise would not know, like Father Boyle and the Homeboys. Years ago a client came to me when he had sold a business and was suddenly a billionaire. He and his wife had two adolescent daughters and wanted to introduce their wealth first through philanthropy. They reflected together on the ways that they had benefited from others' giving, though they may not have realized it; the scholarship that allowed him to go to college, the playground built with private dollars, the children's museum in their town. Their lives were better because of the generosity of others and they could now do the same. Wealth can be isolating but philanthropy could connect them to people and places around the globe, and to each other, in a new way. Their father explained that this was important, "because we are only as good as our connections to one another."

Questions for Further Reflection

1. What do you expect/hope for in engaging your children and grandchildren in philanthropy?
2. Who can best lead this effort?

3. What talents do your next generation have and how can those be harnessed for the foundation?
4. What training or resources are needed for the new prospective board members?

Additional Resources

National Center for Family Philanthropy. https://www.ncfp.org.

Roy Williams and Vic Preisser, *Philanthropy Heirs and Values* (Bandon, OR: Robert D. Reed Publishers, 2005).

Susan Crites Price, *The Giving Family* (Arlington, VA: Council on Foundations, 2005).

Susan Crites Price, *Generous Genes* (Battle Ground, VA: Majestic Oak Press, 2015).

Kelin Gersick, *Generations of Giving: Leadership and Continuity in Family Foundations* (Lanham, MD: Lexington Books, 2004).

Biography

Lisa Parker brings 30 years of experience in philanthropy and non-profit management to her work with philanthropic families. In 1997 she became the president and executive director of the Lawrence Welk Family Foundation, leading the Foundation's initiatives to address poverty and seed the youth-giving movement, and creating youth philanthropy programs for the family's fourth generation. In 2009, she launched San Francisco-based Family Circle Advisors to help families find shared meaning in their giving and to optimize the impact of their grants.

Lisa is an advisor and board member to numerous organizations building and expanding the philanthropic sector, including the USC Center on Philanthropy and Public Policy and the National Center for Family Philanthropy.

CHAPTER 44

How Can You Wisely Develop a Long-Term Strategy for Your Philanthropy?

Barnaby Marsh

In 1930, in the midst of the Great Depression, the economist John Maynard Keynes wrote a paper about economic prospects for future generations. Entitled "Economic Possibilities for Our Grandchildren," he argued to readers that, most likely, the most creative and prosperous days are ahead.

Keynes's insights have implications for philanthropic planning and crafting donor intent. Humans are endlessly creative and driven by opportunity, which means change. In recent years we have seen an increasing array of philanthropic ideas, measures, operations, and ways of supporting new efforts to address some of the world's most pressing problems. In addition, there have been changes in tax law and legislation that affect giving. In the context of dynamic change and innovative practices, a focus on the possibilities of the future can be bewildering, even for those who have extensive experience with philanthropic planning and vision-casting.

Given the inevitability of such changes, how can you wisely develop a long-term strategy for your philanthropy? How do we prudently approach planning when the goalposts and rules of the game are changing, where different generations may see different opportunities and have shifting aspirations, and when the needs and possibilities in society evolve? How much do we acknowledge that the pathway to get there may not yet be known? How much do we let go and allow problems to be solved by others or by future generations?

The first step is to recognize that although the future will bring changes, some things will remain the same. For example, some years ago, I was asked by a well-known billionaire to oversee a study of what society might look like within 50 years. He was doing long-term planning for his philanthropy and wanted to know what trends could be found that could help inform his longer-term planning.

The philanthropist also wanted to know in what ways predictions of the future tended to be right or wrong, and why. His research team had found hundreds of books and articles that made predictions about the future. Just leafing through a few of these was very informative and told a lot about hopes and fears through the ages, besides the awesome power of the human imagination. From Da Vinci's fanciful sketches of flying machines to twentieth-century science fiction of space communities, the array of possible – and wonderful – futures seemed endless. Yet, in the analysis and conclusion, most of our basic human issues and needs remained, even if fundamental breakthroughs in technology, medicine, communications, and other areas had rendered these needs less acute. As one person on my team put it, "there is still poverty in America, even if our poorest citizens now have color televisions, microwave ovens, and cars" – all luxuries that had been aspired to in the 1950s, 1960s, and 1970s.

The main point is, when thinking about the future, the more that some things change, the more that other things, especially human fundamentals, stay the same. The Apple Watch notwithstanding, the 1950s vignettes of soon-to-be-had flying cars, jetpacks, and talking watches remain technological curiosities for an eccentric and rich few. Times and technologies may change, of course, but the basic human experience remains surprisingly constant. Even if and when the robots do (finally) come, we can be fairly sure that there will be more than enough remaining work and problems to be solved by humans to go around, and that the human needs for inspiration, purpose, and fulfillment will probably be as pressing as they are today.

Which brings us back to philanthropy. I am often asked by philanthropists about how to best think about horizons. There is, of course, no one-size-fits-best answer, but the kinds of questions and considerations that this single question leads to are centrally important. Is there realistic hope for future family involvement? If so, what will keep these unique individuals engaged and satisfied? How much flexibility and independence will they have, and what role will the founder's original donor intent play to channel their energy?

These questions lead to a second point: assume that the future will have its own ideas about what is good, right, or necessary. This point becomes evident when you look at the past. The first thing that we notice by looking back is that anticipating long-term possibilities is not easy. Instructive case studies are eye-opening and can help the philanthropist of today to be more thoughtful about what kinds of possibilities can lie ahead. For example, laws change, and societal norms and expectations can change dramatically. Going back just 100 years in the United States, we can see top federal tax rates ranging from 25% to 94%, and laws changing in terms of what qualifies as charitable activity. Recently, a new tax was passed on large university endowments. There are many examples of large private foundations shifting their funding away from the areas of the donor's original intent because staff or even trustees had their own ideas of how the money could be better spent.

One quickly sees the risks and dangers. Philanthropic benefactions without clearly articulated donor intent can result in dramatic power struggles that go on for decades, and the real losers in these struggles are often the charitable beneficiaries. Sometimes, a host institution for a gift assumes more freedom long after the benefaction is made, as in the case of the increasing breadth of uses for the Robertson family's gift to Princeton, originally intending to help encourage students in public service but later used for a very wide array of purposes. This led to a long and very costly lawsuit.

Having an independent private foundation with professional staff is not necessarily easier when it comes to long-term thinking. Professional staff often have agendas of their own, and over time these interests may conflict with those of the founding donor or family. For example, Henry Ford II decided that it was best for him to resign from the board of the Ford Foundation because the directions of the Foundation in the social movements of the 1960s seemed conflict with Henry Ford's basic worldview.

Sometimes, it is not even a matter of shifting fashions and perspectives but merely trying to interpret philanthropic intentions of someone who is no longer living. Consider Englishman James Smithson's large benefaction to establish, in Washington, a new institution for the "increase and diffusion of knowledge." The ambiguity of the gift left its stewards wondering what he had intended. A new school? A new university? A center focused on publishing and disseminating practical knowledge and ideas? Ultimately, a new public museum was thought to be the best option, which may not have seemed to be the most likely possibility to many at the time. Would a public museum have satisfied Smithson? No one knows.

What can we learn from those philanthropists who have been seen as wise in the eyes of history? A crucial lesson is that making space for future generations to innovate and build is important. We can see this in many cases, ranging from John Harvard's supporting the founding of a new college, to Andrew Carnegie's challenge to offer matching funds to build community libraries.

Successful philanthropic efforts (just like all progress) ultimately depend on harnessing the energy and creativity of the leaders and change-makers of each age. Money and a declaration of purpose by itself will not accomplish the most ambitious visions, unless those who are in charge deeply and genuinely embrace and take ownership of the vision. The future, including its innovations, its social movements, and its solutions will always be driven by passionate individuals who are able to inspire and engage others, rather than by those who see themselves as merely entrusted to follow any given set of rules.

This sort of approach, where the donor outlines the "what" of the general vision but leaves open some of the decisions about the "how," can work well because it allows for future creativity. Every sector has its geniuses, whether inventors, pioneers, or those who lead social movements. Philanthropists are generally well-served to identify these change-makers early on, to support them, and to help the fruits of their work create the widest possible benefit. From this perspective, examples of long-term transformation are abundant.

Practically, what does this insight mean to philanthropic families and their most trusted staff who are charged with stewardship? How do we know whether the vision and the compass heading is the right one? One of the vexing problems faced by those who are stewards of great wealth is how to avoid well-intended harm. As the philanthropy history observer Martin Wooster notes in his book *The Great Philanthropists & the Problem of Donor Intent*, examples abound of individuals sapped of their creative potentials and private-foundation structures gone amuck because of the intoxicating aspects of great wealth.

How does one plan for the future prudently and wisely? Although it may seem counterintuitive, some of the biggest possible future potentials are to be found in framing a vision broadly and by allowing a range of ideas to co-exist and to actively compete in its pursuit. Competition of ideas is expensive in the short term because of duplication and what appears to be a lack of co-ordination and focus, but just as in the wilds of nature and in sophisticated economic markets, it is also the surest way to ensure not just survival, but long-term vitality.

One of the billionaires that I worked very closely with, the master investor Sir John Templeton, even went as far as to create three separate large foundations (in three different countries) having identical mandates in observance of this principle. In the long term, what matters is maximizing chances of success, even if it means that in the near term costs are high, and some new directions don't work out. Being able to change course and to reframe a core challenge, and to see fresh solutions, can be built into the DNA of a mandate that serves a bigger vision.

We live in a prosperous time that will lead to even more prosperity in the future. Innovation and change must be our ally, rather than feared. With foresight, wise planning, and some luck, our grandchildren will have possibilities for engagement and fulfillment that are beyond what we can currently imagine. If history is a guide for us, the wisest decisions of today will be those that set lofty goals but that allow the torch of opportunity creation to pass easily from generation to generation.

Questions for Further Reflection

1. Does your family understand, at a deep level, the reasons and intentions for your giving? A few lines written down now could prevent a lot of anguish later.
2. It has been said that the future belongs to those who invent it. In this context, have you thought not only where the need is the greatest, but also where the prospects for innovation and change are the greatest?

3. Consider that in the long term, laws, institutions, and even cultures change. Is your vision conceptualized in a way to anticipate such change?

Additional Resources

Martin Morse Wooster, *Great Philanthropic Mistakes* (Washington, DC: Hudson Institute, 2006).

Martin Morse Wooster, *The Great Philanthropists & The Problem of Donor Intent* (Washington, DC: Capital Research Center, 1998).

Jeffrey Cain, *Protecting Donor Intent: How to Define and Safeguard Your Philanthropic Principles* (Washington, DC: Philanthropy Roundtable, 2012).

Biography

Dr. Barnaby Marsh has privately advised hundreds of the world's most generous individuals on how to achieve greater philanthropic impact. For many years, he worked with the investing pioneer Sir John Templeton to develop novel philanthropic strategies and was a key creativity leader in the development of the $3 billion John Templeton Foundation. In 2015, Barnaby co-founded the elite philanthropic services agency Saint Partners, where he represents wealthy individuals and their families in their long-term strategic giving, including assistance in launching, managing, and producing important philanthropic projects. He holds an AB *Summa cum laude* from Cornell University, and a PhD from Oxford University, where he was a Rhodes Scholar.

3. Consider that in the long term, laws, institutions, and even cultures change. How would you conceptualize [illegible] to anticipate such change?

Additional Resources

Martin Morse Wooster, *Great Philanthropic Mistakes* (Washington, DC: Hudson Institute, 2006).

Martin Morse Wooster, *The Great Philanthropists & the Problem of Donor Intent* (Washington, DC: Capital Research Center, 1994).

Jeffrey Cain, *Protecting Donor Intent: How to Define and Safeguard Your Philanthropic Principles* (Washington, DC: Philanthropy Roundtable, 2012).

Biography

Dr. Ramsay Marsh has [illegible] advised hundreds of the world's most generous individuals on how to achieve greater philanthropic impact. For many years, he worked with the late pioneer Sir John Templeton to develop novel philanthropic strategies and had a key operational role in the development of the $3 billion John Templeton Foundation. In 2007, Marsh co-founded the elite philanthropic consultancy [illegible] Partners, where he represents wealthy individuals and their families in their long-term strategic giving, including assistance in launching, managing, and producing impact-oriented philanthropic projects. He holds an M.Sc. [illegible] and a PhD from Oxford University, where he was a Rhodes Scholar.

SECTION 8

SEEKING SOUND ADVICE

Life is complicated. And it gets more so as wealth increases – particularly when assets are owned in common, structures become more complex, the number of family members increases, and founders plan to pass on operating businesses and financial or real assets. At the same time, the world in which we operate is also becoming more complicated with investments, taxes, regulations, and geopolitical events spinning faster every day.

You can't be good at everything, so it is probably inevitable that you will have to rely on advisors with key technical skill and practical experience. Also, since you will often have only one shot at making certain important decisions (such as a business sale), you might want to talk to someone who has significant familiarity with this particular issue.

But it can be hard to find the right advisor – especially someone with integrity, a good demeanor, the right fit with you, the best set of skills, and the appropriate incentives and motivations. In this section, our authors help you think through the fundamental questions of working with advisors – how do you choose them, which ones are right for your family, how do you use them well, how do you evaluate them and when do you change them?

We start with an essay by Susan Massenzio responding to the question "What types of advisors should you consider?" Even that is not a simple question because the menu can include generalists, specialists, technicians, mentors, coaches, facilitators, counselors, and even family members, all with varying degrees of appropriateness for those roles. Susan looks at all the different sorts of people who can advise families, what specific benefits they can bring, and what you should (and should not) expect from them. She also offers a series of questions that can help families separate the wheat from the chaff and find advisors who will be a positive force in the life of a family, with a particular focus on advisor competence, experience, and goodwill.

In his typical no nonsense, no-holds-barred approach, Philip Marcovici provides guidance on the question "How can you find trustworthy advisors?"

His many years of experience as a lawyer to families of wealth have given him a jaundiced view of many advisor motivations, incentives, and desire for control. He provides great input on reducing conflicts of interest and improving alignment between advisors and clients for the benefit of families.

What do you do when you think you have found a good advisor but you're not sure? Perhaps there are some red flags and maybe just some yellow ones. Stephen Horan and Robert Dannhauser tackle the topic, "How can you avoid the next Bernie Madoff?" Unscrupulous advisors and inappropriate investment products will never disappear, but in a complex investment arena where advisors are often required, Stephen and Robert provide guidance on how to, in the words of Ronald Reagan: "Trust, but verify."

Some families have determined that they could benefit from the integrated objective approach offered by a family office, which then leads to another set of questions such as "Should you choose a single-family office or a multi-family office?" There is a multiplicity of decision factors that should be taken into account, and Kirby Rosplock walks us through a thoughtful, reasoned, and personally relevant way to make this decision. She also offers some handy evaluation tools to understand the choices.

Finally, Hartley Goldstone answers the question, "How do you choose a good trustee?" A trustee makes decisions in the place of others, for the benefit of others. They need to be skilled, trustworthy, experienced, and have good emotional intelligence. Hartley provides guidance on finding, evaluating, and engaging good trustees who will not only execute the technical components of the trust but who will also fulfill the original intent of the settlors and care about the beneficiaries as unique individuals.

At the end of the day, a good advisor is trustworthy. And what kind of person is trustworthy? They are *credible* (you can count on them to know what they are talking about), they are *reliable* (they do what they say they are going to do), you can *talk* to them (you know they will listen and keep confidences), and they are *not self-oriented* (you can be sure they will be focused on your best interests, not their own).[1]

[1]David H. Maister, Charles H. Green, and Robert M. Galford, *The Trusted Advisor* (New York: Simon & Schuster, 2000).

CHAPTER 45

What Types of Advisors Should You Consider?

Susan Massenzio

Beginning Questions

Family wealth is a "high-credence" field. That means that it is not always clear to people using services how results are achieved and how performance is or should be measured. If a dentist does something wrong, you'll probably feel it right away. A wealth advisor's advice may appear right or wrong only long after the fact. As a result, most clients engage with advisors, at least in part, on trust. Personal charm, friendly recommendations, and prestige may trump cold analysis in the selection of advisors.

An advisor relationship is a human relationship. The goal here is not to eliminate emotion. Rather, it is to help you identify three key traits in any advisor you would want to work with: competence, experience, and good intent.

To begin, when meeting with a prospective new advisor or reviewing an established advisor's work, these questions can be helpful to guide the discussion:

- What specific services will I receive (or have I been receiving) from you?
- Who will work with my family and in what capacities?
- How do you differ from other advisors in this space?

What Specific Services Will I Receive (or Have I Been Receiving)?

The first question gets at the crucial matter of what services you can expect from the advisor. Over time, families may come to enjoy personal rapport and closeness with their advisors. But the foundation of any rapport must be tangible services from the advisor to the client, and most of these services in wealth advising take expertise and time to provide.

For example, the backbone of many investment advisors' practices is asset allocation and manager or securities selection. At the same time, they may describe various other services: tax planning, tax preparation, other accounting services, design and facilitation of family meetings, and so on. If an advisor makes these services available, make sure you understand what they are, how they are delivered, and whether you want them. This discussion should help you understand in which areas the advisor feels truly competent and experienced, and which areas are less central to that advisor's area of competency.

Who Will Work with My Family and in What Capacity?

This question gets at the advisor's service model. Most financial advisors work in teams. The team approach can help clients get specialized advice fast and in an integrated manner. It can also make it hard to understand who does what. Ask for specific role definition and clarity. If the people in those roles change over time, that's not necessarily a reason for alarm. You should expect your advisor's practice to grow and change. However, if a key member of the team leaves or is reassigned, or changes take place without communication to you, that may be an occasion for stepping back and re-evaluating the relationship.

How Do You Differ from Other Advisors in This Space?

This question identifies the qualities that distinguish advisors from others. Advisors will often point to what they consider their strengths, whether in investments or planning or family dynamics. Once they do so, it is important to ask for tangible examples of how they deliver them. Again, seek to understand what this advisor identifies as his or her area of core competency. Watch for at least two red flags: first, if an advisor appears to promise to be able to do everything, and second, if an advisor always refers to another team member to get the job done.

Money

Advice does not come free. Part of your task as a client is to evaluate the price for that advice versus its value.

To approach this comparison of price and value, here are some questions that you can ask your own advisors or prospective advisors:

- Since your practice must grow to flourish, what percentage of your time do you spend on seeking new clients?
- What percentage of your time do you spend directly on work with and for your own clients?
- How many clients do you have final responsibility for?

There are no hard and fast percentages to look for in those first two questions. They will often depend on where the advisor is in his or her practice development. Advisors just starting a business will naturally spend more time on marketing. That is why it is helpful also to know how many clients an advisor has final responsibility for serving. Fewer does not simply mean better and more does not automatically mean worse. It all depends upon what you as the client are seeking.

It is also important to ask an advisor, "What are the various ways that you get paid?" Since revenue incents behavior, it is natural for advisors to recommend products or services that make them money.

It is hard to talk about money with anyone, including advisors. That said, it is good practice to discuss fees with your advisor at least once a year and to take the lead in that conversation. There are a few principles and practices that can help you make that conversation productive:

- Make sure fee proposals are clear and written.
- Ask your advisor to put his or her fees in context. For example, based on available marketplace data, where does this advisor's fee structure fall relative to others'?
- Watch how your advisor responds to questions about the fees. How your advisors respond to these questions or this conversation could serve as a sign of their competence, experience, and good intent.

A fair fee and a good fee discussion can bring the advisor's good and the client's good into congruence, and, rather than driving people apart, it can help solidify a productive relationship.

Personnes de Confiance

All these points also apply to the special class of advisors who help families grow their complete family wealth. Some people call such advisors *personnes de confiance*. Others just call them trusted advisors. It is hard to categorize them by a single profession or field, although they may have started out as lawyers, accountants, financial advisors, or psychologists. Sometimes, though, a *personne de confiance* may appear in the guise of a friend, a teacher, a priest, an intellectual, an in-law, or a manager. They often play a key supporting (or number-two) role in families of wealth.

As diverse as they may appear, *personnes de confiance* do share qualities in common:

- An interest in culture: A true number-two recognizes that no family leader, no matter how forceful, can by him- or herself effect lasting change. A system, such as a family, requires agreement and engagement to carry out a visionary's vision.
- A belief in orderly evolutionary change: Sometimes visible change happens quickly. But it is almost always preceded by unseen, gradual

adjustments. Beware of an advisor who promises to change your family culture in the space of a single meeting.

- Subordination of ambition to a higher calling: A number-two is, by definition, not number-one. Some people recoil at the thought of such subordination. But there are many cases in which the quiet efforts of a true number-two have had more positive effects on a family's long-term flourishing than the more noticeable actions of hyperactive number-ones.

The term *personne de confiance* is a high-sounding title. In essence, such an advisor is someone who puts your family – the whole family – first, in terms of preserving and growing all the family's capital. The role is defined by attitude, not skills. Ask yourself: Is there someone in your network of advisors who takes that perspective? If so, hold tight to him or her. If not, start looking for someone who does.

Counselors, Coaches, and Facilitators

One type of *personne de confiance* who can play a large role in the journey of family wealth is the counselor, facilitator, or coach. Such counselors may advise individuals about life or career, or may work with the entire family, say, in preparing for a family meeting or a discussion of governance. Many counselors and coaches are well trained and effective. Some are not. Because there are no generally accepted standards for this role, if you are considering engaging a counselor or facilitator, here are some questions to ask yourself first:

- What are the aspects of your life – individually or as a family – that you would like to improve?
- Do these areas of concern have to do primarily with your career, your family, or your own life?
- Are you willing to make time to meet regularly and to reflect on your meetings?
- Are you willing to be honest and authentic with someone else about parts of yourself, your work, or your family relationships that you may not like?

If the answers to these questions have led you to conclude that you are ready for a counseling relationship, then here are some questions or criteria to consider in seeking out a suitable coach or counselor:

- What is the prospective counselor's training?
- Does the prospective counselor have a medically accepted license?
- What is the prospective counselor's experience? In work? In counseling?
- Does that experience line up with the challenges you are seeking to work on?

Entering a counseling relationship always involves some element of trust, and it is a two-way street. But it does not have to be a pure leap of faith. Consider the idea of committing to just two meetings with any prospective counselor or coach, to assess each other and your possible relationship. If, after two meetings, you both agree that there is a productive fit, then you can proceed to more regular sessions. If not, then neither you nor the counselor has invested a significant amount of time or money in a relationship that would probably not work anyway. These initial two meetings also give you and the counselor some time to explore the possible goals for your work together. Even if you do not keep meeting after that, the work you do in these two sessions may prove useful to you as you continue your journey.

Mentors

There is one more type of advisor to touch upon in the context of family wealth: the mentor. Most mentors today focus their efforts on a task or process of adjustment. A mentor may help you at school or at a new job or at various times in your career. But a true mentor does more than help you *adjust.* A true mentor helps you *evolve.* Families with significant wealth or operating businesses often seek out mentors for the rising-generation members of the family, to help them evolve independent lives, regardless of whether or not they pursue paths related to the wealth or the business.

A true mentor is rare. What are a mentor's characteristics? First, a mentor is experienced. Most often, this experience accompanies old age, but it may be won earlier in life. Second, a mentor is trusted. It takes time and familiarity for someone to become a mentor. Third, as mentioned, a mentor does not focus on just one task or adjustment. Finally, being a mentor takes some wit or even guile. Authenticity is all well and good. But a mentee may not always be ready for the truth. A mentor must know how much to reveal and when. This last point means that you may meet a mentor – or perhaps have already met a mentor – and not quite know it at the time.

Mentorship is not a relationship that can be forced or demanded. After all, Athena, the original mentor, was a goddess. She came and went as she wished. Perhaps the best thing that you can do is to open your heart to the possibility of mentorship. When the heart is ready, the mentor appears.

A Father's Wisdom

I want to end this chapter on advisors with two words of wisdom from the mentor of one of my colleagues, James Hughes. This mentor was his father James Elliott Hughes Sr., himself a model counselor and advisor.

The Beginning of Anything Is Often Farther Down the Road Than We Perceive

Because we are often focused on the present moment and all that's led up to it, we believe that we are either at the beginning or a long way down the road. In fact, the true beginning of any important endeavor – including the journey of complete family wealth – usually becomes clear only after much time and many false starts. Look for a trusted advisor who has the patience to help you find your way to the beginning.

Take Small Steps and Succeed Together before Trying to Tackle the Most Difficult Problems

Often families want to take on the big problems right away. Advisors who encourage this tendency may shine for a moment, but usually those big problems are difficult for a reason. It takes time to understand, much less change, a family's culture. Only success built upon success has a chance of doing so.

Questions for Further Reflection

1. In your life, who has served you as a trusted advisor? What characteristics did that person have?
2. When you consider the different types of advisors described in this chapter, where are the gaps for your family?
3. How might trusted advisors to your spouse or children look different than a trusted advisor to you?

Recommended Reading

- James Hughes, Susan Massenzio, and Keith Whitaker, *Complete Family Wealth* (New York: Bloomberg Press, 2017).
- Niccolo Machiavelli, *The Prince*, trans. Harvey C. Mansfield (Chicago: University of Chicago Press, 1998).
- Herbert Goldhamer, *The Adviser* (New York: Elsevier, 1978).

Biography

Susan Massenzio, PhD is president of Wise Counsel Research Associates. She is a psychologist with extensive experience consulting to senior executives and leadership teams of Fortune 500 financial services firms. She helps firms design effective organizations, develop high potential executives, plan leadership succession, and integrate key leaders into new roles. As an executive consultant, she enables leaders to gain greater insight into their leadership and management styles and to maximize their influence and impact.

Susan has also consulted extensively with family businesses. She helps families make a positive impact through enhanced communication, decision making, cultivation of next generation leaders, and philanthropy. Susan is co-author of *The Cycle of the Gift, The Voice of the Rising Generation,* and *Complete Family Wealth,* all published by Bloomberg Press.

Susan served as the senior psychologist for John Hancock Financial Services, senior vice president for Wells Fargo Bank, and professor and program director at Northeastern University.

Susan holds a PhD in psychology from Northwestern University and a BA in sociology and education from Simmons College. She is a member of the Collaboration for Family Flourishing.

CHAPTER 46

How Can You Find Trustworthy Advisors?

Philip Marcovici

Advisors are almost always necessary, but it is important for wealth-owning families to understand their role, and to manage their advisors in the right way. Finding the right advisor requires that families know what they need and know who they are looking for. And an effective advisor is one who has the interests of their clients at the forefront, and positions themselves as a true trusted advisor.

Letting an advisor "kidnap" the succession process is very dangerous, and all too common in a complex world where leaving it to the experts seems to be the way to go. It is, after all, the wealth of the family involved – not the wealth of the advisor – but there are many situations of advisors becoming the gatekeepers to the family's wealth, using wealth that is not theirs to benefit themselves.

Lawyers and Accountants

Things on the legal, tax, and accounting front are increasingly complex and ever-changing, and there is little chance for any wealth owner to be able to navigate safely without the help of the right advisors.

The first key step is to find the right advisors, and one of the biggest dangers is relying on a lawyer or accountant who does not acknowledge what they do *not* know. It is not at all uncommon to find wealth owners who have turned to their business lawyers or accountants for help in succession and asset protection planning, and to find that the advisor took on the job without having the experience or knowledge needed to do it properly. A superbly competent commercial lawyer may well *not* have the experience and knowledge needed to put together a will or trust, but may turn their hand to it, making a mess of things for the family involved. Good, trusted advisors will acknowledge where they need help, and to be most effective for the family their longstanding commercial lawyers or accountants should stay in the picture, liaising with specialists who can provide the input the family really needs.

Personally, when I use a lawyer or accountant, I like to first ensure that I am using the right person for the right job – I want to know that the lawyer or accountant I am working with has experience and knowledge in the area that I need help with.

Private Banks and Trust Companies

Private banking and wealth management is a big, global business. Private banks generally make their money from managing the liquid assets of their clients, charging a percentage of assets under management (AUM).

For wealth owners, there is no choice but to be very critical about how banks charge, and to consider – where one has negotiating power given the level of assets involved – *not* signing the standard documents that banks put in front of you, but rather to set out your own terms, mandating your advisors to work in a way that makes sense for the wealth-owning family itself. Even where the amount of wealth involved is not enough to dictate your terms to the banks you work with, my suggestion is to agree in writing about the actual service you expect to receive, and to make it clear what your expectations are.

But there is much more than just asset management that an effective private bank can and should provide. A wealth-owning family needs a trusted advisor that is not only able to take charge of asset management in relation to liquid assets, but who is also able to help the family with investments in real estate, art, and anything else the family is interested in. There may also be a family business in the picture, and certainly asset protection, succession planning, and tax minimization will be topics of interest to the family. But if the private bank is focused on income it earns on AUM, will it really be able to help the family in all the other areas of need?

What clients of private banks really need is a trusted family advisor, and continuity in relationships that avoids the family having to re-educate relationship managers given the turnover in staffing suffered (or encouraged) by the industry today.

The wealth owner needs to understand how the industry really works and the failings of those running private banks to truly align their businesses with the interests of their clients. There are private banks and trust companies that get it right, and to find them, wealth owners have to know what they are looking for and ask the right questions.

Independent Asset Managers, Family Offices, and Family Business Advisors

The failings of private banks have led to the creation of independent asset managers (IAMs) and of the multi- and single-family office, and variations on a theme. Pricing abuse, high turnover of relationship managers, misalignment of focus and poor service generally have resulted in many families fleeing the private bank, turning to individuals (who may have left a private bank in favor of an independent firm) to offer them what they do not get from banks.

I believe that family offices, both the single-family office and the multi-family office, are products of the failings of the wealth-management industry to serve the real needs of families.

Defining the term *family office* is not easy, and there are many versions of family offices that bear little resemblance to each other. Today, private banks, law firms, accounting firms, trust companies, and others market family-office services, thereby further confusing the term.

The reality is that every wealth-owning family has a family office, regardless of whether they know it or not, and that it is difficult to find any two family offices that are the same. Someone, in every family, is taking care of things that a typical family office would deal with. A family involved in a family business may have the chief financial officer, or whoever is handling the books for the business, also keep an eye on personal investments, perhaps liaising with asset managers, and also paying bills on real estate and otherwise managing private assets the family holds. In effect, the individual involved is the family office, but the function may or may not be managed in a way that is best for the family, depending on how well structured the role of that individual is.

The more formal family office is one in which a family sets up a single family office – a function put in place just for that family. Here, there is no one model that families adopt, or which is the right one. A senior accountant with the family business coming to retirement might be appointed as the head of the family office function, coordinating the external advisors providing support to the family in relation to assets and succession and asset protection structures. This would be the start of a simple family office, the idea being to have someone keeping an eye on things in a coordinated way.

For many families, the cost of a dedicated single-family office and the distraction of running it makes the idea of a multi-family office of interest. Here the services involved are being provided not just to a single family but to many families.

Wealth owners also have choices when it comes to family business advisors who focus on, among others, helping families develop the right governance approaches, including family constitutions and charters. It is often ideal to work with someone who is able to coordinate with the full team of advisors typical families use. This person can help the wealth owner to actually *implement* approaches that are agreed, by liaising with lawyers and others involved in documenting shareholding arrangements, trusts, partnerships, and other legally binding arrangements that will be critical to the family and the family assets and business.

Conflicts of Interest – Everyone Has Them

Typical private banks have many conflicts of interest, and one of the challenges the industry faces is that clients have increasingly become aware of them. If I have an account with a private bank, they have an interest not only in managing my money but also in directing me to investments in products they have a financial interest in. These may include internal investment products from which the bank earns further fees, or third-party products from which the bank gets some form of benefit, whether through a retrocession (i.e. kickback) or something else. Transactions may give rise to revenue for the bank, and this may create an incentive to churn the account. If I use a trust company that is owned by a bank, does the trust company have an incentive to keep AUM with the bank as a means of enhancing overall revenue? For some banks, the trust function has traditionally been a cost center, specifically for the purposes of expanding AUM.

But if I turn to an IAM, or independent trust company, or to an independent lawyer or accountant, am I assured of freedom from conflicts of interests? In my view, the answer is *always* no. *Everybody* has conflicts of interest of some kind, and for the wealth owner, the best thing is to accept that this is the case, and to be aware of what the conflicts of interest are, so that they can be managed.

There is no replacement for the wealth owner and his or her family really understanding how advisors work. The wealth owner needs them – but needs to manage them, to keep an eye on them, to make sure that they get what they pay for, and to know what they are paying and why.

For advisors, the key to being the trusted family advisor is understanding what clients really need, and aligning interests with the interests of clients. A trusted advisor is one who is not measured by how markets perform and is not a commodity, but someone who is valued for telling the truth and always having the client's interests at heart.[1]

Questions for Further Reflection

1. Does our family understand how our advisors are compensated and what that compensation is? Do these compensation arrangements suggest conflicts of interest that need to be managed?

---

[1]This article contains modified excerpts from Philip Marcovici's book *The Destructive Power of Family Wealth* (Hoboken, NJ: Wiley, 2016).

2. Who has the power to replace protectors, guardians, executors, and others designated to be involved in my family's affairs? Is there a safe and effective approach to long-term governance, or are there risks that advisors can kidnap our family's trust or other structures?
3. Do we have the right advisory resources available to us, allowing our family to obtain the holistic input it needs? Hallmarks of good advisors include acknowledgment of what they do not know, in a complex world where no one has all the answers. Do we have advisors who know the right questions to ask, and who can help us find the specialists needed to find the right answers?

Additional Resources

Philip Marcovici, *The Destructive Power of Family Wealth: A Guide to Succession Planning, Asset Protection, Taxation and Wealth Management* (Chichester, UK: Wiley, 2016).

Biography

Philip Marcovici is retired from the practice of law and consults with governments, financial institutions, and global families in relation to tax, wealth management, and other matters. He is on the boards of several entities within the wealth management industry, as well as of entities within family succession and philanthropic structures. A member of the adjunct faculty of the Singapore Management University and of the Nanyang Technological University, Philip is actively involved in teaching in the areas of taxation, wealth management, and family governance. He is also a member of the Advisory Committee of the Hong Kong University of Science and Technology's Tanoto Center for Asian Family Business and Entrepreneurship Studies. Philip is also a founding advisor to the Cambridge Judge Business School in relation to its Executive Education program on Responsible Business and Wealth Ownership. His website is www.marcoviciasia.com.

CHAPTER 47

How Can You Avoid the Next Bernie Madoff?

Stephen Horan and Robert Dannhauser

Being an effective steward of wealth means you've taken on many important responsibilities and accountabilities. But the complexities of that stewardship go well beyond the capacity of any one person; you can't do it all yourself and be sufficiently expert in capital markets, portfolio management, tax, estate planning, philanthropy, business management, family dynamics, and all the other ingredients of successful wealth management. Your task is to array and manage a team of experts to address your objectives.

Who Can You Trust?

All those experts will bring relatively intangible human capital to bear on your opportunities and challenges, and since you can't literally kick the tires to assure yourself of the quality and suitability of the resources you'll be provided, you'll need other assurances that you've made the right choices for your team of advisors. Smart, technically astute, ethical, loyal people are what you're looking for; you'll make the best choices you can with the information and intuition available to you, and then you'll have to invest some trust that your team has your interests at heart in all that they do.

Bernie Madoff exploded this paradigm for family leaders. As is well known by now, Madoff took advantage of his social and professional profile to abuse the trust put in him by thousands of investors, resulting in billions of dollars lost. Hindsight makes many of the red flags clearer, but it is easy to sympathize with the family stewards who saw Madoff as an industry leader, a fixture in certain social circles, and in many cases, a friend. Trusting Bernie Madoff was a big mistake made by many, but amid the wreckage of lost money and disrupted lives, five important lessons can be learned.

Stewardship Is a Professional Endeavor

Friendships and ease of social interactions should not take the place of evidence of commitment to a professional approach to advice on investments or other technical issues. Does the advisor have a philosophy underpinning their work, and is there evidence that it is consistent over time? Similarly, are there durable processes in place that will guide your advisor's behavior and outcomes? Do the advisor and her employees show evidence of continuous rigorous learning to adapt to changing times?

Your investigation of these issues should inspire confidence that your advisor regards their intellectual capacities as a profession rather than as a more ethereal talent, implying that they are committed to sustained high standards of practice. You should be able to develop this requisite confidence without being deluged by jargon or technical language: beware potential advisors who just can't seem to explain themselves in language you understand.

Trust Your Intuition

At the risk of contradicting the first lesson to not put undue emphasis on likeability, your sense that an advisor is something of a jerk ought not be ignored. The best advisors often evolve to be confidants on a range of issues beyond their initial mandate as they get to know you and your family's circumstances well. This is far more difficult if you find the prospect of spending time with the advisor troubling. More importantly, your antennae's sensitivity to a difficult personality may be an early warning of larger problems ahead.

Demand both the social graces and caliber of expertise you require such as the Chartered Financial Analyst® (CFA), to make an effective working relationship possible, and don't fall to the temptation to make some compromises to have access to singular talent. There are a lot of very smart people in the advisory business and missing one or two from your roster will not predestine your family to suboptimal outcomes.

Insist on Strategy

You should demand a strategic approach to management of your family's assets. An investment policy statement embodies such an approach, capturing the objectives, tolerances, accountabilities, and processes for management of your family's investments in a document that can be shared with family members, advisors, and other relevant parties. The initial development of the investment policy statement can be challenging, testing assumptions and forcing a strategic view of the investment decision-making process.

But that effort is rewarded by having a document to refer to in trying times, which assures objectivity, consistency, and allegiance to strategic objectives when emotions might run high in difficult markets. The investment policy statement (IPS) can also enshrine the checks and balances you've built into your investment governance program, making some of the shortcuts taken by Madoff and his team far less likely. The IPS also anchors advisors in black and white to your objectives, constraints, and preferences, making alignment of their efforts easier and more likely. CFA Institute developed a framework of elements of investment policy statements for individuals and institutions that may be useful as a starting point (https://www.cfainstitute.org/en/advocacy/policy-positions/elements-of-an-investment-policy-statement-for-individual-investors).

Trust But Verify

In the words of the Russian proverb expressed by former US president Ronald Reagan, "trust but verify." Having elected to place your trust in an advisor, you should be vigilant in looking for ongoing clues to support your decision. Separation of duties, prescribed in the investment policy statement, is one important mechanism to be sure that there is independent reporting of the state of your accounts. Paying close attention to investment results is another: CFA Institute has developed an entire professional program around calculation and interpretation of investment performance (the Certified Investment Performance Management (CIPM) certificate) but you can take important first steps by being mindful of results that don't fit with what's happening in the markets, or that are oddly consistent over time, or that the investment advisor just can't explain to your satisfaction. Note that this doesn't mean that investment results always need to be good – there's a time and season to every approach and although over the long term you'll expect superior performance, shorter-term results over a period of months or even a few years may not impress. Investment results should be calculated and reported in compliance with industry standards (the Global Investment Performance Standards – GIPS). You should be able to disentangle the sources of return on your portfolio, including that from exposure to markets and industries, as well as from security selection, and relate that performance to your advisor's strategy. If you're having trouble reconciling your portfolio's returns from your examination of broader returns, take note.

Be a Good Client

The investment policy statement helps build clear context for your advisors' mandates, an important first step. You can (and should) be demanding in your expectation of results, but you should also be realistic about the magnitude of outperformance and timeframe to achieve results, and test your assumptions about these dimensions in dialogue with your advisors early on. Be willing to be vulnerable and tell your advisors when you don't understand them; they owe you clear, thoughtful explanations in language that makes sense to you.

Ignore the temptation to be embarrassed by what you might think are naïve or uninformed questions that are on your mind. Be confident enough to ask about the professional code of conduct to which they subscribe.

Good advisors will appreciate your efforts to engage and appreciate their work, and while micro-managing their mandate won't serve anyone's interests, having a clear understanding of the strategy and the main challenges and opportunities in its implementation is vital. Even the best advisors will sometimes be stumped by your question, more of a reflection on the enormous scope and complexity of wealth management than the knowledge of any one advisor. "I don't know" should be an entirely acceptable response to you, as long as there is appropriate follow-up to find the answers to your questions.

Madoff was a scoundrel. He falsified records and lied to his clients. The aftermath was all the more painful because many families relied on their trust in someone they thought was credible and "one of them." Your advisors have the technical expertise and raw smarts to help you meet your family's objectives. But you need to have capacity to be more than a passive partner to make the most of your advisor relationships and to avoid the occasional crook. The most important lesson of all might be that stewardship of wealth requires more than trust.

Questions for Further Reflection

1. Does the governance of your family's assets allow for the frequency and quality of interactions with your advisors to give you confidence that their mandates are being fulfilled appropriately?
2. Beyond contractual agreements, what systems or documents are in place to give your advisors the context that is useful to their relating their work to your objectives, constraints, and preferences?
3. When did you last hear something from an advisor that you didn't understand? How would your advisor have reacted if you had responded differently to what you heard?

Additional Resources

Ron Rimkus, *Bernard L. Madoff Investment Securities*, CFA Institute Econ Crises, 2017, https://www.econcrises.org/2017/04/20/bernard-l-madoff-investment-securities-2008-2009.

CFA Institute, "CIPM Course of Study," https://www.cfainstitute.org/programs/cipm/courseofstudy/Pages/index.aspx.

CFA Institute, *GIPS Standards*, 2010, https://www.cfainstitute.org/en/ethics/codes/about-gips-standards.

CFA Institute, "Elements of an Investment Policy Statement for Individual Investors," https://www.cfainstitute.org/en/advocacy/policy-positions/elements-of-an-investment-policy-statement-for-individual-investors.

CFA Institute, "Elements of an Investment Policy Statement for Institutional Investors," https://www.cfainstitute.org/en/advocacy/policy-positions/elements-of-an-investment-policy-statement-for-institutional-investors.

CFA Institute, "The Portfolio Management Process and the Investment Policy Statement (2018)," https://www.cfainstitute.org/en/membership/professional-development/refresher-readings/2018/the-portfolio-management-process-and-the-investment-policy-statement.

Biographies

Dr. Stephen Horan leads the development of CFA Institute's education programs, including the globally recognized CFA program, and publications.

The author or co-author of several books, including *The New Wealth Management: A Financial Advisers Guide to Managing and Investing Client Assets* and the *Forbes/CFA Institute Investment Course*, Stephen has also edited the volume *Private Wealth: Wealth Management in Practice.* His articles have appeared in peer-reviewed journals, such as the *Financial Analysts Journal, Harvard Business Review Latin America, Journal of Financial Research, Journal of Wealth Management,* and *Financial Services Review.* He has received numerous research grants, including the 2012 Graham and Dodd Readers' Choice Award.

His award-winning research has been profiled in leading practitioner publications, including *CFA Digest* and *Barron's,* as well as the popular press, including the *Chicago Tribune* and *Baltimore Sun.* He is a frequent columnist in the *Financial Times* and is often cited in the media, including publications such as the *Wall Street Journal,* the *New York Times,* CNBC, *Investment News,* and *Money Magazine.*

Stephen currently serves on the editorial board of the *Journal of Wealth Management* and the *Financial Services Review.*

Stephen earned a PhD in finance at the State University of New York/Buffalo and a BBA degree in finance at St. Bonaventure University.

Robert Dannhauser is head, Private Wealth Management at CFA Institute. Previously, he headed CFA Institute's Global Capital Markets Policy Group and the Standards of Practice Group. Before joining the CFA Institute staff in 2007, Robert held sales, client management, and marketing roles with prominent investment management firms.

He earned the CFA charter, as well as the Financial Risk Manager (FRM) and Chartered Alternative Investment Analyst designations. Robert has a BA in political science from George Washington University; an MBA in finance from the Johnson Graduate School of Management at Cornell University; and an MPH in Health Policy from Rutgers University.

CHAPTER 48

Should You Choose a Single-Family Office or a Multi-Family Office?

Kirby Rosplock

What are the criteria or circumstances that warrant a family to establish a family office of its own (a single-family office or SFO), rather than purchasing those services from a multi-family office (MFO) organization? This article explores these two specific pathways, identifying the setup, offerings, costs, styles, and merits of the SFO model and comparing it to the use of a MFO platform.

What Are SFOs versus MFOs, and How Do They Differ? What Services Are Offered?

The wealth-management industry generally defines a family office as an organization dedicated to serving wealthy individuals and/or families on a diverse range of financial, estate, tax, investment, financial, accounting, and personal family needs. I define a family office as much more: it is a unique family enterprise offshoot created to provide tailored wealth management solutions in an integrated fashion while promoting and preserving the identity and values of the family.

The family office provides a structure that helps a family preserve four capitals: (1) business, (2) financial, (3) family, and (4) social impact or philanthropic. The family office is also a unique family business created to provide tailored wealth management solutions in an integrated way, while promoting and preserving the identity and values of the family.

Why does a family or entrepreneur typically set up a family office? Common goals of family offices include building family capital; organizing, simplifying, and scaling family wealth services to a family group; driving business and wealth transfer planning and continuity; sustaining wealth across generations; managing risk, privacy, and security; and perpetuating shared family values and cohesiveness. Specific needs often addressed by family offices include, but are not limited to, financial planning, tax planning, income protection, life planning, retirement planning, estate planning, investment planning, and capital planning.

Yet those families who decide to set up a family office need to be cognizant that a family office is a business that is built from the ground up and must be maintained over time just as any other business would. It requires a formal business plan, legal structure, a mission statement, strategic plan, an organizational structure, and the administrative and human resource requirements that come with it.

SFOs are designed to serve the bespoke needs of the family; therefore, many services may be provided in-house. As such, the benefits families enjoy include a high level of control, customized and dedicated service, privacy, and a family-first orientation. Family assets of $250+ million are typically required to support an SFO infrastructure on an ongoing basis. Some families establish an office that may be dubbed a coordinator office with less in assets, when they are able to justify the expense and overhead because a key member of the operating team may be running it with only a bookkeeper or accountant on staff.[1] An analysis of strengths, weaknesses, opportunities, and threats (SWOT) when considering an SFO pathway is presented in Figure 48.1.

Strengths	Weaknesses
Control	Attracting/Retaining Talent
Customized, Dedicated Service	Cost Controls
Privacy and Anonymity	Access to Products/Services
Alignment and Integration	Operational Efficiencies
No SFO Competition	Service Level Inadequacies
Patient Capital	Bridging Family Continuity
Wealth Preservation	Urgency Toward Strategic Planning
Family First	

Opportunities	Threats
Open Architecture	Managing Scope
Co-Investments	Controlling Costs
First-Class Service	Compensation Challenges
Collaboration	Generational Mathematics
Sharing/Streamlining Costs	Family Conflict
Peer-to-Peer Exchange	Succession Planning
SFO Best Practice Information & Research	Keeping Family On Board

Figure 48.1 Single-family office SWOT analysis.

Source: Kirby Rosplock, *The Complete Family Office Handbook* (New York: Bloomberg Press, 2014).

[1]Thomas J. Handler, "Twenty-first Century Family Office Structures," Thomas J. Handler, Presented by Family Office Association, 2017.

In contrast, a MFO is defined as a commercial enterprise designed to take advantage of aggregating assets under management (AUM) or advisement from many different, unrelated families, and typically offers a broader array of bespoke services than the average retail private bank, wealth management or brokerage firm. These services may include investment management and oversight, manager selection, due diligence, risk management, aggregated reporting, family education, family governance, capital sufficiency analysis, concierge services, bill payment and/or tax and certain legal advice. MFO services are provided to multiple unrelated families, and a study indicates that they average approximately 83 client relationships, each of whom typically would have a net worth of around $50 million.[2] By pooling unrelated family assets, MFO clients are able to achieve economies of scale, obtain broad, comprehensive services, and gain access to higher caliber professional and advisory talent than what they may be able to afford or justify if they were setting up a family office on their own.

The larger-scale MFOs also may have drawbacks. These may include increased bureaucracy, a lack of personalization and ability to customize, and an institutionalized service offering that is rigid and inflexible to bespoke needs. An analysis of SWOT when considering an MFO pathway is presented in Figure 48.2.

Strengths	Weaknesses
Scale Comprehensive Services Streamlined and Efficient Integration Breadth of Resources Top Talent and Retention Centralized Data Management	Client/Advisor Load (+/–) Institutionalize Service Offering Access to Products/Services Group Think Customization of Personalization Bureaucracy
Opportunities	**Threats**
More for Less Learning Curve Open Architecture "One-Stop Shop" Sharing Costs for Specialty Services Access to Investment Managers, Products, and Research Thought Leadership and Innovation	Getting Too Big Too Fast Maintaining Close Relationships Overpromising Talent Retention and Turnover Ownership and Leadership Alignment Corporate Culture

Figure 48.2 Multi-family office SWOT analysis.

Source: Kirby Rosplock, *The Complete Family Office Handbook* (New York: Bloomberg Press, 2014).

[2]Family Office Exchange, "2012 FOX Multi-Family Office and Wealth Advisor Benchmarking Study," Chicago, IL, 2012.

SFO Setup: What Are the Triggers, and What Does it Cost?

Building an SFO can be a major undertaking and can extend several months or even years, depending upon family, business, and liquidity considerations. The creation of an SFO is typically initiated by some type of triggering event, be it the sale of a company; the exit from a large, illiquid position or holding, such as the sale of real estate; the death, illness, or incapacitation of a key family leader; or the transition of ownership of family holdings from one generation to the next. Most families or entrepreneurs may initially attempt to solve for these types of family office needs with a group of trusted advisors and/or executives embedded in their operating entities. However, the reliance on an informal operating approach may lead to conflicts of interest as well as challenges when/if key staffers leave or eventually wear too many hats within the broader business structures.

The process of setting up a formal SFO requires a great deal of planning to properly scope, design, prototype, test, and launch the office. Typically, family office consultants or advisors are brought in to provide expert guidance, recommendations, and best practices to customize the build-out for the needs of the family. One study reveals that the internal family office costs to operate a SFO on average is 64 basis points (BPs) or 0.64% of AUM. These overhead expenses typically include staffing compensation and benefits, office operations, internal investment management, and internal regulatory, communications, and technology costs.[3] External investment and advisory costs should also be quantified and considered when capturing the full family wealth management expense to establish a family office.

MFO Service Options: Who Decides to Join an MFO, How Much Does it Cost, and What Is the Typical MFO Client Profile?

The option to become a client of an MFO has become far more mainstream over the last 25 years. There are a variety of different types of MFOs, from those that only focus on investment management and may be classified as "outsourced CIOs," to those that actually provide no investment function and may be built off of a professional services platform, such as a law firm or accounting firm, and everything in between. For example, there are several MFOs that were once accounting practices that now operate and primarily offer services related to accounting, bill pay, tax administration, or lifestyle planning.

Most MFOs, however, are full-service and offer both investment management and a breadth of services. A typical client of an MFO may be an individual with anywhere from US$15 to US$500 M net worth, who desires an MFO to

---

[3]The Cost of Complexity, Understanding Family Office Costs, Expanding to Include Investment Cost Data, Family Office Exchange, 2011.

manage an account sized as little as $10 M to as much as his or her whole investable net worth. MFO clients may want more independence from being an operator of their wealth and prefer to delegate to experts or an MFO wealth advisory team to manage their investments and/or wealth management affairs. Particularly for families in transition from one generation of wealth ownership to the next, with no clear family leader or operator to administer the wealth, an MFO can be an invaluable partner. MFOs often will take accounts as small as $5–$10 M and will provide better pricing the more wealth a family designates to them to manage. Other MFOs may have higher minimum account sizes of $25 M or $50 M as they typically only desire to serve a large client whereby they can offer a broader integrated service offering at a premium. Professional service-based firms with no asset management offering may provide a billable hour-type arrangement, retainer fee-based arrangement, or a project-based arrangement for à-la-carte-type services. Again, aligning the services received with the structure of the fee is critical when evaluating MFO providers.

A Case in Point[4]

The Bennington family was an enterprising family into its third and fourth generations, with three main family branches and more than 60 family members. The origins of wealth and business stemmed back to the early 1900s, as gregarious brothers started from humble beginnings to build what would become a large, complex family enterprise with multiple sub-entities and trusts.

Fast-forward to the late 1990s.The death of the patriarch from the second-generation precipitated family owners to consider the long-term viability for the collective family enterprise and the ensuing liquidity. In the early 2000s, the family determined to divest from several key family holdings including real estate and agribusiness, among other holdings. This provided family groups with augmented liquidity and an increased the need for thoughtful wealth management, more comprehensive integrated planning for tax and state considerations, and broader multi-generational family member education, planning, and preparation. The family was at a crossroads.

Although the family remained close, tied by the shared ownership of several of the operating companies for more than 100 years, the family also realized that the different branches had different needs when it came to their wealth, estate planning, philanthropy, and investment planning.

One family, which we will call Branch A, decided they wanted to re-invest the capital into bespoke direct investments, such as commercial buildings, real estate partnerships, pharmaceuticals, etc. They had a more aggressive

---

[4]This is an actual family-office case that has been anonymized to protect the family's privacy and confidentiality. Additional fictionalized data has been added to obscure its identity.

investment approach and wanted to be very hands on with their investments. Plus, they had members of the family being groomed to take on leadership roles within their family. Ultimately after evaluating several MFO options, conducting the business case analysis, and becoming well educated about the family office landscape, they opted to establish their own SFO.

Branch B had more fragmented, dispersed wealth and business ownership. Further, they realized that each family sub-group had different lifestyle needs, investment goals, and risk tolerances. Although they looked at joining with Branch A's SFO, they determined that the approach to investing, the limited services that Branch A was looking to include in their family office mandate, coupled with the divergent legacy goals, made it a poor fit.

Consequently, Branch B did a similar evaluation of the family office space, determined that they did not have enough synergy as a family group to want to setup their own family office and eventually evaluated different MFO providers to suit their individual needs. Some of the sub-family groups from Branch B decided to pool their capital for increased scale to better negotiate with the MFOs to bring down the pricing and to increase overall services. At the same time, the individual sub-groups of Branch B could have their family affairs managed independently under the umbrella of the MFO, allowing them to maintain their level of privacy between the family sub-groups of Branch B.

Branch C took a slightly different approach from A and B. They chose to work with an MFO service provider-type firm that specialized in accounting. They received aggregated reporting, trust accounting support, tax preparation and administration, tax planning, and reporting support and coordination with their financial, investment, and fiduciary advisors. Branch C had a more traditional, conservative approach to their wealth management and opted to keep the bulk of their wealth with legacy financial institutions that had served the family for generations. They were able to supplement the non-investment related services they did not receive from their financial and banking relationships with an accounting-based MFO platform that also helped keep the family connected.

Ultimately, each family branch found the solution that was most appropriate for their needs. The key lessons learned were to focus on the long-term goals for the wealth, investment philosophy, and risk tolerance, understand the price of control and privacy to set up an SFO and to weigh these against the scale, aggregation, and integration that an MFO platform may provide.

Finally, they were able to look at what would build the greatest level of harmony and cohesion among the broader multi-generational family and recognized that giving family members the autonomy to identify an appropriate wealth management solution – whether SFO, MFO, or some variation of the two – allowed the family to better solidify family relations and trust, rather than locking family members into a legal structure where goals, needs, and long-term values could not be aligned.

Closing Thoughts

At the end of the day, there is no right or wrong answer to the family office question, although there are pros and cons to each approach. You must examine your family's needs and expectations realistically and find the solution that is the best fit for you.

Questions for Further Reflection

1. Do you believe your family has the capability and capacity to be a good family office operator? Is there interest, skill, and experience within the family to take on a leadership role?
2. How highly do you value things like control, privacy, and tailored customized services? Are you willing to pay extra for such things?
3. How amicable are relationships within the family? How might an SFO structure be a potential area of conflict or an opportunity to build cohesion and continuity?
4. How fee- or price-sensitive is the family, and are the costs to set up and operate a family office sustainable over multiple generations?
5. What might an MFO platform provide in terms of broader services, integrated wealth, and investment advice, and/or continuity for your family?

Additional Resources

Kirby Rosplock, *The Complete Family Office Handbook: A Guide for Affluent Families and the Advisors Who Serve Them* (New York: Bloomberg Press, 2014).

Kirby Rosplock, *The Complete Direct Investing Handbook: A Guide for Family Offices, Qualified Purchasers, and Accredited Investors* (New York: Bloomberg Press, 2017).

EY Family Office Guide, 2016.

Biography

Kirby Rosplock, PhD, is a recognized consultant, researcher, innovator, advisor, author, facilitator, and speaker in the family business and family office realms. She is Founder/Principal of Tamarind Partners, a family-office consulting firm.

Kirby grew up in a business-owning family as a fourth-generation family member, beneficiary, trustee, board member, and trustee of her family's foundation. For nearly a decade, Kirby also served as director of research and development at GenSpring Family Offices.

Kirby has a BA from Middlebury College, an MBA from Marquette University, and a PhD from Saybrook University. Her dissertation was "Women's Interest, Attitudes, and Involvement with their Wealth" (2007). She is author of

The Complete Family Office Handbook, A Guide for Affluent Families and the Advisors Who Serve Them (Wiley/Bloomberg, January 2014) and its companion, *The Complete Direct Investing Handbook, A Guide for Family Offices, Accredited Investors and Qualified Purchasers* (Wiley/Bloomberg, May 2017).

Kirby is dean of family office at the Purposeful Planning Institute (PPI), a fellow and GEN faculty of the Family Firm Institute (FFI), and a member of the advisory board of Merton Venture Philanthropy.

CHAPTER 49

How Do You Choose a Good Trustee?

Hartley Goldstone

Ongoing guidance along with acts of kindness and compassion on the part of my trustee really changed my life. It turned me around during the lowest part of my adult life.

—A Trust Beneficiary[1]

A decade ago I set out to unravel a riddle: Why do family trusts commonly preserve a family's financial assets, yet fail to preserve either family or trust?

Sound investing and tax tactics are, of course, important. At the same time, my experience is that families who "do" trusts well know that long-term success hinges on the personal relationships that trusts create.

With this in view, it is my intention (1) to show that the relationship between trustee and beneficiary is vital to a family's broader scheme to prepare beneficiaries to live meaningful, productive lives, and (2) to provide guidance for selecting a trustee.

What Issues Go Unaddressed by Trust Documents?

As we begin to unravel the riddle, it helps to be acquainted with an important issue that trust documents by and large fail to address.

Please take a moment to picture Grandma and Grandpa. Years ago, Grandma and Grandpa had a promising idea. With hard work, skill, a talented team, and good luck, the idea has made them wealthy.

[1]The vignettes and quotes throughout this essay are extracted from stories that first appeared in Hartley Goldstone and Kathy Wiseman, *TrustWorthy – New Angles on Trusts from Beneficiaries and Trustees* (Trustscape LLC, 2012).

Grandma and Grandpa love their grandchildren very much. They spend sleepless nights wondering how their good fortune will affect their grandchildren.

Grandma and Grandpa's greatest hope is that wealth will be a helpful resource as grandchildren gain self-awareness, become educated, and pursue their life's goals.

Their greatest concern – what's nerve-wracking to Grandma and Grandpa – is whether a substantial inheritance will ruin their grandchildren and lead to lives of unhappiness, or worse.

Grandma and Grandpa make an appointment with a top-notch tax lawyer who is known for cutting-edge estate-planning strategies. They return home with a binder jam-packed with trust documents that solve a variety of asset-preservation problems. But not one of them speaks to the hopes or concerns Grandma and Grandpa have for their grandchildren.

The takeaway is that most trust documents do not address, other than in a cursory manner, the lifelong trustee/beneficiary relationship created by the trust – a relationship that will make or break Grandma and Grandpa's greatest hopes for their beneficiary grandchildren. But, as we'll see in a moment, the trustee can remedy this.

Here's an action for you to consider: jot down your greatest hopes and concerns regarding wealth's impact on your loved ones. Keep your list close at hand as you speak with potential trustees.

Great Trustees Do More than Manage Assets

Trustees tend to treat beneficiary relationships as legal relationships at the core. "I am the trustee. You are the beneficiary. Our 'dance' together will often be mechanical and sometimes awkward. Occasionally we may break through to something more purposeful."

> A woman in her forties takes me aside at a conference. "My life is successful by almost any measure," she explains. "I am a tenured professor at an Ivy League university. I have a wonderful husband and children. I sit on several non-profit boards and currently chair my family's foundation. The only place that I am treated like a child is when I visit my trustee. I have come to terms with this, but my concern is that my children will have to go through the same thing."

Better to seek a trustee who will see the trustee/beneficiary relationship as a whole-hearted human relationship. Go with this stance, and it becomes clear that Grandma and Grandpa's greatest hopes – that trusts will enhance the lives of his loved ones – are more likely to show up.

A beneficiary is challenged with addictions for much of his adult life. The trust that his late grandfather created purchases a condominium for him, supports his basic needs, and pays for a variety of treatment programs over the years. His father's heartbreak and frustration lead him to alternate among compassion, hostility, and estrangement. Beneficiary, father, and trustee have regular phone contact and occasional "crisis meetings." Son puts together sustained sobriety and other productive steps toward resurrecting his life. Father and son reconcile, and they include the trustee in conversations about how the family's trusts can bring the larger family together.

Selecting a Trustee: Questions to Consider

Here are some common considerations to reflect on when selecting a trustee:

- What are your goals? What do you want the trustee to do?
- Would you prefer an institution? Or an individual? Or some combination?
- How important is geography? Age?
- How about familiarity with specific types of assets in the trust?
- How would you prioritize knowledge of investments, competency in taxation and trust administration, and readiness to engage with beneficiaries?
- Would selecting a family member be a help or a hindrance?
- How about a family friend?
- What kind of factor is the cost of a trustee?
- Do you want the beneficiary to have a voice in this selection?

Will Your Trustee Reach Out to Your Beneficiaries Beyond the Legal and Administrative Duties?

Trustees cannot expect to have an exemplary relationship with beneficiaries anchored in quantitative outcomes alone – no matter how good those outcomes are. It's spending a sufficient amount of time and energy on qualitative matters that brings about flourishing relationships.

A boy of eight became a beneficiary upon the death of his grandfather. His trustee regularly visited the young beneficiary at his home for years before he was told of the existence of the trust. This simple act created the foundation for a lifelong relationship. "The little things that my trustee as an adult did to reach out to me as a child were critical in the development of a rapport between the two of us." That beneficiary is in his 40s today and grateful for the care his grandfather took in selecting a trustee who has been a mentor and friend for 30-plus years.

Trust beneficiaries, especially first-timers, often feel overwhelmed when entering a relationship with a trustee. Anxiety, trepidation, and confusion are natural and can lead beneficiaries to become defensive and adversarial.

How will trustees transcend this when complicated relationships and inherent tensions exist? By initiating conversations carefully designed to address the challenges and realize the enormous potential that every trust relationship holds. Sometimes that requires listening deeply and asking significant questions, other times creating trust-related learning opportunities, and yet other times partnering with a beneficiary to make the best decisions possible. The trustee will seek the beneficiary's ideas and openly discuss his own thinking.

Will Your Trustee See Each Beneficiary as a Unique Individual?

Trust creators are often unaware of the tendency of many trustees, sometimes with the advice of counsel, to treat all beneficiaries of a given trust in exactly the same manner. A common theme among beneficiaries who share positive stories is the impact of trustees who take the time to understand their interests, dreams, and needs. Corollaries include a willingness to listen and be empathetic, even when disagreeing with a beneficiary.

> As one beneficiary summed it up, "The trustees I've had have really taken the time to understand what I'm doing and how I'm doing it. When issues come up we talk. We work together to find the best way to tackle situations ... It has been neat to see how the trust can support different types of people, investments and endeavors over time."
>
> And from a trustee, "If a beneficiary is a little bit unusual, that shouldn't bother someone in my position. I may not always agree, but at the same time it is refreshing that they don't passively accept what I am saying. I enjoy the give and take."

Will Your Trustee Proactively Tackle the Responsibility to Make Distributions?

The Trustee's responsibility for distributions is the nexus for building life-enhancing relationships with beneficiaries. Great trustees are proactive.

Trustees have three responsibilities: administration, investment, and the least understood of the three responsibilities, distribution.

Trustees typically estimate that 90% of their time and energy is spent on administration and investment. That leaves 10% for distribution.

In many cases, trustees approach distributions as an afterthought, meaning nothing happens until a beneficiary requests funds. Upon receiving a request, the trustee moves into action.

This reactive approach can leave beneficiaries feeling like they aren't understood, and trustees tending to be overly cautious out of concern for making mistakes.

A proactive trustee, on the other hand, is one who recognizes the need to spend sufficient time and energy to build solid relationships with beneficiaries.

When contemplating a request for funds, a proactive trustee asks the beneficiary: "What do you hope to accomplish by making this request?" and then "Why is that important to you?" Soon, trustee and beneficiary are brainstorming assorted ways to accomplish the beneficiary's goal. And finally – can the trustee say yes to the request? If not, is there a different way to look at the beneficiary's goal – one that would lead to a request that can be approved?

> A recent college grad asks for help drafting her first business plan. Our conversation includes how the trust might support her dream and what would be required of her to receive financial backing. She does her homework and concludes that the idea is not sound. She goes back to the drawing board to start over again.

Experiences like these build trust. Everyone benefits because the relationship is mutually fulfilling.

Will Your Trustee Honor the Trust Creator's Intent?

Trustees and beneficiaries repeatedly tell us that knowing the intent of the trust creator is crucial. Although trustees are, of course, bound by the trust language, they indicate that knowing what the creator would have wanted provides valuable guidance in making decisions. For beneficiaries, knowing the intent helps them understand their trusts as opportunities for enhancing their lives, rather than simply being the source of funds.

> Said one beneficiary, "It was what I needed personally to hear so that I could make sense of how and why this was happening to me!"

Will Your Trustee Put Your Family's Interests Above All Else?

In our modern world, corporate trustees face a variety of demands, some institutional (e.g. risk management, profitability, need for new clients) and some personal (e.g. career advancement, increased compensation, status). Family members have their own biases. Nevertheless, each must put aside their personal predispositions when wearing the trustee hat.

> James, a beneficiary, has a couple of co-trustees: one a family member, the other a trust company.
>
> James has a long and very negative history with his family trustee. In his late 30s, James has been living in Paris and, according to the family trustee, is always thinking of very creative ways to get money from his trust.
>
> The family trustee doesn't like or trust James, and James knows it. So when James approaches his trustees to ask for money to go back to school to get a graduate degree from the Sorbonne to become a teacher, the family trustee is unable to conceive of James having changed.
>
> His reaction: "Absolutely not! How do we know he is really going to use the money for that purpose?"
>
> The institutional trust officer has a different take: "Because I have not known James as long as the family trustee has, there isn't a negative history between James and me. After considering carefully what I know of James, I believe he is serious about the endeavor."
>
> The trustees and James negotiate a plan that includes accountability on James's part. The trustees make the distribution. James returns to school and indeed shows seriousness about his education. He comes through.

Will your family be able to say, "There was never a shadow of a doubt during the 30 years that we worked together that, although our trust officer was paid by the trust company, he worked for our family's best interests"?

The Final Twist to the Tale

If you can answer yes to all five questions ...

What difference will that make for the trust creator? For the beneficiaries? For generations of your family to come?

Questions for Further Reflection

1. What concerns do you have regarding your current system of trusts? What, if anything, would you like to change?
2. Who or what would be your ideal trustee? Why?
3. What steps can you take to bring your reality closer to this ideal?

Additional Resources

Hartley Goldstone and Kathy Wiseman, *TrustWorthy: New Angles on Trusts from Beneficiaries and Trustees: A Positive Story Project Showcasing Beneficiaries and Trustees* (Trustscape LLC, 2012).

Hartley Goldstone, James Hughes, and Keith Whitaker, *Family Trusts – A Guide for Beneficiaries, Trustees, Trust Protectors, and Trust Creators* (Hoboken, NJ: Wiley, 2016).

Biography

Hartley Goldstone, JD serves as executive coach and consultant for trustees and adult beneficiaries. He has guided many, who are living with trusts successfully, adapt to key roles, while deepening their understanding of trust-related relationships and responsibilities.

Clients hire Hartley to ignite new perspective and performance. They learn practical skills and gain the confidence to actively contribute to the long-term success of intergenerational wealth transfer.

Confidential coaching and individually tailored education is carried out in person, by telephone, or video conference – so there are no geographic limitations.

SECTION 9

FACING THE FUTURE

Baseball's philosopher-king, Yogi Berra, said it best: "It's tough to make predictions, especially about the future."

The world is moving fast and change is inevitable. Some changes will be good for us and some won't. Families rightly wonder how they will fare, what they should embrace, how they should adapt, and how they should prepare themselves.

There are no silver-bullet answers to questions like these. A good place to start when considering the future is the core values of the family. It might be worthwhile to skip back to the questions raised in Section 1 of this book – Thinking Through What Matters Most – to remind yourself about the fundamental beliefs and principles that could be a source of stability and constancy through whatever is to come.

But it is also important for families of wealth to consider the global trends that may affect them, as well as the potential shifts within their own families and communities. The authors in this section offer some interesting food for thought on these topics.

James Hughes looks at the question "What does the future hold for families with significant wealth?" from his long experience and unique perspective. He sees many changes on the horizon, including the definition of family itself, new types of family leadership that will be required, and the increasing importance of female leadership and wealth ownership. He also considers the impact of China on everything and everyone, and the implications of having most family assets in a trust structure.

Fernando del Pino writes a thoughtful personal answer to the question "How can you chart your own path, no matter what everyone else says you should do?" from the standpoint of an inheritor and a wealth owner. He addresses many tricky subjects – including parental favoritism, the danger of advisors, the fading notion of owners, and the burdens and responsibilities of wealth – and provides wise counsel for founders and heirs alike as they look to the future.

James Grubman also weighs in with his advice on how wealthy families should face the many challenges of the future, both within and across generations, and ultimately how they can maintain both stability and resilience in the face of a rapidly evolving world. Navigating the challenges with a flexible, adaptive attitude is one of the strongest contributors to long-term family harmony and prosperity.

Finally, we conclude this section by reprinting a condensed version of a 2015 speech entitled "Lifting the Small Boats" by International Monetary Fund (IMF) Managing Director Christine Lagarde, with her kind permission. In her remarks, she comments on one of the key issues in today's (and tomorrow's) world – global economic inequality – and the related instability and disequilibrium it can bring. This has been an enormously prosperous period for global families of wealth. Other global (and local) citizens have felt left out of the prosperity wave and believe the system is rigged and unfair. From her unique vantage point, Christine raises issues and ideas for policymakers and families of wealth and power to consider about how we might make sure the "small boats" – the livelihoods and economic aspirations of the poor and middle class – are lifted too, for the benefit of all. Food for thought.

No doubt one of the most dangerous sentences in the world of business and investments is "It's different this time." Facing the future means being clear-sighted about the present and the past. That said, conditions do change, and that can require revised strategies – even if the goal is to maintain what was. In this respect, families with long-term vision may even resemble small nations, of which the medieval political philosopher Al-Farabi wrote, "The second lawgiver must legislate differently than the first lawgiver – if he is to do the same thing." Tradition itself springs from and relies upon innovation.

CHAPTER 50

What Does the Future Hold for Families with Significant Wealth?

James Hughes

One of the future trends I believe that families with significant wealth must consider is the new emerging forms of what families are. In the developed world, almost all families are evolving toward defining themselves as families of *affinity*, rather than families of *origin*. Of course, all families begin with two people with two different family names. The multiple new forms of family follow this same definition, while incorporating the husband/wife form as one of many choices.

Inclusivity will become the only process families can follow if they are to mirror the new evolving and emerging social and cultural reality of what families consist of. Thinking this way and practicing this reality will provide the positive attraction to the rising generation of possible new family members; this thought and practice will promise them possibilities for their individual freedoms and growth, inclining them to decide to join the family's journey. It will lead, as a result, to the family's flourishing far into the future.

Another consideration is that families more and more will need to become learning organizations to succeed, even by embedding Chief Learning Officers (CLOs) within their systems. Education, as a didactic exercise, is passé. Only learning will meet the challenges of the augmented economy in which "intangible" assets rather than tangible assets will come to be the foundation of fortunes. Intangible assets are embodied in human, intellectual, and spiritual capital, fused into excellent social capital to permit the family to make the joint decisions necessary to meet the challenges of the future.

All families seeking to flourish must comprehend and embrace the augmented economy and its novelties. The most successful will evolve their family offices and/or professional advisors from managing risk of financial loss toward the thriving of each family member through qualitative assessments, aimed at growing and developing each member's gifts and remediating his or her deficiencies.

To do this, I envision families engaging CLOs just as nearly all successful for-profit and not-for-profit organizations have already done. These CLOs will displace family office executives and outside professionals who have been de facto chief risk officers. These CLOs will be people who embody the highest professional integrity, substantial emotional intelligence, high intellectual consciousness, serious understanding and experience with how families dynamically preserve their financial assets over a period of at least 100 years, and a deep abiding interest in why and how human and family systems flourish. They will also know how to help nurture and grow a family's leaders – those from "in front" who show where the individual family boats need to go to flourish and even more importantly those who lead "from behind" who assure that no boats sink and that all boats rise. These CLOs will be measured by only one metric – "Is every individual member of my family's boat rising, with a result that our entire family is rising?"

A third trend I see of great importance to families with wealth, and to the rest of the world, is the regendering of the distribution and control of property, both tangible and intangible, throughout the developed world.

Birth control, educational, and vocational opportunities, and changing definitions of family are all leading to a redistribution by gender of the control and ownership of property. As a result, societies themselves are being fundamentally changed, since those with the control of property determine the fundamental virtues, values, and directions of those societies. Today, in the developed world, women almost universally inherit equally with their brothers, control their inheritances, and go to university and on to graduate studies and degrees in larger proportion than their brothers. They now, in many families, out-earn their brothers and, in many places in the world, their husbands. Families will thrive who can recognize and discuss these immense new realities of gender and property distribution and control.

The fourth trend concerns China. Everything in the world of the future will be affected by China. Awakening 1.4 billion people must have enormous consequences, particularly when almost all these people are literate and draw upon an ancient culture of great sophistication and depth. Among the things family leaders will want to watch are the consequences of China's one-child policy, which will lead to a rapidly aging population and to many families with only one heir (often a female heir); the enormous wealth transition between generations that is just starting; and the consequences of many of those single children and single grandchildren being deeply imbued by Chinese culture and philosophy while having been sent West for secondary, tertiary, and graduate enlightenment education. These children and grandchildren will form China's new leadership in all phases of its modern and emerging economic, social and cultural evolution.

A related trend, one in which China may be instructive to the rest of the world, is what I call family inversion. Very few women throughout the developed world, exemplified by Japan, are having more than two children – and in many cases only one, or even none. As a result, I believe that the vast majority of privileged families are going to face family inversion and possibly extinction of whole branches in the next 50 years. Many family plans are based on the assumption that the family fortune will be dissipated as new children are born and create more mouths to feed. This family inversion trend could up-end those plans entirely. It could also counter the trend of many investment professionals to recommend greater risk because of the need for growth to match the supposedly Malthusian future of family population increase. Looking forward, demography suggests that the opposite will be true as inversion takes over.

One last trend that I believe will affect the future of families with wealth: Almost all families in the Common Law World of Britain, Canada, Australia, New Zealand, and the United States by their third generations hold 90% of their wealth in trusts. Most think they have headed off many fiscal risks by creating such trusts. What they do not know and are not told is that 80% of the beneficiaries of trusts consider their trusts more as a burden, rather than a blessing. This belief is not because the beneficiaries are entitled or ungrateful. Rather, it is because they are aware that their trustees care nothing or extremely little about them as persons.

Unfortunately, these beneficiaries are largely correct. Trustees generally spend 90% of their time on trust administration and trust investments. They have little or no time (leaving aside interest) to seek to enhance the lives of the trust-founder's beneficiaries. Such trusts are entropic to the core and often lead to family failure. The future of trusts lies in increasing the number of beneficiaries who say that their trusts are blessings. CLOs are people committed to this principle. Founders can commit to this principle by starting their trusts by the following two first sentences (before all of the "Whereases"): "This trust is a gift of love. This trust exists to enhance the lives of its beneficiaries." A founder who starts his or her trust with these sentences greatly increases the likelihood that the trust will become a vehicle to grow a family's human, intellectual, social, and spiritual capitals. And when founders start from this premise and lead with these two sentences, the trustee they seek will appear.

Questions for Further Reflection

1. Are the women and men in your family prepared for the challenge of fiscal inequality?
2. Do your most senior advisors understand the disruptions that the augmented economy will pose? How are they preparing your family to face these disruptions?
3. How could you infuse your family's trusts with humanity, making them blessings rather than burdens to future beneficiaries?

Additional Resources

James E. Hughes, Susan E. Massenzio and Keith Whitaker, *The Cycle of the Gift* (New York: Bloomberg Press, 2014).

James E. Hughes and Susan E. Massenzio, *Voice of the Rising Generation* (New York: Bloomberg Press, 2015).

Hartley Goldstone, James E. Hughes, and Keith Whitaker, *Family Trusts* (Hoboken, NJ: Wiley, 2016).

James E. Hughes, Susan E. Massenzio, and Keith Whitaker, *Complete Family Wealth* (New York: Bloomberg Press, 2018).

Biography

James Hughes, a resident of Aspen, Colorado, is the author of *Family Wealth: Keeping It in the Family*, and of *Family – The Compact Among Generations*, and is the co-author with Susan Massenzio and Keith Whitaker of *The Cycle of the Gift: Family Wealth and Wisdom, The Voice of the Rising Generation*, and *Complete Faith Wealth*, and he is a co-author with Hartley Goldstone and Keith Whitaker of *Family Trusts: A Guide to Trustees, Beneficiaries, Advisors, and Protectors.*

He was the founder of a law partnership in New York City specializing in the representation of private clients throughout the world. He is a current Fellow of Wise Counsel Research (www.wisecounselresearch.org), a Boston-based think tank. He is a founding member of the Collaboration for Family Flourishing. James is a graduate of the Far Brook School, which teaches through the arts, the Pingry School, Princeton University, and the Columbia School of Law. He is a counselor to the Family Office Exchange and recipient of its Founder's Award, the recipient of the Private Asset Management Lifetime Achievement Award, the Ackerman Institute Family Partner Award, and the Wealth Management Lifetime Achievement Award.

CHAPTER 51

How Can You Chart Your Own Path, No Matter What Everyone Else Says You Should Do?

Fernando del Pino

I used to belong to a family business. My late father, Rafael del Pino, started his business, Ferrovial, from scratch and grew it to the large infrastructure business it is today. In 1999 it went public and, coming from a stint at the Chase Manhattan Bank, I joined his family office to help invest the IPO's proceeds. I also joined Ferrovial's board of directors and its executive committee.

In 2007, after giving it a great deal of thought and with my father's blessing, I took the life-changing decision of going solo. I sold my shares in the business, left the board and started managing my own net worth independently. My experience as shareholder and board member of a family business and also as a global investor, together with the experience learned from other family businesses through the activities of the Madrid Family Business Association, which I co-founded nearly two decades ago, have led me through a very interesting journey of discovery, a journey from theory and wishful thinking to practice and reality, from conventional wisdom to common sense. "In theory there is no difference between theory and practice; in practice, there is."

This chapter tries to distill some of the things I have learned.

Perceptions of Reality: Founder and Heirs

Family-business founders have built their very identity around the business. It is not only the fruit of an entire life's labor, but also an extension of themselves, their chosen child. In fact, we could say that "family" businesses seldom exist as such. In reality, they are businesses founded, owned, and run by an individual who happens to have a family. For all practical purposes, it is *his* business, not his family's business. He owns the business but, very importantly, the business owns him at least as much. Therefore, whenever the choice has to be made between sacrificing the business and sacrificing the family (and believe me, that dilemma will arrive), the vast majority of founders will choose to sacrifice the family, as sacrificing the business would be akin to committing some sort of psychological suicide. Often, that feeling also prevents them from leaving their posts in sufficient time to ensure a smooth transition to the next generation.

Many founders have such a controlling nature that they want to control the lives of their offspring from the afterlife, sometimes several generations down the road. Therefore, to the delight of lawyers, consultants, and financial service providers, they sometimes set up all sorts of rigid complex corporate structures depriving their children of their freedom to succeed and to fail and sending them a destructive message of mistrust.

A better path is to educate their children in basic financial and business matters and also emotionally and psychologically to become full owners and full adults, teaching them the responsibility of ownership, but trusting them and accepting that they should lead their own lives, for better or for worse.

Family members should remember that the business affects the lives of many families, starting with its employees. Thus, the owner's responsibility should not be taken lightly, but neither should it be used to blackmail the members of the next generation to oblige them to pursue a path they do not choose to follow. That is a recipe for disaster for everyone – including the business, which the owner intended to save in the first place.

The succession of the founder in a family business is always difficult, particularly when succession is about who becomes CEO. The power and money involved can induce rivalry among siblings, compounded by an emotional factor: being "the chosen one" is regarded as a special act of *love* from the parent/founder, and all children in the world crave a piece of love from their parents (particularly from an absent parent, which is usually – and logically – the case for most founders).

A family in which one sibling is a writer, another is a musician, and the third is an Ivy League MBA trained at a prestigious firm is a consultant's dream. The reality is that siblings often have similar education, background, and capabilities and, most important, they may have similar aspirations. When such aspirations are frustrated, unavoidable and often lasting consequences follow, and it's neither realistic nor fair to expect or demand otherwise.

At the risk of sounding too blunt, due to the inherent conflicts of generational transitions, if peace is to be preserved, most family businesses should be sold by default at every generational change unless there are extremely good reasons to keep it in the family. Every consultant should start by recommending a sale unless he can be convinced that he is witnessing a true exception to the rule.

If the decision is taken to keep the business in the family, it is desirable to provide the necessary liquidity system so that shareholders always remain *volunteer* shareholders and not shareholders enslaved in a golden cage that will bring trouble sooner rather than later. The perfect solution, where feasible, is to have periodic windows to sell shares at a pre-agreed, objective, mechanical valuation method (i.e. multiples are much better than beautiful discounted cash-flow models, which can be so prone to manipulation).

Bankers, Consultants, and Lawyers

Money and conflict in family businesses attract all sorts of service providers, like flowers attract bees. Lawyers, consultants, and private bankers will compete, quite literally, for a portion of the family's wealth. Ross Johnson's character in *Barbarians at the Gate* jokes that "all I want from bankers is a new calendar every year and all I care about lawyers is that they go back in their coffins before the sun goes up." This might be an exaggeration, but it's not totally misguided. A trusted and wise lawyer can be a great asset. However, many lawyers prosper out of other people's conflicts and have incentives for making such conflicts eternal. In this sense family businesses provide a promising field.

The best advice here is to stay clear of legal confrontation whenever possible. Peace of mind is a treasure, life is short, unexpected things happen, and a mediocre agreement is better than a favorable court ruling after long litigation. Remember that money, power, and prestige are nothing compared to inner peace, that the bridges blown up by a bitter legal confrontation may be impossible to rebuild, and that what appears so important today becomes small stuff with the passage of time. Let the breeze blow it softly away.

I've known arguably the best family business consultants from around the world, and although I don't deny that a few might prove harmless or even useful, they are seldom game changers, because deep problems that have been boiling since the distant past cannot be expected to be solved, as if by magic. Written family agreements based on twisting people's arms and denying the elephant in the room are worthless pieces of paper.

Neither are consultants neutral because, regardless of who pays the bill, they have just one client, which is never "the family" nor the business, but an individual; it might be the founder or it might be the chosen (or willing) successor. Given the choice between losing business for telling the truth or subtly supporting the (sometimes hidden) clients' pre-determined agenda, most consultants (family business and otherwise) will take the latter option. It's just human nature. Finally, here's a word of caution. Consultants meddling in a family business conflict can achieve enormous power as family members open up their hearts, becoming extremely vulnerable. Without integrity, disaster looms.

Financial services providers appear as fast as the Road Runner at the smell of an orphan fortune (i.e. an IPO). It is very common for street-smart founders who have become very wealthy by exploiting their talent for doing business to feel completely lost on financial matters. Their natural exit is to lean toward the big institutions and their legions of well-dressed private bankers.

However, with very, very few exceptions, Wall Street is plagued with conflicts of interest and offers nothing more than an intimidating façade, high fees, and mediocre returns. In fact, the job of most private bankers is to discreetly and swiftly pass money from your wallet to their wallet, whereas the hyped "strategists" are just well-paid salesmen with very poor forecasting track records but an enviable capacity to explain why things have happened, *after* they have happened.

A better path is to hire independent value-oriented managers or to hire a family office CIO that follows the three basic tenets: value-investing, aversion to debt, and simplicity. Keeping a fortune for the next generation against the powerful enemies of taxation, inflation, and mediocre returns, and the temptation of debt-financed grandiose deals and eccentric luxury is sometimes as hard as making such a fortune. Don't underestimate the challenge.

Boards of Directors: The Importance of Owners

Teaching all wealth inheritors the basics of value investing (and very particularly the wisdom of Benjamin Graham's *The Intelligent Investor*) is, in my view, the best way to ensure that wealth reaches the next generation. It is not only decisive in the family office, but value-investing principles will also help heirs tremendously in their roles on boards.

Today's corporate culture has killed the notion of owners, with the result being worsening capital allocation decisions, short-termism, and poor counterbalance to CEOs. One symptom of this trend is the incredible 10-fold increase in CEOs' pay in the United States in the past 40 years, after inflation, and their deified status. A more sober view, however, shows that most CEOs lack capital-allocation skills and are used to having asymmetrical risk–reward incentives, which very often push them to engage in unprofitable growth, empire building, or reckless leverage that might put the business in jeopardy.

Moreover, boards chosen by CEOs have their share of yes-men and mutual back-scratchers such that the so-called independent directors are seldom independent, particularly in continental Europe. (Indeed, in my view, the only true independent board member is the guy who has skin in the game, the true partner that shares downside risk.) When educated owners sit on the board, these things happen less often. Family business should exploit the huge competitive advantage of having their boards filled with such educated, motivated, value conscious, long-term oriented owners.

Wealth, Meaning, and Self

Dear heir: Wealth provides comfort and financial independence, potentially opening up a huge field of personal development in the intellectual and spiritual realms without having some of the hardships of everyday life. Beyond financial independence, the benefits of wealth soon start falling under the logarithmic law of decreasing returns. Wealth allows you to help others, for there is more joy in giving than in receiving, but wealth also carries the responsibility of fiduciary duty toward the next generations and may become a burden if low self-esteem, low self-worth, and guilt for unearned wealth get a hold on you. Social pressure can worsen the situation.

Quite paradoxically, in the United States, the cradle of capitalism, freedom, and private property, one of the most basic incentives to prosper – leaving your possessions to your loved ones – is tolerated for everyone but the rich, who seem forced to very publicly and loudly leave relatively little to their children. In Europe and Asia, on the contrary, the culture of inheritance is accepted as the most natural thing in the world.

Instead of setting you free, wealth may enslave you with pride, eccentric luxury, ambition, envy, and moral decay. Don't forget that following the Golden Rule and trying to live a virtuous life – with humility and dignity, temperance, and moderation while accepting one's circumstances with grace – is the key to happiness. In my case, my Christian faith has been a priceless beacon.

Being is much more important than having. Own your life. Make sure your decisions are truly yours. Find yourself, be yourself, march to the beat of your own drum and set good life priorities. Surround yourself with genuine love. Don't worship money, neither by overconsuming nor by hoarding, for it is just a lifeless tool, and do not allow yourself to be defined by your net worth. You are worth much more than that.

I wish you fair winds and following seas in this beautiful journey of life.

Questions for Further Reflection

For Founders

1. Are you aware of how much the business owns you? Are you prepared to sell the business if family peace is at risk?
2. Do you put the same interest, energy, and resources to solve family problems as you do to solve business problems?

For Heirs

1. Are you sure "your" decisions are truly yours? Do you really own your decisions?
2. What is your definition of success/failure? Does it coincide with your parents' definition?

Additional Resources

On Business and Investing:

Benjamin Graham, *The Intelligent Investor* (New York: Harper Business, 1949).

Fred Schwed, *Where Are the Customers' Yachts?* (New York: Simon & Schuster, 1940).

Warren Buffett and Lawrence Cunningham, "The Essays of Warren Buffett," *Cardozo Law Review* 19, no. 5 (1997).

On Life:

Edward Garesché, *How to Live Nobly and Well* (Manchester, NH: Sophia Institute Press, 1999).

Richard Foster, *Freedom of Simplicity* (New York: HarperOne, 1981).

Biography

Fernando del Pino is CEO/CIO of Myway Investments. Prior to that he worked at the Del Pino's Family Office (1998–2004) and at the Chase Manhattan Bank. He has belonged to the board of directors and executive and audit committees of Ferrovial (1999–2007) and to the board of the Rafael del Pino Foundation (2000–2012). He also co-founded and chaired the Madrid Family Business Association and later remained as board member (2000–2015). He belongs to the advisory board of Magallanes Value Investors and to the Ethics Committee of Altum Faithful Investing. Since 2011 he writes monthly columns in Spain's leading financial journal (also posted in his bilingual blog, www.fpcs.es). He lives in Madrid, Spain, with his wife and four children.

CHAPTER 52

How Do You Balance Family Stability with Resilience Over the Generations?

James Grubman

Financially successful families face many challenges within and across generations. Navigating these with a resilient, adaptive attitude is one of the strongest contributors to long-term family harmony and prosperity. How do families maintain both stability and resilience in the face of a rapidly changing world?

Keep in mind that the transition to wealth by the first generation is the initial challenge to be navigated in the family. There are myriad choices about how to spend or give, how to parent, and how to communicate in the midst of wealth. How these choices are handled will influence whether the second and third generations will be ready for adulthood. If the founding generation has been willing to weave together elements of their past and their present in flexible ways, the family will be well-suited for preparing the next generation and for wise decision-making within the family. On the other hand, parents too strongly wedded to the past or too quick to chase the pleasures of affluence will have set the family on a path undermining the family's future.

As the rising generations of the family enter adulthood, those family members raised with wealth (the "natives" of wealth, compared to first-generation "immigrants" to wealth) will in turn influence the blending of the family's heritage with a willingness to adapt to changing conditions. This is the second major challenge for the family. Hold too tightly to the past, and the family will harden and crumble. Dive too eagerly into each passing trend of materialism, and the family will find itself untethered from its valued roots.

In certain ways, families must operate like Janus, the Roman god of beginnings, transitions, and passages (from whose name we get the first month of the year, January). Janus is typically depicted with one face looking to the past and one face toward the future. Like Janus, families must carry from the past the values and skills the family's founders developed from their experience of scarcity or adversity. Looking forward, these values and skills must then be adapted for changing conditions as the family takes in new members, encounters new financial or business stressors, and copes with unanticipated social pressures.

To accomplish this balance of stability and resilience, it can be helpful to focus on three central questions:

1. What should we maintain from our heritage that has served us well?
2. What should we let go of that no longer serves us?
3. What new practices or ideas should we take on that will serve us for the future?

For the first question, think about which traditions, rituals, values, and skills are fundamental to the family. These have likely helped steer the family (and perhaps the business) through challenging times. Perhaps elements of faith, spirituality, or social commitment are integral to these values. Prudent financial management and avoidance of extravagance may be core skills. There may be family rituals around holidays, transitions, and anniversaries that bring people together and renew the bonds of relationship. These traditions, values, and skills should feel so embedded in what makes the family unique and prosperous that letting go of these feels like risking the family's identity.

Second, think honestly about which elements of the family's heritage may be nostalgic, sentimental, or tied to times or places that have gone by. These may feel emotionally important to some in the family, but the skills or lessons linked to those events may no longer be as relevant to the world of today or tomorrow. For example, many families tell cherished stories of frugality during the early days, or how they handled major setbacks in the business using clever or risk-laden strategies. These are the legacy stories of the immigrant journey to success and wealth. Yet, times may have changed enough that those strategies no longer fully apply. Or, they have been superseded by more sophisticated strategies available to the family now. Like parables, keep the lessons of those wonderful stories but be willing to place them in the past.

Finally, talk in depth about the family *as it stands now.* Who is a part of the family now who might not have been anticipated in the past? Are you more diverse, dispersed, or multi-cultural than the family's origins ever would have predicted? Does family life encompass experiences far beyond its traditional roots? If so, you must make a place at the table for a broader range of viewpoints, experiences, adjustments, and opportunities than your heritage would have envisioned. Like Janus, look ahead. What resources or networks does the family now have that are likely to be utilized in hard times in the future? How is the family adapting to the modern world in ways that are the *new* life lessons, values, and skills? These are likely to be contributing to the family's current and future resilience alongside the family's heritage and traditions.

Think of the following examples as you imagine blending past, present, and future for your own family's adaptability:

- A southern European food products family with a tradition of autocratic male leadership gradually transitions to a family council headed by dynamic women, yet the family proudly upholds its ethnic heritage, identity, and rituals.
- A North American family enterprise in the automotive industry develops franchises on three continents and prepares for disruptive change in the business. Within the family, they welcome in-laws from the cultures where the new factories and business units are being developed, gathering every two years in the Midwest for a three-day family assembly and barbecue.
- A family enterprise stretching back five generations struggles like many families to communicate and collaborate about the issues they must handle in the modern era. A young family member with entrepreneurial skills develops a technology platform for communicating securely and easily, then discovers the application has commercial potential for similar family enterprises. A new venture is born alongside the family's traditional businesses.

Balancing stability with resilience is neither easy nor simple under the pressures of everyday life, particularly with affluence. If the family constantly re-tells old familiar tales of the past but isn't adding to them with new examples of success and spirit, the present may be withering in favor of cherishing the past. It may be time to re-evaluate the family's willingness to take risk, to explore new ventures, and to support those who want to look ahead more than behind.

Alternatively, if the family is chasing so many trends that a sense of focus has been lost, it may be time to re-group, do strategic planning, and find your center again. It also may be time to create new rituals that celebrate the family and its connections. Time and distance may have weakened the connections needed to sustain the family. Re-establishing the core values, rituals, and traditions of the family may help regain a sense of grounding and cohesion.

No one person in the family can accomplish the blending of past, present, and future. Although individual family members or leaders may have vision for what must be done, maintaining family resilience requires dialogue crossing generations and family branches. The three questions described earlier must be debated, positions must be heard, and consensus must be found. Achieving the balance between heritage and adaptation requires the family to share in a vision.

Like Janus keeping watch over both tradition and adaptation, prosperous families can face the unique challenges that come with wealth – guided by cherished values yet able to respond to a constantly changing world.

Questions for Further Reflection

1. What are the cherished traditions of your family? Have some of these started to drift away or be neglected? What would be required to re-activate them in a fresh way, relevant especially to younger family members?
2. How willing are you to adapt some of the values of the family for the perspectives of younger family members? Could you engage in a dialogue to discover what might recapture their energy and commitment?
3. Look past the changing forms of modern communication to find their underlying substance. There may be stronger connections than you may think. Are there ways to advocate for traditional values while making room for new interests?

Additional Resources

Starting or renewing a family-meeting process is often the first step in working together on the blending of tradition and adaptation. For help with family-meeting planning and facilitation, see the following white paper:

Dennis Jaffe and Stacy Allred, "Talking It Through: A Guide to Conducting Effective Multi-generational Family Meetings about Business and Wealth," dennisjaffe.com, 2014.

For more discussion on the adjustments needed as families move from the wealth-creating generation to subsequent generations, see the following book:

James Grubman, *Strangers in Paradise: How Families Adapt to Wealth Across Generations* (Boston: Family Wealth Consulting, 2013).

Biography

Dr. James Grubman is a consultant to multi-generational families and their advisors about the issues that arise around wealth. He helps families establish healthy patterns of communication, governance, and parenting for succeeding generations. He is the author of the renowned book, *Strangers in Paradise: How Families Adapt to Wealth Across Generations,* and co-author (with Dennis T. Jaffe, PhD) of *Cross Cultures: How Global Families Navigate Change Across Generations.* He has been published widely and quoted extensively by *The Wall Street Journal, The New York Times, CNBC,* and other media, including Malcolm Gladwell's 2013 book, *David and Goliath.*

James holds Fellow status in the Family Firm Institute and the Purposeful Planning Institute, and he is a member of several US and international estate-planning organizations. He maintains specialty interests in neuropsychology and legal issues affecting wealth management. His global consulting practice, Family Wealth Consulting, is based in Massachusetts.

CHAPTER 53

How Can We "Lift the Small Boats" Too?

Christine Lagarde

Recently one morning, I almost choked on my yogurt when I saw the front page of a leading business newspaper. There it was – a league table of the world's best-paid hedge fund managers. It showed that the highest earner was able to pocket $1.5 billion. *One* man, $1.5 billion!

Together, the 25 best-paid hedge fund managers earned a combined $10.9 billion, even as their industry suffered from largely mediocre investment performance.

This reminded me of a famous Wall Street joke – about a visitor to New York who admired the gorgeous yachts of the richest bankers and brokers. After gazing long and thoughtfully at these beautiful boats, the visitor asked wryly, "Where are the *customers* yachts?" Of course, the customers could not afford yachts, even though they dutifully followed the advice of their bankers and brokers.

Why is this relevant right now? Because the theme of growing and excessive inequality is not only back in the headlines, it has also become a problem for economic growth and development. I would like to take an economic perspective on this situation. I will *not* focus on the yachts of the super-rich, who have become the face of a new Gilded Age. It is not immoral to enjoy one's financial success.

But I would like to bring into the discussion what I would call the "*small boats*" – the livelihoods and economic aspirations of the poor and the middle class.

In too many countries, economic growth has failed to lift these small boats, whereas the gorgeous yachts have been riding the waves and enjoying the wind in their sails. In too many cases, poor and middle-class households have come to realize that hard work and determination alone may not be enough to keep them afloat.

Too many of them are now convinced that the system is somehow rigged, that the odds are stacked against them. No wonder that politicians, business leaders, top-notch economists, and even central bankers are talking about excessive inequality of wealth and income. And these concerns can be heard across the political spectrum.

My key message is this: reducing excessive inequality – by lifting the small boats – is not just morally and politically correct, but it is *good economics.*

You do not have to be an altruist to support policies that lift the incomes of the poor and the middle class. Everybody will benefit from these policies, because they are essential to generate higher, more inclusive, and more sustainable growth.

In other words, if you want to see more *durable* growth, you need to generate more *equitable* growth. With this in mind, I would like to focus on two issues:

1. The causes and consequences of excessive inequality.
2. The policies needed for stronger, more inclusive, and more sustainable growth.

Causes and Consequences of Excessive Inequality

Imagine lining up the world's population from the poorest to the richest, each standing behind a pile of money that represents his or her annual income.

You will see that the world is a very unequal place. There is obviously a vast gulf between the richest and the poorest. But if you look at the changes in this line-up over time, you will notice that *global* income inequality – that is, inequality *between* countries – has actually *fallen* (i.e. improved) steadily over the past few decades.

Why? Because average incomes in emerging market economies, such as China and India, have risen much faster than those in richer countries. This shows the transformative power of international trade and investment. The massive global flows of products, services, people, knowledge, and ideas have been good for *global* equality of income – and we need more of that. So we can further reduce the gap *between* countries.

But – and this is a big "but" – we have also seen *growing* income inequality *within* countries. Over the past two decades, inequality of income has *risen substantially* in most advanced economies and major emerging market economies, especially in Asia and Eastern Europe.

In advanced economies, for example, the top 1% of the population now accounts for about 10% of total income. And the gap between rich and poor is even wider when it comes to wealth. Oxfam estimates that the combined wealth of the world's richest 1% is equal to that of the other 99% of people. In the United States, over one-third of total wealth is held by 1% of the population.

If you put all this together, you see a striking divergence between a *positive global* trend and mostly *negative* trends *within* countries.

China, for example, has been at the sharp end of both trends. By lifting more than 600 million people out of poverty over the past three decades, China has made a remarkable contribution to *greater global equality* of income. But in the process, it has become one of the world's most unequal societies – because many rural areas remain poor and because income and wealth have risen sharply in the cities and at the top levels of Chinese society.

In fact, economies like China and India seem to fit neatly into a traditional narrative, which says that extreme inequality is an acceptable price to pay for economic growth.

Body of Evidence

But there is a growing body of evidence that countries should *not* accept this Faustian trade-off. For example, analysis[1] by my colleagues at the IMF has shown that excessive income inequality actually *drags down* the economic growth rate and makes growth *less* sustainable over time.

The IMF research[2] demonstrates that you need to lift the small boats to generate stronger and more durable growth.

It shows that, if you lift the income share of the poor and middle class by 1%, then gross domestic product (GDP) growth *increases* by as much as 0.38 percentage points in a country over five years. By contrast, if you lift the income share of the rich by 1%, then GDP growth *decreases* by 0.08 percentage points. One possible explanation is that the rich spend a lower fraction of their incomes, which could reduce aggregate demand and undermine growth.

In other words, our findings suggest that – contrary to conventional wisdom – the benefits of higher income are trickling *up*, not *down*. The poor and the middle class are the main engines of growth. Unfortunately, these engines have been stalling.

A recent Organisation for Economic Co-operation and Development (OECD) study, for example, shows that the living standards of the poor and lower middle class in advanced economies have been falling relative to the rest of the population. This kind of inequality holds back growth because it discourages investment in skills and human capital – which leads to lower productivity in a large part of the economy.

---

[1]Jonathan D. Ostry, Andrew Berg, and Charalambos G. Tsangarides, "Redistribution, Inequality, and Growth," IMF Staff Discussion Note SDN/14/02, February 2014, https://www.imf.org/external/pubs/ft/sdn/2014/sdn1402.pdf.

[2]Era Dabla-Norris, Kalpana Kochhar, Nujin Suphaphiphat, Frantisek Ricka, and Evridiki Tsounta, "Causes and Consequences of Income Inequality: A Global Perspective," IMF Staff Discussion Note SDN/15/13, June 2015, https://www.imf.org/external/pubs/ft/sdn/2015/sdn1513.pdf.

Drivers of Excessive Inequality

So, the consequences of excessive income inequality are increasingly clear – but what about its causes?

The most important drivers of extreme inequality are well known – technological progress and financial globalization.[3] These two factors have tended to widen the earnings gap between higher- and lower-skilled individuals, especially in advanced economies.

Another factor is the over-reliance on finance in major economies such as the United States and Japan. Of course, finance – especially credit – is essential to any prosperous society. But there is growing evidence, including from IMF staff,[4] that too much finance can distort the distribution of income, corrode the political process, and undermine economic stability and growth.

In emerging and developing economies, extreme income inequality is largely driven by an inequality of *access* – to education, health care, and financial services. Let me give you some examples:

- Almost 60% of the poorest youth population in sub-Saharan Africa has fewer than four years of schooling.
- Nearly 70% of the poor in developing economies give birth without access to doctors or nurses.
- More than 80% of the poor in developing economies do not have bank accounts.

Of course, another major factor is low social mobility. Recent studies have shown that advanced economies with lower levels of mobility across generations tend to have higher levels of income inequality. In these countries, parents' income is a major determinant of children's income. It suggests that, if you want to move up in society, you need to grow up on the right side of the tracks. This doesn't sound fair.

Policies for Stronger, More Inclusive, More Sustainable Growth

Policymakers (and the private citizens who are responsible for voting them or their masters into power, at least in the world's democracies) can, in our view,

---

[3]These two factors feature prominently in the academic literature and public discussions about inequality. The results of our latest note on the Causes and Consequences of Income Inequality confirm the findings in the literature (Dabla-Norris, Kochhar, Suphaphiphat, Ricka, Evridiki Tsounta, "Causes and Consequences of Income Inequality: A Global Perspective").

[4]A recent IMF note on Rethinking Financial Deepening shows that, after a point, financial development damages growth. See Sahay et al., "Rethinking Financial Deepening: Stability and Growth in Emerging Markets," IMF Staff Discussion Note SDN/15/08, May 2015, https://www.imf.org/external/pubs/ft/sdn/2015/sdn1508.pdf. An IMF Working Paper and a recent BIS paper argue that it is possible to have too much finance.

generate a swell under the bow of the small boats. There are recipes for stronger, more inclusive, and more sustainable growth in *all* countries.

The *first priority* – the number-one item on the list – should be macroeconomic stability. If you do not apply good monetary policies, if you indulge in fiscal indiscipline, if you allow your public debt to balloon, you are bound to see slower growth, rising inequality, and greater economic and financial instability.

Sound macroeconomic policies are the poor's best friend – and so is good governance. Endemic corruption, for example, can be a strong indicator of profound social and economic inequality.

The *second priority* should be prudence. We all know that actions need to be taken to reduce *excessive* inequality. But we also know that a *certain* level of inequality is healthy and helpful. It provides incentives for people to compete, innovate, invest, and seize opportunities – to upgrade their skills, start new businesses, and make things happen.

At their best, entrepreneurs have what economist John Maynard Keynes called "animal spirits" – a sometimes-boundless confidence in their own *unique* ability to shape the future. In other words, standing out from the crowd is an essential driver of prosperity.

The *next priority* should be to adjust policies to country-specific drivers of inequality, including political, cultural, and institutional settings. No more one-size-fits-all but, rather, smart policies – potential game changers – that could help reverse the trend toward greater inequality.

Smart Fiscal Policy

One potential game changer is *smart fiscal policy*. The challenge here is to design tax and spending measures that have minimal adverse effects on incentives to work, save, and invest. The objective must be to promote both greater equality *and* greater efficiency.

This means widening the tax revenue base by – for example – clamping down on tax evasion and reducing tax relief on items that disproportionately benefit the rich.[5] In many European countries, it also means reducing high labor taxes, including those made through cuts to employer social security contributions. This would provide a strong incentive to create more jobs and more full-time positions, which would help stem the tide of part-time and temporary jobs that have contributed to rising income inequality.

On the expenditure side, it means expanding access to education and health care. In many emerging and developing economies, it means reducing energy subsidies – which are costly and inefficient – and using the freed-up resources for better education, training, and stronger safety nets.

---

[5]Half the rich world's governments allow their citizens to deduct the interest payments on mortgages from their taxable income.

Promoting greater equality and efficiency also means relying more on so-called conditional cash transfers. These are immensely successful anti-poverty tools that have contributed significantly to the reduction in income inequality in countries such as Brazil, Chile, and Mexico.

During my recent visit to Brazil, I had the opportunity to visit a *favela* and witness first-hand the so-called *Bolsa Familia* program. This program provides aid to poor families – in the form of pre-paid debit cards – on condition that their children go to school and take part in government vaccination programs.

Structural Reforms

In addition to these smart fiscal policies, there is another potential game changer – *smart reforms* in vital areas such as education, health care, labor markets, infrastructure, and financial inclusion. These structural reforms are essential to lift potential economic growth and boost income and living standards over the medium term.

If I had to pick the three most important structural tools to reduce excessive income inequality, it would be *education*, education, education. Whether you live in Lima or Lagos, in Shanghai or Chicago, in Brussels or Buenos Aires, your income potential depends on your skills, your ability to harness technological change in a globalized world.

Another important tool is *labor market reform*. Think of well-calibrated minimum wages and policies to support job search and skill matching. Think of reforms to protect workers rather than jobs. In the Nordic countries, for example, workers have only limited job protection, but they benefit from generous unemployment insurance that requires jobseekers to find new positions. This model[6] makes the labor market more flexible – which is good for growth – while safeguarding the interests of workers.

Labor market reforms also have an important *gender dimension*. Across the globe, women have been facing a triple disadvantage. They are less likely than men to have a paid job, especially in the Middle East and North Africa. If they do find paid employment, it is more likely to be in the informal sector. And if they eventually get a job in the formal sector, they earn just three-quarters as much as men – even with the same level of education, and in the same occupation.

Worldwide, there are about 865 million women who have the potential to contribute more fully to the economy. So the message is clear: if you care about greater shared prosperity, you need to unleash the economic power of women.

---

[6]For more information on the Nordic model, see Olivier Blanchard, Florence Jaumotte, and Prakash Loungani, "Labor Market Policies and IMF Advice in Advanced Economies During the Great Recession," IMF Discussion Note SDN/13/02, March 2013, https://www.imf.org/external/pubs/ft/sdn/2013/sdn1302.pdf and "Jobs and Growth: Analytical and Operational Considerations for the Fund," International Monetary Fund, March 14, 2013.

You also need to foster *greater financial inclusion*, especially in developing economies. Think of micro-credit initiatives that turn poor people – mostly women – into successful micro-entrepreneurs. Think of initiatives to build credit histories for people without bank accounts. Think of the transformative impact of cell-phone-based banking, especially in sub-Saharan Africa.

Conclusion

All these policies and reforms require leadership, courage, and collaboration. Politicians, policymakers, business leaders, and all of us need to translate good intentions into bold and lasting actions.

There are many cynical voices out there, questioning the need for action in these areas and declaring defeat well before the battle has begun. We must be able to prove these cynics wrong – by focusing minds, by forging partnerships, and by setting the *right goals*.

On all these issues, I see an important *role for the IMF*. Our key mandate is to promote global economic and financial stability. This is why we have been deeply involved in development – by helping our 188 member countries to design and implement policies and by lending to countries in times of distress, so they can get back on their feet.

It is often said that we should measure the health of our society not at its apex, but at its base. By lifting the small boats of the poor and the middle class, we can build a fairer society and a stronger economy. Together, we can create *greater* shared prosperity – for *all*.

This is a condensed version of a speech entitled "Lifting the Small Boats" by International Monetary Fund (IMF) Managing Director Christine Lagarde, delivered at the Grandes Conferences Catholiques in Brussels on June 17, 2015. It is used with permission.

Questions for Further Reflection

1. Is the combination of higher, more inclusive, and more sustainable growth a good goal?
2. Will the world be better and safer for everyone if the small boats can also benefit from the rising tide? Can excessive inequality put that at risk?
3. What are some examples of the small boats in your community or in the rest of the world? What can we do to help ensure the benefits of global growth are shared?

Biography

Born in Paris in 1956, Christine Lagarde completed high school in Le Havre and attended Holton Arms School in Bethesda, Maryland. She then graduated from law school at University Paris X, and obtained a Master's degree from the Political Science Institute in Aix en Provence.

After being admitted as a lawyer to the Paris Bar, Christine joined the international law firm of Baker & McKenzie as an associate, specializing in labor, anti-trust, and mergers and acquisitions. A member of the executive committee of the firm in 1995, She became the chairperson of the Global Executive Committee of Baker & McKenzie in 1999, and subsequently chairperson of the Global Strategic Committee in 2004.

Christine joined the French government in June 2005 as Minister for Foreign Trade. After a brief stint as Minister for Agriculture and Fisheries, in June 2007 she became the first woman to hold the post of Finance and Economy Minister of a G-7 country. From July to December 2008, she also chaired the ECOFIN Council, which brings together economics and finance ministers of the European Union, and helped foster international policies related to financial supervision, regulation, and strengthening global economic governance. As Chair of the G-20 when France took over its presidency for the year 2011, she set in motion a wide-ranging work agenda on the reform of the international monetary system.

On July 5, 2011, Christine became the eleventh managing director of the IMF, and the first woman to hold that position. On February 19, 2016, the IMF executive board selected her to serve as IMF managing director for a second five-year term starting on July 5, 2016.

She was named Officier in the Légion d'honneur in April 2012.

A former member of the French national team for synchronized swimming, Christine is the mother of two sons.

Conclusion

We hope you have found the questions and answers in this volume valuable. They were intended to provoke thought and discussion, to stretch your mind, and perhaps even challenge long-held beliefs. We also wanted the ideas to be practical enough to resolve thorny questions and to offer hope that resolution is within reach.

We are grateful to the families who have been brave enough to express their questions aloud, to the advisors who have identified the critical issues families face, and, of course, to the contributing authors who have shared new ways of thinking and meaningful advice from their wealth of experience. We see this book as a sort of community project where people pool resources and exchange ideas. No single person has all the solutions. No single family has yet faced all the issues. But together we can find answers to the key questions that challenge us all.

Most of all, our aim has been to give you ways to think about these questions for yourself, because the answers that you come to today may, appropriately, be very different 10 years from now.

For these reasons, we encourage you to return to this book from time to time as your family changes, as your business evolves, as the world around you shifts. Scan the table of contents to see which questions speak most to you. Review chapters for the questions that have been of importance to you and remain so – and see how your own thinking has changed. Think of yourself in dialogue with these authors – not as experts speaking to you in monologue but as other intelligent people trying to think through these difficult matters with clarity.

As you make this review, ask yourself these simple questions to crystallize your thinking and your learning:

In the areas of family and wealth,

- What is going well that you want to continue doing?
- What actions or decisions are no longer serving you well that you want to stop?
- What ideas or practices appear to hold promise that you would consider starting?

Finally, here at the end, we want to emphasize one more question, which is, in a way, the question that hangs over the entire book and indeed over the entire endeavor of managing family and wealth – the question whose answer makes all the rest worthwhile: "What is your true wealth?" Give yourself a moment to think about your answer to that question. Let that answer be as tangible or as intangible as seems right to you, for it will guide how you apply everything you learn from these pages.

About the Editors

Tom McCullough is chairman and CEO of Northwood Family Office and a longtime advisor to families of significant wealth. He has spent over 35 years in the family office/wealth management field. The combination of this background, along with his own family's desire for a truly integrated, objective, and customized service, led Tom to start Northwood Family Office in 2003. It has become one of the leaders in its field and is regularly recognized as the "#1 family office in Canada" by *Euromoney* in its global private-banking survey. Prior to founding Northwood Family Office, Tom was a senior executive and member of the executive committee at RBC Wealth Management. Tom is a frequent speaker and passionate advocate of the family office and other solutions to the issues faced by families of wealth. He is an adjunct professor of Private Wealth Management and teaches in the MBA program at the University of Toronto's Rotman School of Management, as well as the Rotman Family Wealth Management program designed specifically for family members. He is co-author of the book *Family Wealth Management*, published by John Wiley & Sons (2013). Tom is an entrepreneur-in-residence at Western University's Ivey School of Business, a member of the editorial board of the *Journal of Wealth Management*, and a Fellow of the Family Firm Institute. He is also chair of the CEO group of the Wigmore Association (http://wigmoreassociation.com), a collaboration of eight independent family offices from around the world. He holds an MBA from the Schulich School of Business at York University as well as the CIM (Chartered Investment Manager) and CIWM (Certified International Wealth Manager) designations. He is married, has two adult children, and is involved in a wide range of philanthropic endeavors.

Tom can be reached at tm@northwoodfamilyoffice.com.

Dr. Keith Whitaker is president of Wise Counsel Research, a think tank and consultancy focused on families with significant wealth. Keith has consulted for many years with leaders of enterprising families, helping them plan succession, develop next generation talent, and communicate around estate planning. With a background in education and philanthropy, he enables family leaders to better understand their values and goals as well as to have a positive impact on the world around them. *Family Wealth Report* named Keith the 2015 "outstanding contributor to wealth management thought-leadership." Keith has served as a managing director at Wells Fargo Family Wealth, an adjunct professor of management at Vanderbilt University, an adjunct assistant professor of philosophy at Boston College, and a director of a private foundation. He was also a special assistant to the president of Boston University. Keith's writings and commentary have appeared in *The Wall Street Journal*, *The New York Times*, *The Financial Times*, *Claremont Review of Books*, and *Philanthropy Magazine*. His *Wealth and the Will of God* appeared in 2010 from Indiana University Press and he is co-author of *The Cycle of the Gift: Family Wealth & Wisdom*; *The Voice of the Rising Generation*; *Family Trusts: A Guide for Beneficiaries, Trustees, Trust Protectors, and Trust Creators*; and *Complete Family Wealth*, all published by Bloomberg Press. Keith holds a PhD in Social Thought from the University of Chicago and a BA and MA in Classics and Philosophy from Boston University. He serves on the board of directors of the National Association of Scholars.

Keith can be reached at keith@wisecounselresearch.org.

Index